Charles Higham is the author of many bestselling Hollywood biographies, among them: *Audrey: The Life of Audrey Hepburn, Bette: The Life of Bette Davis, Cecil B. DeMille, Errol Flynn: The Untold Story* and *Kate: The Life of Katharine Hepburn*. His latest book is *Wallis: Secret Lives of the Duchess of Windsor*.

By the same author

Kate: The Life of Katharine Hepburn
Audrey: The Life of Audrey Hepburn
Bette: The Life of Bette Davis
Cecil B. DeMille
Errol Flynn: The Untold Story
Wallis: Secret Lives of the Duchess of Windsor.

CHARLES HIGHAM

Brando

The Unauthorized Biography

GRAFTON BOOKS

A Division of the Collins Publishing Group

LONDON GLASGOW
TORONTO SYDNEY AUCKLAND

Grafton Books
A Division of the Collins Publishing Group
8 Grafton Street, London W1X 3LA

Published by Grafton Books 1989

First published in Great Britain by
Sidgwick & Jackson Ltd 1987

Copyright © Charles Higham 1987

ISBN 0-586-20455-5

Printed and bound in Great Britain by
Collins, Glasgow

Set in Melior

For Mitch Douglas

Preface

The evening of December 3, 1947. The opening-night audience at the Ethel Barrymore Theater in New York City is at fever pitch. The word is out that Tennessee Williams's new play, *A Streetcar Named Desire*, will be the sensation of the season. Tickets have been at a premium for weeks and lines have run around the block for standing room. A din of excited conversation fills the lobby. Much of New York society is present. From out of town the news has come that the drama breaks every law of the theatre and shows raw sexual passion on the stage for the first time. And that one of the actors in it is so impressive that he will soon become a leading figure of the Broadway stage.

The dark red velvet curtain lifts. The audience sees the set of a two-storey corner building on a street in New Orleans on a steamy late spring evening. White frame houses with clumsily built outside stairs and galleries and gables appear in a vividly realized perspective of the city. The backcloth evokes the turquoise sky of twilight. The audience can sense the presence of the Mississippi, running brown and sluggish behind the ancient warehouses. The sound of black voices is accompanied by blues played on a distant piano. A white and a black woman sit on the outside steps of the apartment building with its wrought-iron balconies. Two men stroll around the corner. One is tall, lanky, with a prominent nose. The other, upon whom everyone in the audience is focused, is of medium height, with powerful, muscular shoulders and arms, a

5

broad, sculptured chest, and sturdy legs. His face has an extraordinary innocence and openness. There is an animal-like quality in the way he moves. He conveys power and pride in his masculinity – a physical confidence that comes from possessing a perfect physique and an uncomplicated, outgoing, brutal nature. He exudes enjoyment of food, alcohol, laughter, and pleasure.

His clothes are designed to emphasize his muscles. His T-shirt, a size too small, is soaked in sweat, and shows off his carved, sharply defined weightlifter's pectorals. His jeans are cut tight, revealing the outline of his genitals.

Women are riveted by him. There is scarcely a female in the audience who does not lean forward to stare hard at him, and many of them, though they would have been the last to admit it, are quite visibly aroused. The actor stands for a moment, enjoying, drinking in the audience's interest, fully aware of the effect he is creating and relishing it. He carries a blood-stained package of meat. Then he takes the package and heaves it at the drab girl – his wife – who stands on the first-floor balcony ready to greet him. She utters a cry of shock at the contemptuousness of the gesture but, used to being treated so, catches the package and gives a frail, girlish laugh. She calls out to him, 'Where are you going?' When he tells her he is on his way to the bowling alley, there is so completely vulgar a disdain combined with a kind of lazy self-indulgence in his manner that in an instant everyone in the theatre grasps the character.

It was the beginning of an unforgettable evening. Scene after scene excited the first-night crowd. And despite the excellent performances of Jessica Tandy, Kim

6

Hunter, Karl Malden, and others in the cast, it was this young, unknown player who carried the occasion from first moment to last. As Stanley Kowalski, the crude, violent, and dangerous young mechanic who humiliates and subdues the elegant, defeated southern gentlewoman Blanche DuBois, Marlon Brando played with a savage, primitive dynamism that went beyond any of his predecessors in realistic theatre. Overnight, he changed the face of acting in America forever.

Before his advent, American actors had taken their cues from the European and British stage, characterized by theatrical gentlemanly eloquence, flawless diction, and exquisite manners. They declaimed their speeches, clinging to a nineteenth-century style of delivery, sometimes even walking down to the footlights to address the audience directly. Brando, in contrast, imported from the American heartland a farm boy's instinctive earthiness and animalism.

On the surface, he was, of course, the ideal Stanley Kowalski. He answered the description Tennessee Williams had written in the play's directions before he even met the actor. In his private life, Brando even emulated Stanley. Women have commented on the bluntness of his approach to sex. One described how, when he visited her on the set of a film, he indicated to her by a nod that they should go to his dressing room. They did, and he removed his clothes without saying a word and made love to her. Other women mentioned how he would call them in the middle of the night, feeling aroused, and then drive to their homes, walk through the front door, strip, and throw them on the bed.

He could be cruel, dropping women without warning and taking up with them again when he felt like it. Yet, in many ways, he was unlike Kowalski. He was a thinker, interested in philosophy, mysticism, and psychology. He could be warm, loving, and generous to women; so captivating that years later they would threaten or attempt suicide in efforts to get him back. His charm was so irresistible that former girlfriends still mist with tears at the mention of him. Or they will laugh, happily, over some remembered practical joke or touch of humour of his that long ago enlivened their lives.

Brando electrified those he encountered. When he walked into someone's psyche, he left his mark forever. He had Kowalski's animal magnetism taken to the ultimate degree. He had, and has, an extraordinary honesty, the rarest of all qualities among motion picture stars. Most actors weave fantasies about themselves, reinventing their pasts with the aid of press agents and concocting qualities for themselves that are creations of their imaginations. Their egocentricity is so absolute that they have virtually no interest in other subjects. Brando is an exception to the rule. Except in joking, he has not lied about his past. He is more interested in other people than in himself. He would far rather read a book on sociology than an article about himself. He has never subscribed to a clipping service, nor has he kept scrapbooks. In this, also, he is almost unique among the Hollywood set.

It is the secret of his greatness as an actor that he has played with an empathy and an instinctual understanding that not even the greatest 'technical' performers could possibly match. Laurence Olivier, almost certainly the finest actor of three generations in England, has unhesitatingly stated that he gives first place to Brando. Certainly, none of the major American male performers – Robert De Niro, Al Pacino, Dustin Hoffman, and Paul Newman – would hesitate to say that he is their model. They have stripped away the veneer of generations of sophisticated playing to act through the guts of a character and with the raw emotional force that Brando exemplified from the beginning of his career.

Like many major artists in any field, Brando has worked essentially for himself. He feels that actors who play for an audience, trying to please it, are cheating their art. He has to satisfy himself first and foremost. If people can understand what he is doing, well and good. If not, he shrugs and accepts it.

He has always detested Hollywood and has chosen to be an outsider in Los Angeles. He hates what he believes to be the fantasies, foolishnesses, and above all the hypocrisies of the movie business. An old-fashioned liberal, he feels he has no truck with commerce; in fact, he has given most of his money away and lives with extreme simplicity. The Oscar, which he has won twice, for *On the Waterfront* and *The Godfather*, strikes him as a symbol of a fatuous business. Such views have scarcely endeared him to the movie industry, but with a combination of masochism and a shrewd awareness of his unlimited public appeal, the Hollywood he despises has paid him incredible sums over the years, including $3.5 million for less than twenty minutes in *Superman*.

For him, love and sex are the meaning of life. He told Adriano Botta in *L'Europeo* in March 1973: 'I have loved a lot in my life. I still do. I have had many women. I like love. I insist on enjoying sex. Should sex and desire die in me, it would be the end. It doesn't matter if I have almost never been happy with a woman. Nor does it matter that with every woman my relationship has ended up in nothing. I face love every time as a necessary good or a necessary evil. Sometimes

I even approach sex and love with boredom. But I must make love and give love, whatever the price. It is a matter of life and death.' He has almost never developed the slightest admiration for a female co-star; the exceptions are Vivien Leigh, the touching and fragile Blanche DuBois of the screen *Streetcar*, and Maria Schneider, the tortured nymphet of *Last Tango in Paris*. Brando is not a social being. He has said, 'I don't like people. I don't love my neighbour. Every time I put any faith in love or friendship I only came through with deep wounds. Today I am truly a person not open to relationships; this isn't a lie, but a very true fact. I am deeply lonely: alone. I enjoy life, up to a point, but I no longer have dreams. Death and old age are events which I accept and await with all feasible serenity. To a certain extent at times I make of them the purpose of living: I work towards the point at which I can accept them with equanimity.'

He has always admitted to making stupid films because he needed money to help other people. He hasn't seen himself as a saint because of this; it has simply been his decision in life.

Marlon Brando's torn T-shirt, his tight jeans, his extreme physicality have influenced generations up to today. Only Gene Kelly in musicals matched him as a revolutionary of style. His lack of technique, his inability to memorize lines after his earliest career, his insolent distaste for the profession of acting itself, and his outright contempt for movies have added to his mass popular appeal and have enhanced his image as an eternal rebel.

A classic school dropout, his hatred of authority stemmed from a childhood of constant conflict with his father. Marlon Sr was a correct businessman who dressed like a clothing model, smoked an avuncular pipe, raised his children by the Good Book, but philandered relentlessly in private. He deprived his wife of the chance for a career on the stage, so that Brando may have had an urge to fulfil her frustrated dreams. Becoming an actor was, for Brando, not merely a way of earning a living when he had neither the physical nor intellectual skills for any other profession. It was an act of revenge.

His street clothing, unconventional for actors in New York City at the time, was a symbol of his desire to slap down his father's neatly necktied, impeccably strict appearance. He assumed the look of a predatory male animal, his T-shirt and jeans deliberately designed to emphasize his potency.

After the earliest years, and until the serious efforts he made in *The Godfather*, *Last Tango in Paris*, and *Apocalypse Now*, he whored for years for money to support causes or divorces, ironically becoming the highest paid and most admired of actors in the process. At his best, as in *The Men*, *Streetcar*, *On the Waterfront*, *Julius Caesar*, *Reflections in a Golden Eye*, and *The Godfather*, he was a consummate actor, who entered completely into the roles he played. At his worst, as in *Candy*, *The Missouri Breaks*, and *The Formula*, he was among the laziest and most indulgent of the major stars. But Brando is always fascinating to watch. Despite his open contempt for the profession that supported him, he remains an actor with a rare capacity to become the person he is playing, and to be the model, the idol of millions. When it came time in *The Godfather* for Al Pacino to play his first scene with Brando, Pacino was found pale and shaking with nerves. Asked what the problem was, he is reported to have said, 'You don't understand. I am acting with God.'

Brando's chameleon capacity to take on colours, textures, patterns of speech, was his special art in both private and public life. He remains the most expert and inventive of mimics for his friends.

When I called France Nuyen, the beautiful French-Chinese star of *The World of Suzie Wong* on Broadway, who was in love with Brando, she said to me, 'You *are* Marlon, aren't you?' She added, 'It would be just like you to pretend you're an author, writing a book about you.' I protested vainly that I wasn't Brando. 'You did this to me some time ago,' she went on in gentle accusation. 'You said you were a Russian producer who was making an epic about the Chinese-Russian conflicts of the nineteenth century and you wanted me to play a princess. You said you went up to the house you live in on Mulholland Drive – your Russian accent was so perfect – and that a ferocious Marlon Brando jumped out of the bushes at you, snarling! Then when I called your bluff, you relaxed, laughed loudly, and said you were testing me, to see what I thought of you after all these years – *really* thought!'

Even when I finally met Miss Nuyen, she was laughingly uncertain whether, some 130 pounds lighter, Marlon had achieved a miraculous disguise. Russian accents have been Marlon's speciality, in the countless similar practical jokes he has played on his friends. At one stage, he convinced the Oscar-winning writer and director Daniel Taradash that he was the grand old Russian actor Akim Tamiroff. Sometimes he might be an authority on insects, or a lepidopterist, or an inspector reporting on a fly plague, or . . . the list goes on and on. His love of mischief remains childlike and irresistible. When he hasn't fought directly with the press, he has delighted in teasing his unhappy interviewers, pulling their legs, mocking their seriousness. Nobody who saw it could forget his interview with Dick Cavett in the early 1970s, in which he unsettled his understandably nervous host by ribbing him on his commercial break cues, mocking his constant reference to notes below the camera frame and sharply exacerbating Cavett's characteristic smiling tense unease.

But while Brando has made fun of those who earn their living from – or from writing about – the media, he has been deadly serious about the things that have mattered to him. The causes and activities of AIM, the militant American Indian Movement, in its sometimes violent demonstrations against the white man's breaking of treaties, preoccupied him for years to the exclusion of practically everything else. That movement could not have persisted without Brando's financial support. He was the strongest backer of Russell Means and Dennis Banks, AIM leaders, both of whom were arrested and imprisoned. He was involved in manic episodes, most notably the AIM-supported seizure of a Roman Catholic novitiate in the winter snows of Gresham, Wisconsin, in which he and his companions lay under siege for three days and nights of rifle fire. He provided aid, comfort, the means of escape, and sanctuary in his houses in Los Angeles and Tahiti to Dennis Banks, when that activist was under federal warrant of arrest for incitement to riot in a courthouse in Custer, South Dakota. He could easily have been tried and imprisoned himself for assisting a fugitive from justice, but he correctly calculated that the government wouldn't risk making a martyr of him and thereby enhancing the Indian cause.

He travelled to India for UNICEF, entering the horrifying heart of the Bihar famine areas, surrounded by the dead and dying. He aided the Black Panthers and the cause of Martin Luther King, and underwent intensive FBI investigation for his activism in the 1960s and 1970s. In his adopted Teti'aroa, an atoll off Tahiti, he has done his utmost, in the face of treacherous weather conditions, to provide a self-supporting community using the natural resources of palm woods, leaves, and local stones. He has been involved in an experimental ocean plankton farm that might point the way to underwater feeding for the impoverished of the Third World. He has explored windmill technology and the possibility of opening a University of the Sea, and he has given his patronage to many distinguished scholars from all over the world. His virtually unknown work on the ecology and history of the Society Islands has brought in academic field missions that have produced fascinating results.

By contrast with his semipolitical career and his varied but extraordinary passage as a classic American star, his personal life has been a disaster. He told *L'Europeo* that, if he were asked to sit in judgement on himself, he would absolve Marlon Brando the actor, but he would condemn Brando the man to a lingering death, appropriate to his megalomaniac character. Clearly, he was referring to the infernal (and touchingly human) mess he has made of his marriages and love affairs. His first wife, Annie Kashfi, with her suicide attempts, her breakdowns, her seizures, her attacks of hysteria and violence, seems to have been provoked by him into a state of mind that bordered on insanity, their conflict reaching its peak in a prolonged and garish custody struggle over their son. His second wife, Movita, clashed with him less picturesquely in a child-support struggle. Rita Moreno, the fiery Puerto Rican actress, tried to kill herself over him. Two of the women he was involved with died by violence: Anne Ford, the respected dress designer, was murdered at the hands of unknown killers, while Pina Pellicer, the Mexican actress with whom he starred in *One-Eyed Jacks*, committed suicide. His close friend, the leading Hollywood attorney Norman Garey, shot himself; his beloved Wally Cox died of heart failure brought on by a combination of drink and drugs. And Brando's parents died unpleasant deaths: his father from a malignant melanoma, and his mother from the effects of years of drinking.

In many other ways, fate has struck him serious blows. Film after film was drastically affected by weather. Wind and rain, pursuing him diabolically throughout his entire life, finally put paid to his Tahitian paradise in a series of shattering cyclones. The surprising thing is that, despite misfortunes which would have destroyed most men, he has managed to retain his sturdy midwestern horse sense and a feeling for the comparative value of things. Perhaps it is the knowledge of his humanness and lack of pretence, and the absolute sincerity of his finest performances, drawn from life rather than celluloid, that have endeared him to millions and made him one of the few stars whose name on a marquee ensures bankability and international success. Like Garbo, Brando requires no Christian name. His name readily provokes a smile, a laugh, a thoughtful word or two, wherever it is mentioned. Whether he likes it or not, Marlon Brando is one of the immortals. And this is his epic story.

1

Omaha in 1924 was a city still smarting from the memory of grasshopper plagues when the sky was green and humming with living clouds that drifted in, ate the crops, and left thousands without sustenance. A city that had survived fire and tornado and typhus and influenza epidemics to become fat and sassy five years before the Wall Street crash. A city alive with men in straw boaters and women in cloche hats and flags and bunting and carts groaning with produce. A city that had brutally swept out the Indians who owned its fertile soil, fought the federal government to make the sluggish Mississippi waters navigable, and voted a cowboy in a ten-gallon hat to be its roaring mayor.

Muscles counted for more than brains in Omaha. A man was judged by his size, his house, and his money. A woman was expected to stay home, knit, sew, crochet, and try to look pretty as late in life as she could. The Bible was the only reading matter found in most households; the story went around Omaha that when a new encyclopedia salesman out of New York knocked on fifty Omaha doors in a day, he was told, 'We already have a book.' Rotarians, Elks, Shriners, and Masons dominated the brown, drab office buildings with their glazed glass partitions, linoleum floors, and noisy typewriters.

Newfangled radio was discouraged in many Episcopalian and Baptist homes. The most popular movies offered stalwart heroes, melting heroines, and vamps or villains who got their comeuppance in the last reel.

Omahans had a stubborn, suspicious disregard for the industrial East, with its sweatshops, its labour unrest, its high-hat airs. Contemptuous of Big City corruption, they clung to the old rural values of share and share alike, help your neighbour, and gang up against the big guys.

The Brando family were pure Omaha several generations back on the father's side. Marlon Sr was twenty-seven in 1924, a spick-and-span product of the Shattuck Military Academy of Minnesota, where he had excelled at swimming, football, and in the Crack Squad, one of the three best parade-drill teams in the nation. Shoulders thrown back, erect as only a military man could be, he marched to work every morning for Western Limestone Products in his homburg, dark suit, well-pressed white shirt, plain tie, and brightly polished patent leather shoes. He grew a neat moustache, attended church on Sundays, and generally minded his manners. Yet behind the immaculate Episcopalian front he was another creature entirely.

He had a temper inherited from his folks, the Brandows (formerly Brandaus), a Dutch-Alsatian family that settled in New York State in the early nineteenth century. His father, gruff Eugene Brandow, was National Lead Company manager in Omaha. Marlon Sr, who changed his name to Brando, philandered, stealing away to Chicago for lusty fornication in the brothels or husbandless boudoirs of the Windy City. A teetotal Omahan at home, he drank on the sly out of town. Speakeasies knew him well, in the Prohibition towns he visited on his 'business trips'.

His wife was another creature entirely. Dodie, born Dorothy, came to the marriage under a shadow. Pretty, fair, sturdily put together like her husband, she was

18

cultivated, sensitive, tender, and fond of the arts; some thought her 'Bohemian'. She read books, loved classical music and New Orleans jazz, sported brightly coloured cloche hats, and had a childlike love of fun and laughter and risqué jokes. She also enjoyed acting on the stage.

Her family past was dark. Dodie's grandmother, the beautiful Julia, had married Dr Myles Gahan, a bedrock Episcopalian, devout Mason, and governor of Grand Island's St Francis Hospital. Dr Myles settled down with Julia in Grand Island, Nebraska, in a big white frame house that was often opened up for showers or galas or charity dinners. But rumours circulated of Dr Gahan's cruelties, his sadistic treatment of his devoted wife, and it was said that his children – Bessie, his eldest, Vilma, June, and Myles Jr – lived in fear of their formidable father.

In 1896, Bessie married William Pennebaker, bookkeeper and later treasurer of the Cripple Creek Mining Company. In 1898 and 1899, Bessie gave birth to two daughters, Dorothy (Dodie) and Elizabeth (always called Betty).

The year Betty Pennebaker was born, Dr Gahan quit the family home, abandoning his wife and children. He moved to Omaha; not a word did he write them from that day on. Grand Island was scandalized. And soon his fellow Episcopalians were to have more fodder for gossip. Dr Gahan, pillar of his community, was broke. He had secretly disposed of his real estate. So when Julia filed for divorce, she found she had a huge mortgage to pay off, and her husband had a mere $1,300 to his name. Julia did the only thing possible for a pretty, impoverished woman in those days. She found a new husband, a farmer named O. O. Hefner. Then, to escape wagging tongues, she carted herself and her brood off to Omaha.

When Dorothy married Marlon Sr, Dorothy's sister Betty married Oliver Lindemeyer, a rubber tyre executive from California, and moved out West, where Dodie visited her from time to time.

Marlon and Dodie's first child, Jocelyn, was born in 1920; their second, Frances, three years later; and Marlon Jr, their youngest and last, on April 3, 1924, in the Omaha Maternity Hospital. From the day his mother tenderly carried him in his swaddling clothes into the three-storey white-clapboard, elm-flanked house on Mason Street, the boy was a star. He was nicknamed Bud, Jocelyn was dubbed Tiddy, and Frances Fran or Franny. Bud liked to imitate everything and everybody as soon as he could toddle. If he could climb up to a shelf, you could be sure he would fall from it; feet first of course, but in a way that suggested he was having a fit. He was mischievous, comical, outgoing, gorgeous, and irresistible: a baby prince.

When he was three the Brandos moved to 1026 South Second Street, a bigger house in a fancier part of town. The backyard offered an enormous elm that Marlon could see from his third-floor room; his father built him a treehouse in it. There was another elm out front. Marlon went to kindergarten from age four. His favourite place was the monkey house at the zoo, where he became fascinated by the primates, observing their habits with fierce interest.

Julia Gahan died before Bud was born; he scarcely knew his paternal grandparents, Eugene and Marie, before they passed away, but he was crazy about his grandmother Bessie ('Nana') Hefner and his Aunt June. Bessie was a Christian Science convert and a champion speedreader who could get through an entire novel in

20

an hour. Dodie would take him and his sisters to visit with Bessie or June in Grand Island, to enjoy the simple pleasures of their table. Because Bud and Frannie were closer in age, they had more in common with each other than they did with Jocelyn. They would run away regularly on Sundays, leaving their shoes on the running board of the family car to announce their disappearance. Jocelyn often had to search for them herself; she would invariably find them roaming around the stores in downtown Omaha. She took them to school in harnesses until they learned better.

Sometimes five-year-old Bud Brando would shinny up the mantelpiece, pose there, clutch his chest dramatically, and fall from some imagined Indian arrow. The family competed to see who could eat fastest, hold their breath longest, tell the biggest lies, or sink fastest in muddy sand before hollering for help. Bud delighted in exploring neighbourhood rubbish dumps looking for rusty bicycle wheels, abandoned corsets, broken umbrellas, hairbrushes, or dead birds and cats. When his pet chicken died, Dodie arranged for the bird to be buried near the river. Bud disinterred it and brought it back to the kitchen, depositing it on the table. He was sent back to bury it again (he didn't).

He often got into scraps with neighbourhood kids. He was as jumpy as a gopher on a hot griddle. Dodie said later, 'One day the mother of a little boy in our neighbourhood came to our house in a towering rage and complained Bud had been beating her son. As soon as Bud learned the boy was younger than he, and he was about six, he left him alone. They became bosom friends, and (twenty years later) Bud was the best man at his wedding.'

She also recalled, 'Even as a boy, Bud had a great desire to travel, to see faraway places. When he was a child, he'd often start on mysterious journeys all by himself. But he never got very far. One day I helped him pack for his final trip. He wouldn't tell me where he was going. He took a skillet and some eggs with him as provisions for the journey, but he forgot to take butter. He had to cook the eggs in the skillet without any butter, and came back to wash the skillet. That ended his journey; he stayed.'

Dodie's obsession was the Omaha Community Playhouse, which she had helped to found just before Marlon was born. Much as she loved her children, she was bored by the drudgery of housework, and, fanciful and lighthearted in temperament, found escape in the charming rough-and-tumble of an ambitious semi-professional theatre. Under the able direction of Gregory Foley, the Playhouse was run in a brisk communal spirit. Business leaders, fashionable ladies, clergymen, and physicians all pitched in with money and social support, helping to make scenery and costumes, flinging charity showers and holding meetings to discuss what plays they would present. Foley was influenced by the new theatre in Europe that dispensed with all but the most minimalist scenery, and this revolutionary approach on a midwestern American stage caused even the distinguished periodical *Theatre Arts* to sit up and take notice.

Dodie was the biggest name in the Playhouse. By all accounts, she had great charm, style, versatility, and presence on the stage. And the repertoire, in which she also played a hand as assistant producer, was extravagantly varied and ambitious. In 1925, she was the star of *Liliom*, Ferenc Molnár's fantasy play about a girl in love with a fairground employee and their experiences in a world between life and death. Her acting was described in the *Omaha World-Herald* as 'memorable'.

In Arthur Wing Pinero's romantic drama *The Enchanted Cottage* – which was filmed in Hollywood many years later starring the Playhouse's own Dorothy McGuire – she was a tragically ugly girl transformed into beauty for love of a disfigured man. Like her son in later life, Dodie showed a mastery of the art of makeup and gesture, concealing her natural beauty in the distorted face and hunched, awkward posture of a psychically and physically ruined heroine. When her true looks emerged in the transformation scene, the *World-Herald* announced that 'the audience gasped'.

When Marlon was nineteen months old, Dodie took him to Los Angeles to visit her sister Betty Lindemeyer. She reported back to the paper on seeing a production of *Outward Bound* while she was there: 'Good, but not as good as ours.'

Even Marlon Sr deigned to appear on the stage in 1926, as a swaggering, hairy-chested, bloodthirsty pirate in *Captain Applejack*, 'an Arabian Nights adventure by Walter Hackett,' that was described as 'a highly seasoned, bubbling dish,' with a plethora of vamps, ladies fair, its handsome hero and its moustachio-twirling villain. Dodie appeared in the fall of that year in the title role of Eugene O'Neill's *Anna Christie*. As the waterfront girl trying to find some meaning in life, she made her strongest impression to date. The *World-Herald* critic wrote on October 26, 'Mrs Brando far excels her earlier work. Anna is old in her youth, with the knowledge of life's injustice and its bitterness. The sincerity of the character and of Mrs Brando's interpretation of it lies in the fact that Anna speaks the truth and *is* the truth, ugly though it may be.' These words would equally apply to the unaffected realism that her son would bring to his best performances.

The constant work at the Playhouse took Dodie away

from her children. 'I became mother to Fran and Bud,' Marlon's sister Jocelyn said.

Dodie was in Channing Pollock's play *The Enemy*, as the bewitching Pauli Arndt, expertly handling an Austrian accent. She passed on to her son her gift of mimicry. Assistant director of *The Enemy* was a slight, very handsome boy called Henry Fonda, who had been hired, at Dodie's recommendation, when the Playhouse was founded. (Henry's Aunt Jane was a major figure of the Playhouse.) Many years later, Fonda repaid the debt by recommending Jocelyn for the only female role in the World War II Navy play *Mister Roberts*, in which he starred on Broadway. She was very successful in the part. In January 1928, Hank, as he was known, co-starred with Dodie in Eugene O'Neill's *Beyond the Horizon*. A composite photograph of the cast in cameo cutouts shows Fonda, dreamy and liquid-eyed, with the face of a poet; Dodie looks square-jawed and determined, her face framed in a pretty white cloche hat.

Jocelyn, Frances, and Marlon were in the audience for the elaborate Festival of Nations that Dodie helped produce, given for the International Folk Art Society of Omaha and held at the City Auditorium. A picture of Dodie at the time shows her looking pensive, leaning dramatically against a door in a long white Isadora Duncan scarf. She was also producer of a much-admired production of J. M. Barrie's *A Kiss for Cinderella*, in which Dorothy McGuire, the most talented member of the children's theatre, played touchingly opposite Henry Fonda.

Dodie's problem was that she was fond of the bottle. Whether her alcoholism sprang from the stresses of trying to run a full-scale local theatrical career, a large house, and a growing family all at the same time or was the result of her husband's notorious philandering is uncertain. It was ironic that, just when her tippling of bootleg liquor and visits to speakeasies became a serious hazard to her career, she turned up in the starring role of the drunkard's wife in the hoary old moral temperance drama *Ten Nights in a Barroom*. The *World-Herald* wrote, 'When Mrs Brando ... does her song number, you are instructed not to throw things that will hurt. Her fearful earnestness in singing "Take Back Your Gold" is one of the most amusing elements in the performance. The melancholia of her Julia is deliciously comic.' The irony didn't go unnoticed. Even today, old Omahans prefer not to be quoted as they speak in whispers of Dodie's drinking habit.

In 1930, Marlon Sr obtained a better job, with the Calcium Carbonate Company of Chicago, and the family reluctantly dislodged itself from South Second Street and moved to Evanston, Illinois. To leave the Omaha Playhouse just when she was winning attention in serious theatrical circles was quite a disappointment for Dodie. Young Hank Fonda had already left town and was clearly set for Broadway and beyond. There was no theatre in Evanston to speak of.

The Brandos' rented house in Evanston was at 1044 Judson Avenue, just a couple of miles from Chicago's northern border. The 1000 block was very grand. Among the residents were Bishop George Stuart, one of the early leaders of the ecumenical movement, and a member of the World Council of Churches, who always walked with his head up high as though he were talking to the Lord himself, and Andrew McNally, grandson of a partner in Rand McNally, which published the Mother Goose series and numerous atlases and maps. Marlon liked to imitate these distinguished gentlemen with their haughty airs; Stuart and McNally looked down on the Brandos as social inferiors.

It was a two-storey frame dwelling in one of the classic streets of the town, with proper homes and looming old mansions on either side. The Brando home – rented, never bought – faced east, which meant that, despite the shade of a big elm tree at the front, it was as hot as the inside of a Franklin stove in the summer morning hours. The house was close to the beach of Lake Michigan, to the neighbourhood schools and bustling Main Street.

It was a handsome residence. The fireplaces were pure marble. The living and dining rooms were big and airy. The kitchen, the centre of the family's life, had not only a fat-bellied stove but also an extensive icebox, and a boot room with a wood chest for winter storage upstairs from the fruit and storm cellar. Even the garage was something. It was a brightly painted slatwood structure with sliding doors and glass panels and a salt box, Marlon's favourite refuge, where raccoons and possums made their home.

Marlon and his sisters enjoyed running up and down the hardwood staircase with its maple banister, racing through the master bedroom and the two children's rooms on the front of the second floor south side. They invaded the maid's room and fooled around with her sink, toilet and bed.

Marlon Jr's bedroom was on the north side. Smaller than the other rooms, it looked out on the backyard. The children relished the attic, an unfinished, rustic, musty place with low ceiling boards jutting out at irregular angles; it afforded a perfect place to seek refuge and listen to the wind whistling off Lake Michigan. Frances wrote later in the block newspaper, 'It was there, under the eaves [that] the enclosed spaces were ideal for hiding or imagining perils or simply [indulging in] childhood dreams.'

Evanston was a 'thrilling, even glamorous environment,' Frances continued. She added that the town was just the right size for kids to encompass as they flew freely about on their bikes. They enjoyed risking their necks over scary trails on high clay mounds along the Metropolitan Sanitary District canal located several miles away along the city's western border. With neighbourhood kids, the Brandos discovered treasures in trash cans; they played scrub, and kick the can, and several versions of hide-and-seek. All summer, in decorous bathrobe and slippers, they trailed down to the beach at Greenleaf Street. They dived from the dangerous pilings and the broken-down pier, or shouted at the crazy lady on Sheridan Road by the lake. They sneaked into houses that had been left vacant and explored them from cellar to roof, making up ghost stories or other fanciful tales about the empty rooms. They roller-skated and followed the neighbourhood bagpiper and organ-grinder and could hardly wait for the Good Humor man. The sight of an elderly woman driving a Detroit Electric auto (she had a generator in her garage) would have them in transports of delight.

Bud was always the centre of attention, the star of the neighbourhood block. Richard Stockton recalled the family very well: 'I remember one time his sister said he had been walking in his sleep the night before, and I had never heard of such a thing and I was wondering what on earth they were talking about.' Ruth Woolf, who lived at 414 Greenleaf, said, 'I remember Bud. He used to go exploring – too far! I used to chase him off my garage roof.'

Milton Avgerinos, a young Greek-American, was probably Marlon's closest boyhood friend. Milton

27

remembered him, as everyone else seems to have, as 'a free spirit. An individualist who would do anything he wanted.' He recalled that he and Marlon were constantly at each other's homes and were fond of each other's parents. They were always getting up to various pranks. Milton remembered running with Marlon to the fire alarm box a block from Marlon's home, pulling the alarm, and running back to the house. They raced up the stairs, hid in the bathroom, and watched through the window the thrilling sight of red fire trucks screaming down the street in response to the alarm.

Milton shared pleasant summers at Lee Street Beach with Marlon. The two would wander through town sunburned and seeking the relief of dime ice cream cones at the local soda fountain. Other times they spent enveloped in the rich, plush seats of the local movie theatre for a mere six cents a ticket. Sometimes there would be musicales in Dodie's living room, when she would play the piano, and Milton, Bud, and the other neighbourhood kids would join in a group sing. Jocelyn would lead the children in hastily prepared playacting sessions.

Winters were as much fun as summers, Milton remembered. He and Bud could earn nickels digging cars out of the snow or winning bets in snowball-throwing competitions. They did have a major mishap one Christmas. Milton, Bud, and their friends realized that discarded Christmas trees made great forts after they were sawed into pieces. Spare branches would be used for bonfires. Some of the trees were very large. On one occasion, Milton was carrying the top of a tree and Marlon the bottom. The tree was about seven feet long. As they were struggling with all of their ten-year-old strength to manage this unwieldy prize, an automobile slammed into the tree and threw them over with it. They were badly cut and bruised.

Milton recalled that there was no way that Bud could be kept indoors against his will. If he was placed in his room for misbehaviour, which was often, he was amazingly skilful at removing the screen from the window no matter how carefully it had been hammered on by his father.

On Saturdays, the children went to see the matinees at the Main Theatre, and on Sundays they went to the Varsity, Valencia, or Howard movie shows. They loved the talkies, especially Westerns with cowboys and Indians, movies that, to his later shame, Bud cheered loudly. He dressed up in a cowpoke outfit and swaggered convincingly in imitation of Hoot Gibson or Hopalong Cassidy. Few children in Evanston could match him when it came to acting out being hit by an Indian arrow. He alarmed little girls as he fell down the house steps into flower bushes, twisting in all too convincing agonies of death.

Marlon attended Lincoln School, just two blocks away from his parents' house, on the corner of Main and Forest. Soon after he enrolled, the family moved to a handsome apartment at 524 Sheridan Square. Built in 1896, the school was architect John T. Wilson Jennings's masterpiece. It looked like a castle, with its turret, mullioned windows, and ancient grey stone. Lincoln was part of the elementary system, with a creative arts programme that leaned heavily on Northwestern University's Fine Arts Department.

The dominating presence was Supervisor Frederick W. Nichols, a bearded, perfectionist scholar and former sheepherder, who had become so dissatisfied with the general textbooks available that he wrote and published his own. The school staff was admirable. Mildred Milar was Marlon's fourth-grade teacher. She remembered Marlon coming to school neatly dressed

29

in a fresh white shirt, tan pants, and oxfords. Mildred Milar said, 'His mother would send him so well dressed. But by the time he reached the classroom, he would have had a scuffle of some sort in the playground. His shirttail would be out, his hair all tousled, like a curly chrysanthemum on top. Usually, he had been fighting for the underdog in the yard, the guy who seemed to be losing.' By contrast, Mrs Milar said, Jocelyn was 'like a little doll,' and Frances was 'more of a conventional conformist than Bud. It bothered Fran that he got into these scuffles. They were very close.' Another teacher recalled striking up quite a friendship with this 'bright little boy, Bud,' whom she would find sitting on a tile bench outside her classroom. He would be sent there to prevent him from disrupting a class in session: a quietly effective discipline. 'He was just a mischievous little kid,' the teacher said. 'Full of pep and life.'

One of his classmates was the frail little ten-year-old Wally Cox, whose mother was an author of mystery stories and of a novel about itinerant Scandinavian farm workers entitled *Seedtime and Harvest*. Wally was always being picked on because he lacked athletic ability. He could put up his fists and fight but very often would wind up on the yard covered in dirt. Marlon took his part, protecting him. He loved Wally. They were complete opposites: Bud was brawny and physical, Wally was a thinking reed. One of Marlon's teachers recalled, 'Bud came in one day filthy black from top to bottom. Somebody had said something about Wally and he had rolled Wally's critic around in the coal shed. He looked like a Negro.'

Young Bud would take on anybody, and on one occasion impulsively smashed in a small glass window in an Evanston hotel when a big party was in progress.

A classmate said, 'We were playing kickball or some such game and the ball got slammed into Bud's face. I guess he thought I was responsible. He pulled out his little dingus and tried to pee on me.' A boy who was with Marlon in sixth grade remembered 'walking home with Bud, jumping hedges, the usual things'. Another classmate, Nan Prendergast McChesney, said, 'He loved to tease the girls. One time, he chased us with a garter snake. He was always in *some* kind of trouble.' He would clown around constantly, put frogs in his sisters' beds, clash with them in pillow fights, scrap with the neighbourhood kids, and find every excuse to be a cutup.

In the late afternoon and evening, Marlon liked to listen to the radio, sitting enthralled with his sisters at the adventures of the Lone Ranger, Jack Armstrong, and Little Orphan Annie. After that, the kids had cups of cocoa and off to bed. It was a pleasant life, healthy and vigorous, and Evanston, with its airs and graces as the sophisticated lady of the North Shore, primped and fashionable, with its picturesque homes and spacious lawns, was an idyllic setting to grow up in. It was conservative, Republican, rearguard, dominated by the ladies of the Women's Temperance Union, who even made merchants stop making ice cream sodas because of the supposedly intoxicating effects of the fizzing soda water. It is claimed that the ice cream sundae was invented in Evanston to overcome the temperance ladies' objections.

2

Dodie would have liked to have had more children, but her husband had sexually neglected her. In addition, she suffered the loss of her acting career. In a city ruled by temperance workers, a woman like Dodie, who drank, got whispered about. It was soon to be common knowledge in Evanston that she was an alcoholic, that she continued to buy bootleg liquor in the Prohibition years. Already, the seemingly idyllic family life of the Brando clan was falling apart. And Dodie was faced more than ever with a painful subject she had tried to ignore: Marlon Sr's womanizing.

The façade of the Brandos' family happiness shattered when Bud was twelve and his father came home from a romantic encounter in Chicago with his undershirt and shorts smeared with lipstick. Dodie drunkenly screamed at him, and he responded by beating her brutally. Bud threatened to kill him. It was an ugly scene that was to be repeated many times in the years to come.

Bud lost his respect for his father as soon as he was old enough to understand the man's true nature. He resented his father's hypocritical insistence on the double standard. His mother's fits of crying, as she flung herself on her bed and sobbed her heart out over her husband's cruelties and infidelities, hurt and angered the boy.

At last, in 1938, Dodie Brando had become such a scandal in Evanston that they had to move again. The two girls visited with their Aunt Betty in Santa Ana,

California, for a while, and so did Bud. Marlon Sr left his job and became first a manager at Chemical Carborundum, which fed cattle with chemicals for better beef, and then at Shellmaker, which supplied calcium for chickens to improve the strength of their eggshells. He snapped up a farm near Libertyville, another satellite town of Chicago, less haughty and more rural than Evanston. Bud entered the tenth grade of Libertyville Township High School. He played snare drum in the band but otherwise took little interest in the school. He was fairly good at track, but his lack of discipline quickly forced him off the team. Legend has it that he was in school plays, but the Libertyville High magazine shows that he never went beyond fooling around as a member of the Curtain Raisers, the team of backstage hands employed for dramatic productions. Only Franny of the three Brando children actually acted at Libertyville. Marlon flunked typing class, largely due to his absenteeism. His typing teacher confirms that he scored 'minus thirty words a minute' on his test. As he was at Evanston, he was a classic cutup. Glenn Miller, a former classmate of his, said, 'Bud was contrary to the norm. In those days, kids dressed nicely and properly for school. But when Bud turned up, it was in a ripped T-shirt.'

Frank Underbrink, son of the high school's head teacher, remembered, 'Bud would take off and ride the rails, then call his parents collect after a few days of wandering and ask for the money to come home. Marlon Sr and Dodie were worried sick about him. I remember they came to see my dad, in our living room, and I recall them saying, "We don't know what to do with the kid."'

A young, handsome would-be actor named Don Hanmer was around the Brandos a good deal in 1940, awkwardly courting twenty-year-old Jocelyn, whom he later married. They had met at the Lake Zurich Summer Playhouse, where Jocy was working. Hanmer has vivid memories of the family at the time. He said, 'While Marlon Sr was away on his business trips, Dodie would let the whole house go. Everything was all over the place. Then Dodie would suddenly say, "Oh, God, I gotta make a hole in the house." Which meant picking the things up and putting them away because Bud's dad was on the way home and he wouldn't like to see the way the farm looked. She was such a free and easy person. I loved her.'

Hanmer will never forget the first day he met the family – all cutting up when father was absent. 'Bud was sitting at his drums, beating away like a madman to a Gene Krupa record. When Jocelyn said to him, "I want you to meet Don, Bud," Bud barely looked up and kept banging away. Fran came tearing in dressed in jodhpurs and said, "Hi, Don!" and out she flew. Then Dodie ran in and shouted, "Hi, Don, dinner's ready!" And she put her two fingers in her mouth and made the loudest whistle that I ever heard! It was total madness!'

He added, 'Bud came over one afternoon to see Jocelyn in a play at Lake Zurich. He was talking to me and Jocy when all of a sudden he fainted. Everybody in the theatre was in an uproar. He was the centre of attention. Of course, he wanted to be! He finally came to. Of course, he hadn't "fainted" at all.'

After Don and Jocelyn became engaged, Don often played football with Bud in the farmyard. He enjoyed that, but there were times when he found the kid disconcerting. Young Marlon had developed his custom, mentioned by just about everybody, of studying people minutely, down to the last detail of their clothing and demeanour, as though to catalogue gestures, movements, and mannerisms. He would draw on this knowledge when he became an actor. Hanmer said, 'We would all be sitting at the dinner table and suddenly I'd notice Bud was staring at me and studying me and would make me feel uncomfortable. Then suddenly he'd make a remark about me, a remark that was probably pretty close to being on target. I found that kind of directness embarrassing. I was pretty gauche at the time. I felt uncomfortable with this kid.'

Don's and Jocelyn's wedding took place at the farm. The Hanmer parents were there from Chicago, along with Marlon Sr and Dodie and Bud and Fran. Hanmer said, 'I felt like an ape at the ceremony. My hands felt enormous. I guess many guys feel like that when they're married. I was so awkward in those days. They had this huge Great Dane, Dutchie. Dutchie barked all through the ceremony. It was very distracting. When it got to the point where the preacher said, "If there is any one among you who objects" – or something to that effect – "speak now or forever hold your peace," there was a silence and then Marlon Sr very loudly cleared his throat. Jocy and I nearly jumped out of our skins! After we were pronounced man and wife, we walked out to the car to drive to Lake Zurich for our one-night honeymoon. Bud came out after us and stood beside the auto and without warning began to sing "Auld Lang Syne". We thought it was rather strange.'

The Hanmers were so short of money they had to stay at Libertyville for some time while both tried to make some headway on the stage. Hanmer recalled terrible quarrels between father and son. They would be on the porch when Marlons Sr and Jr would start screaming at each other. Dodie would say to them, 'Can't you speak in a normal voice to each other? Can't you just have a discussion?' Then the pair would walk into the front yard and a minute later the screams of anger would be louder than ever.

Julia Cameron, a former Libertyvillan and now a *Los Angeles Herald Examiner* columnist, recalled that Bud's first date at fourteen was a fellow high school student. Miss Cameron remembered her as not particularly attractive, 'small, worried . . . with a depressive nature and a voice like the drip of a faucet'. Years later, Marlon's grandmother Bessie told Truman Capote, 'Ah, Bud. He always went for the ugly ones!' If that is true, then he certainly broke the rule later on.

One of Bud's most miserable memories of that period was when his father forced him to milk the family cow. He was supposed to go to the prom that night, and to his disgust the cow shat on his shoes. Try as he might, he couldn't get rid of the smell, and the rest of the evening was painfully embarrassing.

He constantly rebelled against authority. According to the Reverend Douglas Wright, a former schoolmate, he lit a fire in the classroom. One day during band practice the conductor said that he was annoyed with the orchestra, and, 'if the directions I gave were wrong, I deserve a kick in the pants'. He didn't mean that seriously, but, Wright said, 'For Bud, that was too big an opportunity to pass up. He placed a good, hard kick in the conductor's pants. Bud was banished from the band.'

Bud had now become rather fat and roly-poly, and Marlon Sr gave the boy dumbbells and barbells. Pressured by his father, Bud was busily involved in bench presses, arm curls, flies and bent-over rowing movements. Within a year, he was already showing signs of a muscular physique. Much as he disliked the gruelling drudgery of body-building, and his father's insistence that he continue with it, he at least had the pleasure of earning the admiration of other boys and the admiring glances of young girls. It cannot be said that he entered into the training with any more intrinsic discipline than he entered into anything else in life.

Marlon Sr finally realized that it was impossible to discipline the boy so long as he lived at home and went to school as a day pupil. So, in 1942, Marlon Sr decided to send his difficult son to his own alma mater, Shattuck Military Academy at Faribault, Minnesota. Marlon hated the idea of this. Although America was at war following the Japanese attack on Pearl Harbor on December 7, 1941, he didn't share most young boys' ambition to be in the service. In fact, he was quite indifferent to the flag-waving jingoistic atmosphere pervading the nation. But he had no alternative. He had to accept his father's unpleasant ruling. He took the Union Pacific Railroad with a change of trains in Chicago to Faribault's Rock Island Depot, arriving on September 1. He was driven across the Fourth Street Bridge, past St Mary's School and the Treasure Cave Blue Cheese Factory to the top of the hill where the military academy stood. Three hundred yards down the drive, he passed under an archway where he caught his first glimpse of Shattuck's orange and cream quarry limestone buildings covered in a rich growth of native ivy.

Soon he was listening to the commanding officer's welcoming address, filled with the inevitable homilies about loyalty, dedication, and patriotism. Marlon found that his fellow students were almost all sons of graduates and, like himself, members of the Episcopal Church. Marlon was assigned to room 142 in Whipple Residential Hall. His roommate was young John (Jack)

Adams. But his closest friend was the lean, genial Dick Denman, who had arrived at the same time. Denman roomed right across the corridor.

The daily schedule was a torment to a free spirit like Marlon. The students were wakened at 5:45 each morning. After their shower, they had to lay out their uniforms, shine their shoes, and brush their hair. Following inspection, they had to report for early morning drill, which involved jumping jacks, sit-ups and push-ups, and dozens of other calisthenic exercises. They marched to breakfast in the dining hall, wolfing down a hefty meal of cereal, eggs and bacon, toast and coffee, and prepared for classes, which started promptly at 8:30 A.M. Lunch was served at noon. In the afternoon, there were military hikes and exercises, including infantry drill in setting attack and defence formations. From 3:30 to 5:30, there were compulsory athletics, covering a whole range of sports. Immediately after that, there was a full hour of military formation drill, followed by dinner from 6:30 to 7:00. Classroom study went on from 7:30 to 9:00, with lights snapped out at 9:30 P.M. The only break in this gruelling regime was on Wednesday afternoons; the only female company the boys enjoyed was a very occasional, fully chaperoned date with girls from St Mary's School. Marlon's favourite date was the attractive Barbara Wright, whose mother knew Dodie very well. They took country walks (with a chaperone!) and danced together at the military proms. There was nothing serious in their relationship: just a light-hearted, adolescent boy–girl friendship.

The advantage of this daily grind was supposed to be that it turned out fit young men for active service. Despite his lapses from discipline, Marlon worked hard at Shattuck to make something of himself. He was extremely popular. His good humour, irreverence towards his teachers, ready smile, and no-nonsense, down-to-earth lack of pretence made him an ideal classmate. And of course his athletic ability ensured him outright admiration all round. He was a strapping five-feet nine-inches tall, 156 pounds of well-defined brawn. Dick Denman remembered, 'Bud could run like a deer for long distances. He was a swimmer without peer and was on his way to being the best footballer at Shattuck in his time.' In his first year, he emerged strongly at swim meets, doing well in the 400-yard freestyle dash and on the 160-yard relay team. He was substitute on the B squad as right halfback on the football team. Hudson (Hockey) Mealey, later a University of Minnesota football great and a star of the Shattuck team, said, 'Bud was always horsing around. He could have been a terrific athlete. He was very fast on his feet and had a magnificent physique. But he didn't hold to his form.'

Marlon was also a member of the Crack Squad, which his father had joined in 1916. This was a precision-drill team whose members were considered the school elite. To join it was Shattuck's highest honour; the squad had never been defeated in intercollegiate competition. To be part of the squad involved two hundred hours of flat-out training for just twenty minutes before parents at the annual parade. Marlon Jr's membership in the squad was one of the few accomplishments that his father ever appreciated.

But soon, his nature reasserted itself. In his second year, he injured a knee in a scrimmage on the football field, following a touchdown. Once out of the hospital, he used an exaggerated limp. According to Shattuck's civilian headmaster Nuba M. Fletcher, Bud worked his limp for weeks, 'Anything to duck out of assignments, classes, duties.'

However, Marlon did find one discipline he enjoyed. He enlisted with the Shattuck Players, under the guidance of English Department head Earl M. (Duke) Wagner and assistant teacher Frank H. (Buzzy) Below. Dick Denman said, 'Bud wanted to be an actor. He excelled in English classes where Shakespeare was the staple. He would read Shakespeare far into the night.' Denman added, 'He not only understood the words but the deep meanings in them. He was very successful in acting on the stage. He was able to pick up on the writers' perceptions. But then he had an odd thing he would do. He would change the lines as he saw fit. His dramatic instructors weren't too thrilled when he did that.'

Marlon first appeared in *A Message from Khufu*, a melodrama about an archaeological expedition to Egypt that was inspired by the story of the discovery of the tomb of Tutankhamun. He played Ben, the dashing hero, and he was described in the school newspaper as 'a new boy who shows great talent'.

He appeared in the farce *Is Zat So?* and a play about ghosts, *Four on a Heath*. In the latter play, he was a highwayman strung up from a gallows with a rope around his neck. Just released from the school hospital after his football injury, he made it to the theatre despite his limp, arriving just before the performance was to begin. The limp gave considerable realism to the performance. The audience applauded loudly, and the review was a rave.

Over the years, rumours, fuelled by Marlon himself, had it that he was responsible for a variety of pranks, smoking in the gymnasium, making a firecracker bomb that scorched the parquet floor, cutting the bell rope in the tower and sending the bell crashing down on somebody's head, and emptying a chamber pot out of a dorm window. All of this was the invention of press agents. However, it is true that he often cut classes, and on one occasion did start a small fire on one of the floors of the building, using a flammable hair tonic. When he dropped out of the Crack Squad by pretending to be lame, he infuriated headmaster Fletcher. Finally, Fletcher warned him that he would either have to turn up for regular inspection or go back to the hospital and stay there. Fletcher said, 'When inspection came, Marlon wasn't there. We checked the hospital. He wasn't there either. We found out he had just decided to go downtown. He broke probation. That was a serious offence.'

He was expelled immediately and told to pack his bag and go home. This was a considerable shock to his girlfriend, Barbara Wright, who still lives in Faribault. She feels today that his sudden removal was like 'an execution'. Though nothing serious had come of their innocent romance, she was very fond of him, and was the envy of many of her fellow pupils at St Mary's School because of Marlon's looks and physique. The boy's dismissal was a great shock to everybody at Shattuck as well. The cadets were crazy about young Bud and immediately made a massive joint petition to have him reinstated. Headmaster Fletcher was impressed with this show of loyalty and love, and offered Marlon the chance to come back and finish his studies the following summer term. But Marlon had no interest in that. He had already become bored with Shattuck.

He returned to Libertyville and his father's wrath. It was a severe blow to Marlon Sr that his son was such a loser. To be expelled from military school was a great

41

dishonour, especially in wartime. Marlon Jr was nine-teen now.

And there was worse to come. Marlon was pronounced 4F at his draft medical exam. The appropriate records are locked up in the old Army storerooms in St Louis and inaccessible; according to Marlon, he pretended to be psychologically disturbed and convinced a psychiatrist, who confirmed his problem and excused him. Another explanation is that his football injury had left him with permanent cartilage damage and he would not have been able to stand up to pack drill or route marches. Whatever the reason, he was delighted, since he was totally without interest in joining the service.

Instead, he worked as a day labourer. But he found the constant ditchdigging and construction work intolerable. So he decided he would go to New York and try to bum his way into the theatre as some kind of an actor: the only pursuit he had any aptitude for or interest in. Jocelyn – Don was now in the Air Force – had already moved there and had made some headway on the stage. She had actually appeared in a Broadway play, *First Crocus*, while Fran, who had also moved away from home, had started to paint in Greenwich Village. Dodie hoped Marlon would succeed as Jocelyn had. Marlon Sr was contemptuous of his son's desire to join his two sisters to take up a career as an actor, quite forgetting that he himself had had a brief fling on the stage in Omaha. Although he accepted his girls going on the stage, acting wasn't, to Marlon Sr, a man's job: it was something for 'faggots or fairies'. No doubt this contempt for the profession stimulated Marlon all the more to seek a life on the stage.

3

Just past his nineteenth birthday, at the end of May 1943, the stocky, muscular kid in T-shirt and dungarees arrived in New York. 'The first thing he did when he got off the train,' Frances Brando said, 'was to have his shoes shined. And then he felt so sorry for the shoeshine man he gave him the five dollars in his pocket.' The city was filled with servicemen in uniform. The bars were so crowded you often had to reach over somebody's shoulder to order from the bartender. A current joke had it that you were lucky if you didn't find yourself drinking out of somebody else's glass.

At night, the city assumed an eerie aspect. There was talk of possible bombing attacks from Germany, and the dim-out was in force, which meant that every building had to be darkened as the sun went down. The Statue of Liberty's torch was subdued for the duration. New Yorkers were surprised to see, as they strolled the night streets, the unfamiliar stars.

That week in 1943, Manhattan was a clean, glittering, soaring city of transcendent energy and vitality. The streets were filled with men of all ages in uniform, all the way from gold-braided generals to willowy sailors in virginal white bell-bottoms. Only the very young, the elderly, or the physically handicapped wore civilian clothes. The crowds swarmed through the sun-filled canyons of stone, under a brilliant blue sky. The hotels, in particular the Astor and the Biltmore and the Savoy Plaza, were hubs of activity in the overcrowded town. So booked up were they that a room could only be obtained for a maximum of five nights. For the well-heeled, there were the glamorous nightclubs, the Copacabana, the Stork Club, or the Latin Quarter. Older officers favoured the Persian Room, where the elegant pianist-chanteuse Hildegarde played wearing long satin gloves. Most popular of all was the Rainbow Room, high up in Rockefeller Center, where there was dancing to a swing orchestra surrounded by heavily curtained windows.

Girls in those days wore garish make-up, their hair piled high under fancy hats fashioned like cauliflowers, tulips, vases, or lampshades. Their costumes had square shoulders, with pleated swinging skirts equipped with deep pockets. Handbags were slung over shoulders and were large enough to pack a lunch in.

Despite the war and the fact that meat, coffee, sugar, canned goods, and nylon were rationed, and women had to paint their legs brown because of the shortage of stockings, the atmosphere was one of intense and antic gaiety. A man on furlough, physically fit from weeks of training, irresistible in his uniform, had the world at his feet.

Swing set the tone of the wartime city. Along with the yells of street vendors selling chestnuts, lemonade, orange juice, or candy, and the insistent scream of the traffic, the sounds of Benny Goodman, Glenn Miller, the Andrews Sisters, Gene Krupa, and Frances Langford filled the air from a thousand jukeboxes. There were even bands in hotel lobbies, furiously screeching away. Every cab driver played music from his car radio very loud, to the delight of the smooching couples in the back.

Marlon, able-bodied, husky, and healthy, was a complete outsider with practically every other kid of his own age in the service, but this didn't bother him at all. With his duffle bag slung over his shoulder, he cheerfully made his way to Frannie's rented pad on Patchin Place in Greenwich Village.

He was barely able to make his way through the clutter of canvases, easels, palettes, and art books. Frannie was lonely and depressed, and Marlon had to work hard to cheer her up with his antic humour. 'Her boyfriend, an early date from Libertyville, had become a Naval pilot and had been killed in action,' Don Hanmer recalled.

Marlon loved Greenwich Village, with its proliferation of all-night book stores and galleries and coffee bars and quiet squares where poets read their work aloud and old men gathered to play chess on Sunday afternoons. Greenwich Village was leafier, more appropriately named in 1943 than it is today; informal, pleasantly scruffy, it was a quiet oasis in bustling, brassy Manhattan. A young man could spend a day browsing among old books or used records or simply contemplating the sky and the leaves and the people passing.

The focus of activity was Washington Square. Bustling restaurants such as the Samovar, the Purple Pup, the Pirate's Den, Gallup's, and Polly Holliday's were the most popular. In these crowded and smoke-filled meeting places, the intellectuals gathered to talk politics, philosophy, art, music, psychology, and literature. Foreign movies were preferred to local ones. Chess was the most favoured game. Marlon, who had, despite his natural athletic ability, no interest in participatory or spectator sports, felt easily comfortable amid their intellectual scene. While he may have been somewhat inarticulate, he had the capacity to listen. He absorbed an enormous amount of information and became a cheerful expert on everything. Greenwich Village became his university, and the bearded denizens his mentors.

'Bud was thrilled at being free from all the restrictions which he felt were a greater imposition than other people think they are,' Frances said. 'He just went head first into everything. He lived a typical Bohemian life, stayed up all night, went to parties. Everyone he met, he took very seriously. He believed they were what they said they were. Every odd, bizarre thing was marvellous. He was open to everything.' But, she added, the disillusionments he suffered taught him to see deceit and insincerity in people. He studied gestures and speech; he was a master of mimicry and could manage any accent: French, Spanish, Italian, Yiddish, Greek. 'He would bring almost anybody home to spend the night at the studio,' Frances said. 'Just because they didn't have any place to sleep.'

Jocelyn was out of town that spring, touring as an understudy to Dorothy McGuire in *Claudia*; Don Hanmer was to appear in Moss Hart's patriotic all-American Air Force show, *Winged Victory*, which would open at the Forty-fourth Street Theater in November.

Marlon settled into the comfortable, easy flow of Village life. There, his T-shirt and jeans and scuffed tennis shoes seemed quite normal. His silent, moody strength, square-cut physique, and crooked, mischievous schoolboy smiles, at once sexy, secretive, and challenging, fascinated everyone he met. Women fell over each other to go to bed with him.

In those first weeks, he met a stunning girl named Cecilia d'Artuniaga Webb, known to everyone as Celia. Small, dark, intense, and adoring, with big, liquid brown eyes, Celia was crazy about Marlon. They began seeing each other regularly.

That spring, after working briefly as a lemonade salesman on Fifth Avenue and an elevator operator at Best's department store, Marlon enlisted in the drama classes of the New School for Social Research on West Twelfth Street. The New School Dramatic Workshop, under the direction of the great Erwin Piscator, was the magnet for many aspiring young actors arriving in New York City. The Workshop had been established in 1940 and already was filled with much of the young, raw talent that would emerge spectacularly in the years to come. Among the students of the mid-1940s were such future luminaries as Harry Belafonte, Shelley Winters, Walter Matthau, Tony Curtis, Rod Steiger, Ben Gazzara, Elaine Stritch, and even Tennessee Williams.

Entering the New School's building was quite an experience for the young Brando. Designed by the internationally celebrated Joseph Urban and built in 1931, the New School was a marvellous example of Bauhaus architecture. The building featured spectacular murals by Thomas Hart Benton and the Mexican artist José Clemente Orozco. Even the reception room for new arrivals on the third floor was stunning. It was completely surrounded by Benton's works, illustrating the Old South, the lumber industry, the growth of the West, the rise of the coal and iron industries, the emergence of American industrial power, and aspects of life in the Big City.

In those days, most of the students were formally dressed, in coats and ties, even in the hot late-spring weather. Marlon, with his T-shirt and jeans, stood out, and drew either shocked or admiring stares from most of his fellow pupils. He was introduced to Piscator and his wife Maria Ley. A small, intense disciplinarian

47

with piercing, pale blue eyes and an intensely Teutonic manner that grated on Marlon's nerves, Piscator was a refugee from Hitler's Germany; he had conceived the Dramatic Workshop as the creative centre of all American theatre. He had been a member of the Communist party and had run into considerable controversy in Berlin; moreover, he had had considerable difficulty immigrating to the United States in view of his political background, and even the support of Albert Einstein, Max Reinhardt, and Sinclair Lewis had not resulted in his being granted citizenship.

In Germany, Piscator had revolutionized the theatre by stripping away the old, timeworn techniques of heavy, emphatic scenery, staging, and acting and instead using bare stages, realistic lighting, and naturalistic performances. This theatrical innovator, whose thinking had even influenced Dodie Brando's Omaha Community Playhouse, would now accept her talented son into his workshop.

The Dramatic Workshop was, in the words of the New School's historians, Peter M. Rutkoff and William B. Scott, 'much more than a school ... less than a drama company'. Piscator ran it with an iron hand. His faculty was extraordinary. Theresa Helburn, pillar of the Theater Guild; Harold Clurman and his wife, Stella Adler; the theatrical historian John Gassner; and the feisty Lee Strasberg were among the brilliant teachers. George S. Kaufman, Paul Muni, and Sinclair Lewis were sponsors and occasional lecturers. The distinguished composer Hanns Eisler and the great conductor Erich Leinsdorf also taught there; the term courses included acting, voice, and speech as well as dancing, indoor calisthenics, and lectures on the history of drama.

The atmosphere in classes was intensely concen-

48

trated. This was long before the era in which students would shift around in class, whisper, get up and go out and come back again, or sample drugs. No one would have dared even sneeze in a Piscator session. Piscator demanded unequivocal obedience, absolute dedication and passion, and if one of the boys or girls failed to demonstrate these, he would be ruthlessly weeded out and his departure recommended in no uncertain manner. Marlon chafed at this gruelling imposition on his life, but he could see no other future open to him, and certainly to be a member of the Dramatic Workshop was an accomplishment in anyone's career.

As for Stella Adler, Brando would never forget her first entrance into the class. She walked into the room with a commanding poise, magnetism, and imposing presence. Her parents, Jacob and Sarah, had dominated the Yiddish theatre in New York throughout much of the early part of the twentieth century. Tall and majestic, with masses of fair hair, staring blue eyes alive with wonder and surprise, and a theatrical voice that harked back to the Broadway mode of thirty years before, Stella, then in her mid-forties, was a creature held in awe by almost everyone. Her only real enemy was Lee Strasberg, whose system of teaching acting was very different from her own. On a visit to Paris in the 1930s, Miss Adler, with her husband, had met and had been permanently influenced by the legendary Russian teacher Konstantin Stanislavsky. From Stanislavsky she had learned that the actor must take his inspiration from a scene's intrinsic truth. Instead of relying on effective memory – the recollection of events in his own experience, as Strasberg wanted – Adler insisted the actor become the instrument of the playwright's vision, not imposing his ego on the play. Such a thesis was the opposite of Strasberg's, who believed in drawing everything from the actor's own entrails, as a silkworm draws silk. Miss Adler taught her students that the playwright provided the truth to which the actor must adhere; out of this adherence would come a performance that would be the equivalent of everything the artist had envisioned. Brando said later, 'Stella had the deepest influence upon me. She influenced my personal and my professional life. I am devoted to her. As a teacher, she has an infallible instinct for character and for knowing what people are. The spectrum of her talent is reflected in all she does.'

Flamboyant, adorable Stella was larger than life. She once said to her husband Clurman, waking him from a slumber in which he tossed restlessly in the grip of nightmares, 'Don't sleep like a great man. Just sleep!' When he informed her he was ten thousand dollars in debt, she said to him, 'You are underplaying the part. A person in your position should be one hundred thousand dollars in debt!' She said of Brando, 'I taught him nothing. I opened up possibilities of thinking, feeling, experience, and I opened the doors, he walked right through. He never needed me after that . . . He lives the life of an actor twenty-four hours a day. If he is talking to you, he will absorb everything about you, your smile, the way your teeth grow. His style is the perfect marriage of intuition and intelligence.'

What Stella saw in Marlon was his lack of pretence, his hypersensitivity to experience and his ability to concentrate on everything with the instinctive sharpness of an animal – absorbing people, places, and objects. Unburdened by intellect, he had none of the problems of rationalization that can handicap a performer. Not only did he have in abundance the physical beauty, virility, and animal magnetism necessary in any male player who might one day become a star, he also had the brute wisdom of the semi-educated, and the public would be able to identify with him. Whatever he might lack in polish or technique (he was no John Gielgud in the making, certainly, nor was he a young Olivier) he could more than make up for with an innate earthiness and an instinctive possession of the common touch.

To most of his friends, he was simply a character and a cutup, whose life consisted of hamburgers, hot dogs, Cokes, bedding girls, and going to see funny movies. No one remembers him inside an art gallery or a concert hall. His closest friend at the time, other than Celia Webb (Marlon, who had a tendency to lisp, had a problem pronouncing her name), was the twenty-year-old Darren Dublin, slight and twinkling, who was in the drama class with him. Darren skimmed cheerfully along the surface of things, not taking life too seriously, fond of chasing nubile young women, full of bright talk. The two men hit it off at once. 'What did we do for entertainment in the evening?' Dublin said. 'We fucked girls. Apart from that? We'd go to movies. He liked Laurel and Hardy pictures.' Marlon would double up with laughter, holding his stomach, at Laurel's frail, sublimely stupid klutziness and Hardy's chubby, roly-poly exasperation. From the great comedians this sexy kid learned the skill of minimalism: the art of deadpan.

That summer, Dodie had split with Marlon Sr. Still drinking heavily, she moved, at her family's suggestion, to Manhattan where, for $150 a month, she rented a sprawling, dowdy brown ten-room apartment in a brick building on the corner of West End Avenue and Seventy-seventh Street. As embarrassed as ever by her drinking, Marlon saw little of her, only occasionally gathering with the rest of his clan for dinner at her home. He was always anxious in her presence for fear she would pass out at the table. Don Hanmer returned on furlough that fall to rehearse for *Winged Victory*, and he and Jocelyn moved in with Dodie to help take care of her. Frannie stayed on in the Village with Marlon. Marlon's antics fascinated Hanmer. He recalled a typical display of eccentricity: 'I was just out of rehearsal for the show and here comes this guy with a paper bag on his head. I could see by the shape of him it was Bud. This paper bag had two little holes for the eyes so he could peek out. I said to him, "Bud, what the hell are you doing with a brown paper bag over your head?" and he replied, "Hiding from – ", he mentioned some girl's name. "She wants me, and I'm trying to hide from her." I thought, "Hiding? and he has *a paper bag over his head*?"'

In October 1943, Marlon began appearing in Drama Workshop shows at the New School. The students were featured in a series, *The March of Drama*, in which theatre authority John Gassner lectured and individual scenes were performed by the young actors. Critics, talent scouts and agents haunted these productions, looking for new actors of merit. The performances took place in Joseph Urban's magnificently designed New School auditorium. The amount of study, rehearsal, and performing the students had to do was incredible, and Marlon was in everything. Just to list his weekly performances is exhausting. His first appearance was on October 29, 1943, in George Bernard Shaw's *Saint Joan*. On November 5, he was Bartley, the old woman's son in John M. Synge's *Riders to the Sea*. Just a week later – so tremendous was the pressure of the compulsory repertoire – he was Prince Anatole Kuragin in Piscator's condensed version of Tolstoi's *War and Peace*; on November 19 he was a second workman in Georg Kaiser's expressionist play *Gas*, and a mere week later Golya, a student, in another Gassner illustrated lecture scene from *On the Eve* by Alexander Afinogenov. On December 10 he was Nikita in Tolstoi's *The Power of Darkness*, and on January 7 – there was a badly needed break for Christmas – he was in a class improvisation session under Erwin Piscator's gifted thirty-year-old assistant, brisk, efficient, crop-haired Chouteau Dyer.

On January 21, Marlon appeared in Gerhart Hauptman's fanciful melodrama, *Hannele's Way to Heaven*, about a girl rescued from drowning whose mind is filled with fantasies of the hereafter. Marlon played her lover, the schoolteacher Gottwald, who in the opening scene carries her limp, water-drenched body on to the set; later he becomes the dark angel who haunts her dreams. In one scene, Brando entered dressed dramatically from head to foot in black, carrying a bunch of bluebells, then flung off his cloak to show a tunic of pure gold. His realistic acting style contrasted sharply with the affected quasi-mysticism of the play. George Freedley of *The New York Morning Telegraph* said that Marlon's was the best performance of the evening. Two nights later, Freedley reviewed *Twelfth Night* saying of Marlon's Sebastian: '[He] handled the part . . . satisfactorily, though it would have been interesting to see what he might have done with Feste or Orsino.' Marlon also played a giraffe in a children's play, *Bobino*, by Stanley Kauffmann, at the Adelphi Theater, was the star in two plays of Molière cobbled together as *Sganarelle* and appeared in many other New School productions.

The records of the New School Drama Workshop show as many as seventeen absences in just twice that many days in March and April, and Piscator and Chouteau Dyer were severely aggravated by his behaviour. 'My husband loved Marlon like a son,' Maria Ley Piscator, now eighty-eight, said. 'But Marlon didn't want to work. It hurt Piscator terribly.' Marlon showed no sign of guilt at his frequent class-cutting, and began telling people his newfound conviction that acting was 'for the birds'. One of Piscator's students, the well-known actress Elaine Stritch, remembers her intense feelings for Marlon at the time, when she was seventeen. She had come from twelve years in a convent and was staying in the strictly regulated confines of a Roman Catholic finishing school run by nuns on Ninety-first Street.

She fell in love at first sight with 'this extraordinary-looking young man, so different from the young guys I went with back home. There was something very sensitive, very artistic and wonderful about him, like a figure in a romantic novel.' Elaine was trying very hard to look grown up. She wore fancy hats with veils like Stella Adler's, and did her best to project the persona of a dignified and mature woman. She smoked cigarettes and behaved as dramatically as possible. She drank too much red wine. The truth is, hers was a terrific act: she was a virgin who knew nothing about the world. Her idea of an affair between a man and a woman was based on old Irene Dunne–Charles Boyer pictures, in which the hero and heroine went to small Italian restaurants with chequered tablecloths and bottles on them and whispered romantic nothings to each other in the semidarkness. She admits, 'I knew how to kiss and hug. But as far as physical contact with a guy, no way! I was going to be actress. It was first things first.'

She was terrified of Marlon because 'he had gone through that school like a dose of salts'. According to Elaine, he even took out the ugliest, fattest bucktoothed girl in class. When Elaine warned him that would only confuse the girl because he had no intentions of being serious with her, he laughed the idea off, saying that the fat girl was 'all things to all people, and similar bullshit'.

He was determined to carry the shy Elaine off to bed. He called the Reverend Mother of her convent school, and the old nun was excited, thrilled when she heard his voice because she had heard so much about him from Elaine. She came running down the stairs to the smoking room, the only place in the Ninety-first Street convent where the students were allowed to enjoy a cigarette, exclaiming loudly, 'It's Marlon! It's Marlon!' Elaine said to her, 'You're acting like he's asking *you* out!' Elaine rushed to the phone in a dither of excitement; Marlon said he would like to take her out for her birthday, February 2. He picked her up at the convent school. She looked forward to a Dunne–Boyer evening at an Italian restaurant with violins. Instead, 'Au contraire . . . He took me to the public library!' Elaine says he did it because of his 'wicked' sense of humour. 'He knew the books would bore the shit out of me!' From the library, he carted her off to a synagogue, and to Presbyterian, Russian and Greek Orthodox churches, studying her reaction as a devout Catholic and gleefully noting her discomfort. Finally, they did go to a Greenwich Village restaurant, where she drank so much wine she could hardly raise her fork. And very late, he took her to 'the rawest, filthiest, dirtiest nightclub with a floor show you could imagine'.

She was in a state of shock. By the time it was midnight, she was a complete wreck. At last, Marlon asked her if she wanted to come up to his apartment and see his new cat. Completely innocent, she went upstairs without a tremor, wearing fur coat and boots because of the snow. He sat her down on the couch and disappeared behind the curtain leading to his bedroom. She sat there frozen and began playing with the cat. Marlon called out to her to take her fur coat off. She said she wouldn't. Suddenly, the cat let out a howl like a soul in pain, and Elaine cried out, 'What's the matter with the cat?' Marlon replied from behind the curtain, 'She's in heat! If the smell's bothering you, open the window!' Wondering what she would do next, Elaine was still frozen on the couch when, without warning, Marlon emerged from behind the curtain dressed in pyjamas. That was enough. Elaine fled down the stairs. By now, it was three A.M. Her convent school had closed at curfew time, two A.M., and when she banged on the door, the Reverend Mother had to throw on her habit and let her in. Elaine burst into tears. She told the old nun everything and was advised, 'Just say a prayer to Our Lady and she'll straighten you out.'

However, prayer proved useless. Elaine remained hopelessly in love. Marlon didn't forgive her for that first date and didn't speak to her for a year. When they appeared in plays together, the situation was 'unendurable' for her.

Among those who had heard about Marlon was the Music Corporation of America (MCA) agent Maynard Morris. In those days, the slight, high-strung Morris was constantly looking around the drama schools to find new and exciting young clients. Not only was Morris struck by Marlon's presence, electricity, and sexual magnetism as Sebastian in the Shakespeare play, but his friend, the small, energetic Mayer Mishkin, who was in the talent department of Twentieth Century-Fox pictures, was also very impressed by the performance. Mishkin recalled, 'Everybody in the cast of *Twelfth Night* looked pure "drama school" until this

56

kid came on. His voice was unusual. He was strange, different, a kind of renegade. When the show ended, I turned to Maynard, who was sitting behind me, and said, "That guy is interesting," and he replied, "He is. I just took him on as a client."'

Mishkin arranged for Marlon to come into the office at Twentieth and meet the casting chief, Joe Pincus. Like most theatre people, Marlon had a contempt for Hollywood, feeling that nothing of merit came out of it. He certainly didn't want to try out for a movie – unless, of course, it was a huge part – but he went in for the test to please Maynard Morris.

Marlon sat in various positions on a stool, full-face, profile, three-quarter-face, so the director, Burk Symon, could see whether he was photogenic. He found the experience ludicrous; much as he liked Mishkin, the test bored him to tears. To relieve the tedium, he pulled a yo-yo out of his pocket and started playing with it. Mishkin said, 'I asked him, "What are you trying to do? Get me fired?" So Marlon said, "Okay, I'll do the test again." Right in the middle of the next take, he pulled an egg out and did a disappearing magic trick with it! He achieved his purpose. My boss, Joe Pincus, said, "Don't send that test anywhere. Throw it out!"'

Harry Belafonte, also a student at the New School, said that at the time, 'I was one of the few black guys there, and Marlon was one of the handful who befriended me. The only way we could afford to see Broadway plays was to share a ticket. I'd see the first half and Marlon would take over after intermission. Sometimes it was the other way around. Afterward, we'd go to a local café and have a nickel cup of coffee and compare notes.'

Belafonte recalled that some weeks they would play

large roles, some weeks small. One particular actor irritated them with his conceited behaviour. Cast in *Twelfth Night*, in a role that required a padded stomach, the actor found the lining filled with itching powder supplied by Marlon and Harry.

In addition to Darren Dublin and Celia Webb, Marlon formed another close friendship that year: with Carlo Fiore, who was also a student at the New School. He insisted on calling Carlo Freddie. Born of immigrant Sicilian parents, just over twenty at the time, Carlo was lean, sinewy and dark, a moody, bright youth who had dropped out of college early to help support his family by steam-pressing clothes in the Garment District. He wore zoot suits several sizes too large for him, with enormous pads to disguise his narrow shoulders, and pompadour haircuts slicked down with grease; he sported a broad Brooklyn accent. The two met for the first time at Pennsylvania Railroad Station, where, along with Elaine Stritch, Darren Dublin and the other class members, they were heading for Sayville, Long Island, for the three months at the New School's Summer School under Chouteau Dyer and Maria Piscator. Fiore never forgot Marlon arriving on the platform, dressed up for a change in a well-ironed button-down oxford shirt and well-pressed tan slacks and carrying two expensive leather suitcases. The only sign of his Bohemianism was his well-scuffed pair of tennis shoes. As the train drew out of the depot, Marlon, grinning his schoolboy's mischievous grin, introduced himself to Carlo in the parlour car. He invited Carlo to join him and the other students, most of whom were laughing and kicking up a storm, but Carlo hung back shyly. Marlon liked him for his reticence. They were friends at once.

Sayville turned out to be a joy. The wooden, semicolonial theatre building overlooked a small private beach scattered with driftwood and a bay that was bright blue in the summer sunshine and sparkling with yacht sails. Swimmers were shouting and throwing coloured beach balls. Fields ablaze with wildflowers surrounded the property's stables, barns and gardens. The students raced to the basement storeroom and picked up bed frames, linen, and blankets, setting up house with startling speed in any room that would accommodate them. A few found places outside the building. Marlon settled on the barn as his 'place of residence' for the entire summer season. The barn had every advantage. It had a ladder that could be drawn up, rendering the hayloft inaccessible to intruders when girls were lured in there. It was comparatively cool, with a cross-breeze from the sea. And of course there was something irresistibly romantic about the idea of making love in a hayloft.

Marlon dragged his and Carlo's bed frame pieces, bedding, and linen across the lawn to the barn. Inside, the barn smelled sweetly of straw and summer weeds; the ladder rose all the way up to a trap door in the ceiling; there was plenty of room in the loft to set up the beds. There was even a small arched window through which they could see danger approaching. What more could a man ask for? Too excited to sleep, the youths talked until sunrise.

It was a pleasant season. Marlon appeared in *Ladies in Retirement*, as the nosy Cockney boy Albert Feather, who pries into a murder committed by an unhappy spinster, Ellen Creed (Chouteau Dyer). Elaine Stritch and a new and gorgeous actress named Blossom Plumb were the crazy Creed sisters Emily and Louisa. Marlon worked backstage in *Charley's Aunt*, listed along with

Blossom as an 'assistant,' and he rehearsed for his former role of Sebastian in *Twelfth Night*.

Marlon didn't take his work too seriously. His modest fees were being met by Dodie, who wanted him to be a good actor, fulfilling all of the ambitions she herself was never able to realize. He had pocket money to burn. He managed to borrow an automobile, drove himself and Carlo riskily fast, swam naked in the ocean at night, made love, sometimes sharing the girl with Carlo, consumed hamburgers, chips, and hot dogs. He bummed his way through most of the classes, reducing Chouteau Dyer to exasperation.

Dodie arrived at Sayville to visit with Marlon in June. She felt the lure of greasepaint and was very pleased indeed when Chouteau Dyer, at Marlon's suggestion, decided to include her in the class as by far its oldest member. She asked for and obtained the leading role of the doctor in a one-night performance of *Cry Havoc!*, a play about women in the armed services in which both Blossom Plumb and Elaine Stritch were featured. At first, she was eager, excited, and anxious to see Marlon working. She was relieved to find that he still wasn't drinking anything – beyond a very occasional beer.

But for Dodie, there was the constant tension of working with young actors and actresses who enjoyed drinking both by day and by night, and who remained miraculously unaffected by alcohol during their performances. Like all alcoholics, it was a terrible strain to see others enjoying liquor when she could not. Frustrated by her husband's sexual neglect, and a woman of great passion and sensuality, she inevitably found herself drawn to the many handsome youths resident at Sayville. But at her age, almost twice their own, it would have been extremely undignified to reveal her feelings.

It was therefore a delight to her when she found that Carlo Fiore showed clear signs of attraction to her. He was one of those rare young men who found middle-aged women irresistible. But she still didn't want to make the first move.

Carlo told Marlon he wanted 'to fuck Dodie'. Marlon wasn't pleased, but said nothing. That same night, at a party held in the theatre for the entire company and crew, Carlo danced with Dodie again and again. As they held each other close under the multicoloured lights, Carlo felt himself aroused. Dodie responded, but she was still nervous about allowing herself to be drawn into a sexual situation with a man young enough to be her son.

Towards midnight, Marlon and Carlo drove Dodie to her motel two miles away on the edge of town. Back at the theatre, they parked their car in the lot and strolled across the lawn to the barn. Marlon said to Carlo, 'I can see you want Mother. Why don't you go to bed with her?' Carlo looked ashamed and embarrassed, and said he wouldn't do such a thing. Marlon, who had asked the question in a tone of heavy seriousness, suddenly burst out laughing. He was testing Carlo; he certainly didn't want his mother to have an affair with his friend. Dodie and Carlo saw little of each other after that.

Marlon was still unforgiving of Elaine Stritch. Not only was she nervous around him, but she also resisted sleeping in a dormitory with the other girls because of her modesty about undressing. One of the students built her a kind of tiny annexe off the kitchen, with a window that led through the wall. One night, she was saying her rosary when Marlon burst through the door. He was carrying a prop gun from *The Petrified Forest*.

Elaine had had many nightmares that he was going to kill her for refusing him her favours. When she saw the gun, she was horrified. Grim and unsmiling, Marlon walked up to her bed, stepped on her stomach in his bare feet, and went through the kitchen window. He opened the icebox, took out a bottle of milk, drank it, and returned, stepping on her stomach again. 'He left me in a pool of sweat,' Elaine said, laughing affectionately after forty years. 'That son of a bitch!'

Rehearsals of *Twelfth Night* continued. Carlo appeared as Antonio in the play; Darren Dublin as Sir Andrew Aguecheek. Marlon was cutting up more than ever, defying Chouteau Dyer's anxious discipline. The fact that Piscator himself was absent in New York encouraged Marlon to abandon the self-control he had learned from Stella Adler. The dress rehearsal was a disaster. When Piscator turned up that night to address the cast, he gave them hell. Dodie lashed out at Marlon for his performance, dragging up all his mistakes in the past, storming off to her lodgings, packing up and departing for New York, telling him that she wouldn't talk to him again until he stopped being a boy and became a man. She said to Marlon, 'If you won't take acting seriously, you'll go into the feed business with Pop!'

Marlon did manage to concentrate on his part, and the actual performance of the play saw him in better form; the local reviews were quite respectful. Meanwhile, he was being distracted by Blossom Plumb, who was tall, blonde, and pretty. Still calling Celia in New York, he was consumed with Blossom in Sayville. But she held back and, unlike every other girl he approached, refused to succumb to his charms. When Marlon was lying innocently with Blossom on top of his bed in the barn, holding her hand gently and not attempting to make love to her, he got his comeuppance from Piscator. The great teacher opened the door and, seeing them together, announced that they were to come to his office immediately. There he told them that they were expelled. Marlon shrugged, but Blossom was heartbroken. She protested that nothing had happened, and Marlon seconded her, but Piscator was adamant that they must both go. Her parents came to pick her up. Marlon continued to date Blossom occasionally in New York during the next few months. According to Mrs Piscator, her husband later regretted his decision and said that Marlon was probably the most promising actor he ever taught.

Back in New York, Marlon moved from Greenwich Village to West End Avenue, with Dodie, who had gone back to the bottle. According to Don Hanmer, Dodie would vanish on drinking sprees for days at a time. Nobody knew where she went. Sometimes, Marlon or his sisters found her in some flophouse or dive. She would then return to West End Avenue and maintain sobriety for a while. Then she would slip off the wagon again. On one occasion, Hanmer said, Marlon, Frannie, and Jocelyn decided to try to find out where their mother kept her booze. After searching through all ten rooms of the apartment, they found no trace of a bottle. They raked through ceiling lamps, closets, chests of drawers, everywhere. At last, Dodie came home. Marlon and the girls said, almost in unison, 'Where did you hide it? The bottle . . . where did you put it?' Dodie laughed. 'It's very simple! Look under the towel on the bathroom floor!' They stared at her. She went on laughing as she said, 'One thing I know. None of my children ever picks up the towels from the bathroom floor!' Everybody broke up and hugged Dodie. 'She was a great gal,' Hanmer says. 'Very gutsy, very funny.'

Maynard Morris began pushing Marlon. The MCA agent praised his client's talents wherever he could. Brando learned to trust Maynard as he trusted few others. He spent long hours in Maynard's outer office, hoping for jobs to make some money to get by. He still cared little for acting.

Morris's associate Edith Van Cleve was another influence in Marlon's life. Tall, blonde, elegant, she adored him, and he was full of respect for her. She was convinced he was ready for Broadway.

Both Maynard Morris and Edith Van Cleve saw in this actor who was quite indifferent to thoughts of fame and fortune, who openly despised the egotism and selfishness of most of the theatre people surrounding him, an amazing natural talent that thrilled and enthralled them. Marlon was different from anyone they had ever handled as a client. Although he sought work to support himself, he seemed not to care whether he would ever be a leading man, let alone a star. They had constantly to push him ahead. Lazily overrelaxed, too often relying on his physical beauty to carry him through social and professional situations, he had the essential make-up of a semi-intellectual and the form and manner of a star athlete. Both agents knew the combination would finally be irresistible – but Marlon totally disbelieved them.

Edith Van Cleve decided that Marlon was, after such very limited experience, poised for Broadway. She found the play *I Remember Mama*, a series of sentimental sketches strung together by John Van Druten, one of Broadway's most polished gentleman playwrights, from Kathryn Forbes's popular book, *Mama's Bank Account*. Morris handed Marlon the script. Farsighted, and resistant to wearing glasses, Marlon asked Stella Adler if she would read it for him. She did, and told him he would be ideal as Nels, the fifteen-year-old son of an immigrant Norwegian family in San Francisco, who dreams of being a doctor and blossoms into manhood in the final scene.

Dodie, Jocelyn, Frannie, and he acted out a dramatic run-through of the play at West End Avenue. They all thought it was sentimental rubbish, and Marlon responded to the material with complete indifference when he forced himself to read it. But to please Stella and Maynard he read for John Van Druten and for the producers, Richard Rodgers and Oscar Hammerstein II. According to De Witt Bodeen, who later adapted the play for the screen, and who was present at the reading, 'Neither Dick nor Oscar was impressed with Marlon. But Van Druten was. He directed his play. He insisted Marlon play Nels.'

'Although he didn't like the dialogue,' Bodeen adds, 'Marlon tried very hard at rehearsals. John Van Druten was a terrific help.' Van Druten instilled in the company a sense of family, to which Marlon responded. Marlon was fascinated by the veteran Oscar Homolka, who played the father of the clan, shuffling around the stage with his nose buried in the script, refusing to put it away, even at dress rehearsal. And Marlon was intrigued also by the effortless command of another veteran, Mady Christians, cast as the mother.

Marlon was attentive at rehearsals, although his diction was badly slurred, and the British Van Druten, accustomed to words being spoken so clearly they could be heard in the back row of the upper balcony, had politely but insistently to ask him to speak up. He didn't always obey. But it was clear to Van Druten that he had made the right choice. In fact, for all of the virtuoso technique of the two principals, Marlon threatened to upstage them just because he had no theatrical style or obvious technique at all. He appeared to have wandered in off the street. The hint of Norwegian in his accent was just right, and the open-faced, chunky, pink-cheeked look inherited from his Dutch, Alsatian, and Irish ancestors made him ideal for the part.

Before the play opened, Marlon was asked by the theatre publicity man to provide a brief autobiography for the programme notes. Mischievously, he scribbled out, 'Born in Calcutta, India, but left there at six months of age.' And so read his first professional programme biography.

Dodie, who was at home during one of her drinking spells, was not present at the opening night at the Music Box Theater on October 19, 1944. Her absence must have been, for all his pretended indifference to his career, an agony for Marlon. However, Celia, Darren, and Carlo were present, along with Frannie and Jocelyn. The theatrical director and teacher Robert (Bobby) Lewis attended the performance. He said, 'This boy came down the stairs, and I thought, "It's an understudy they found on the street." He had no technique – nothing, and then I realized he was something new in the theatre – a completely fresh, real person, who made the rest of the cast seem theatrical.'

Marlon invited all of his friends to the West End Avenue apartment that night. Most of Marlon's gang were, Fiore said, 'shy, sensitive, frightened people, or outlandishly uninhibited exhibitionists. A sensible, serious person who wandered off the street wouldn't be welcome there.'

Marlon took Carlo to see Dodie in her bed where she had removed herself from the festivities. Bifocals perched on her nose, she was reading the steamy pages of *Lady Chatterley's Lover*. She told Carlo, 'I'm going back to Bud's father. It's just as well. I've put the family through a lot of hard times because of my drinking.'

It cannot be said that Marlon made a sensation in *I Remember Mama*. He was simply one of a large and expert cast, and no critic echoed Robert Lewis in singling him out in contrast with the others. The *New York Times* critic Lewis Nichols didn't mention him at all. Wolcott Gibbs in *The New Yorker*, after praising Mady Christians, Oscar Homolka, and the actress Joan Tetzel as 'nearly perfect,' added, 'So are the nineteen other people in the cast, and in this space we won't discriminate.' However, Robert Garland in the *New York Journal-American* said, 'Marlon Brando is, if he doesn't mind my saying so, charming.'

But Marlon's personal reputation went beyond any public or critical attention he might have received. The world of the theatre was abuzz over this extraordinary, fresh, and seemingly innocent talent. Women in particular went back again and again to the performance just to see him, so potent was his sexual attraction.

As for Marlon, he still had very little time for the play or the character he was performing. When he realized that it was set for a very long run, instead of being pleased, he groaned to his family and friends that he would now be a prisoner for an indefinite term. He had to find some way to alleviate the deadly tedium of repeating the same lines and business night after night and twice on matinee days. He developed a lifelong habit of rearranging the words he had to speak or making stage crossovers that were not in the directions, indulgences that greatly irritated the older members of the cast.

Deciding to play a prank on Oscar Homolka, Marlon put salt in his sugar shaker in the dinner scene. Homolka always emptied the whole sugar bowl into his coffee. This usually brought laughs from the audience. This time he swallowed the coffee and spat it out – Marlon was convulsed with laughter and improvised a line in which Nels apologized for the gag. Homolka didn't speak to him for months.

After the show each night, Marlon would meet Darren Dublin in the alley, or Blossom Plumb, who had moved to New York, or Celia Webb, or Carlo Fiore. Dublin recalls, 'We'd go to a little spaghetti joint he was crazy about.' It was called the Professor's. Some say Marlon was broke at the time. Dublin denies it. 'He always had money in his pocket. He was generous. People borrowed from him. I was broke. When I got through the two dollars a week my father gave me, I'd see his wallet lying on a table and I'd just go over to it and take out some bills. He saw it, and he didn't care.' One time, Marlon saw Darren in a suit that looked familiar to him. Darren had taken it and had it cut down to fit him. Darren remembered Marlon would never send anything out to get washed. 'He'd rather just take my underwear or my shirt and if it didn't fit he'd find another.'

One night Marlon, Carlo, and Blossom were talking in the West End Avenue apartment when, without warning, Marlon said, 'Goodbye,' and climbed over the sill into dense fog and disappeared. Convinced he had fallen, Blossom was hysterical. She called out into the fog. No reply. Carlo said, 'He's just playing a game. Ignore him.' They strolled into the kitchen. After some time, Marlon jumped in out of the fog. Blossom screamed at him, Fiore recalled, but Fiore just said, 'How did you do it?'

'I clung to the rainpipe.'

'It's rusty and rotten. Suppose it had given away?'

'That never occurred to me.'

68

Fiore described another incident. He woke up in the maid's room one morning after he and Marlon had been to bed with two girls. Their dates had left, and Marlon was in the bed with him. He was appalled to see Marlon's hand crawl down Carlo's stomach and fasten on his penis. But Carlo quickly realized that Marlon was mistaking him for one of the girls. The moment Marlon realized what he had in his hand, he let out a yell. 'Holy shit!' Marlon exclaimed. 'I thought I was in bed with a broad!'

'That's what I thought you thought,' Carlo replied.

4

I Remember Mama was a great success. Its warm, humanist sentimentality and gallery of vivid character portraits ensured it the support of a wide public, and it became a particular favourite of the women's clubs, which attended by the busload; matinees were always sold out weeks in advance. The run continued spectacularly for just under a year. The fact that he was in a Broadway hit was helpful to Marlon's career, though, as always, he was unconcerned with his own achievement. He would much rather have been in a new political play, or in Ibsen or Strindberg or Shakespeare. Van Druten had to return during the run to redirect Marlon's performance when it threatened to fall into flatness and dullness – which was often. When the decision was made to take the play on tour across the country, Marlon was the only member of the cast who did not go on the road. The thought of indefinitely acting this role of a simple Scandinavian youth was intolerable to him.

Having gone back for a time to live with her husband, Dodie now returned to New York. Marlon became increasingly exhausted by her comings and goings – her sudden unexpected bursts of temper and crying jags. Marlon Sr, cold, authoritative, and distant in Chicago, was of no help. A few days after *I Remember Mama* closed on Broadway, Dodie fell down on the floor drunk at Marlon's feet. He was so embarrassed and ashamed and miserable that he let her lie there and left the West End Avenue apartment. That night, she disappeared again. He had had enough. He moved to the Park Savoy Hotel, where he stayed for several months. His companion there was his former girlfriend Celia Webb, who, like all the other women in his life, would drift away from him, return to him, and then drift away again. She, like the others, couldn't resist it when he asked her back, so strong was his sexual magnetism and his charismatic personality. There could be no commitment on either side in these relationships: neither Marlon nor his girlfriends expected anything serious to result from these casual liaisons. If these women felt pain at Marlon's inability to make in them any kind of serious emotional investment, they chose not to show it. And Celia Webb was no exception to this rule. She knew that any kind of emotional dramas or demands would drive him away from her permanently.

Stella Adler, still passionately convinced of Marlon's genius and constantly overriding his own indifference, urged him to appear in a new play by Maxwell Anderson, *Truckline Café*, which was to be co-produced and directed by her husband Harold Clurman. By now, Stella and Marlon had become more than mentor and follower. They had become friends. Marlon was a frequent visitor to the homes of Stella's immediate family, her brilliant mother, doyenne of the Yiddish theatre, who gave some private instruction herself, and Stella's brothers Jay and Luther Adler, accomplished performers both. In the company of this extraordinary family, Marlon could at last feel what great theatre could be. He picked up, consciously or not, a rich range of gesture and emphasis from his minute and thorough study of these marvellous thespians at home and in their appearances on the stage. He absorbed everything but at the same time learned from the Adlers that to overanalyse or intellectualize in performance was fatal in developing a rapport with an audience. Acting came from the guts or it didn't come at all.

Set in a roadside diner on the ocean highway between Los Angeles and San Francisco, *Truckline Café* dealt with the restless lives of assorted travellers who stopped there. Stella wanted Marlon for the part of Sage McRae, a returned World War II serviceman who shoots his unfaithful wife and throws her in the sea, returning to the roadside café to give himself up. Among those cast were Karl Malden, Virginia Gilmore, and Ann Shepherd as the erring Tory McRae.

Co-producer of *Truckline Café* was the young Elia Kazan, who was also destined to be dominant in the young actor's career. Born in Constantinople, the stocky, feisty, harshly intelligent thirty-six-year-old Green-American was a force to be reckoned with in the theatre. An actor graduate of the Group Theater, he had made his mark as a director in 1942, guiding Tallulah Bankhead through the antic excitements of Thornton Wilder's play *The Skin of Our Teeth*. And he had already made an impression in the movies with his touching evocation of a New York City childhood, *A Tree Grows in Brooklyn*.

Clurman and Kazan were dubious about hiring Marlon for the part of Sage McCrae, but Stella was adamant that he must be given a chance. She told Clurman, 'This young pup will be Broadway's best actor within a year.' Reluctantly, the producer and director called him in for a reading. Marlon was equally reluctant. The play didn't impress him. He felt that its manufactured situations and stilted, quasi-literary dialogue would ensure it a rapid oblivion. But he didn't have the temerity to question Stella Adler.

At the first reading he was inept. Entering with round

shoulders, head bowed, hands thrust into the back pockets of his jeans, he mumbled his lines so badly that Kazan, who was never noted for his patience, asked him sharply to speak up. Clurman also lost his temper with him, demanding that he at least try to improve his diction. Kazan groaned and said that this was the worst actor he had ever seen. Already frustrated because he couldn't get Burgess Meredith for the part, Kazan thought both Stella and Harold were out of their minds to even consider Marlon.

However, Clurman saw in this young, withdrawn, brooding sensitive actor with his child's face and muscular boxer's physique a potentially powerful presence in the theatre. He was determined to work with this new talent; Marlon won the part. Maynard Morris's energetic associate Edith Van Cleve asked Marlon how much he wanted a week. Marlon said instantly, 'Five hundred dollars.' Somehow, he had found out that that was the fee Burgess Meredith would have received. She told him it was out of the question. He insisted. She screwed up her courage and called Kazan, who was incredulous and almost hung up on her. But the determined agent somehow forced him up to $275 a week, which was a decent salary at the time.

Clurman, according to his custom, spent long hours talking with Marlon, in an effort to understand this actor's strengths, weaknesses, and personality. He became fascinated by Marlon's capacity to absorb the personalities of everyone he met, to sum people up briefly, cryptically, exactly. He knew Marlon resented acting as an inferior occupation; that he was in the grip of machismo guilt about this supposedly soft profession. But Clurman also knew that Marlon was compelled to be an actor to escape himself. Marlon poured out his anguish in those long nocturnal meetings: his misery over his mother and his harsh, adulterous father, the pain of his childhood, the struggle to build his physique.

Clurman knew that Marlon's constant lying, pretending, teasing, his imitations and practical jokes were his way of dealing with his emotional turmoil. Clurman even thought he understood why Marlon mumbled. 'Marlon was unable to voice the deepest part of himself,' he said. 'It hurt too much. Because Marlon's acting had its source in suffering, the display of which he unwittingly resisted, it acquired enormous power.'

Once rehearsals of *Truckline Café* began, Clurman could see how Marlon had prepared himself for the part. Marlon had been starving himself to acquire the gaunt, hollow-eyed look of the tortured ex-soldier. Yet this conscientious effort towards truthfulness was counterbalanced by the actor's perverse laziness. Again and again, Clurman had to prod Marlon to enhance the dramatic force of his playing. Unable to hear Maxwell Anderson's words, the director had to move to the back of the orchestra, and Anderson, beside himself, would look at Clurman as much as to say, 'Who is that idiot on the stage?' Clurman would scream, 'Louder! Louder!' until he was hoarse. Finally, in desperation, he ordered Marlon to scream. Marlon let out a blood-curdling shriek that shocked Clurman to his feet. 'Okay!' Clurman shouted. *'Don't stop screaming!* You see that rope there? Goddammit, *climb the fucking thing!'* Marlon, startled by this unexpected violence in his mild-mannered director, expertly shinnied up the rope. Then Clurman told him to slide down it and roll on the floor from one end of the stage to the other, screaming and screaming. At that moment, Clurman ran up the steps to the stage, hauled back and kicked Marlon with all the force that his lightweight frame could muster. Marlon leapt up, bristling with rage, ready to kill him. The performance was born.

During the following three weeks of constant rehearsal and discussions among actors and director of the play's meaning, Marlon, who had come to hate Clurman, at last began to improve. He grew thinner and thinner, dropping down to a mere 135 pounds. Clurman ordered him to gain weight so that his early entrance from the beach in swim trunks wouldn't be too embarrassing. He stuffed himself full of hamburgers and french fries until he gained a few pounds. By the time dress rehearsal came along, he was feeling like hell. But he was working very hard now. Although he could easily have jumped in a shower fully clothed to show himself drenched in sea water in the final act, Clurman insisted that two men with buckets soak him, just as he went upstairs to the stage; in order to give him the shock of sudden cold. And when he entered, his teeth were chattering: it was a touch he thought of himself. As he delivered the big speech about the murder, dripping wet, shivering, the effect was extraordinary. When he spoke the words, 'I shot Tory . . . and then gave her body to the sea. I swam out to the end of the pier . . . Do you know what it feels like to be a murderer?' the audience was stunned. Even Kazan had to admit that he played with great power.

Yet, on the first night at the Belasco Theater, on March 2, 1946, he began awkwardly, mumbling so much through the first act that people began to get restless, asking each other aloud what he was saying. Most of the play bored the audience, but Marlon again rose to his big dramatic moment. As he sat at the table, cradling a hot cup of coffee, waiting for the police, tears streaming from his eyes, he not only acted the part, he lived it. The restive spectators were utterly still during the long speech. With the New York theatre crowd's traditional instinct for new talent, the spectators were electrified as they recognized the stunning performance of an extraordinary actor. As he made his final exit, he hit on a very good idea. The playwright indicated that Sage McRae should go willingly to his inevitable destiny in the gas chamber. Marlon walked as though he were dancing, happy to be destroyed. It was the final note of triumph in an unforgettable performance. The audience jumped to its feet and gave him a standing ovation.

The play didn't run. The reviews killed it. However, Marlon received considerable praise for his performance. Howard Barnes in the *New York Herald Tribune* wrote, 'Marlon Brando and Ann Shepherd bear the brunt of the melodrama with considerable skill.' Louis Kronenberger said in *PM*, 'As the young murderer, Marlon Brando is quite effective in a difficult emotional scene.' Vernon Rice said in the *New York Post*, 'Long after ... the play [is] forgotten we shall remember ... the poignant playing of Ann Shepherd and Marlon Brando as the ill-fated husband and wife.' But the consensus was thumbs down on Anderson's play itself. Lewis Nichols in *The Times* said that Anderson must have written it with 'his left hand in the dark of the moon'. No critic differed with that judgement.

On March 6, Clurman and Kazan published an advertisement in *The New York Times* announcing that they would close the production on March 9. Stating that no other course was possible in view of the notices, they charged that this misfortune was due to the stranglehold exercised by reviewers who rendered gifted directors and producers powerless. 'There is a black-out of all taste except the taste of these men,' the directors said. They added: '*Truckline Café* has faults, but is the kind of play that, in our opinion, every theatre lover should see. That is why we did it ...' George Jean Nathan dealt with their complaint in his 1947 Theater Yearbook. Summarizing the failure of the Anderson drama, he wrote, 'There is much truth in what the Messrs Clurman and Kazan say, though they have committed the error of picking the wrong play about which to say it, and so have made what they say nonsensical.'

During the play's brief run, Marlon became friendly with his fellow actors Kevin McCarthy and Montgomery Clift, who had already made their mark in the theatre. In home movies taken by McCarthy in Bedford Village, Marlon, bare to the waist, can be seen climbing a tree, trailing a stick through water, carrying Kevin's two-year-old son James, fooling around with Karl Malden and the up-and-coming actor Barry Nelson. He plays games with a very young and skinny Montgomery Clift, who was also born in Omaha, puffing smoke through a girl's skirt between her legs in a poster advertising the British film *Stairway to Heaven*, coming up behind Monty, who is reading a newspaper with a torn hole in the middle, and touching him suggestively, then flirting with him, dressed, like Monty, in a woman's flowered hat, two falsies stuffed into his shirt, making limp-wristed gestures, to which Monty responds in kind.

Despite the closing of *Truckline Café*, Marlon was still in luck. During the brief run, Guthrie McClintic, husband of Katharine Cornell, then at the height of her career as First Lady of the American theatre, had caught his performance. With him was the actress Mildred Natwick, who remembers how impressed they both were. 'Marlon was wonderful,' Miss Natwick said. 'Guthrie and I decided at once he would be perfect for

77

the part of Marchbánks, the young poet in George
Bernard Shaw's *Candida*, which Kit Cornell was about
to do for the third time, with me as the character
Prossie.'

Marchbanks, the delicate, tortured, poetic youth in
love with an older woman married to a minister, had
been played by Orson Welles and Burgess Meredith in
previous Cornell productions of the play. Meredith had
made a sensation in the 1942 production. It was a hard
act to follow, but Mildred Natwick recalls that
McClintic felt a stronger, more virile Marchbanks was
called for. And, of course, Marlon's strikingly lean and
gaunt appearance in *Truckline Café*, his expression of
tortured love, weighed heavily with the producer-
director.

Marlon was impressed by the thought of appearing
in a George Bernard Shaw play. He had, of course, been
in *Saint Joan* at the New School and he knew Shaw's
reputation as a champion of anti-establishment values.
Although the play *Candida* did not appeal to him
strongly, he was flattered by the opportunity to work
in the drama.

Even Marlon Sr was reluctantly impressed that his
son would be in a Shaw play. He flew to New York to
attend the first-night performance. At last, he was
beginning to yield in his grim opposition to his son's
acting career. And he was due for a vacation in Manhattan anyway. Dodie was too drunk to show any real
interest, but both Jocelyn and Frances were overjoyed.
They may have had mixed feelings about *I Remember
Mama* and *Truckline Café*, but Shaw was another
matter.

Mildred Natwick remembers, 'Marlon was always
very nice to me at rehearsals. Very polite, very subdued. Sometimes, he would let the performance down

somewhat, and Guthrie McClintic would bawl him out. But he would pull himself together again.' Marlon managed to suppress his natural athleticism to become the frail and fanciful poet. He 'became' what Shaw described: a strange, shy youth of eighteen, slight, effeminate, with a delicate childish voice, and a hunted, tormented expression and shrinking manner that showed the painful sensitiveness or very swift and acute apprehensiveness in youth, before the character had grown to its full strength. There was an odd parallel with *Truckline Café* in Shaw's description of Marchbank's clothes ('He has apparently ... waded through the waters.'). There was a damp, ragged look about Marlon's blue serge jacket, tennis shirt, and blue trousers that echoed his bedraggled third act appearance in the Anderson play.

On the first night at the Cort Theater, on April 3, 1946, the other actors, led by Miss Cornell and Sir Cedric Hardwicke, played with the precision and timing, the careful emphases of seasoned veterans. But Marlon was late entering on his first cue, and the cast stood in silent agony for a moment, unable to cover the awkward gap with lines or stage business. At last he appeared, pretending to be trembling with nerves, reaching for his face in an awkward, shivering gesture. Cast and audience were in a state of excruciating suspense. A prompter whispered his opening line, 'Glad to meet you, sir,' addressed to Sir Cedric Hardwicke, but seemingly Marlon didn't hear it. Shaw's stage direction called for him to back nervously against a bookcase. He took too long doing this. The expression on Katharine Cornell's face was indescribable. But of course, he hadn't forgotten his line. It was cunning of him to hold everyone in suspense. When he finally spoke the words, not a soul in the theatre was unaware of him. As he talked on, awkwardly, through the scene, to the words, 'I am so ill at ease with strangers,' it was obvious to everyone in the cast that he had successfully upstaged all of them. What chance did the elegant, seasoned precision of Katharine Cornell or Sir Cedric have against such a realistic player as this? And to add insult to injury, at the curtain call, he got by far the loudest round of applause.

The reviews, however, were mixed. Lewis Nichols in *The New York Times* wrote, 'Marlon Brando emphasizes the weakness and banks the fire [of Marchbanks], the result being a somewhat monotonously intoning poet.' John Chapman of the *New York Daily News* said, 'A new young actor named Marlon Brando managed to make something different, something a little more understandable out of the trying role of Marchbanks, the baby poet ... The role ... can be "horror, horror, horror." It can be too effeminate. It can be shouted ... Mr Brando achieved a believable, lovesick introvert by playing very quietly. His intensity was within him, where it should be.'

Marlon Sr, when he came backstage with Dodie, felt compelled to greet his son with pride. That night, there was a modest celebration at the West End Avenue apartment. But before long, Marlon Sr's unpleasant personality reasserted itself. Carlo Fiore recalled a scene several days later, on a Sunday, in which the family gathered for afternoon coffee and Dodie, crossing her legs, accidentally exposed the underside of her thighs. 'Adjust your dress!' Marlon Sr snapped, humiliating her in front of everyone. To make the occasion even more awkward, Marlon Sr coldly ignored Carlo Fiore, refusing to say a word to him all afternoon. Finally, Marlon and Carlo escaped to take the huge old family Great Dane Dutchie for a walk in Riverside Park.

When Marlon asked Carlo what he thought of his dad, Carlo responded with his true thoughts. He thought him 'a snob, a bully, and a bore'. When Carlo said, 'I wouldn't kick off my shoes, stretch out my legs, and pick my nose in his company,' Marlon said, 'My father's insecure. He's a frightened man.' Marlon described his father as fearing the loss of control over his family, giving that as the reason for his laying down ultimatums. 'I *hate* ultimatums!' Marlon said.

At last, Marlon Sr returned home. When *Candida* closed after a number of performances and opened in Chicago for a limited run, there were increased tensions between father and son, and Marlon chose not to stay in his father's home. Mildred Natwick recalls, 'Marlon often let the performance go in Chicago. He would forget lines. Guthrie lost his temper with him. But he improved once again.'

Back in New York, Marlon took up with a new girlfriend. While still seeing Celia Webb, he also dated Faith Dane, a tall, voluptuous, dark girl who was to play the bugle in a striptease scene in the musical *Gypsy* in 1959. Everett Greenbaum, later a well-known television writer, was just out of the Navy at the time, spending long hours in Washington Square Park among the chess players, when he ran into Faith. 'Faith told me,' Greenbaum said, 'she was in love with this man who looked like a poet but was built like an animal. She wanted me to come over and see him. It was Marlon. He was living at the time in a maid's room at 43 Fifth Avenue.'

Greenbaum remembered that Marlon was sharing this apartment with an eccentric Russian violinist name Igor. According to several of Marlon's friends, he at first adored the crazy Slav, who was filled with energy and mischief. But Marlon finally grew tired of him and decided he wanted him to leave. When the Russian proved reluctant, Marlon cut open his violin and put horse manure in it. Igor left.

This was the period when the Palestine issue was in the news. Day after day, the newspapers reported a furious controversy that had arisen when Great Britain allegedly blocked the immigration of many thousands of Jewish refugees from a war-damaged Europe to the traditional Holy Land. Marlon heard that an acquaintance of his, the accomplished playwright Ben Hecht, author of *The Front Page, Twentieth Century* and *Jumbo*, was completing a drama, *A Flag is Born*, an elaborate political pageant with music by Kurt Weill, that was to star the legendary stage and screen actor Paul Muni. The drama was to aid the American League for a Free Palestine, and was to support a show of arms against the British government. The play depicted the heritage of the Jews and their persecution, which continued even after Nazi Germany had been defeated. It was a powerful drama, and for the first time Marlon was unequivocal in his desire to act a part. Intensely pro-Jewish, to a great extent because of his adoration of the Adler family, and concerned always with the problems of minorities (he was already an intellectual liberal in the making), Marlon was determined to play David, a militant Jew who raises the call to arms against England. In a final curtain speech, David passionately exhorts the world to support the freedom and future of Palestine.

Hecht cast him at once along with Broadway veteran Paul Muni in the lead. And Hecht enlisted Marlon in his Nyack, New York, celebrity baseball team, pulled together to raise funds for the Palestinian cause, which played to capacity crowds, introduced by a brass band led by conductor Boris Morros and accompanied by six

82

elephants. On the team, all dressed in sailor suits, were, among others, Harpo Marx, Robert Sherwood, Marc Connelly, and Charles MacArthur. In one game, they played in drenching rain on a field of deepening mud; wallowing around like the tar baby, Marlon had seldom had such a good time.

There was an additional bonus for Marlon in the production of *A Flag is Born*: It was directed by Stella Adler's brother Luther. Yet, despite all the reasons why he should give his utmost to the part, and despite the fact that he was out on street corners speaking out in favour of the establishment of a Jewish state, Marlon, with his odd perversity, mumbled through rehearsals to the point of driving Luther to fury. Stella, as always, stepped in, insisting that Luther be patient, that Marlon was underplaying, keeping his counsel, and at the same time quietly digging into the character. She was vindicated when, during one rehearsal, the exasperated Ben Hecht, fond as he was of Marlon personally, felt compelled to act out a scene as David himself. Marlon told him with characteristic boldness that the playwright's interpretation of the character was 'shit'. He then pulled all the stops out and gave a stunning interpretation that delighted both Hecht and Adler, and even won the respect of the somewhat difficult-to-please and imperious star Paul Muni.

But at other times, Muni was extremely irritated with him. Marlon told Fiore, 'He thinks I'm some kind of screwball, fooling around in the theatre.' Muni accused him of being too slow on his cues. Marlon felt it was unnatural to speak too rapidly on top of lines, and he disliked the idea of constantly 'feeding' the star. At one rehearsal, Muni screamed, 'Goddamnit, you can drive trucks through the spaces between the cues!' and he marched offstage. It was only with considerable effort that Luther Adler was able to persuade him to come back.

Marlon was fascinated by Muni's oddities and also by those of his wife, Bella, who had a motherly obsession with Muni's well-being. Terrified he would catch cold, she was constantly wrapping him in shawls in the draughty theatre. She and Muni would spend long periods tortuously discussing the complexities of the role. Whenever he felt that he wasn't 'getting' the part, Muni would insist on having artists from Palestine draw the face of his character so he would have a model to work on. He fiddled around with beards of every size, shape, and colour; he fought with Luther Adler over his big speech addressed to the world's diplomats, describing it as 'peroration on peroration on peroration,' and taking weeks to memorize it. The biggest problem lay in the dramatic final scene in which Muni was to die on stage. Marlon was supposed to cover Muni's face with the flag of Israel, deliver the curtain speech, and march offstage to Kurt Weill's triumphant music. But Muni, disobeying Luther Adler, whispered to Marlon that he shouldn't cover his face at all. The egotistical actor wanted to be seen by the audience at the end of the play.

At the first night, at the Alvin Theater on September 5, 1946, Muni, much to his annoyance, found that Marlon did cover his face. The next night, Marlon was amused to see the flag gradually moving down the actor's head as Muni surreptitiously pulled it. A few people in the audience noticed and tittered audibly. Bit by bit, the supposed corpse, determined not to be upstaged, revealed first his forehead, then his nose, then his mouth, and finally his chin. When the curtain came down, Marlon walked off, thinking, as he later told Fiore, 'What a fucking ham!'

The play was an immediate success. The reviews were excellent. Brooks Atkinson in *The New York Times* led the applause. He spoke of a play that conveyed 'the agony and grandeur of human beings'. Although he had reservations about the 'pageant-like quality' of the evening, Atkinson had nothing but praise for Paul Muni in what he called 'one of the great performances of his career'. Ward Morehouse in the *Sun* said, 'Marlon Brando, the young actor who was so generally acclaimed last season, is a bitter and impassioned David . . .' William Hawkins in *The New York World Telegram* talked of him as 'a sternly hopeless David, whose accusations sear when his bitterness bursts out . . .' Robert Garland in the *Journal-American* spoke of Marlon as 'the bright particular star of the Ben Hecht pageant. First in *Truckline Café*, and then in *Candida*, and now in *A Flag is Born*, he is rapidly fulfilling the brilliant promise he made as the short-trousered Nels in the long-lasting *I Remember Mama*. His David is enduring in the memory.'

At last, here was a performance to which Brando was totally dedicated; political theatre set him on fire as a performer. Marlon's curtain speech, fiery, ferocious in its intensity, delivered with magnificent eloquence, brought the audience to its feet night after night. He was a sensation, and people came back to see the play for him alone time and time again. Paul Muni, a difficult, withdrawn, and sullen man when crossed, was infuriated at being upstaged by this mere newcomer. But eventually, basically decent, he was forced to stand back and accept the fact that Marlon was at the very least his equal as a performer. He learned to endure the fact that Marlon's applause was louder than his own and that the youth had the kind of raw, untutored genius that no amount of professional trickery and ingenuity could ever match. During the run of over a hundred performances, Marlon never let the evening down.

The play caused a major international controversy. Ben Hecht was savaged by the London press, which greatly resented his criticism of British policy in the Middle East. He was charged by the *London Daily Express* with being 'a Nazi at heart'. This bias was seen in newspaper after newspaper. And then, while the run was still going on, Ben Hecht made a very serious mistake. He took out a full-page advertisement in the *New York Herald Tribune* and fifteen other newspapers congratulating Jewish terrorists for blowing up British trains, slaying British soldiers, and rifling British banking institutions. He excoriated the World Zionist Movement for weakness in support of the cause. *Time* magazine attacked him for this. The Zionists abandoned him. Such leading Jewish figures as Edward G. Robinson and the journalist Dorothy Thompson gave up on his cause. His support for the guerrilla fighters lost him friends in every part of the world. This was a considerable shock to Marlon, who was torn by his disapproval of terrorism and his loyalty to Hecht. Marlon, as it turned out, seldom saw Hecht again.

5

It was during this charged period in Marlon's life that he again met Wally Cox, his boyhood friend in Evanston. Wally was to become the closest person in the world to him, the one man for whom he would feel an enduring love, and to whom he gave more of himself than to anyone else. Theirs was a brotherhood that lasted a quarter of a century until Cox's death.

After leaving Evanston with his ever-wandering novelist mother, Wally studied botany at City College in New York in 1942. While Marlon was at Shattuck Military Academy, Eleanor Cox was stricken with partial paralysis and Wally had to work as shoemaker, silversmith, and puppeteer to support her. Despite his frail and delicate appearance, he surprisingly passed an Army physical and was sent for basic training to Camp Walters in Texas. But he couldn't stand up to the life and collapsed with a heatstroke while working as combined messenger, hospital worker, and barracks guard. Honourably discharged 4F, he returned to New York and enrolled in the School of Industrial Arts at New York University.

One afternoon, Marlon was with Frannie at a grocery store on Seventh Avenue. In a typically frisky mood, Marlon was holding a delivery cart with one hand, trying to make Frannie get into it so he could take her for a ride down the street. Never able to cope with Marlon's eccentric humour, she said this was behaviour 'for kids' and he should forget it. They were arguing violently when Wally suddenly appeared.

Although he hadn't seen Wally since the age of eight, and more than fourteen years had elapsed in between, Marlon recognized him immediately and shook his hand. He said to Wally, 'Frannie's acting like a stuffed shirt.' Wally agreed. To show up what a poor sport she was, he offered to take a ride in the cart himself. He was so small and bird-boned, he easily fitted into the cart. Delighted, laughing loudly, Marlon pushed him down the sidewalk.

Their friendship blossomed at once. Everett Greenbaum, Wally's other close friend, says, 'From that day on, Wally always called Marlon "Marlon Brando, the actor." He'd say to anyone, myself included, things like, "Oh, wait a minute, I gotta talk with Marlon Brando, the actor."' Greenbaum recalled that Marlon and Wally would sit by the hour and try to answer the questions of life – marriage, life, death, everything that went on. He says, 'They were both great observers of people. They could imitate animals, people, both of them. What bonded them? Humour, curiosity, a hunger for knowledge, particularly scientific things, inventions. They were the only people I ever knew who read *Scientific American* from cover to cover.'

They made an odd couple: Marlon, who, at twenty-three had put on even more muscle weight by now and at 165 pounds looked more square and powerful than he had in his Shattuck days, and Wally the shrimp. They were like the figures in the advertisement: the boy who had sand kicked in his face and the man he became after taking a course with Charles Atlas. Marlon took Wally to parties full of theatre people. They seldom shaved, lived in jeans and T-shirts, and were constantly teasing each other, Wally ribbing Marlon over his obsessive weight-lifting, Marlon ribbing Wally over his skinny arms and legs. Marlon called Wally

'Walrus,' because of his solemn demeanour. As a result, Wally had cards printed and handed out to people in which the only word on them was 'Walrus', followed by his phone number. If anyone picked on Wally, he had Marlon to answer to. Marlon was at once Wally's champion, bodyguard, and confidant.

Marlon was fascinated by Wally's burgeoning comedic gifts. Wally would tell stories at parties involving brilliant mimicry. The two of them would yodel, whistle together in two-part harmony, and then Wally would give long, solemn monologues about his misadventures. These were especially funny because they were delivered in a voice of monotonous, droning self-pity. The crowd, led by Marlon, would double up laughing as Wally told endless stories about a boyhood friend called Kion, and his misadventures. Wally's klutziness was his stock in trade. In many ways, he reminded Marlon of Stan Laurel. Wally's slow burns were wondrous, and he was a master of timing in delivery. Yet he never seemed to be working at his art. Everything about Wally was spontaneous, natural, unforced. Marlon, who had to work so tortuously to achieve his results on the stage, was in awe of this little man whom he considered a genius. And Wally's unselfish tending of his invalid mother commanded Marlon's respect; there was so much resonance with the Brando family.

At the time, Cox was forming a partnership with a nice-looking stringbean named Richard Loving, who was dating Frannie and would soon marry her. Marlon had brought them together, and they started a jewellery business in order to scrape up some money. Loving recalled, 'Wally taught me how to saw metal, silver, how to solder, how to, well, manufacture is rather too strong a word, let's just say make hand-made jewellery.' The figurative jewellery was fashioned mostly of sterling silver; they designed cufflinks in different ingenious forms, including ice tongs, or earrings in the shape of lions or horses. Some other businesses bought supplies from them, but it was difficult to make a living in the field. They were doing just slightly better than starving.

Wally lived in a depressing apartment on Tenth Avenue, right across from Dick and Fran, who occupied a third-floor cold-water flat in Hell's Kitchen on West Fifty-fifth Street. Loving said, 'Wally's was one of the most awful-looking apartments I've ever seen in my life . . . It was just a total mess. Sort of for derelicts. It was furnished with just beds and a mattress on the floor, and a couple of work tables. It was disgusting.'

Disgusting or not, the flat was a favourite haunt of Marlon's. He would often bring girls there while Wally conveniently slept on the mattress in the living room. Sometimes, Marlon would drop by to see his brother-in-law and Wally working on the jewellery together. Because Marlon used the apartment for dates, many people believed they were sharing the flat and various women.

Dick and Frannie Loving's apartment was no better than Wally's. Don Hanmer recalls, 'It was one of those pads with one room after another like a railway carriage. They were called railroad flats in those days. It was filled with junk. The only way you could get in was through the kitchen. But you had a hard time getting to any of the other three or four rooms because they were piled high. I mean there were tables, chairs, boxes, barrels, God knows what. You literally could hardly squeeze your way through. Unless you wanted to climb over, like going over the Alps. It was a madhouse.'

Darren Dublin recalls, 'It was around this time that Marlon bought a motorcycle. He taught me to ride it. Later, I broke my wife's leg when she and I were on it. Somebody opened a car door and we ran into the door.' At the time, Dublin adds, 'Marlon and I were living at the Park Savoy on Fifty-eighth Street behind the Essex House. My dad had asked me to contribute money to our home, and I said I was moving out instead. Marlon gave me five bucks for the first week's rent. We each had one little room and shared the bath with six tenants on the floor.' They ate mostly at the Horn and Hardart on Fifty-seventh Street, but Marlon's favourite place was The Professor's. 'Marlon always paid for us,' Dublin said. 'He was the only one of the three of us who was really working.'

At the time, Dublin remembers, in addition to dating Celia Webb and Faith Dane, Marlon was 'seeing Stella Adler's daughter Ellen. She was wild about him.' Marlon's life became a kind of French farce, with hot and cold running girls, each one demanding most of his time.

Marlon's ever-vigilant agents heard that the tempestuous forty-four-year-old Tallulah Bankhead was looking for a suitable leading man for a theatrical production, *The Eagle Has Two Heads*, a melodrama by the French poet and dramatist Jean Cocteau. Adapted by Ronald Duncan, the play had been produced in London in the fall of 1946, followed by Cocteau's own production in Paris. It was the story of a nineteenth-century queen of a Ruritania-like country who sexually consumes and then destroys a handsome and impassioned young poet. Edith Van Cleve pushed Marlon for the part on the basis that he had been so excellent as the lovesick Marchbanks in *Candida*. Tallulah had just broken with her polished leading man and lover Donald Cook, who had been starring with her in a summer tour of Noël Coward's *Private Lives*, and she was eager for a new co-star.

Tallulah decided that she should 'audition' Marlon, who had become friendly with Robert Lewis. She asked Lewis to set up the meeting, which, she was sure, would lead inevitably to the casting couch. Marlon decided he should visit with Lewis at his house in Connecticut before he went on to Tallulah's. Lewis gave Marlon detailed instructions. From Grand Central Station, he should go by train to Stamford, where Lewis would pick him up and drive him to Lewis's house at Pound Ridge, New York. Lewis made it clear that Marlon must be on time, because the Oriental houseman insisted upon guests' punctuality at lunch.

Lewis arrived at the train station. Marlon wasn't on the train. Nor was there any message from him when Lewis called the house. The fact was that Marlon had forgotten where he was supposed to be going and had wound up in Bedford Hills. When Marlon called Lewis, the director told him to stay right where he was. Lewis drove over and picked him up, finding him in the midst of a quarrel with a truck driver. Marlon was accompanied by Blossom Plumb, whom Lewis later described as having '[a] dead white face, dank hair . . . her dress ending in a pool of blood on the floor.' When they finally arrived at Pound Ridge, the infuriated houseman presented a ruined lunch. After the meal, the three went up to the terrace to enjoy cigarettes and chat about Tallulah's wayward ways.

It was a warm, sunny day. Lewis wasn't surprised when Marlon stripped to undershorts and basked in the heat, but he was quite surprised when Blossom Plumb removed everything except her panties. Lewis nervously warned Blossom and Marlon that they should be careful with their cigarettes because the masses of dry leaves below could easily catch fire. However, they ignored his advice and threw half-lighted cigarettes into the scattered autumn foliage below. Lewis made his way into the garden and picked up the cigarettes. He then formed a circle of ashtrays around Marlon and Blossom, but it was useless. Over went the cigarettes again, and down went the unfortunate host to retrieve them. Finally Blossom Plumb took off into the woods and didn't come back. Lewis began to discuss Tallulah with Marlon, watching Marlon's cigarette constantly and praying he would use an ashtray. He didn't.

Warning Marlon that there could be a conflict of personalities between him and Tallulah, Lewis suggested that there be a two-week escape clause in the contract. He then drove Marlon to Tallulah's country home, Windows, in Bedford Village. She had poured a fortune into the house, remodelling it, filling it with antique furniture along with her portrait by Augustus John. Her silver and linen were of the finest. She had put in a swimming pool and had planted a garden with 5,000 daffodils, 1,000 gladioli, 150 rose bushes, and hundreds of other flowers. Her staff included a butler, a cook, and numerous other help. She gave parties at which she consumed enormous amounts of alcohol, told bitchy and extravagant stories, and traditionally made off with the best-looking man present.

After Lewis made the introductions, Bankhead looked Marlon up and down with a cattle farmer's eye. Satisfied, she puffed away at her cigarette, emitting so foul a breath that it almost knocked Marlon over. Disgusted by the stench of liquor that only reminded him of his own mother's drinking, he asked Tallulah rather prissily, 'Are you by any chance an alcoholic?'

She replied in her famous husky drawl, 'No, darling, just a heavy drinker!' She began discussing the play with him. He told her he wasn't impressed with it. She wasn't interested in hearing his opinion; did he want the part? As they sat on the couch, she reached down to pick something up and clutched at his ankle. Her hand crawled slowly but surely up his leg under the jeans, while he sat there like a stone. Later, he told Bobby Lewis, 'I was interested, from an engineering point of view, to see if it was possible for her to gain her objective through that difficult route. It was!'

However, he insisted later, nothing happened. Not only was Tallulah considerably older than he, but she wasn't his type and her heavy drinking and bad breath would have turned him off in any case. But he decided to go ahead with the part and managed to get the escape clause in his contract as Lewis had suggested. Again, Tallulah attempted seduction, in his dressing room, while rehearsals were going on. It was useless. He rejected her again without much subtlety, pitching himself into a head-on quarrel with her that seldom stopped from first rehearsals on. He delighted in shocking the supposedly unshockable actress. One time, seeing her in a restaurant, he shouted out, 'Tallulah, how the fuck are you?'

The play opened in New Haven, and by the time the first performance took place, Marlon already wanted out. He deliberately acted in a manner that would provoke a break. In the first act, Tallulah had to deliver a seemingly endless soliloquy – her chief reason for undertaking the play in the first place. Marlon was supposed to do absolutely nothing but listen to this interminable speech. Instead, he walked around the throne room, made faces at the audience, flicked invisible dust off the furniture, made finger signs at friends in the wings, picked his nose, zipped and unzipped his fly, and scratched his ass.

In another scene, Marlon had to climb a flight of steps and begin crying. In view of the play's absurdity, he felt more like crying from boredom. He had managed tears easily in *Truckline Café*, but now his only solution was to put Vick's VapoRub on the banister rail before the scene began. He smeared it all over his eyes when his back was turned to the audience, and Tallulah was so shocked by the smell, she whispered to him, right on stage, 'Why don't you stay home in bed instead of spreading germs all over the place with that goddamned cold?'

Marlon staggered all over the stage in the poisoning scene, seemingly fighting the effects of the toxic potion, only falling to the floor when the audience's gales of laughter were completely out of control.

After that opening-night performance, Tallulah made a last-ditch third effort to seduce her handsome co-star. She invited him to her hotel suite, where he found her dressed in a semi-transparent black silk negligée that outlined her breasts. She was drunk, and began talking nonstop. Soon she was groping him with such violence that he turned and fled. As he did so, he announced, 'I forgot to mention. I'm a virgin!'

After that, he began to taunt her backstage. Outside her dressing room, he would suddenly emerge farting or doing dozens of sit-ups and push-ups. 'He's driving me nuts!' she would scream, 'with those goddamn nipups!' Marlon called Edith Van Cleve almost every day, begging her to get him out of the show before the two weeks expired. When the production moved to Boston, Marlon at last got his wish. The twenty-eight-year-old Helmut Dantine took over, to terrible reviews. The infuriated Tallulah put it out through the grapevine that Marlon was uncontrollable, uncooperative, and untalented. Knowing Tallulah, few listened.

At about this time, in Key West, Florida, Tennessee Williams was writing the final draft of a play entitled *The Poker Night* that would later be renamed *A Streetcar Named Desire*. It was the story of a lost lady, Blanche DuBois, who comes to stay with her sister in New Orleans, disrupting the household in the process, and provoking the anger and lust of her brother-in-law, the brutal, selfish, physically powerful Stanley Kowalski. Blanche, the thirty-year-old Southern belle whose scandalous seduction of young boys is hidden behind the façade of a seemingly chaste and delicately civilized schoolteacher, was Williams's most accomplished portrayal to date of a tragic character. Much of the playwright himself was poured into her: like Blanche, he was a victim of an addiction to mindlessly brutal men. Stanley, the violent and cruel animal whom Blanche's sister Stella marries, was modelled upon the muscular savages with whom Williams was obsessed. Along with the drama of the play's action, there was a powerful subsidiary theme: the dying culture of the South swallowed up in the harshness and vulgarity of the modern world.

Williams's agent, Audrey Wood, succeeded in interesting Irene Selznick, wealthy daughter of MGM's Louis B. Mayer and wife of David O. Selznick, in producing the play. Irene Selznick wanted Elia Kazan to direct it because his production of Arthur Miller's *All My Sons* had impressed her greatly. She knew he could bring the requisite qualities of passion, intensity, and ardent realism to the production. However, Kazan, who was looking for a change of direction, was reluctant to take it on. It was only when his wife Molly proved persuasive that he changed his mind and accepted.

Casting was the usual headache. John Garfield was everyone's first choice for Stanley. But he wanted to do Jan de Hartog's play *Skipper Next to God*, which was being mounted at the same time, and he imposed impossible demands on Irene Selznick to perform in *Streetcar*. He wanted the right to leave the play at any time during out-of-town previews, New York performances, or on tour, to make any movie he wanted. He also sought to be guaranteed the role of Stanley in an eventual film version. Finally, he would only commit to the performance for a few months. Irene Selznick gave up.

Dozens of actors were considered. Burt Lancaster was a strong possibility, but Hal Wallis had him under contract and wouldn't release him. Edith Van Cleve pushed Marlon and so did MCA agent William Liebling, Wood's colleague, who had been delegated the task of finding actors for the leading roles.

Elia Kazan was dubious but said that at least he would be willing to have Marlon read. Edith pleaded that Marlon was terrible, as Gadge Kazan well knew, at all readings. But Kazan insisted.

Not excited by the prospect of working with Kazan again, Marlon failed to return Edith Van Cleve's numerous phone messages. These calls were all relayed through Marlon's friends; at the time, to preserve privacy, he did not keep a home phone, making calls from a pay telephone in the lobby of his building. Finally, flat broke, hungry, and unshaven, Marlon turned up at Liebling's office, more to please Edith than because of any enthusiasm for the job. He had never even seen a Tennessee Williams play.

Liebling looked over Marlon in his T-shirt and jeans

and at once saw Kowalski. He took hold of Marlon's arm and said they were going to see Irene Selznick at her offices at the Henry Miller Theater. As they walked, Liebling described the part to Marlon who, instead of responding, said, 'Do you sing?'

Liebling replied that he did. Marlon suggested they harmonize. In barbershop fashion they sang 'Dear Old Girl the Robin Sings Above You,' which Liebling recalled from his former days on the vaudeville stage. When they reached the office, Marlon picked up the script and took off.

The play fascinated him, but he hated the part of Stanley, even though he looked, acted, sounded, and even reacted like him. The selfish, brutal, violent devil in Stanley disgusted him. Nevertheless, he could see that the part would give him the chance for an acting tour de force.

Concerned about his ability to play Stanley, Marlon held on to the script for a week. He was still traumatized by the experience with Tallulah, and dreaded any further stage work. At last he called Kazan to say he just couldn't go ahead. The line was busy. He thought some more, and decided he was hungry, poor, and he owed it to Edith Van Cleve and William Liebling to try. When he was summoned to the lobby phone, it was Kazan, who in his typically abrupt manner said, 'Well, what is it, yes or no?' Marlon said, 'Yes.'

A few days later he read for Kazan, who called Irene Selznick, then in California, and told her, 'However risky and unreliable, Marlon will be a very interesting Stanley. I'm sending him to meet Tennessee.' Liebling and Edith Van Cleve jointly provided the train fare. Celia Webb accompanied him for moral support.

Williams was renting a shingle-roofed bungalow overlooking the sea at Cape Cod, midway between

North Truro and Provincetown. He was living there with his Latin lover, familiarly known as Pablo. They shared the house with the producer Margo Jones and her assistant Joanna Albus. This crowd spent much of the time sitting around drinking straight scotches and telling dirty stories. The electricity and plumbing were not working, so at night the only light was supplied by candles and the occupants had to relieve themselves in the bushes.

Once again, Marlon got lost, and arrived in a town some miles from his destination. The bedraggled couple finally turned up an astonishing three days later to be received by an impatient and irritable Tennessee Williams. However, once he saw Marlon's physique in jeans and T-shirt and his sullen, sexy, stubborn face, Williams was ecstatic. He knew he had his Stanley Kowalski. He wrote later, 'He was just about the best-looking man I had ever seen, with one or two exceptions.' Whoever played Stanley had to be the epitome of crude, raw masculinity and sexual potency. Williams saw him as five foot nine, a muscular mesomorph with bulging deltoids and biceps, a powerful chest and thick, stocky legs. It was as though he had dreamed of Brando before they had actually met; he had seen him only once on the stage, in *Candida*, and although Williams himself had studied at the New School with Piscator, he had never seen Marlon in student performances. Now he could see that Brando met every requirement for the part.

And for good measure Marlon even managed to fix the plumbing and electricity. He put his hand down into the overflowing, filthy toilet and released the blockage, then, using a penny, fiddled successfully with the fuse box. Then Marlon went to work on the reading. With Williams feeding him the lines, he breezed through scene after scene with startling authority, and the playwright was beside himself. Margo Jones was so impressed, she yelled, 'Get Kazan on the phone right away! This is the greatest reading I ever heard!' Marlon wasn't overjoyed. He knew perfectly well he would be cast; he never doubted it. That night, he and Celia slept on the living-room floor. Williams mischievously wrote in his memoirs that he resisted making a pass at Marlon. ('I have never played around with actors. It is a point of morality with me. And anyhow Brando was not the type to get a part that way.')

Next day, Marlon took a long silent walk along the beach with Tennessee. Communication between the two men was slight from then on. They had little in common beyond the play.

On his return to New York – Tennessee loaned him the twenty dollars' fare – Marlon went to see Irene Selznick at her elaborate Fifth Avenue apartment. She had just returned from California. Given Marlon's disdain for the Hollywood her father Louis B. Mayer and husband David O. Selznick represented, he wasn't in a mood to be impressed. He prowled around the apartment restlessly, looking at the expensive things, feeling uncomfortable amid the luxury. He rambled on about his part in front of Irene, mentioning his dismissal from Shattuck, grinning, carrying on like a schoolboy. He was testing Irene to see if she would fall for his schtick. When she didn't, when he saw that she was firm and intelligent and nobody's fool, he began to behave differently. He slipped it to her that he had no time for Hollywood; she took it generously to mean that he wouldn't want an out clause as Garfield had demanded; actually, he was making a quiet dig at the expense of her father and husband. (She was divorcing Selznick at the time.)

Irene knew a Stanley Kowalski when she saw one. She approved Marlon and signed him at $550 a week, the equivalent of $2,500 a week today and the exact sum that Marlon had instructed Edith Van Cleve to obtain. Jessica Tandy, whom Irene and Tennessee had seen in one of his plays in California, was cast as Blanche DuBois, and Karl Malden as Mitch, Blanche's awkward and stumbling suitor. Kim Hunter was Stella. With so strong a cast, and Kazan at the controls, it was clear that a theatrical event was in the offing.

Rehearsals began on October 5, 1947, running from 7:00 at night to 3:00 A.M., in the dank and cavernous old hall that had once been famous as the New Amsterdam Theater Roof at the time of the Ziegfeld Follies. As always, Marlon was tense, nervous and irritable in rehearsal, boring anyone who would listen with a spiel that John Garfield should have been cast after all.

Kazan explained to Marlon that Stanley sucked on a cigar all day because he couldn't suck on a teat and needed 'the confidence of resurgent flesh'. He saw Stanley as 'naïve, slow, meaning no harm'. Stanley's code was simple and simpleminded: he was a hoodlum aristocrat, wanting to bring the fake genteel Blanche down to his animal level; he was 'dissatisfied, hopeless, cynical, content with physical pleasures so long as nobody got more, able to equate only through his sex'. He had his household in perfect order and didn't want to be invaded by a phony, corrupt woman. He not only poured his beer, he nursed it.

Kazan taught Marlon how to bring the props to life: the cigar, the torn T-shirt, the jeans, the beer bottles, the trunk full of Blanche's clothes. Stanley was completely self-absorbed to the point of fascination. 'He hates his wife Stella's airs. He is supremely indifferent to everything except his own pleasure and comfort.'

The question of enjoyment was particularly important. Stanley fed his own ego. He was a hedonist, but what did he enjoy? Sex equalled sadism. It was his equalizer. He conquered with his penis.

Marlon agreed. He told Kazan, 'Stanley is one of those guys who work hard and have lots of flesh with nothing supple about them. They never open their fists . . . They grip a cup like an animal with a paw around it. They're so muscle-bound they can hardly talk. Stanley doesn't give a damn how he says a thing. His purpose is to convey his idea. He has no awareness of himself at all.'

Despite his understanding of the character, Irene Selznick remembered that Marlon had 'great difficulty with his lines, seemed under great pressure and was often late'. Audrey Wood recalled how 'sleepless, unshaven and pale' he was much of the time. One morning he held up the cast for hours. When he at last turned up, Kazan went over to him but instead of berating him put his arms around him and gave him some money to buy food. Marlon went out and ate a hamburger and came back – while everyone waited.

Irene Selznick was upset by these delays and asked Kazan what was troubling Marlon. Kazan explained gently that Marlon always had these terrible struggles with his roles. She must be patient. For days, Kazan went on training Marlon, telling him not to worry about being letter-perfect or enunciating his lines exactly. Marlon gave bits of speeches, confused or transposed scenes, lost his cues, and reduced the disciplined Jessica Tandy, who was cast as Blanche, to discreetly concealed exasperation.

Kazan pressed on. He sat still, silent, in taut concentration in the orchestra. He waited and watched. At times he would run to the stage and quietly make a tiny adjustment that solved a seemingly insurmountable problem. More and more, as time went on, Marlon responded vibrantly to Kazan's inspiration. As their actor–director relationship crystallized, Marlon even began to socialize with Elia and Molly, often playing High Card with their young daughter for hours.

During the rehearsals, Marlon joined the Actors Studio, which opened at that time under the direction of Robert Lewis, Lee Strasberg, and Cheryl Crawford. The founders had longed for a revival of the Group Theater in which they had cut their teeth in the dramatic arts. They wanted an ongoing workshop where talented actors could learn together, the funds raised from friends in an atmosphere of cooperation. Lee Strasberg worked only with beginners, though it was later claimed that he had been from the outset the guiding light in the studio. Among those taking Lewis's classes were Marlon, Montgomery Clift, Maureen Stapleton, Jerome Robbins, John Forsythe, Karl Malden, Patricia Neal, and Beatrice Straight.

The studio moved that year from a Fifty-fourth Street dance studio to 1697 Broadway. Marlon still liked Bobby Lewis, and he worked, contrary to his later published statements, with complete dedication in class. Marlon caught up with his old friend Montgomery Clift at the time. After Marlon left *The Eagle Has Two Heads* in New Haven, Clift had met him on the train to New York and they enjoyed a searching conversation about their mutual concerns and the problems of being an actor. But by now, years after their clowning in Bedford Village with the McCarthys, they had mixed feelings about each other. Marlon, with his quirkish sense of humour, his fondness for practical jokes and his streak of extreme vulgarity, found Clift no longer prankish but snobbish and withdrawn. He told Kevin McCarthy, 'The guy acts like he's got a Mix Master up his ass and doesn't want anyone to know it.' There was a peculiar scene one evening after *Streetcar* rehearsals when Marlon and Ellen Adler were at a party. Monty was constantly lighting Ellen's cigarettes, and Marlon was becoming irritated because he usually let her light her own. Suddenly, Marlon brutally pulled Ellen from Monty, shouting, 'She's my Jew!' The sombre and tortured Monty was furious.

As well as dating Ellen Adler, Celia Webb, Faith Dane, and Blossom Plumb, Marlon was seeing the still virtually unknown sexy, young, slim Shelley Winters. At the time Winters was a student at the Actors Studio, where she saw Marlon often, and was belting her way through *Oklahoma* on the stage. Very talented, self-obsessed, with a dose of the street smarts, she had her pick of men.

Shelley and Marlon began to date that fall. She asked if she could see him rehearse. He told her to come in as discreetly as she could, as Kazan hated being watched when he was working. However, Kazan recognized her from class as she skulked in wearing a black scarf and a heavy black overcoat, and ordered her out to fetch some coffee. For several more rehearsals, that was her job.

She commuted between watching *Streetcar* at the New Amsterdam Roof, running in to the St James Theater, sometimes arriving minutes late for her performance in *Oklahoma*, and attending lessons at the Actors Studio. One night, she recalled, Marlon invited her to Wally Cox's apartment on Tenth Avenue. Marlon was living in Murray Hill at the time. She described in her memoirs climbing up to the cold-water flat, noting the dismal furniture, consisting of an orange crate and brick desk, paint cans and brushes everywhere, a kitchenette with metal table and unmatching chairs. Wally Cox served a dinner of canned tomato soup, cold cauliflower and sour cream, brown rice, and kasha. The light was supplied by candles in beer bottles. The cheap wine was spiked with gin. After dinner, Marlon worked out with barbells in front of the others. He was following a Charles Atlas course including bench presses, curls, and squats, determined to bring his physique to even greater perfection for the upcoming performance. Later that night, Shelley Winters claimed, Wally Cox closed the sliding doors to the living room, leaving her alone with Marlon, who told her that the only way to keep warm on that freezing night was to get into bed. She agreed. 'My body generates a great deal of heat,' he said, and Miss Winters found he was telling the truth.

Despite dividing his amorous attentions among five women, working hard at the Actors Studio, attending the many parties around town, and doing his best to take care of Dodie during her visits to New York, Marlon still summoned up much energy in preparing *Streetcar*. According to Carlo Fiore, his strength built so formidably after the faltering start at rehearsal that Kazan became uneasy, feeling that Brando's power, his sexual magnetism and attack, would throw the emphasis of the play away from Blanche. Such a shift in direction would make the male audience identify with Stanley as the villainous and dangerous antagonist, instead of with Blanche as protagonist. If that happened, then males would tend to sympathize with Stanley's brutality. Kazan knew Williams must have the final word on the subject. When Tennessee saw a rehearsal, he was excited and told Kazan, 'That boy Marlon must be given his head.' Carlo Fiore was astonished when he attended the rehearsal of the rape scene in which Stanley violently ravishes Blanche. Carlo saw that the gentle and thoughtful Marlon had converted himself into a primitive monster. He said, '[Marlon's] T-shirt disclosed the heavily muscled torso of a truck driver, he mumbled like a moron, he scratched his asshole, digging in deep to get at the itching, and to show that he had a perpetual hard-on, he wore tight jeans to outline the bulge of his genitals.'

Marlon's friend Carlo was frequently backstage during rehearsals, and he was as distracting to Marlon as was Shelley. Marlon was appalled by Carlo's addiction to cocaine (later, he was also to become an addict to heroin), his endless sniffing and sneezing, and finally Kazan lost his patience and asked Carlo to leave the theatre. Later that day, as they walked down Forty-second Street, Marlon expressed his disgust for his friend's habit. He told him there would be tickets for him for the opening night, but he should 'go away and take care of himself before then'.

Nevertheless, it was Marlon who began to see a psychiatrist. It had already become fashionable in the 1940s to go into therapy, and Dr Bela Mittelman was among the most favoured shrinks in New York at the time. Marlon was tortured by doubts about his adequacy for the role of Stanley and badly needed help in finding his confidence. In addition, Marlon's complicated emotional life, his sexual compulsion, and his agony over his mother and hatred for his father caused him extreme stress. Mittelman helped. Sometimes, worn out from his activities, his sessions with Mittelman, and his Actors Studio involvements, he would again let the performance down at rehearsal, and drove Kazan to the point of wanting to beat his head against the wall. But the work went on.

6

Streetcar opened out of town at the Shubert Theater in New Haven. Jo Mielziner had designed a vividly effective stage setting, evoking the cramped, dreary ugliness of the Kowalskis' New Orleans apartment. The set was seedy and squalid, with no door, merely a shabby curtain between two rooms. Defying the bluenoses, Kazan had decided to go beyond Odets or Miller in his conveying of naked sexuality. The scene in which Stanley carried Blanche off to bed surpassed in its graphic realism anything anyone had seen on the stage before. Movies were handicapped at the time by the Motion Picture Code, which insisted on married couples being placed in twin beds, dressed in pyjamas, and allowed to embrace only with their feet on the floor. There was no similar censorship in the theatre, and Kazan took full advantage of it. Surprisingly, the sanctimonious Louis B. Mayer didn't object to his daughter Irene's involvement in so sensational a project. He was pleased to see her present the sort of material he would shudder to find on his desk in Hollywood.

For all the late-night last-minute rehearsals, for all of Jo Mielziner's expert guidance of the physical side of the production, and for all of the gruelling hard work contributed by the cast, *Streetcar* was a technical shambles in New Haven. The complex lighting scheme, suggesting different times of day, the transparent backdrop screens made of gauze through which glimpses of the Vieux Carré could be seen, looked marvellous. But lighting cues were transposed, a breeze began to move the backdrop, and there was an uncomfortable moment or two when the cast failed to pull together as a unity. Nevertheless, the play lost little time in exercising its power. The darkening twilight of a late spring day; the sound of black entertainers from a nearby barroom; the tinkling of the piano; the voices of people overlapping: this was stagecraft at its finest. When Marlon entered in the opening scene in Navy jacket and blue jeans with bulging crotch, carrying a red-stained butcher package, the audience was riveted. When he shouted the line 'Hey, there! Stella, baby!' and threw the meat at her, it was obvious that a star had been born. So raw a sexual presence had never been seen onstage in America before. And Marlon – pushed, coaxed, reassured, argued with by Kazan – acted with an intensity and passion he had never previously achieved.

Scene after scene had a brutal power, reaching a peak in the big quarrel scene between Blanche and Stanley. Jessica Tandy, whose dislike of Brando matched that of Blanche herself, let fly with uncontrolled savagery, and he responded in kind. The play's violent action, always sustained by the writer's art, was followed by the agonizing coda of Blanche's exit to the mental asylum. And that in turn was followed by Marlon's unforgettable playing of the victory scene, in which, as Stella cries wildly over her sister's madness, Stanley voluptuously, soothingly kneels beside her and offers her the one thing he can securely and unequivocally give her: sexual pleasure. As Marlon whispered, 'Now, honey, now, love, now, now, love . . .' and the blues piano swelled along with a muted trumpet, the audience was absolutely still for moments. Then came the applause which was strong, enthusiastic, but not quite as ecstatic as producer, director, and cast had wished. Many in the audience were shocked – admiring, yes, but shocked just the same. Women in that more inhibited age felt tense and awkward at being actually aroused by Marlon; men were rendered uncomfortable, made to identify with an ignoble savage. Tennessee Williams had taken the daring step of insulting both sexes by inference: women for clinging to romantic daydreams, men for lacking romanticism in their bluntly physical approach to sex.

Louis B. Mayer led the flood of admirers that poured into Irene Selznick's suite at New Haven's Taft Hotel, where she gave an after-show party. But there was a disappointment: the local reviews were mediocre. The critics were unable to appreciate the originality and audacity of the master work. But word-of-mouth ensured bookings for the New Haven run. Even people who didn't usually go to the theatre were drawn in by the promise of a vicariously erotic experience.

Boston and Philadelphia bookings followed. Once again, reviews were mixed, but by this point nobody cared. The public was discovering *Streetcar* and nothing could stop the play now. Marlon dragged Tennessee off for an evening celebration in a Greek restaurant in Philadelphia. While Marlon gobbled the heavy, greasy food, Williams watched him, unable to eat a bite. Marlon never said a word.

At the New York opening, from the moment he tossed the butcher package, Marlon held his audience spellbound. Encouraged by his out-of-town success, stimulated by the enthusiasm of Kazan, pricked by the rivalry of Jessica Tandy, he was at his most authoritative and powerful that night. He was male sex personified. In a rare commitment to the text, he altered no line or piece of business. When the curtain fell, the audience jumped to its feet and applauded and shouted ecstatically.

Irene Selznick's after-show party was held at the 21 Club. Her friend, the Hollywood director George Cukor, who knew everybody, compiled the guest list, which included almost everyone who mattered in New York. On Irene's instructions Marlon did the unthinkable and wore a suit and tie for the occasion. Among others present were his parents, both dressed to the nines and exuding familial pride, Jocelyn and Don Hanmer and Frannie and Dick Loving. Wally Cox was there, but Marlon was unable to persuade Cukor or Irene to invite Carlo Fiore or Darren Dublin. Just after midnight, someone brought in the papers. Everybody stopped talking as Irene read Brooks Atkinson's rave review in *The New York Times*. Almost all the other papers were equally enthusiastic. Next day, the line at the box office went around the block.

Overnight, Marlon was propelled into the first ranks of theatrical stars. William Hawkins's review in the *New York World Telegram* said, '[He] plays the blunt and passionate Stanley Kowalski with an astonishing authenticity. His stilted speech and swift rages are ingeniously spontaneous, while his deep-rooted simplicity is sustained every second.' Richard Watts, Jr, in the *New York Post* wrote, 'I have hitherto not shared the enthusiasm of most reviewers for Marlon Brando, but his portrayal of the heroine's sullen, violent nemesis is an excellent piece of work.' The ultimate rave came from John Chapman in the *New York Daily News*, who said, 'The company, headed by Jessica Tandy, Marlon Brando, Kim Hunter and Karl Malden, is the answer to a play-goer's dream. Mr Brando is magnificent as the forthright husband, in his simple rages, his simple affections, and his blunt humour.'

Film offers poured in, but Marlon, who still could muster no respect for Hollywood movies, told his MCA agents he had not the slightest interest in moving to the West Coast. Reporters from *Theater Arts*, *Life*, *Look*, and other magazines found him extremely elusive when they sought interviews, and the press agents working for Irene Selznick had enormous difficulty in pinning him down to talk with the press. He had little interest in engaging the star-making machinery of newspaper gossip columnists, paparazzi, and commentators on the stage. Occasionally, he would submit to an interview, filling it with nonsense about some philosophy of life and sarcastically made-up facts about himself. At one point, he told an interviewer that he liked 'people and cats, Babylonian jewellery at the Metropolitan Museum of Art, ancient tombs, medieval armour, and landscape paintings'.

During the play's run, Marlon lived very much like Stanley Kowalski. Instead of moving into a comfortable apartment in keeping with his new status and $550-a-week salary, he shifted from Murray Hill to a one-room uncarpeted flat in a shabby brownstone on Fifty-second Street, in the midst of nightclubs, greasy-spoon restaurants, and jazz dives. The grimy windows opened on to a constant din of traffic, car horns, screaming neighbours, early morning garbage carts, and the jangling of swing and jazz bands. His room was bare, depressing and ugly, and he shared a filthy communal bath with other residents. His only furniture was a couple of mattresses, some grubby pillows, and a noisy hi-fi set on which he incessantly played 78-rpm Gene Krupa records. In the corner were barbells and dumbbells and a low wooden workout bench. When he went out, it was invariably by motorbike. He would take his girlfriends, led by Celia Webb, on the back of the seat, and once he took Tennessee Williams, who wrote to his friend Donald Wyndham that he had had the exciting experience of being rushed off on a nocturnal trip with his knees gripping Marlon's buttocks.

Carlo Fiore was a frequent passenger on these spins around town. Marlon especially enjoyed racing through Central Park, slowing down only when police cars emerged, kicking out the parking brace against the pavement, making sparks fly. He announced his engagement to Celia Webb at the time, but this was merely a gag to overexcite the columnists. Neither he nor Celia had any illusions about the nature of their relationship. It remained lighthearted, superficial, and uncommitted, like all his other liaisons with women. But they agreed that they should say something to the constantly calling gossips who filled the society columns with absurd and meaningless news. When the columnists swallowed this nonsense and regurgitated it in print, their opinions about the gossip industry were only confirmed.

Deeply troubled by Carlo's new addiction to heroin as well as cocaine, Marlon struggled to make him break the habit. Whenever Carlo stayed at Fifty-second Street, Marlon hid his money so his friend couldn't find it. It was only when Carlo's withdrawal symptoms became unendurable that Marlon would take Carlo up to Spanish Harlem and buy him a fix. Once when Carlo seemed to have vanished, Marlon tracked him to his poverty-stricken home on Jefferson Street, Brooklyn. Fiore was so ashamed of his lodgings he wouldn't let Marlon in; Marlon took him to a workmen's cafeteria on Broadway and Myrtle Avenue, filling him with coffee in an attempt to spark up his spirits. Suddenly, Marlon realized that the time had dragged on and it was almost seven o'clock. *Streetcar* started at eight. Breaking every speed limit, Marlon drove Carlo to the theatre, raced through the stage door and on to the stage. Since he was wearing jeans and T-shirt anyway, he didn't have to change.

Marlon was often bored and restless during the twenty minutes in which he was offstage in the play. He worked out with weights, made his way into the alleyway beside the theatre to talk to Carlo or other friends, or made love to girls in his dressing room. He often returned barely on time for his cue, and the rest of the cast had to endure his cavalier attitude. Sometimes, they would conspire and switch lines and action in an attempt to 'throw' him when he returned. But with amazing speed he would grasp what they had done and turn the tables on them, making up a line on the spot which would in turn throw them. The audience seldom suspected what was going on.

Marlon liked to box, taking on various members of the theatre staff or crew in the theatre boiler room who were prepared to put up their fists. He was a clumsy, inept pugilist for all of his strength, and he was easily outmatched by his understudy Jack Palance and by his favourite opponent, Nick Dennis, who played a small part as one of Stanley's poker partners in the play. Small, well trained, compact, and muscular, Dennis was very good with both fists, whereas Marlon never remembered his left. Even Carlo, who was thin and lacked the muscles necessary in a boxer, could easily slip under his guard.

One night, during his twenty minutes offstage, Marlon took on Nick Dennis in his toughest sparring bout yet. Expert in the right cross, Dennis slammed hard into Marlon's face. Blood ran from Marlon's nose all through the rest of the play, appalling Jessica Tandy as he kept pressing a blood-soaked handkerchief to his face. After the last curtain call, Marlon walked to the hospital. When he checked in, doctors told him his nose was broken. Mrs Selznick, Kazan, Malden and just about everybody Marlon knew trailed in to see him. Marlon enjoyed the attention, and he enlisted the help of a nurse to dress bandages around his head so that he resembled an Egyptian mummy, his eyes staring out with exaggerated pain. As soon as his visitors left, he slipped off the bandages and laughed at their discomfort. As for the nose itself, he was quite happy to leave it in its broken state. He felt that it rendered his appearance more virile and striking, and that people would come to the theatre just to see it.

In 1948, Marlon 'adopted' a young dancer named Sondra Lee, familiarly known as Peanuts. He added her to his list of concurrent girlfriends, then suddenly decided he would prefer her to be a kind of kid sister to him. Joseph Sargent, later a well-known film director, remembers an incident at the time. He was having a candlelight after-show dinner with Sondra in her basement apartment, when suddenly there was the sound of a huge roaring motorcycle drawing up. Sargent could hear a man's footsteps slamming down the steps, followed by a beating of fists on the door.

Marlon walked in. Sargent was flabbergasted. He had never expected to meet the hottest new actor in America. He was amused when Sondra introduced Marlon as 'Phil'. Clearly, Marlon had asked her to do so, since Marlon was labouring under the illusion that he could keep their relationship a secret and that nobody would recognize him. Sargent played along with this nonsense, also addressing Marlon as Phil. Apparently, Marlon didn't suspect that Sargent knew who he was. It was an exhausting and tiresome masquerade. But after the introductions, there followed a halting, awkward, monosyllabic conversation. It was a frustrating situation for Sargent because he was eager to continue his date with Sondra – alone – to its much hoped-for conclusion. Clumsily, Sargent said the obvious: 'I absolutely loved you in *Streetcar*.' Marlon mumbled his thanks, leaving Sargent to grope for the next line. 'Marlon didn't help,' Sargent says. 'He just sat there. Sondra didn't quite know how to pick up the pieces. She did her best, she made jokes and they kidded around a little bit. And she tried to convey to him that he'd knocked at the wrong time. But he wouldn't move.'

The awkward conversation dragged on and on. Sargent became increasingly irritable because he hardly needed Marlon to interfere with his affair. But later, he says, he realized 'how dear Marlon was and how sensitive. He was being protective of Sondra, like a big brother. Terribly insensitive to me, but decent towards her. However, at the time, his behaviour seemed to me totally presumptuous. I was completely pissed off with him. Ultimately he left, but boy oh boy! It was forever.' Marlon's relationship with Sondra was no more serious than his others. They soon drifted apart, met again, and again drifted apart.

Another friend of Marlon's at that time was the publicist Eddie Jaffe. Jaffe never worked for Marlon, but they had a strong admiration for each other. Marlon's relationships with men were as casual as his relationships with women. He and Jaffe simply saw each other on and off, on the most superficial level. A former copyboy, journalist, and legman for gossip columnist Walter Winchell, the tiny, skinny Jaffe, who liked to conduct his affairs from his bed, was one of Marlon's favourite characters. They had first met at an Israeli benefit at Manhattan Center around the time of

A Flag is Born, and Marlon enjoyed going up to Jaffe's big single room with a piano, where Jaffe would play jazz music. 'Marlon had a habit of taking his dirty socks off and putting them in my chest of drawers, taking out a clean pair and putting them on,' Jaffe said. 'He never returned them.' Jaffe continued, 'He would eat oranges and leave the peels all over my place. Sometimes, he would climb over the rooftops to friends' apartments on Fifty-fourth Street and just squeeze the oranges and leave the peels in the sink.' Jaffe remembered that once *Streetcar* became a hit and Marlon became famous, women pursued him constantly. They would find his apartment and trail up there looking to get laid. They would flock to his dressing room or wait for him in the alley outside the theatre to catch him.

Jaffe said that Marlon was constantly indulging in new practical jokes. He loved calling people up to tell them Jaffe was dead. 'One night,' Jaffe recalled, 'he took a girl I was going with, and she came back two days later crying and said he was horrible to her, and she'd never go with him again. She said he had left her alone most of the evening while he went downstairs and decorated the communal toilet with toilet paper all over the place. When the girl returned to me, she promised complete fidelity. But two nights later he came by again, and again she left with him.' Jaffe adds, 'Why were women so attracted to him? Because he exemplified the brutality he had onstage in *Streetcar*.'

Marlon liked to play jokes on sober, ultra-serious Jessica Tandy. One night, in Jaffe's presence, he ran into some drunken sailors and told them that if they went over to Jessica's dressing room at the theatre, she was available for a free lay. Fortunately, they were stopped at the stage door. On another occasion, he offered to take Jessica on a ride somewhere. She expected to be picked up in a comfortable car, and was appalled when she saw his motorcycle. Jessica refused to ride with Marlon.

During the run of *Streetcar*, Marlon continued to find time to work at the Actors Studio where performances were solely for the other students. One play in which he appeared was *Reunion in Vienna*, by Robert Sherwood, in whose *The Petrified Forest* he had, of course, acted at Sayville. The part of the Archduke Rudolph in this fanciful comedy was as far removed as it could be from Stanley Kowalski. However, Marlon admired John Barrymore, whom he went to see in silent films at the Museum of Modern Art, and Barrymore had made a great hit in the screen version of the play.

Lewis explained to Marlon that he wanted him to act in full uniform, with sword, moustache, monocle, cigarette holder, and Austrian accent. But Marlon was exceptionally undisciplined, as so often before. He would lose his monocle or the tasselled belt he wore, or he would fail to have his costume pressed. Finally, it came time for the performance on a Sunday night. He was immaculate now. Without warning, disobeying Lewis's direction, he slapped the actress Joan Chandler, who was playing his romantic fancy, seized her, kissed her with extreme and comic violence, and then said the line, 'How long has it been since you were kissed like that?' His use of the exaggerated theatrical style of a lost generation was received by his fellow students with rapturous applause.

In addition to *Reunion in Vienna*, Marlon also appeared in improvisations. In one scene he played a prisoner in a concentration camp to director Alan Schneider's guard. Escaping from the camp in the hastily pulled together scene, Marlon, Schneider said,

117

'jumped me and I wasn't about to get my back broken ... if I hadn't stopped he would have killed me.'

In another improvised scene, Eli Wallach was a Federal agent looking for drugs in Marlon's room. Marlon ran in and screamed, 'What the fuck are you doing?' He added, 'I'll knock the shit out of you!' and, ignoring Wallach's protests, hurled him off the stage. Eli came running, arms flailing, and Marlon burst out laughing. That defused the tension of the moment, and Eli joined the laughter.

However undisciplined Marlon was during rehearsals, he did pursue his craft with dedication to expand his understanding of acting. In her history of the Actors Studio, Cindy Adams recounted that 'when Kevin McCarthy cut his hand the first person up was Marlon – not to help – to see. He had to learn from it. What did it look like, feel like? He gazed deeply into that cut, looking at the exposed little tendon, holding Kevin's hand himself to perceive the mysteries of life.'

Wally Cox continued to occupy centre stage in Marlon's life – he was more important to Marlon than any of his women. Marlon was determined, more than anything else, to launch Wally's career. Nervous, shy Wally still kept on muddling away at his costume jewellery work with Dick Loving. He was delighted when they sold enough to make forty dollars a week. At a party one Sunday night, Wally was persuaded to do one of his monologues, an imitation of a noncommissioned officer in charge of army recruits. It was terrific, and Marlon led the laughter and applause. Late in 1948, towards the end of *Streetcar*'s first year, someone suggested that Wally take some of his monologues to Max Gordon, genial proprietor of the Village Vanguard in Greenwich Village, where, in an uncomfortable, crammed atmosphere, with wall-to-wall tables, audiences could judge new talent and confirm success or failure by the loudness of their applause. Gordon hired Wally on the spot. Wally's first night at the Vanguard in December 1948 was torture for him and for Marlon. Rather than focus attention on the stage, the audience shouted, gave orders to waiters, clinked glasses and dishes all through his act. Finally Marlon screamed at everyone to be quiet. They obeyed, and Wally repeated his act. He then got a standing ovation.

It was around this time that Wally took to emulating Marlon and his motorcycle. After nervously riding all over New York on the back of Marlon's bike, Wally finally bought a motorcycle of his own, dressing up absurdly in leather, jeans, or coveralls – just like Marlon. Here was this charming wimp weaving through traffic as though he were a hot-rodder. Wally basked in the irony of it all. Later, he even bought Marlon's motorcycle.

In 1948, Jocelyn came into her own as an actress. She and her husband Don were so impoverished, they had to use photo bulbs for heat in their toiletless cold-water flat on West Sixty-ninth Street. So, when she landed the only female part in *Mister Roberts*, destined to be a major success on the stage with Henry Fonda in the lead, Marlon was overjoyed. For weeks, Jocelyn walked up and down the bare floorboards learning her lines, while Don listened intently along with their baby son David. Marlon would drop in whenever he could to listen to Jocelyn, cue her, and make useful suggestions, or to babysit four-year-old David when Jocelyn and Don went out.

So, when *Life* magazine photographed Marlon and his family at home in 1948, it depicted a happy and optimistic moment of the younger Brando clan. They all faced the camera head on: little David, Jocelyn, attractive and fair-haired, Don, standing straight up, with a black T-shirt under his cheap, grey two-piece suit, Frances, seated on the floor, her legs apart and her hands folded between them, in a shirt and slacks; Marlon in a suit of the same cut as Don's, with a white T-shirt under it; and Dick Loving seated on the sofabed with his daughter on his knee. Thus was Marlon portrayed just before he achieved true national stardom. However widely celebrated the Broadway career he was then enjoying, it could not compare with the exposure he would soon find in Hollywood.

7

Other stars, when they began their careers, were only too eager to give as many interviews as possible, particularly to the fan magazines that would feature them in glamorous two-page picture layouts at the beach, by the swimming pool, or dancing at nightclubs and attending lavish premieres and parties. Marlon regarded this treatment as appropriate only to what he considered the frivolous pursuits of Hollywood. He didn't think it suitable for a serious actor in the theatre to lend himself to such nonsensical displays. However, he did want to help out the hardworking press agents for Irene Selznick and the Ethel Barrymore Theater, so he made himself available to a select group of journalists. Following the *Life* magazine Brando family story, he played his recorder through mouth and nostrils for various reporters, displaying a range that ran from 'The Sheik of Araby' to 'Greensleeves'. Journalists dutifully noted his deliberately silly running commentary about tribal music as he thudded away at his bongo drums. For the more intellectual press, he would provide superficial and meaningless comments on Freud, Spinoza, or Schopenhauer. The bitchier columnists would note that he was more likely to be found reading porno books, the Charles Atlas body-building course, or his mother's well-worn copy of *Lady Chatterley's Lover*.

He allowed himself to be photographed working out with his dumbbells and barbells, or splashing cheerfully in the swimming pool of a Manhattan hotel, where he liked to join in water polo or handball games. Much as he disliked the press, at least his meetings with them provided something of a break from the boredom that was setting in that year. By now, Marlon had grown weary of performing in *Streetcar*, as he had become tired of *I Remember Mama*. As always, he came to resent matinée days when he had to do the play twice, and he found it more and more difficult to retain any degree of freshness in his acting. Much to Irene Selznick's annoyance, Kazan was not available to come back and brush up the cast. So irritable was Marlon by the time the summer of 1949 came along that he refused to rehearse with Uta Hagen, who was to take over the part from Jessica Tandy during Miss Tandy's summer vacation. Anthony Quinn, who would soon replace him, had to help Miss Hagen.

Marlon also declined to travel with the show, either to the provinces or to England. Irritable and exhausted, he continued to reject every play and film script offered him.

He lived on very little money. Despite his animosity towards Marlon Sr, the young actor detested handling finances and handed over all but $150 of his $550-per-week *Streetcar* salary to his father for investment. Most of the income went to a farming project, Penny Poke Ranch in Nebraska. Even in the face of his father's total failure to make a success of the property, Marlon continued to support the investment with seeming indifference to its financial outcome. Marlon even told interviewers that his father was performing investment miracles for him.

A Streetcar Named Desire finally closed on Broadway by mid-1949, and Marlon went off to Paris by ship. It was his first trip overseas, and, like most young and intellectually inquisitive men of his postwar generation, he had a lust to imbibe European culture firsthand. He was familiar with the works of the new school of existentialists headed by Jean-Paul Sartre and Simone de Beauvoir and was also fascinated by another literary figure in their circle, Albert Camus.

Whereas most newly arrived stars would have checked into a good hotel and made arrangements to notify the local press, Marlon was relieved to find that the French had never heard of him and that his Broadway reputation had not crossed the Atlantic. Instead of merely staying in an inexpensive pension, Marlon deliberately chose to enter the lower depths. He checked into a Left Bank hostelry that was the Parisian equivalent of a flophouse. The young actor's idol was Arletty, the glowing star of Marcel Carne's masterpiece *The Children of Paradise*. She was cast as Blanche DuBois in the French production of *Streetcar*, and when Marlon saw the performance he was dazzled by her command of the role – he found it more authentic in its seedy grandeur than Jessica Tandy's. He went backstage to tell her what he thought of her. Confronted with this unkempt, badly shaven American youth in jeans, Arletty was appalled. She came from a tradition in which stars dressed like stars, people got themselves up to go to the theatre, and nobody came backstage without an invitation. She snubbed him, and he was mortified.

He spent his evenings not in the various grand theatres like the Comédie Française or the Marigny where Jean-Louis Barrault and his wife Madeleine Renaud were presenting a brilliant theatrical season, but in sleazy cafés or bars in Montmartre or Montparnasse. He even became a companion to the shelterless beggars who roamed the city streets rifling the trash cans for scraps of food. When Marlon's agent Maynard Morris happened to be strolling in Paris one night,

Morris was astonished to find himself accosted by a figure in shabby clothing, wearing a cloth cap, surrounded by an indescribable collection of riffraff. It was Marlon.

After several weeks in Paris, Marlon began to experience a disillusionment with the city. Despite his opposition to American political policies – especially regarding the reinstatement of former Nazis to positions of power in the German government, and evidence of a new American colonialism in other parts of the world – he still objected to the pervasive French enmity for Americans in general. He decided to tour the rest of the Continent.

He took the express train from Paris to Rome with a reservation for a tiny, cramped roomette so constructed that, when unfolded, the single bunk was placed over the toilet. The luggage had to be jammed in under the same bunk next to the bowl. It was difficult for him to sleep because of the constant rattling, banging, and rolling of the express as it roared through the night. Soon after the train crossed the border into Italy, Marlon woke up with a start, feeling a need to relieve himself. He swung himself out of the bunk and managed to raise the bed and hook it to the wall. But he lost his balance and his urine splashed all over his suitcases. He pulled the bed down again and tried unsuccessfully to sleep.

When he arrived at the grand, marble-floored Stazione Termini in Rome, his suitcases smelled so foul that more than one cab driver refused him a ride. At last, he found a taxi in which the driver was asleep over the wheel. He piled in with his cases and tapped the driver on the shoulder, ordering the man to take him to a cheap pensione.

Brando had always admired Italian movies, and he

was especially fond of the neo-realistic films of Rossellini and De Sica because they conveyed so much more meaning than did the studio fare coming from Hollywood. These directors vividly portrayed the lives of the Italian working class. Indeed, after the chilly French, Marlon found the Italians open, unpretentious, warm, wildly attractive and intoxicatingly humorous, sensual and joyful. To his surprise, Catholicism, which he had always thought of as a repressive force, didn't seem to inhibit the voluptuous southern indulgences of the Romans. Rome provided an unforgettable spectacle of ruins, fountains, streets crammed with buzzing, honking automobiles driving at reckless speeds, the screams of street vendors, and the gilded, overpowering magnificence of St Peter's, the Vatican museum, and the Sistine Chapel. But tourist attractions, however splendid, held little appeal for this young Bohemian on the loose. He was drawn instead to the rich subculture of the city, and spent hours, as he had in Paris, at sidewalk cafés, laughing, talking with the local intelligentsia, and picking up the luscious local girls.

He travelled to Naples and then by boat to Sicily. Exploring that island rich with legend, abrim with the stunning vitality and beauty of its denizens, he at last came to a kind of paradise in a great field filled with thousands of richly scented flowers. Pulling his shirt off, he lay back in the blossoms, absorbing the Sicilian sunlight. He fell asleep, in the grip of a perfect dream. Many years later, in an interview in *Playboy* magazine, he said that this experience was perhaps the only true moment of happiness he had ever known.

Quite apart from his enthralling discovery of Europe, to which he would return again and again over the years with mingled feelings of relief and pleasure, there was the important discovery that to be anonymous was the greatest of all pleasures. He instinctively knew that fame and everything that went with it were curses on the human spirit. And he knew with a kind of sombre, painful sense of awfulness, that inevitably his chosen profession would result in even wider acclaim and notoriety. He wanted neither; he considered even then deserting the theatre for the life of a day labourer, a carpenter, a digger of ditches. But then he remembered the humiliations of his days in such occupations. The idea of working for any kind of boss was intolerable to him. Maybe, with any luck, his father's farm would pay off and he could assume the life of a pre-Industrial Age agrarian.

He returned to Paris for a brief stay. One morning, the clerk at the pension desk handed him a package that had been airmailed from Hollywood. He groaned inwardly when he saw the postmark. He opened the envelope as he strolled out into the street. The covering letter came from MCA's West Coast office. He was not familiar with the signature – Jay Kanter. Just twenty-one years old at the time, New York-born Kanter was beginning his professional life as an agent with the company, hoping to capture the interest of the few clients assigned to him by bringing them potential properties. Marlon read the letter. Kanter explained in it that Stanley Kramer was about to embark on a new movie entitled *The Men*, and that he wanted Marlon for the leading role. A six-page outline of the script was enclosed.

In spite of himself, Marlon was intrigued. He considered the thirty-five-year-old, New York-born Kramer as the only producer in Hollywood worth talking about. He had admired Kramer's expert, hard-hitting, and brutally accurate portrait of the rise of a prizefighter, *Champion*, and, still more, his version of Arthur Laurents's stage play, *Home of the Brave*, in which Kramer blended white and black actors – a courageous action at the time – to expose the anti-black prejudices that existed in the armed forces.

As he strolled down the boulevard, Marlon began reading the outline of *The Men*. He was moved by the story. Based on the experiences of a paraplegic war veteran, it was an account of the young and sensitive Ken Woziak, who, crippled in battle, had become bitterly withdrawn at first and later discovered in the tough, unsentimental camaraderie of a hospital ward a way to become a human being again. Woziak's relationship with his fiancée, later his wife, is agonizing. He is uncertain of his sexual potency – his ability both to satisfy her sexually and to father children. The tensions and conflicts of the story seemed to Brando to have powerful possibilities. And for once in a Hollywood film, the story had social significance. Brando said later, 'It had what I felt was an important dramatic situation. Take this guy and this girl, the guy completely helpless, worse than a baby or an animal. It's impossible to realize such terrible frustration and helplessness unless you've lived like that.'

He cabled his acceptance to Kanter and returned to New York. He began telling people that perhaps there was hope for the American film, that Kramer was giving Hollywood an inoculation of realism, and that all of the best pictures didn't necessarily come from Europe. He arrived home to unhappy circumstances, however. Jocelyn's marriage to Dan Hanmer had fallen apart while she was on tour in *Mister Roberts*. And Dick Loving and Frannie were having a problem making a go of things in their depressing apartment in Hell's Kitchen. Moreover, not only was the Nebraska farm doing badly, but Marlon Sr was experiencing reverses in his cattle feed business due to inefficient management and difficulties in handling his staff. When Marlon next saw him and Dodie in New York, he realized with sadness how they were ageing: Dodie's blonde hair was streaked with grey now, and her body, at fifty-two, was definitely showing the effects of drinking. But at least she had joined an Alcoholics Anonymous group in Chicago.

Marlon said later that he went to Hollywood in a state of extreme anxiety and discomfort. In those last days before his departure, he was deep in intensive sessions with his psychiatrist, Bela Mittelman. He was concerned that his face wouldn't photograph well, despite evidence to the contrary in the magazines. He didn't think he would be at ease in California, and, like all stage people, he couldn't shake off the sense of selling out that accompanied trips to the West Coast. However, there were certain compensations. His grandmother Bessie (Nana) and Aunt Betty and Uncle Ollie were still living in California, in the pleasant, unpretentious suburb of Eagle Rock, and he looked forward to seeing them again. And, of course, he was eager to meet Stanley Kramer, to see if the man lived up to his reputation.

He was met at the train station by Nana, Betty, and Jay Kanter. Kanter was very well tailored and smooth: not the sort of person Marlon would normally relate to easily. But from the instant they met, somehow they had total rapport. Marlon trusted him completely, looking into his eyes and seeing the character within. Kanter had arranged for him to stay with Stanley Kramer until he was settled in; Marlon still hated hotels, finding them very depressing. He and Kramer liked each other at once, even if the meticulous and orderly producer admittedly found Marlon a rather dishevelled houseguest. He says, 'I was very fond of Marlon, but he *was* disorderly, and bathroom privileges caused some friction.' Marlon's entire wardrobe consisted of one woollen suit with tears in the seat and knees, three pairs of jeans, and three T-shirts. His socks needed darning.

He despised Hollywood from the beginning. The sprawling city of Los Angeles with its palm trees and white, hard sunlight was unappetizing to him. He told reporters that he ate gazelle's eyes for breakfast, was born in Outer Mongolia, that Hollywood was notable for 'putrid glamour,' and that the only reason he was there was because he didn't have the moral strength to turn down the money. And he characterized the town this way to a columnist: 'Hollywood is a frontier town ruled by fear and love of money, but it can't rule me because I'm not afraid of anything and I don't love money. People around here are trapped by success and wealth. Hollywood is one big cash register.'

At the studio, Marlon was introduced to a man who was to become another very good friend. Jack Cooper was the slight, slender, sweet-natured publicity man for the Stanley Kramer Company, which had been set up to make independent productions for United Artists studios. Normally, Marlon detested and despised press agents, but he saw that Cooper was an exception to the rule and a thoroughly decent person, devoid of pretence.

Cooper, who was sensitive and considerate of Marlon, coaxed him gently into doing a series of interviews with the local press. The empresses of Hollywood gossip were Hedda Hopper and Louella Parsons. Marlon refused to wear a suit to see them, and when Hedda interviewed him, mumbled something incomprehensible that had her snapping angrily at him.

Aware of these women's extreme right-wing politics and strict approach to morals, he felt a barely concealed contempt for them. After talking to them meaninglessly for hours, he described Hedda as 'the one with the hats,' and Louella as 'the fat one'. Louella Parsons wrote of him, 'As far as I'm concerned, he can drop dead. He has the manners of a chimpanzee, the gall of a Kinsey researcher, and a swelled head the size of a Navy blimp, and just as pointed – as far as I'm concerned he can ride his bike off the Venice pier.'

Jack Cooper's widow Marie, also a good friend of Marlon's, recalls, 'Everybody was curious about Marlon because of his reputation as an eccentric. Jack never found him eccentric. He found him very delightful, very open, a little bashful and very, very sensitive.'

However, she adds that Marlon was impossible with the press. As an example, when reporters asked him about his mother, he would reply, 'She's a drunk.' Jack Cooper would have to kick him under the table. When he was asked about his background, he would say, 'It was horrible.' Everybody in the Kramer Company was astonished. Marlon hadn't learned to lie. His honesty was so complete that nobody in Hollywood knew how to deal with him.

After two weeks with Stanley Kramer, Marlon went to stay at his Grandmother Nana's home in Eagle Rock. He immediately proceeded to disrupt the household. He refused to get up early to accommodate Aunt Betty, who went off to her job as an interior decorator at 8:30 A.M. He wouldn't eat the breakfast she prepared of cereal and toast and fresh fruit, but instead cracked a couple of eggs open and drank them. He sucked pomegranates or oranges and dropped the skins and pits wherever he happened to be. Out at night with various girls, he would return in the small hours, waking up the family as he raided the refrigerator.

On the other hand, he behaved perfectly when he went to have dinner with Jack and Marie Cooper. Marie recalls that one night she prepared for him a solid meal of chicken, potatoes, vegetables, and a salad. He was as eager as a schoolboy as he sat down to tackle the meal, exclaiming, 'Gee, this is real wild!' Mrs Cooper said, 'I made a lemon meringue pie. I went in to fix the coffee before I ate mine, and when I came back part of my slice was missing from my plate. I looked at Marlon. I knew he had eaten it. But when the coffee was served, he wouldn't touch the sugar! He told me it was bad for his weight! He asked for the saccharin, and when I said we didn't have any, he shook his head. And that after eating a second helping of pie!'

Marie Cooper adored Marlon. 'He had a very poetic quality about him,' she says. 'Those deep-set greenish hazel eyes that look right through you. He was the most unactorish actor I've ever known. He loved our cat, Dapper Dan, a Siamese. You should have seen the way he picked him up, kissed him and petted him! And the day after we had him to dinner he sent me a beautiful note with flowers. I'll never forget him.'

In preparation for his role in *The Men*, Marlon conferred with the director Fred Zinnemann, and he met with some of the veterans on whom so much of the story was based. He decided to move into the Birmingham Veterans' Hospital at Van Nuys, where, in the paraplegic ward, he could get to know the injured soldiers firsthand. This was admittedly a rather difficult undertaking since these men were tough, seasoned, and naturally contemptuous of such softies as movie actors. Moreover, the idea of being observed and imitated by a physically normal man could have easily provoked feelings of jealousy and bitterness among them, and the circumstances could be read as exploitative. Fortunately, Kramer had already foreseen this probability, and had ensured the cooperation of three of the men as technical advisers. One of these was Ted Anderson, who, like Bud Woziak, the character played by Marlon and named by the writer Carl Foreman to match Marlon's own nickname, was a first lieutenant who had been hit in the back by a bullet while on combat patrol. He spoke to the others and assisted in the integration of both Marlon and the 'real' actors, Jack Webb and Richard Erdman. Several of the veterans were also to play parts in the film. Of those, Arthur Jurado turned out to be a natural performer – a powerful, charismatic, muscular man, whose paralysis was all the more moving because of his superb upper-body condition.

Marlon spent six weeks, from morning to evening, lying in a hospital bed at Van Nuys or wheeling himself around, learning the techniques of operating a wheelchair. He had a urine bottle strapped to his leg: he learned how the veterans dealt with the muscular weakness in their lower torso that made urination or defecation an ordeal. He determined the problems of sexual intercourse for these men. Surprisingly, some of them were capable of erection and penetration, but the problem for those men was that due to the loss of sensitivity it was very difficult for them to climax, and sometimes they would unsettle their sexual partners by spending exhaustingly long periods in intercourse. Almost every one of the paraplegics was a former college athlete, and the lack of activity and mobility created a sense of anger and resentment among them, revealed in an edgy, communal gallows humour.

Somehow Marlon managed to win over these sceptical and contemptuous soldiers. He had the common sense not to show pity; he was direct in his approach to the men, learning to play ball with them, joining them in the hospital's swimming pool for water polo, racing with them in the wheelchairs. At night he would meet with them at their favourite watering hole, the Pump Room, on Ventura Boulevard in Sherman Oaks. The paraplegics liked the Pump Room because the bartenders and waitresses knew them all by their first names, and there was a specially built front door wide enough to allow them to get their wheelchairs through without difficulty. (The bar was re-created in the film.) In order to learn his wheelchair manoeuvres, Marlon never walked in there with them, but joined them in his chair. One night, a woman walked over from the bar and said to Marlon, her eyes full of pity, 'You poor man. Wouldn't you like to walk again?' He recognized her at once as a fake evangelist who had a reputation of sorts in the San Fernando Valley. He glanced up at her with his deadly quizzical smile, his eyes seeing right through her, signalling, 'Leave me alone, lady.' But she didn't. Blindly, she pushed on. 'I can make you walk . . . I have the power!' she proclaimed. Marlon stared at her. She began singing a religious hymn. By this stage, the other veterans were struggling not to burst out laughing. They loved the way Marlon was leading her on.

She cried out, 'Feel the power of God, surging up through your toes, your ankles, your legs, your thighs! Your muscles are incredibly strong now!'

Marlon started to shift theatrically in his wheelchair. She went on, 'I can see your body responding! It's the power, the power!' Marlon went red in the face, started to grunt, struggled upward with sweat streaming off his face. The woman said, triumphantly, 'I knew it! The

133

power is with you!' And Marlon let out a long sigh and stood up, pretending to be a little shaky. Then, slowly but surely, he began to dance around the room, terminating with a frenzied jig that had all of the veterans hysterical with laughter.

The day *The Men* started shooting, Marlon moved from Eagle Rock to share co-actor Richard Erdman's modest Hollywood Boulevard apartment. Erdman had the role of Leo, the raffish, horse-race-loving, sardonic vet in the film. His predecessor as Erdman's roommate had been Luther Adler, who had directed him in *A Flag is Born*. Marlon was glad to catch up with Luther and talk about Stella. And according to Erdman, Marlon was excited to find the collection of Judy Garland records at the apartment. The place was filled with the sound of her singing, and Erdman recalls that Marlon 'loved Judy's passion, her vibrancy, her attack'. Marlon and Dick took turns using the living-room couch depending on their arrangements with women; Erdman did the cooking and Marlon cleaned up. Erdman got to know Marlon very well, and recalled that many girls, led by Shelley Winters, were around Marlon at the time. He also remembered that Marlon, after attending only one day's rushes, disliked the way he looked on film. 'He thought of plastic surgery,' Erdman said. 'There was something about his eyes he didn't like. The way he smiled. He'd come over to me and say, "Why do you smile like that all the time? What are you smiling about? It's a sick thing to do." I told him I smiled because I was a basically happy character, as a person and an actor. He thought that was stupid.' Erdman said, 'Marlon had a lot of problems. He'd mope and sulk and you didn't know what was bothering him. And then he'd be the happiest, craziest nut in the whole world.'

Erdman continued, 'Most of the time he lived with me, I thought, the guy's selfish. If it's good enough for Marlon, it's important. If it ain't for Marlon, it don't exist. However, he would occasionally do things that would disprove that. He'd entertain me with stories for hours. And that wasn't selfish. But at times he could be self-indulgent and obsessive and demand you "play" with him constantly.'

There was a sequence in *The Men* – subsequently cut from the film – in which Leo wins twenty thousand dollars at the racetrack. 'It was my big scene,' Erdman said. 'Marlon was kidding and clowning around behind the camera, and it was very distracting. I couldn't concentrate. Here I had this very difficult physical scene that involved flipping out of bed, wheeling around the ward in a chair, and he wasn't paying attention as the script called for. I was so exasperated by his fooling, I finally said, right there on the set, "Come on, Brando, you had some help from me in your scenes, and now I need some help from you." He settled down and was very serious and very helpful.'

Marlon was not impressed with Everett Sloane, who played the irritable and difficult Dr Brock, based on Dr Ernest Bors of the Birmingham Veterans' Administration Hospital. Given an impossible part to play, saddled with a long explanatory opening speech about paraplegia, Sloane, so inspired in Orson Welles's *The Lady From Shanghai*, was miscast in this new picture. The part called for bad temper hiding warmth and decency; Dr Brock cannot show pity for his patients, but he is essentially compassionate. Sloane played the part on only one level of coldness. He had had a nose job, his splendid, hawklike member reduced to not much more than a pathetic beak on his face. It was a disaster for Sloane and haunted him right up until his tragic suicide. 'That nose used to drive Marlon crazy,' Erdman remembered. 'Marlon would say to me, "Do you know what he sees when he looks in the mirror? He sees a piece of shit in front of his face."'

Sloane did not admire Marlon either. He came from the school of acting that called for immediate decisions, no probing into the meaning of roles, and acting done off the top of the head. So he had no patience with Marlon's insistence on more and more takes to make a scene perfect, his endless digging into the character he was playing, his moods of anguished meditation. Jack Webb was also at odds with Marlon's acting methods. Cast as an embittered, aggressive veteran, Webb had a sharp tongue and a cynical manner. Marlon's introspective sensitivity grated on him constantly. All he wanted was to get on with the work and go home. By contrast, Marlon found a warm and sympathetic friend in the real veteran and amateur actor Arthur Jurado. He was impressed with Jurado's complete absence of heroics in dealing with his own paralysis, and the way in which he managed to maintain his magnificent torso, more splendid than Marlon's own.

But even Jurado, who had never acted before, was bothered by Marlon's slowness on the set. 'Acting for the camera was strange to Brando,' Stanley Kramer said. 'It took him a while to learn to hit his marks, to know his lines. But, with so many nonactors about, none of whom knew what they were doing, his inexperience was never a problem.' Marlon respected the director Fred Zinnemann, who said, 'He had an extraordinary instinct, a sensitivity that made him cross the barrier to understanding these handicapped men. And, with his great cleverness, he quickly understood how minimalism was required in movie acting. His soft-spoken voice, so often incorrectly called a mumble, was ideal since the sound-track picks up everything perfectly.'

The result of this concentrated effort was a movie of considerable force, vitiated only by Everett Sloane and by the sentimental portrait of the veteran's wife played by Teresa Wright. The ending was softened, with a rapturous reunion of the troubled couple accompanied by swelling musical chords, giving an otherwise honest film an unfortunate touch of Hollywood falsity. As a result, Marlon, who had given all of himself to the playing, was never entirely satisfied with the finished results.

During the last days of shooting, Marlon again visited with Jack and Marie Cooper, and even slept at their house, with the beloved cat Dapper Dan sharing his couch. He spoke to his hosts of his compassion for the Jews – which had been given expression in *A Flag is Born* and his appearances at benefits for Israel – and of his love and respect for the Adlers and Harold Clurman. 'You know, it makes me feel very inferior, not being Jewish,' he told Marie. She and her husband were deeply moved by the sincerity of this statement. They already thought of him as one of their own family. He was so totally natural and unspoiled. He resembled no other actor they had ever dealt with: far from being egotistical, he seemed to be much more interested in them than he was in himself.

Shelley Winters had arrived in Hollywood from New York a year before, and was already rapidly making her mark as an up-and-coming young actress. She remained funny, tough, ambitious, and full of wild and extravagant stories about her romantic adventures. Marlon's friends state without exception that she was strongly attracted to him and pursued Marlon single-mindedly, determined to make him take her seriously.

In her memoirs, she insists that the feeling was mutual, and that Marlon, if anything, was the aggressor in the relationship. Whatever the truth, Marlon did begin dating her again during the making of *The Men*. He asked her to accompany him when he was invited to a big Christmas party at the Hollywood Hills home of Norman Mailer. Marlon was in the middle of *The Naked and the Dead* (he was still reading it several months later) and was interested in Mailer. He wanted to meet Charlie Chaplin, who was also on the guest list. Since he had moved from Dick Erdman's back to Eagle Rock with Nana, Ollie, and Betty, he called Shelley, who was very excited, and asked her to drive him to the party.

As it turned out, Marlon was too shy to talk to the two people he had come to meet: Mailer and Chaplin. Instead, he chatted with the black bartender. He hated the party. The reactionary actor Victor McLaglen, who had once formed a Nazified band called the Hollywood Dragoons, was harassing the liberal Montgomery Clift, accusing him of working with 'Commies'. Several people were heckling Chaplin on the same ground. Disgusted with the atmosphere of conservatism and feeling his usual discomfort at the party, Marlon told Shelley he wanted to leave. As they got to the door, the host intercepted them. 'Where are you going?' Mailer asked. 'You didn't meet anybody.' And Marlon snapped, 'What the fuck are you doing in Hollywood anyway? You should be in Vermont writing your next book!' The next day, Marlon left by train for New York.

During the shooting of *The Men*, he had been offered an opportunity to do the screen version of *Streetcar*, but he was not particularly interested in repeating the performance for the movie. He felt he had dredged up everything there was to be got from the part. Moreover, always intensely concerned with the complete honesty and integrity of any project he might be involved with, he feared the sort of compromises that Hollywood might impose upon the play. He decided not to make a decision until Warner Brothers, which had been successful in obtaining the rights, had resolved the numerous censorship problems with the Production Code office headed by Joseph Breen. He cannot have been pleased by the absurd suggestion that Olivia de Havilland and Joan Fontaine should play Blanche DuBois and Stella Kowalski.

In Manhattan, Marlon moved in with Darren Dublin and his wife Flo to a condemned building on Tenth Avenue between Fifty-fifth and Fifty-sixth streets, just across the street from Wally Cox's equally depressing quarters. It was the severe winter of 1949 and there was no heating or water in the dilapidated structure. The only light was supplied by candles. Marlon's room was not much more than a clothes closet with a tiny bed in it. With no work in the offing, and some months to go before *The Men* was cut and released, Marlon began to drift.

He met a new girl, Roberta Haynes, who quickly became an addition to the ranks of Celia Webb, Blossom Plumb, Faith Dane, Ellen Adler, Shelley Winters, and his other women. She was a gorgeous, dark-haired actress with brown eyes and olive skin. In her early twenties, her hair tumbling around her waist, she looked like a Polynesian beauty, but her real name was Roberta Schack, a Jewish girl from Los Angeles who had been briefly married to Jay Kanter and who had been appearing on Broadway, replacing Leora Dana in *The Madwoman of Chaillot*.

Marlon had learned about her from Jay, and called her to ask her for a date. She agreed without much hesitation. They met, Roberta recalled, at the Bird-in-Hand Restaurant on Broadway. He arrived on his red motorcycle, in black cap and leather jacket, smiling broadly. She liked him immediately and agreed at the end of the evening to a second date.

This time he picked her up at her apartment, in driving rain, and hailed a taxi for her because he didn't want her to get wet. He went ahead of her on the motorcycle. Roberta recalled fooling around the fountain in front of the Plaza Hotel with Marlon in the early hours of the morning. Their affair was a brief one because Roberta went on the road tour of *Madwoman* to Boston. During that out-of-town run, she decided to spend a weekend in New York. Since Marlon was away at the time, his room in Darren's apartment was vacant, and Roberta stayed in it, because she had given up her own place. 'In the middle of the night,' Roberta remembers, 'Flo came in and tapped me on the shoulder, saying, "Marlon's home." And I remember saying to her, "Well, tell him to go away . . ." and Flo left and came back. She said, "He doesn't want to go away. He wants to sleep with you." And I remember getting up out of bed, my hair was in curlers, and I thought, What should I do, go to a hotel or take the curlers out of my hair? And I took the curlers out of my hair and that was how I really got to know Marlon.'

Roberta kept in touch with Marlon on and off during her tour. Then she returned in the spring of 1950 and found he had moved to another apartment on East Fifty-second Street, where he had one room with a bed, a small bathroom and a Pullman kitchen, all extremely tiny. She said, 'We would go to movies at the Museum of Modern Art. I remember walking down the street with him in the springtime and buying bags of cherries off the vendors. One time, he borrowed some money from me, about nine dollars. He never seemed to have any cash. He returned the money, of course. He wanted to see me in *Madwoman* when it came back to New York and played a season at the City Center. I got him a ticket for a matinée. Backstage, everyone was very excited and peered out through a hole in the curtain. I asked what was going on, and they said, "Marlon Brando is out there." I said, "I know. I got him the ticket!"'

Roberta Haynes continued, 'We never did much on dates. It was a hot summer. Marlon came to my apartment and showed me how to sit under the shower with cold water running. We would spend hours like that as he played simple melodies on his recorder.' She remembered finding lots of messages from Shelley Winters at his apartment. 'Marlon took them all and threw them in the wastebasket,' she said.

At the beginning of 1950, Wally Cox opened and closed quickly in a musical show, *Play Me a Song*, in which he earned rave reviews for his monologues. Marlon, who was present at the first night and at the party afterwards, did his best to get the press to take notice. To one reporter, he said of Wally, 'He is an old, fragile, beautifully embroidered Chinese ceremonial robe, with a few little 3-in-1 oil spots on it!'

That July, twenty-six-year-old Marlon began taking out the attractive Tamar Cooper, daughter of Jack and Marie Cooper, who recounts being whirled around Central Park by him on his motorbike. When police stopped them, they were instantly impressed and let him go. 'By then, everybody knew who Marlon was,' Tamar says. He was, she recalled, wonderful to her, taking her out everywhere, introducing her to the city, where she planned to be an actress.

That summer, Warner Brothers concluded a deal

with Elia Kazan (who had enhanced his reputation in Hollywood with an excellent movie about an epidemic in New York, *Panic in the Streets*) and with Marlon, who had since overcome his earlier reluctance to make the screen version of *Streetcar*. Jessica Tandy's name was not considered box-office, even though she had appeared in several films, and it was decided to cast Vivien Leigh, who had played Blanche DuBois in London. At first, Kazan had been reluctant to take on the screen version. But when Tennessee Williams insisted, he finally gave in. Even so, he embarked on the picture with considerable misgivings. The Breen Office demanded that all references to Blanche's marriage to a homosexual be eliminated. Her own nymphomaniac interest in young boys must go: it was 'perverse and unacceptable'. The rape scene would have to be either modified or eliminated. Much to their annoyance, Williams and Kazan, working with the writer Oscar Saul, had to make one modification after another in the script. They fought consistently to keep the rape scene in. Finally, Kazan said he wouldn't go ahead unless the rape was included, albeit by 'suggestion and delicate inference' rather than in 'a semipornographic presentation'. The Breen Office yielded, but only if Stanley Kowalski would seem to be punished by losing his wife's love at the end. There must be an implication that the couple would part. Although all parties reached a form of agreement by the late summer of 1950, there is no question that the film was handicapped because of the moral restrictions required in Hollywood at the time. It goes without saying that Marlon was exasperated by these interferences. However, in the press interviews he gave he skilfully avoided discussing the actual merits of the finished work.

Marlon had the partial consolation of good reviews

for his performance in *The Men*, which opened at the Radio City Music Hall in July 1950. Bosley Crowther in *The New York Times* wrote, 'A trenchant and stinging performance as one of these disabled men who struggles against his bleak frustrations towards a calm readjustment to life is given . . . by Marlon Brando, making his screen debut . . .' Otis L. Guernsey, Jr, said in the *New York Herald Tribune* that Marlon 'lives up to all expectations as the ex-lieutenant gradually and painfully bringing himself back from despair. His irritability and emotional wavering seem the real outward manifestations of an inward struggle . . . His progress from a drugged, bed-ridden state through gymnastics and other treatment to the point at which he can take his place in the world, symbolized by driving a car and changing a tyre by himself, is a reenactment which has the audience straining with him all the way.' Dissatisfied though he was with the finished picture, Marlon grudgingly admitted to friends that he was glad his work was appreciated, even though he had little or no admiration for movie critics.

Despite the fact that he was triumphant in his first film role, and had come off the tremendous success of *Streetcar* on Broadway, Marlon did not appear in any kind of city-to-city promotional tour. The era of talk shows on television had, of course, not yet begun. Even radio interviews were virtually unknown. Once he had gone through the obligatory meetings with the various columnists led by Hedda Hopper and Louella Parsons, whom he so despised, he left for Hollywood via Libertyville, where he visited with his parents and then proceeded with his father to the Penny Poke Ranch at Broken Bow, Nebraska, to look over the pathetic cattle-breeding business that Marlon Sr was futilely struggling to run.

He continued on to California, where he stayed with Jay Kanter at his home in Beverly Hills. Meeting with Kazan in Hollywood on *Streetcar* proved fruitful. Although he remained dissatisfied with the changes in the script from the theatrical version, Marlon remained devoted to the director and would never have worked with anyone else on the film adaptation. It was there that he first met Vivien Leigh, with whom he was very impressed, and her husband Laurence Olivier, who was at the same time starring for director William Wyler in a film version of Theodore Dreiser's novel *Sister Carrie* at Paramount.

Before the shooting began, Marlon took the unusual step for a star of going over the set, checking out props for authenticity. As he explored the carefully re-created stained walls, cheap furniture, and worn carpet, he expressed his approval or disapproval. He sat in every chair, tested the bed, turned the water on and off in the sink and bath, and fingered the filthy drapes. The clothes in the closet looked too neat, so he rearranged them, pulling the shoulders down off the hanger sides and tossing a couple of pairs of trousers and a skirt on the floor. Then he went to the prop room, and picked up some medals, which Stanley would have won during the war, got hold of a fishing rod and tackle, and spread newspapers on the kitchen floor. Finally he said, 'Okay. Now this is Stanley's flat and I'm ready to live in it!' Kazan relaxed; they could begin the first day's work.

Marlon played his usual practical jokes during the shooting. People suspected him of putting urine in a beer bottle that one of the cast unwittingly drank from. When an electrician came in with a tarantula he had caught and put in a jar, Marlon noted that Kim Hunter, who was re-creating the role of Stella, was visibly upset. Later, when he obtained a fake spider from Cockney prop man 'Limey' Plews and lowered it through Miss Hunter's dressing-room window, it elicited quite a scream.

Whereas the fight scenes on the stage had been ingeniously faked, those in the film could not be. Marlon was injured in the course of a staged fight with actors Karl Malden, Nick Dennis, and Rudy Bond. They were supposed to push Marlon under a shower; the scene was done over and over again and Marlon had to keep replacing his clothing. As the men locked in the struggle, Marlon dislocated his right shoulder, which had already been injured at Shattuck. He was rushed to Cedars of Lebanon Hospital. When he returned to the set some days later, he had to play the scene in which Stanley falls to his knees and begs Stella not to leave him. Kazan insisted on numerous takes to get the scene right, and although he had strapped football pads to his knees under his jeans because of his high school injury, his old knee problem reappeared and he had difficulty walking for a day or two.

In addition to the very physical requirements of film acting, Marlon encountered another obstacle during shooting: Vivien Leigh. She played several scenes in a mannered, artificial style, her accent false and affected. She was repeating her London performance and taking direction at night from Olivier, whose approach to acting was quite different from Kazan's harsh, realistic style. Moreover, she was suffering from tuberculosis, so by the end of shooting each day, she was ready to collapse, retiring to bed as early as 9:00 P.M. At first, she and Marlon did not get along. She was irritated by his constant need to delve into the character, to find something fresh after his long experience of playing Stanley on the stage. And he was completely unaccustomed to her British correctness, her constant 'please' and 'thank you,' her greeting of him every time he came on the set (she always arrived first) with 'Good morning,' or 'Good afternoon.' He would respond abrasively, 'Why are you so fucking polite?' He simply didn't understand the manners of an English lady. However, as shooting continued, Marlon softened, and Vivien won his sympathies. He had the rare quality in physically strong men of being tender and considerate in the face of physical weakness. Knowing Vivien was ill, he did everything possible to cheer her up with jokes and funny faces; soon, her acting style merged with his own, and she wound up giving one of the finest performances of her career. Anne Edwards reported in her biography of Miss Leigh, 'Brando would sing folk songs in a pleasant voice to the cast and do imitations of Olivier as Henry V. Larry was difficult to mimic, but Brando was able to imitate him perfectly.'

In one scene, Marlon sprained his thumb, hanging on too hard to a bowling ball. Production lagged, partly due to his injuries, partly due to Vivien's sickness. To keep fit, Marlon worked out at the studio gym with Burt Lancaster – although the two actors never became friends. He constantly raided the apple-vending machine and munched apples through the shooting. When Kazan scolded him genially about this, he said, 'What do you want me to do, eat the script?' His eccentricities were widely commented on. Despite the heat of summer, he insisted on keeping the gas heater on in his star dressing room. The truth was, he was simply chronically absent-minded and forgot that he hadn't turned it off.

As Vivien Leigh warmed up to her part and Marlon found new resources in himself to bring Stanley alive again before the probing eye of the camera, Kazan was pleased with the results.

At the end of the shooting, Marlon surprised everyone by accepting an invitation to dinner with Olivier and Vivien. They were amazed when he turned up in a suit and tie, immaculately groomed. He respected them that much, and they adored him for making the effort to be 'British' and correct for the occasion. They laughed, and told him to take his tie off, and he complied with delighted relief. They had had little opportunity to talk to him over the weeks of filming. Now, they found that despite the vast differences between them in class, education, nationality, and background, they had much in common. All three hated pretence, phoniness, the absurdities of Hollywood at its worst, the inquisitiveness of the gossip columnists, and the whole tragic comedy of life itself. It was in every way a wonderful evening, and none of them would ever forget it.

While David Weisbart began cutting *Streetcar* at the studio, Kazan went to shoot the opening scene of Vivien walking to the streetcar on location in New Orleans itself. Marlon returned to New York the moment he gave his last tiresome press interview. It was to be some years before he saw the Oliviers again.

8

In that same year, Marlon acquired a sinister pet, which he installed in his new cold-water flat at 53 West Fifty-seventh Street, opposite Carnegie Hall. It was a raccoon named Russell, for a boyhood friend of Wally Cox's. The animal wasn't housetrained, and it would urinate and defecate all over the depressing living room. Russell smelled so noxious that he ruined more than one of Marlon's carefully planned romantic encounters. He would scratch people without warning and bite them with his razor-sharp teeth. Not a soul except Marlon could stand Russell. Marlon loved to see the wide-spread havoc this four-legged monstrosity caused. When Russell once crawled on to a window ledge above Fifty-seventh Street and hung there by his claws, Marlon's friends prayed he would fall, but Marlon summoned the fire department, and the fireman climbed up the ladder to rescue the beast. He delighted in asking reporters who came to interview him, 'Any idea how I can get my coon fucked?'

Meanwhile, Wally Cox, who had won a starring role in a television play called *The Copper* for Philco Television Playhouse, once again moved in with Marlon. The two men had an electric toy man that walked and spoke, an electric train, a chess set, and a Monopoly game at which they both cheated. During several leisurely weeks, Marlon rode buses instead of taxis, ate a counter breakfast every morning of three poached eggs, toast, and coffee, wandered in Central Park, picked up his hometown newspaper from the out-of-town stand in Times Square, took his lunch from a mobile hot-dog stand, played ball with friends on Delancey Street, joined boys in their early teens swinging on playground bars, sat brooding on the New York pier looking at the ferryboats, hung out at his favourite restaurant, a Chinese joint run by Henry Foon at 48 Mott Street, or talked with Chinatown's mayor Shavey Lee, posing for photographs with him in the lobby of the grand old Sun Sing Theater.

He decided that if he was going to return to Europe, and he very much wanted to, he must develop at least some minimum skills in French, Spanish, and Italian. So he returned to the New School, quickly mastering these languages with his amazing gift for mimicry.

He also decided to rejoin the Actors Studio, which, despite threatened suppression in the McCarthy era, continued to flourish as a major seedbed of theatrical talent in the nation. Kazan was still the leading light of the studio, running his classes with an iron hand, though he frequently clashed with Lee Strasberg, another egotist of fierce, driving intensity. The Studio had recently produced Alexander Knox's melodrama *The Closing Door*, and Ibsen's *Peer Gynt* with John Garfield in the title role. Among the students at the time were Martin Balsam, Frank Silvera, Eli Wallach, Henry Silva, Jo Van Fleet, and Barbara Baxley. Marlon worked hard, not only appearing in plays but staging them as well. He made a decent job of Act 1 of Ibsen's *Hedda Gabler*, with Thelma Schnee in the title role. Taking a leaf out of Tennessee Williams's book, Marlon chose to set the play not in a bleak Scandinavian house but in a crumbling postbellum southern mansion, cleverly evoked with the most economical means to suggest an atmosphere of broken mirrors and magnolias.

He also played the ageing pedantic Professor Sebryakov in Chekov's *Uncle Vanya*, in which he made a grand entrance with stooped shoulders, weighed down with textbooks and notepads. Another Actors Studio alumnus, Vivian Nathan, recalled, 'He had done his homework [on the play]. He was deep in thought. He adjusted his pince-nez, reached for one of his books, and you saw he had to check something he knew was in the second book. As he took a pencil and paper the book dropped. Then he tried to reach for it and he couldn't and another book dropped . . . that was what everyone watched.'

Meantime, Frannie and Dick Loving were struggling on in New York. Jocelyn, now divorced from Don Hanmer, was planning to move to California to pursue a film career after a short run of the play *Golden State*.

Elia Kazan had in mind an interesting property for Marlon. It was *Viva Zapata!*, the story of the legendary Mexican revolutionary patriot. The screenplay was by John Steinbeck, who had begun work on it in the summer of 1948 with research in Mexico that was interrupted by periods of heavy drinking. At the end of that year, Steinbeck and Kazan had flown to Mexico City to do more investigations. Work on the script was slow, tortuous, and protracted. By April 1949, Steinbeck had finished a first draft, and he went to Hollywood to work on revisions. The property was contracted by Darryl F. Zanuck at Twentieth Century-Fox, who insisted on further changes. What Steinbeck had produced was impeccably authentic, but it was not a workable shooting script. Steinbeck tried again; work dragged on into 1950. It was a never-ending struggle to lick the material. The problem from the beginning was that Zapata's history was intractable, remote, and cluttered with incident. It was not until well into 1951 that the unhappy author at last delivered an acceptable draft to Kazan, who forwarded it on to Marlon.

Even after all this work, the script was dense and more literary than cinematic. Even more problematic was the fact that Steinbeck had failed to supply a forceful emotional line that would carry the film from beginning to end. From the opening of an improbable confrontation between an Indian delegation including Zapata and the dictator Porfirio Diaz, the story proceeded in fits and starts, never achieving the sweep and impact necessary for a good action picture. It became a dry vehicle of vaguely liberal ideas, glorifying a ruthless man who in fact stopped at nothing, including fire, pillage, and murder, in his attempt to lead his people to freedom.

Nevertheless, Marlon saw the script as a suitable vehicle for himself. The idea of Indians protesting against their removal from their land to make room for the sugar barons struck deep into his consciousness. It appealed to him that this was the story of an orphaned peasant who agitated against land control, and he saw in it a means to convey his own pro-labour views.

Marlon devoted himself to exhaustive research on Zapata. However, he almost lost the part. Zanuck was annoyed that Kazan had sent Marlon the script because he disliked his acting style. Irritated by his mumbling, insecure delivery of lines, unimpressed by *The Men* and *Streetcar*, Zanuck had in mind Tyrone Power or even the less well-known Anthony Quinn. (Quinn eventually played Zapata's brother.) But when Kazan said he wouldn't consider making the picture without Marlon, Zanuck reluctantly agreed that Marlon should do a test, a rather humiliating requirement of an actor in Marlon's position. The test was also designed to see how Marlon matched up with Julie Harris, who had made a powerful impression in *The Member of the Wedding*. Kazan wanted Miss Harris; Zanuck didn't, but was prepared to give her a chance as well.

Marlon and Julie Harris, who were fully costumed for their roles, played a scene between Zapata and his bride. Zanuck detested it. He cabled Kazan in New York, 'I DON'T UNDERSTAND A GODDAMNED THING THE SON OF A BITCH SAYS. CAN'T YOU STOP HIM FROM MUMBLING?' He felt strongly that both Julie Harris and Marlon were absurd cast as Mexicans. For Zanuck, Marlon was no more than an Illinois farm boy who looked ridiculous trying to be Latin.

Kazan again persisted in his defence of Marlon for the role. Zanuck agreed to test him one more time, along with a contract player, Jean Peters, who had won a beauty competition and whom the studio was grooming for major stardom. (She would later achieve international fame as Mrs Howard Hughes.) This time Marlon was given Mexican features by a new friend, make-up man Phil Rhodes, and trained by a diction coach, who gave him a kind of semi-Spanish accent. Jean Peters looked slightly more convincing than Julie Harris as a Mexican in the new test, and Zanuck finally consented to go ahead with these two players. By now, even Marlon began to have his doubts, feeling he was too young and corn-fed American for the role.

There was some haggling over price between Kazan and Jay Kanter, but Marlon finally got one hundred thousand dollars to play Zapata. This was a very large sum indeed for those days, and word was out that *Streetcar* would be a box-office hit. Zanuck hated paying that much money, but with both Kanter and Kazan on his back, he finally gave in.

Marlon took a train to Los Angeles and thence to

Mexico to become acquainted with the villages where Zapata had spent his life, meeting old people who remembered the rebel patriot, studying photographs of Zapata's face with its lean, hard lines, so unlike his own round, babyish countenance. Marlon steeped himself in the atmosphere of the Mexico of the first nineteen years of the century, exploring pictorial histories of the revolutionary period. But in the meantime, there was bad news. When Kazan went to see the Mexican authorities, led by the cameraman Gabriel Figueroa, they told him that the script was unacceptable because it was too left-wing and that they would not permit the picture to be made in their country. As a result, much to Marlon's and Kazan's annoyance, a good deal of the potential realism of the film was destroyed in a single blow. It was either a question of cancelling all plans or relocating filming to Texas, where El Paso and surrounding towns just north of the Mexican border might provide something approaching the right impression on the screen.

Kazan decided to go ahead in Texas. He picked out suitable areas including McCallan, Del Rio, and Roma. Shooting was scheduled to start in June 1951, a mistake in view of the severe summer temperatures. But the mood among those connected with the project was that momentum needed to be maintained, or the film would never be made.

As always, Kazan began preparation by having the cast rehearse at Twentieth Century-Fox studios for two weeks before beginning production. The director created makeshift versions of the sets, and the cast had to wear full wardrobe for these run-throughs. Miss Peters recalls that she hated the dress she was made to wear, designed to conceal her authentic American figure and give her the plumpness of a Mexican girl. Kazan and

Marlon worked hard on softening her native briskness and toughness. Kazan even insisted she bend her false eyelashes down instead of curling them upwards. He experimented with Marlon's make-up, making it darker and insisting Marlon wear contact lenses that had the effect of reducing the expression in his eyes. After much discussion, Marlon was overruled in the matter of the large, bushy moustache he had grown to match that of Zapata in the old photographs. It was trimmed to meet leading-man specifications of attractiveness.

The company left for Texas, some by plane and others, like Marlon, by train. While on the Sunshine Express from Los Angeles, he took his lenses out of his pocket to show them to a young female fan he met in the parlour car. She disappeared with them and he couldn't find her. The production manager was furious when Marlon arrived in El Paso to announce that they were gone. In fact, he looked much better without them. His eyes were quite dark in black-and-white photography, and he and Phil Rhodes had worked out an effective Indian look by enlarging his nostrils with plastic bands in his nose and by glueing up his eyelids in a slant.

Anthony Quinn said, 'Marlon was a very peculiar young man. An original young man. He never seemed to want to talk to me. To have a normal conversation. It was always a pretend conversation.' Quinn added that Marlon would get into the car to go to the location and would say, 'How far are you goin', Mister?' He was pretending to be a hitchhiker, and making believe that Quinn was a driver picking him up on the road. On other days, he would assume different parts. Kazan wanted the two men to spend a lot of time together, to become close because they were acting brothers; this, Kazan felt, would give their scenes together a deeper warmth and intimacy. However, Quinn said, 'I didn't feel totally comfortable with Marlon. Our egos just didn't jibe.

'Finally, one day, we were standing away from the camera and Kazan insisted we talk. We couldn't think of what to talk about. We just looked at each other. Suddenly, Marlon said, "How about going over by the cactuses?" I said, "No." But then I did walk over with him, and he began pissing and suggested I join him. "At least we can relieve ourselves together,"' he said.

Jean Peters recalls a curious episode in Texas. 'One night, Marlon climbed up to my window and serenaded me. He played his recorder. I didn't hear him. I was asleep. Next day, he asked if I had heard him. I told him I hadn't. He said, "I nearly broke my neck!"'

According to Miss Peters, Marlon and Kazan constantly changed the script, coming up with all kinds of new business. She enjoyed Marlon's humour, his playfulness. Sometimes, while they were waiting to start a scene, he would write a line of verse and she would write another, until they had composed a complete poem. She hated Roma, where many scenes were shot. They would drive out there from McCallan every morning, in station wagons, in temperatures of 105 degrees, from their non-air-conditioned hotels, along dusty roads for as much as two hours at a stretch. The trip was made even more unbearable by the heavy and stifling period clothes.

Back in Los Angeles, shooting at the Twentieth Century-Fox ranch in Calabasas, Peters and Marlon got to know each other better. But there was no question of a romance. Marlon had already met and become deeply attracted to a gorgeous thirty-three-year-old Mexican extra in the movie, Movita Castenada, who had played Tahitian girls in the 1935 film version of *Mutiny on the*

Bounty and in *The Hurricane*. Warm, intense Movita engaged him on a deeper emotional level than any of the other women with whom he was still involved.

Miss Peters recalls that Russell the raccoon was present during the shooting. She said, 'Marlon had him on a chain and would play with him as though he were a dog. I was driving Marlon to Twentieth Century-Fox from the ranch in my brand new convertible when all of a sudden Russell got loose and bit me in the ribcage. I swerved the car. I was scared. It was a terribly hot day, and I was dying to get home. Marlon asked me if I could stop at a drive-in café, and I remember saying, "How can you eat in all this heat?" Marlon replied, "It's not for me. It's for Russell. He's hungry." We got to the drive-in, and Russell had a milkshake, holding it in his little paws and lapping it up. He didn't do it too well, and he spilled the milkshake all over my new car. I wasn't pleased.'

Although Marlon's friend, cameraman Sam Shaw, took pictures showing Jean playing with the beast, her feelings about Russell never changed. 'He loved my straw bag,' she said. 'He would stick his paw in it and pull everything out. A comb, a brush or a lipstick.' She was glad to see the last of Russell. She remembered that, whereas Marlon breezed comfortably through even the most difficult scenes ('He could do the alphabet and make it work') she was irritated by many of the lines and in particular the scene in which Zapata proposed to her. 'It was very stylized,' she said. 'The words were hard to say and hard to feel you were doing naturally.' But, she added, 'Marlon kind of set me back on my heels because he was so believable. He had the fire and excitement.' She added, 'Marlon would give a scene full-blast even if he was off-camera and I was in close-up. He'd never let down, as many actors do sometimes out of exhaustion or fatigue. And he would often amuse me, help to relax me. Once he spilled something and I said, "Don't be such a slob!" with a laugh, of course. He replied, "I am not a slob." He spoke in the elegant accent of a duke or a prince, and he was so precise and prissy! He added, "I can be the most perfect gentleman you've ever seen." And he did the perfect imitation of how a perfect gentleman would sip his coffee. It was magnificent.'

Back in New York at the end of the summer, Marlon and Elia Kazan were faced with a daunting problem. They were appalled to discover that after all their struggles in making *Streetcar* to overcome the countless censorship difficulties, Warner Brothers had made severe cuts during their absence in Texas without consulting them. The studio had effected these changes to squeeze the picture by the Roman Catholic Church's Legion of Decency without being saddled with a dreaded C-rating, which would have meant the picture had been condemned by Cardinal Spellman. In an angry confrontation with Jack Warner, Kazan swore he would never make a picture for the studio again. Finally, Kazan was so inflamed by the situation that he dashed off a long article for *The New York Times*. Producer Charles K. Feldman and Warner begged Kazan not to go ahead with the piece, but he was determined to publicize his cause. In the article, he pointed out that *Streetcar* had been booked into Radio City Music Hall and the Breen Office had supplied its seal of approval, but then the booking was cancelled without warning.

Kazan's editor, David Weisbart, with whom he had worked every day on the picture, had been dispatched to New York to do a complete re-edit. Meeting with a prominent Catholic layman, Kazan was informed that the cuts had been authorized by the Church. He sat down to watch the altered film. A reference to a kiss on the mouth had been trimmed. The wordless scene in which Kim Hunter as Stella descended the staircase to her husband Stanley had been completely re-edited. There was another cut just before Stanley's sexual assault on Blanche. The end result was that Stella had been virtually transformed into a saint, a direct contradiction of Tennessee Williams's characterization, which portrayed her as a realistic combination of good and bad.

Kazan's *New York Times* piece appeared, but proved futile. The re-edited version of *Streetcar* was the one that eventually was shown. What little respect Marlon might have had for the Hollywood establishment dissolved at that point.

Streetcar premiered at Radio City Music Hall to very good reviews and strong box office results. Bosley Crowther said in *The New York Times*, 'No less brilliant than [Vivien Leigh] is Marlon Brando, in the role of the loud, lusty, brawling, brutal, amoral brother-in-law.' *Time* referred to his filling the screen with 'virile power'. Then, Marlon received his first Academy Award nomination for the performance (he would eventually lose to Humphrey Bogart, who won for *The African Queen*). Vivien Leigh, Karl Malden, and Kim Hunter would all win the award – Miss Leigh for best performance by a woman in a starring role and the others for best supporting actor and actress. As an indication of Marlon's indifference to Hollywood and its ceremonies, he did not even attend the awards presentation.

Not long after that, Kazan found himself embroiled in a much more serious matter. Marlon was shocked to learn that Kazan had been subpoenaed by the US House of Representatives Subcommittee of the Committee on Un-American Activities in Washington, DC, to speak of his role in alleged Communist infiltration of the Hollywood motion picture industry. On January 14, 1952, Kazan testified, declining to name all but two names of Communist party members who had been with him under the same political banner between the summer of 1934 and the spring of 1936, when he left the party. Then Kazan returned to the Old House Office building and rashly named all the other names.

Whatever Kazan's motives, for many people of a liberal stamp his under-oath charges earned him permanent ostracism in many quarters. Among those he named were the actors Art Smith and Morris Carnovsky, Carnovsky's later wife Phoebe Brand, Lewis Leverett, J. Edward Bromberg, and Paula Miller (Mrs Lee Strasberg). He also named the playwright Clifford Odets, claiming later that both Odets and Mrs Strasberg had given him permission to name them. Be that as it may, his statement severely damaged both their careers; Odets himself turned informer to save his own career. Kazan listed all of his pictures and stage productions, giving a breakdown of each in turn to show that they had no Communist content. At times, his litany reached the absurd. Describing *A Tree Grows in Brooklyn* in order to show it had no Communist content, he said, 'There is pain in the story, but there is health. It is a typically American story, and could only happen here, and a glorification of America not in material terms, but in spiritual ones.' He was on shakier ground with *Deep Are the Roots* ('a very frank and somewhat melodramatic exploration of relations between Negroes and whites'). In dealing with *Boomerang*, the story of a miscarriage of justice, he stated,

'This shows the exact opposite of Communist libels on America.' In describing *Gentlemen's Agreement*, a version of the well-known novel about anti-Semitism, he said, 'again it is opposite to the picture which Communists present to Americans.' And yet, as he very well knew, much Communist propaganda was dedicated to showing American racism. And he couldn't resist pointing out that *Pinky*, about a black girl who passed for white, was liked by almost everybody 'except the Communists, who attacked it virulently'. As for *Viva Zapata!*, he said this was 'an anti-Communist picture'.

Kazan's testimony secured him release from any further investigations, a sanctimonious expression of appreciation by Representative Francis E. Walter, and a vote of approval for bringing the attention of the American people 'to the machinations of the Communist conspiracy for world domination . . . I feel that you have made a considerable contribution to the work of the Committee in whatever we can do.'

News of his informing on fellow professionals came as a shock to most of Kazan's friends, including Marlon. Evidently, Marlon decided to allow his abhorrence of such behaviour to be overcome by his loyalty to the director who had given him his start. Karl Malden also found it in his heart to excuse the naming of names. But many did not forgive, accusing him of trying to save his career at any cost. The great actor Sam Jaffe never spoke to Kazan again; some actors snubbed Kazan on the street. Marlon was attacked when it was learned that he would work with Kazan again. Years later, there was an ugly incident in New York. Lou Gilbert, who had appeared in *Viva Zapata!*, ran into Marlon at the Actors Studio. When he wouldn't talk to Marlon, Marlon walked out. Then

Gilbert hesitated, running after him to apologize. Marlon yelled at him, 'Leave me alone, or I'll kill you!'

In the summer of 1952, Wally Cox, unable to endure Russell any longer, moved out. He said, 'I didn't mind him eating my shoes. But when he started gnawing through my suit to get at the candy in my pockets, I gave up.' Wally was about to embark on a TV series, *Mr Peepers*, for NBC, about a young general science teacher baffled by the problems of existence. The show became an instant and overwhelming success. It reached 32.8 in the Nielsen Ratings and was put in the choice 7:30–8:00 Sunday night spot. Marlon was overjoyed.

At the same time, plans were afoot at Metro-Goldwyn-Mayer for a screen version of Shakespeare's *Julius Caesar*. John Houseman, the former associate of Orson Welles, who had presented the play at the Mercury Theater in the 1930s, was contracted to produce it for the screen as a second picture under contract. Joseph L. Mankiewicz was hired to direct, and the decision was made to mingle an American and a British cast. There was no question that John Gielgud was the first and only choice as Cassius; he had just the right 'lean and hungry' look called for by the Bard's description. Houseman, who had been impressed by Louis Calhern's performance as a crumbling bigwig in John Huston's *The Asphalt Jungle*, decided that he would make an excellent Julius Caesar. Mankiewicz suggested James Mason as Brutus, and others cast were Deborah Kerr as Portia and Greer Garson as Calpurnia.

With almost all of the parts filled, there came the major question of who would play Marc Antony, a role that called for an actor of great physical power, eloquence, and attack. Mankiewicz had in mind using Paul

Scofield, an English classical actor who was then playing opposite Gielgud in *Much Ado About Nothing* in London. But even though plans were advanced for a test of Scofield, who had been fitted for costumes, Houseman felt uneasy. Scofield was an intellectual actor, lacking in great sexuality and physique, and was quite unknown to American audiences. Houseman suddenly had an inspiration. How about Marlon Brando? The producer had never forgotten seeing Marlon in *A Flag Is Born*. The tremendous effectiveness of Marlon's final speech over the flag-covered body of Paul Muni, bringing the audience to its feet night after night, had stunned him. Surely Brando could bring the same commanding presence to the crucial sequence of the address to the Senate over Julius Caesar's dead body. It was a gamble, but if it paid off what a sensation the casting would create!

The test of Paul Scofield was cancelled on the spot. Mankiewicz called Marlon and asked him if he would be interested. Marlon replied, 'Oh, my God!' thinking he wasn't up to it, but immediately became fired by the idea. Marc Antony fitted into Marlon's picture of the revolutionaries against dictatorship he most wanted to play. For a month he worked hard, listening to recordings of every British actor he could find. At the end, he was ready to prepare a special tape for Mankiewicz to take to Hollywood. But after the director heard the tape, he said, 'Marlon, you sound exactly like June Allyson. We've got a lot of work to do.' His lisping, somewhat feminine soft voice was such a contrast with his rugged face and figure.

Marlon tried again. At the second hearing two months later, in the new pad Marlon had rented opposite Carnegie Hall, Mankiewicz was satisfied. This time, Marlon had the requisite power and eloquence.

The scene chosen, Marc Antony's speech to the Senate after the assassination, was very effectively delivered. (For Marlon, the final line of the speech provided a nostalgic recall to Sayville and his appearance in the play *Cry Havoc*: 'Cry havoc, and let slip the gods of war!') When the tape arrived in Hollywood, studio chief Dore Schary listened to it. He couldn't believe Brando could achieve such heights of eloquence, and indeed suspected that Laurence Olivier had made the recording. The matter was settled. Marlon was cast.

Brando agreed to work for a minimum salary to help Houseman. He returned to Hollywood and again stayed with Jay Kanter. Readings began. At the first of these Marlon was timid, possibly overwhelmed by his remarkable fellow actors. He turned up in a striped sweatshirt with a rolled umbrella and talked, in Houseman's words, like 'a stuttering bumpkin only remotely acquainted with the English language'. However, as the readings and rehearsals went on, Marlon became more assured. He was tremendous in the oration to the forum: The 'Friends, Romans, countrymen' speech had seldom been delivered with as much passion or intensity. His face, with its broken nose and sharply chiselled chin, looked more convincingly 'Roman' than anyone else's in the cast. He felt at ease with the plump, imposing Houseman and the loquacious Mankiewicz, especially since the director chose to shoot the film in sequence. Marlon had always hated having to play his parts piecemeal, out of order, trying to build a line of character through conflicting and disorganized schedules.

At last, there came the great sequence of the oration itself. He worked diligently with John Gielgud, who selflessly imparted to Marlon the techniques learned in a lifetime of phrasing and building within a speech. In the end, Marlon absorbed and reflected his tutor's artistry. He also reached a conclusion of his own about the interpretation of the speech. He came to Houseman in a state of great excitement and exhilaration. He had for some time been questioning himself on the necessity for 'subtext,' what Houseman called 'the need to enrich and strengthen a role through subjective exploration beneath and between the author's lines'. Houseman recalled, 'Now suddenly he had discovered that with a dramatist of Shakespeare's genius and in a speech as brilliantly and elaborately written as Antony's oration, it was not necessary nor even possible to play between the lines, and that having, in his own mind, created the character and personality of Antony, he must let Shakespeare's words carry the full flood of his own emotion from the beginning to the end of the scene.' Houseman pointed out that the oration did have a subtext: the ambivalence between Antony's feeling for Caesar and his exploitation of that feeling to sway the mob for his political ends.

The Forum scene took a week to shoot. Marlon had to repeat the speech, in whole or in part, over and over again, so that the reactions of the crowd could be blended in. According to Houseman, Marlon never once lost his energy or concentration, pleaded fatigue, or questioned the constant work. Mankiewicz's direction and the careful editing, combined with Brando's sheer power of personality, carried the sequence and made it unforgettable. At the end of shooting, Gielgud offered Marlon a chance to appear with him in London in a season of classical plays. With typical perverse humour, Marlon replied, 'I'm sorry, I can't do it. I've promised to go scuba diving in the Bahamas!'

Julius Caesar was a bold venture for all concerned, since Shakespeare was considered to be a deterrent to ticket sales. Alas, it proved not to be an exception to the rule. The box-office response was lukewarm, and reviews were tepid. Whatever Marlon felt about Hollywood, he couldn't deny that on this occasion every effort had been made by MGM to achieve an artistic and distinguished film. Today, it seems dull and stilted, with Brando's performance easily the liveliest thing in it. Oddly, Mankiewicz has said, in retrospect, 'When I cast Marlon Brando as Marc Antony in *Julius Caesar*, it was the stuff stand-up comedians lived on for months – all mumbles.' Nevertheless, Marlon was nominated for an Oscar for the role.

During the shooting, Marlon saw a good deal of old friends. High on the list as always were Jack and Marie Cooper. Mrs Cooper remembers, 'One night, Jack was playing the piano in the living room and I was sitting and reading. There was a knock on the front window. I looked: nothing there. Then there was a knock on another window. I went, no one there. Then the back door. I opened it. It was Marlon, laughing. He looked like a Roman figure on a coin.'

Marlon also developed more fully an existing friendship with the slim, tweedy, somewhat intellectual extra, bit actor and stand-in Phil Rhodes, who shared Marlon's deep admiration for John Barrymore. Rhodes delighted in imitating Barrymore, and recorded certain speeches made famous by the late actor, which Marlon would listen to for inspiration in his dressing room between scenes. Marlon got Rhodes a job as his stand-in during the picture. Among Rhodes's many talents was also the art of make-up, but he still didn't have his union card. Later, he was to become Marlon's make-up man in picture after picture.

During the shooting, the locally respected painter Kenneth Kendall made some expert sketches of

Marlon, observing him in every possible pose and gesture. He executed a skilful oil painting of Marlon as Marc Antony in scarlet toga and gold laurel leaves that the MGM publicity department wanted to hang in the lobby of the Four Star Theater in Los Angeles, where the picture would play. But the actor hated it. 'Marlon was horrified when he saw it,' says Ken DuMain, who took over from Rhodes as Marlon's stand-in during the last two weeks of shooting. 'Marlon said, "That painting's shit."' He responded similarly to Hollywood sculptor Constantine's bust of him with his mouth open, saying, 'It makes me look as if I'm about to suck every cock in Hollywood!' At the same time, a vicious forged photograph of Marlon in a sexual encounter with Wally Cox gained wide underground circulation in Hollywood; the faces had been cleverly superimposed on other people's bodies in a studio lab. The forger of this piece of smut was never identified.

Yet another friendship forged during *Julius Caesar* was with Louis Calhern, who played Caesar. According to the playwright John Patrick, a close friend of Calhern's, 'Marlon developed a hero worship for Lou, which I fervently shared.' Tall and imposing, acting both on and off the screen in the grand manner, Calhern fascinated the young actor, who was in every way his opposite. Patrick recalled his first meeting with Brando, at breakfast at the Beverly Hills Hotel. Marlon, he remembered, said, after the waiter took the order, 'How does it feel to order another human being around?' Patrick replied, 'It feels wonderful. It reassures me I'm no longer an unwanted kid and I've come a long way.' Marlon said, 'I'm never going to let material things become important to me. I'm never going to own a car, a home, or a swimming pool.'

At the time, Patrick said, Marlon 'rented a car that

I'm sure had once been owned by the Mafia . . . it was full of bullet holes. I borrowed it from him once, to my regret. In order to get the door open, you had to brace your foot against the body and pull with all your strength on the door handle, at which point it would fly open, throwing you off balance.'

In the last month of making *Julius Caesar*, Marlon rented a modest imitation Spanish house on Laurel View Drive in the Hollywood Hills which, Patrick said, 'looked as if it were inhabited by ghosts'. When Patrick came visiting on one occasion, the front door was open and, since nobody answered the knock, the playwright simply walked in and found Marlon in the basement, playing bongos. Later, when Marlon cooked a steak for the two of them, they had to share the only steak knife in the house.

Marlon's relationship with Movita had progressed so far at this time that she had followed him from New York to Hollywood. She seldom visited the set because it made Marlon nervous to have her watch him work. Instead, she would spend her days hovering about his dressing room or at the house. Always she was ready to provide affection, warmth, and Latin passion for her lover. Regardless of what she wore, Movita looked gorgeous, exuding the exotic appeal that so attracted Marlon. She never yielded to the pressures of gossip columnists who yearned for stories of Marlon Brando's romantic life.

Her resolve to keep their affair private even withstood emotional flare-ups between them. By now, Marlon was a big enough celebrity that young and attractive starlets were drawn to him. One of these was the beautiful and vivacious Rita Moreno, then virtually an unknown dancer-actress under contract with MGM who had won small parts in such films as *Pagan Love*

Song and *The Toast of New Orleans*. She and Marlon began a romantic involvement that did not go unnoticed by Movita. While Rita was ideally his type of woman — dark, smouldering, intensely Hispanic — Rita still very much took second place to Movita, and Marlon returned with Movita to New York at the end of shooting, where she persuaded Marlon to let her decorate the Fifty-seventh Street walk-up. According to Carlo Fiore, Movita was signalling through this act of redecoration her desire to marry Marlon, to make something permanent of their relationship according to her Roman Catholic precepts. Ultimately, Marlon resisted the idea of being pinned down, as was his pattern with all women.

9

While resting in New York from his struggle to master Shakespeare, Marlon had some good news: Jocelyn, who was dating and would soon marry the novelist Eliot Asinof, and had just appeared successfully in a run of Eugene O'Neill's *Desire Under the Elms* on Broadway, had landed a picture contract with Columbia. She was already on her way to Hollywood. And then, Stanley Kramer, with whom Marlon wanted to work again despite his dissatisfaction with the compromises in the released version of *The Men*, contacted him to suggest a new picture, *The Wild One*.

The story of *The Wild One* originated in an actual incident, the raid of a gang of motorcyclists on a small town called Hollister, near Los Angeles, in 1947. Frank Rooney had written a detailed account of the episode for *Harper's*, which he had entitled *The Cyclists' Raid*. Kramer told Marlon the story had value because it dealt with the problem of rising violence in American society that stemmed from the pressures on young people driven to rebel even to the point of endangering their own lives.

Increasingly involved in liberal causes, Marlon instantly agreed to the project. Despite his personal dislike of Erwin Piscator, he had been influenced, along with his other fellow students of the New School Dramatic Workshop, by Piscator's left-wing views. His natural love of the underdog, evinced in school, was now expressing itself in his passionate interest in the political and social rights of minorities. He was one of the many sponsors of the Scientific and Cultural Conference for World Peace held at the Waldorf-Astoria in New York City on March 25–7, 1949, and attended it with his sister Jocelyn – an event that the House Un-American Activities Committee viewed as totally Communist in backing, inspiration, and expression. Many of the sponsors of the Conference, Jocelyn included, later had career problems merely because they had been supporters. When a complete report on the Conference was published in HUAC summaries in 1951, the heading read, quite bluntly, 'The Communist "Peace" Offensive'.

Of course, Marlon had no sympathy whatever with the totalitarian system that operated in the Soviet Union, but he did hold strong liberal views about the repressive forces in most societies. And because he believed that American social and political conditions were responsible for the nurturing of violence and criminal acts, he was instantly riveted by the theme of *The Wild One*. And he liked the contrast between this movie and *Julius Caesar* – not to mention the fact that he could ride his own motorcycle in the film.

He asked who would direct the film, and as with *The Men*, found that Kramer had reached the interesting decision to hire a foreign-born director for a very American subject. Kramer believed that a European eye would bring freshness and immediacy to this local theme. He engaged the Hungarian-born Laslo Benedek, whose sympathy, warmth, and integrity had impressed the producer. As it happened, Benedek had had an experience which, along with reading *The Cyclists' Raid*, had provided a special inspiration for him. While he was at Malibu Beach, his car had been surrounded by black-leather-clad motorcyclists, in helmets and goggles, shouting menacingly as they circled the vehicle before Benedek was able to make his escape. A first-draft screenplay was prepared by Ben Maddow, who had written John Huston's urban thriller *The Asphalt Jungle*, starring Brando's favourite Louis Calhern. However, Maddow was soon replaced by John Paxton, whose screen work was equally strong.

Marlon returned to Hollywood with Movita at the beginning of 1953. This time, he found a house in the Pacific Palisades. He liked the almost-completed script, requesting only a few changes, and had several meetings with Kramer to agree on basic principles of realism regarding the portrayal of the story as it actually happened. Benedek recalls that when he first met Brando, the star, in T-shirt and jeans, never sat down in the office, but roamed about, looking at pictures of his wife and daughter, his daughter's finger-paintings, and just about every other object in sight, pouring out an endless list of questions and declining to discuss the actual picture at all.

Mary Murphy, the attractive, gentle young actress cast as the storekeeper's daughter who becomes involved with the motorcycle gang and falls in love with its leader, had an almost indentical experience. 'Everybody left the office, and I was sitting there by myself. In walked Mr Gorgeous,' she said. Again in T-shirt and jeans, he prowled around the room looking at her; if he hadn't been so nice about it, she would have been put in mind of 'a mountain lion looking at its prey'. She knew, she said, she was being 'put on the block,' but Marlon had a 'wonderful sense of humour. He chatted to me about all kinds of things, told jokes to put me at ease, picked things up, put them down.' As with Benedek, whom he also had never met before, Marlon was testing these people, seeking out their true characters, wanting to make sure he could work with

171

them. Unlike almost every other star, he was incapable of being as self-centred as he was self-absorbed. He always reached out to others, seeking, looking for answers. His curiosity wasn't merely investigative. He wanted to judge how comfortable he would be with his fellow players and his director.

Before shooting began, Marlon characteristically plunged into homework. He went to Hollister with Stanley Kramer, Laslo Benedek, and John Paxton so that he could absorb the physical background – even though the film itself would not be shot there. On each occasion, he rode his motorbike to the scene and back. He arranged to meet with actual cycle gang members, questioning them endlessly on their histories, backgrounds, and hopes for the future. His restless eyes missed nothing. He learned exactly how they cut their hair, how they liked to flex their muscles in tight T-shirts, how they felt an almost sexual thrill riding their metal steeds, carrying their girlfriends on the seats behind them. He listened to their slang, their broken, semi-articulate speech with its peculiar idioms and rhythms. He learned about the macho bragging they indulged in, the meaningless fights for supremacy, the constant teenage tests of strength, from arm-wrestling to push-up contests to races on dusty roads. He agreed with both producer and director that actual gang members should be blended into the cast, as with the veterans of the Birmingham Hospital in *The Men*.

But during this intensive research, feeling his way deeper and deeper into the character he would be playing, Marlon received some disturbing news. The dreaded Breen Office refused to approve the final draft of John Paxton's script. Kramer and Benedek appealed directly to Jack Viszard, the Breen-appointed censor in the matter. They told him this interference with screen freedom was a denial of the First Amendment and an outright scandal. Viszard responded that he was upset by the sympathetic treatment of the motorcyclists, that if a gang like this invaded his own city he would 'shoot first and ask questions later'. The producer and director tried to explain that after they had spent a week of working on an assembly line or as garage grease monkeys, this freedom and camaraderie of the road was all these toughs could look forward to. Viszard wasn't interested. He felt the film glorified violence. As a result, Paxton had to emasculate much of the film's message, and when Marlon was given the revised draft, he was furious. He told Kramer and Benedek they had sold out, saying, 'This is not the script I read and liked and committed to.' However, he said he would go ahead because he had promised to. While making no bones about his contempt for the compromise involved, he informed Jay Kanter that he wouldn't try to break the contract.

There was worse to come. Viszard demanded that Brando narrate a gratuitous introduction to the movie, the gist of which was that this episode of the raid was a one-time happening, and that such a thing could never happen again. But for Brando, the whole point was that it *could* happen again; that it would happen again; that incidents like this would become typical as ordinary young men became increasingly crushed by society's pressures and deadened by the boredom of their lives. By speaking the introduction, Marlon would betray the very theme to which the moviemakers had committed themselves.

Still Marlon adhered to his contractual agreement. Benedek said, 'You can imagine how Marlon felt. He hated the Breen Office, us, the whole world. But he understood that the stupid prologue was the price we had to pay to get the film made at all.'

Marlon found a way of showing his contempt for the opening statement. He assumed a semi-amateurish southern accent for the occasion, making faces all through the recording in the studio. It was his way of saying, 'This isn't me talking. It's someone else.' Benedek said, 'It was his own way of saying to the Breen Office, "Screw you."'

The first scene shot was the important one in the local café in which Johnny, Marlon's screen character, gets into conversation with the waitress, Kathie, played by Mary Murphy. Marlon disliked the speech written for him by John Paxton, and he was also aware that Miss Murphy was uncomfortable with her own dialogue. After several takes, Marlon threw up his hands and told Benedek that he had decided to improvise a speech. Benedek was annoyed; the picture had to be made in twenty-four days with the lowest possible budget. Those were the only terms the studio would accept before backing the production. Time was money, and Marlon's delays simply could not be tolerated. Marlon delivered a new speech on the spot. It was filled with biker slang, halting, tense, entirely real. Benedek yielded. He allowed Marlon to go ahead. He instructed Mary Murphy to listen carefully, improvising her own response. As a result, both she and Marlon helped create a memorable sequence. And the spontaneity of her reaction, at once nervous and attracted, was precisely what Marlon had wanted. Nor was that attraction entirely acted. 'I had such a crush on Marlon,' Miss Murphy said. 'But there was always Movita.'

In order to help Mary Murphy identify completely with her part, Marlon took her for rides on the back of

174

his motorcycle, spinning her around corners and even over sidewalks and along dirt tracks until she felt every bone in her body was shaken. She was much more comfortable in her elegant British car. After a very hard day's work, she was glad to drive home and relax. But on a particular evening, she had an unpleasant shock. As she started up the automobile, she heard an unsettling sound of something rattling loose in the wheel. Tired and upset, she called one of the crew members, who investigated the problem. He unscrewed the right front hubcap and discovered that a number of large stones had been placed inside it. She was determined to find out who was responsible. Finally, Marlon admitted, laughing like a schoolboy, that he was the culprit. She forgave him immediately.

The schedule grew more and more torturous, stretching late into night after night. Marlon never complained. And he was sympathetic, thoughtful, seeking ways in which to overcome the censorship of the script. As usual, he didn't like to rehearse lines, only the physical action, watching the camera moves and the essence of scenes rather than concentrating on every word of the script. At times his changes irritated the director. In one sequence, in which Johnny, the bike rider, discovers that the sheriff is his girlfriend's father, he began scratching his nose for no particular reason. Benedek pointed out that this nose-scratching was distracting and unnecessary. Marlon replied, 'If my nose itches, why the fuck can't I scratch it?' Benedek responded that it intruded, it was out of place. Marlon shrugged and accepted the direction. In the final scene, Johnny is shown with a half-smile, giving a stolen statue to his girlfriend. Marlon felt this was a phony 'Hollywood' ending. But Benedek argued that it was touching and real and also humanized the character. Again, Marlon accepted Benedek's counsel.

Benedek was so exhausted after twenty-four nights with almost no sleep that he literally burst into tears on the last day of work. Even Marlon, with his powerful physique and iron farm boy's constitution, was worn out. And his dissatisfaction with the picture was never overcome. He gave several interviews saying that it 'missed badly,' that 'only the violence was shown and not the true pathos of the subject matter'. Even Benedek concurred that the film was less than it should have been because of censorship. But the reviews were on the whole respectful. Hollis Alpert in the *Saturday Review* said, 'The nice thing about Mr Kramer's movie is that it doesn't preach or ever state directly what the sources of the trouble are. It's done largely through implication and is helped no end by an astonishing performance on the part of Marlon Brando.' *Newsweek* took a less favourable view: 'Playing a role that is twice as tough and taciturn as his Kowalski . . . Brando gets to smile at the film's end and to show a touch of normal human emotion. Otherwise his performance is unrelated to anything except an enigmatic exercise in the sinister.'

The Wild One was not one of the big successes of its period at the box office. But it achieved a deep and lasting influence. A whole generation of youths modelled themselves on Marlon in it. Around the world, teenagers began buying leather jackets, riding cycles, slicking down their hair with grease, and working out in gyms to build their muscles, talking in the script's lazy, throwaway slang. Marlon's sullen, slouch-shouldered, powerful presence became a symbol and a force of the 1950s. Even James Dean, Montgomery Clift, and dozens of lesser actors emulated the Brando style. Alas, Marlon took no pleasure in this. He was particularly disappointed with James Dean, who fell futilely in love with Marlon after viewing *The Wild One* and besieged him with phone calls. Marlon introduced Dean to a psychiatrist and took an older-brother's interest in him. He was bothered by Dean's slavish imitation of his character in *The Wild One* and much preferred James Dean the individualist to this round-shouldered, surly, mumbling caricature of himself. He felt that Montgomery Clift damaged his reputation by trying to be a surrogate Brando. 'He's more fucking me than I am myself,' he once told Carlo Fiore.

Marlon was so disappointed with *The Wild One* that he said he wanted to retire. He bragged emptily that Penny Poke Farm in Broken Bow, Nebraska, would furnish him a lifetime income, when in fact it was sinking into disaster. It had carried with it his entire personal fortune, and he was loyally trying to cover for his father once again. He talked about making *Pal Joey*, the Rodgers and Hart musical, with Mae West, but nothing came of it. There was a possibility he might do *Prince of Players*, a ponderous script about the great actor Edwin Booth, but this also fell apart. He owed a picture to Twentieth Century-Fox, but would accept nothing they offered.

Dick Loving and Frannie had settled in Mundelein, Illinois, in an old and draughty farmhouse surrounded by beautiful country and forest. The farm consisted of several buildings, one of which Loving used as a painting studio. Marlon briefly visited with them that summer.

After some time with his sister and brother-in-law in the country, Marlon decided to return to the stage. He told Edith Van Cleve, who was still representing him in New York, that he had elected to pull together a scratch company for an Eastern Seaboard tour. The play he wanted to star in was Shaw's *Arms and the Man*, in which he would appear as the pompous Bulgarian general Sergius, with his friend William Redfield in the showier part of Bluntschli. Carlo Fiore and another friend, Sam Gilman, were given parts. Carlo agreed to join the company, but only on condition that he was able to get his fixes of cocaine during the run; he promised he would not take heroin. Marlon unhappily agreed. Phil Rhodes joined the team, along with the actress Janice Mars. Movita stayed behind in New York.

Morton Gottlieb, who later produced *Sleuth* and *Same Time, Next Year* on Broadway, handled the tour, which began in July 1953 at the Theater-by-the-Sea in Matunuck, Rhode Island. The audience, excited by the idea of seeing Marlon Brando in the flesh, packed the house, and Herbert Ratner's direction was praised by the local press. The company moved on to Falmouth, Ivoryton, and Framingham, while gossip had it that Marlon and Janice Mars were involved with each other. However, Marlon seemed to regard the whole trip as not much more than a paid vacation. His performances were drastically uneven, sometimes excellent, more often inadequate. And much of the time, he was drained by the effort of holding together a company so largely composed of personal friends with modest acting talents and broad American accents that it seldom, if ever, conveyed the right Shavian atmosphere. The amateurishness of the production would undoubtedly have ruled it out for Broadway, but at least it served the purpose of relaxing Marlon after his experience with *The Wild One*.

New York at the end of the tour brought more problems. Carlo Fiore was again trying to kick the drug habit, and Marlon loaned him the money to take off to Fire Island where he could be dried out in a special retreat. By working part-time as a waiter, Carlo was able to return the money, but in no time he was hooked again. Disgusted, Marlon took off to Europe with William Redfield, for two months of bumming around Paris, only to be turned off the French liner *Ile de France* because he had lost his passport. He considered doing a screen version of *Mister Roberts* with Jocelyn repeating her role as the nurse, but this plan, like so many others, collapsed. Instead, he asked Elia Kazan for ideas. The director suggested he might read a script written by Budd Schulberg, *On the Waterfront.*

On the Waterfront was to become famous for several reasons: as Marlon's first Oscar-winning performance, as a masterpiece of American film, and as a colossal box-office success. It put Marlon once and for all in the very front rank of international stars. But to many liberals of the Brando stamp, it was to become infamous as an example of a glorification of treachery and whitewashing of McCarthy-era testifying. It was not only directed by an informer, Kazan, but it was written by one; Schulberg had named many of his fellow writers as Communists in a recent hearing of the Un-American Activities Committee. Moreover, it featured Lee J. Cobb, who had helped damage several actors by naming them earlier that year, including Lloyd Bridges and Sam Jaffe. Many of Marlon's friends and colleagues, most notably Kim Hunter, had had their careers affected by the blacklist. Yet he had never spoken out publicly against the Un-American Activities Committee. And now he had committed to working with three who had named names. It is ironic that some interpreted the character he portrayed, the waterfront worker Terry Malloy, as an informer rather than a decent man who wanted to draw attention to vicious criminal strike-breaking methods by blowing the whistle and risking his own life.

The film had originally been planned with Kazan and Arthur Miller, while at the same time Schulberg had discussed the possibility with Columbia of dramatizing Malcolm Johnson's Pulitzer Prize-winning series of articles, *Crime on the Waterfront*. After a disagreement with Miller, growing out of Miller's disapproval of Kazan's cooperation with the House Un-American Activities Committee, Kazan joined forces with Schulberg. Kazan had once been a longshoreman and had learned much of the reality of life on the docks. Schulberg joined him in research along the piers of Hoboken, New York Harbor, and other locations. Investigative reports had revealed that the waterfront was under the control of rival gangs. Ten per cent of all harbour profits were pocketed by criminals. Unless longshoremen gave kickbacks to hiring bosses, they couldn't work. Kazan and Schulberg met with the well-known waterfront priest Father John Corridan, whose language combined colourful baseball slang and Christian piety in equal parts. Another waterfront figure, the insurgent Arthur Browne, taught them much about life on the piers. For a year, the research went on, along with hours of discussions at Schulberg's Pennsylvania farm and at Kazan's townhouse on East Seventy-second Street. The two men took the script to Darryl F. Zanuck, who hated it. Zanuck was uncomfortable about the co-authors' political background, and felt that there was a certain phoniness in the material. In addition, like so many studio chiefs, he disliked movies that dealt with the lives of the underprivileged, and, although he had allowed John Ford to do *The Grapes of Wrath* and *How Green Was My Valley*, and Kazan to do *Pinky*, the story of a poor black girl, he was now convinced that audiences were looking for pictures about the rich and glamorous. Zanuck invited the two to Hollywood, let them sweat through a three-day train journey, kept them waiting a week at the Beverly Hills Hotel, and then killed the project.

Jack Warner didn't want the picture, and neither did Paramount or MGM. The new wide-screen spectaculars Cinema-Scope and Cinerama ruled the day. A black-and-white picture about labour problems seemed the last thing Hollywood would want to undertake. Finally, Sam Spiegel, who had had a great success with *The African Queen*, showed an interest in the property and set up a deal with United Artists. The script was sent to Marlon, who initially decided against it; it was passed over to Frank Sinatra, but United Artists would only agree to finance Sinatra to the tune of half a million dollars. That was when Marlon was approached again. Spiegel, according to Schulberg, 'wined, dined, wooed, and seduced' the star. 'Kazan reminded Marlon how he had fought to give him the lead in *Streetcar*.' Marlon gave in.

The deal with United Artists then fell apart, and Columbia rescued the project. That studio's ferocious boss Harry Cohn hated political movies, but he said he would cast Marlon 'reading a telephone book'. Eva Marie Saint made her screen debut as the delicate, nervous heroine, and Rod Steiger was cast as the hero's mobster brother.

Marlon decided he had to research the lives of longshoremen on the spot. He hung out on the docks, helped load crates, and got to know the workers, who gradually came to trust him. The filming started in Hoboken in the savage winter of 1953.

Simultaneously, Marlon's private life ran into stormy

181

weather. Movita, who had been living with him for some time, was unable to find in him the complete emotional commitment and single-minded devotion that she so needed. She wanted to marry him; she wanted her future secure with him; she didn't want him even to look at another woman. She wanted her total affection returned. These were precisely the terms Marlon could not offer her. Lusty, virile and free, he wanted to be his own man. The quarrels between the couple that resulted from this conflict were violent and constant. Finally, Movita walked out of West Fifty-seventh Street and returned to California; she had had enough.

Making *On the Waterfront* was an endurance test for all concerned. Marlon left Fifty-seventh Street each morning at the hated hour of six, already dressed for the part of the waterfront worker in order to save time going into Wardrobe, riding the Hudson tubes rather than his motorcycle or the studio limousine. He felt that by joining other itinerant workers on the train, he would get a strong sense of the lives they lived. He hired Carlo Fiore as his stand-in. Their friendship, so badly damaged by Carlo's drug-taking, had been renewed. As the winter weather worsened Marlon proved to be less democratic and more willing to accept movie-star privileges. While the small-part players and crew had to drink coffee from paper cups while clustered around improvised fires lit in garbage cans, Marlon and Carlo enjoyed the comparative comfort of the Hoboken Hotel, washing their frozen hands and feet under hot water in the bathtub, or eating steak, baked potatoes, and apple pie à la mode.

During the shooting, a stevedore was hurt by a falling crate and Marlon offered to help out. Brownie, the work gang leader, gave Marlon the injured man's bail-ing hook. Karl Malden said, 'It was dangerous work requiring a good deal of experience. Without a word, Marlon took hold of the next crate.'

Kazan made sure that real longshoremen were blended with the cast, often choosing men inexperienced in acting to stand next to Marlon for authenticity. In his chequered woollen jacket, greasy tie, and rough work pants, he was barely distinguishable from the real-life dock workers.

Eva Marie Saint, like Mary Murphy before her, was sweet and unassuming, overawed by Brando and in need of his constant support. She and her husband Jeffrey Hayden, later to be well known as a television director, became instant friends with Marlon. Marlon had lunch every day with Eva, which helped overcome her nervousness and shyness. He was aware that her fragile quality and intense, consuming integrity were exactly correct for the part she played.

The biggest scene in the film, the one that became legendary, was when Rod Steiger, as Marlon's brother, talked with him in a moving cab, and Marlon delivered the line, 'I coulda been a contender. I coulda had class. I coulda been somebody, instead of a bum, which is what I am.' Shot in a local studio, it was a sequence that caused endless friction between Marlon and Kazan. Marlon hated the scene. It was not until years later that he understood the universality of it, telling a *Playboy* interviewer that everybody in life felt they could have been a contender, that regret and disappointment were part and parcel of the human condition. At the time, when the scene was actually being shot, Marlon felt it was false and phony. He couldn't believe that his character's brother could actually pull a gun on him, and he told Carlo Fiore it was bullshit. Fiore suggested that the scene would play better if

Marlon would look at the gun with shocked disbelief instead of fear. Much to Kazan's annoyance, Marlon took Fiore's advice and played the scene as Carlo had suggested. He still wasn't entirely comfortable with it, but at least it made better sense now. Even so, the scene had to be shot again and again until both actors, who were in many ways at odds with each other, were satisfactorily melded. The result was among Marlon's most sensational moments on the screen. The sequence, due to his carefully realistic playing, had a moving force and honesty.

Rod Steiger recalled, 'I remember making this sequence. When we came into the studio, there was a set of one half of a taxi cab. There was supposed to be a back projection of a New York street moving behind the rear window. But it hadn't arrived, and Kazan was furious.' As a result, Steiger added, it was decided to shoot the scene in very close with a blind over the back window, to disguise the fact that the back projection wasn't there. 'Gadge [Kazan] decided to make the best of the situation. The fact that the camera had to stay in so tight on our faces "made" the scene. We shot it over and over again.' Steiger said that both of them improvised a good deal in the scene. The final outcome was a compromise between Budd Schulberg's script and their own additions.

Shooting continued. The Hoboken winter grew more and more brutal. The cameraman, Boris Kaufmann, had to shoot in actual snow, a challenge in those days before fast film became generally available. Even the interiors were shot on location. The crew had to drag equipment six floors up and squeeze it into the tenement room occupied by Eva Marie Saint's character.

There was some tension between Marlon and Eva Marie Saint during the film's making. In one scene

Marlon was not satisfied with her acting when she failed to respond to him with what he considered sufficient sharpness and anger for the situation. In a break between shots, he deliberately, and with sadistic humour, tortured her verbally until at last, as Kazan ordered the cameras to roll, she screamed, clawed, and kicked Marlon. It was what Marlon wanted, and at the end she, Marlon, and everybody else broke up with laughter.

In mid-production, Dodie arrived, already ill from liver and kidney problems brought on by her drinking. But with the alcoholic's capacity to conceal personal disintegration, she was seemingly chic, elegant, and in very good shape. Fiore recalled that she arrived on a damp, drizzling day, while a sequence on a rooftop between Marlon and Eva Marie Saint involving a cage full of pigeons was being undertaken. Marlon was extraordinarily tender and considerate to his mother. He may have been instinctively aware that she had only a very few months left to live.

It was almost certainly the stress of this knowledge, plus the break-up with Movita and his uncertainty about how the picture was going, that made Marlon more than usually testy in the last three weeks of the film. During the shooting, Marlon became involved with the young and attractive fashion designer Anne Ford. They first met a few days after commencement of production. It was ten P.M. on the Saturday after Thanksgiving when Marlon, who had run into Anne at actor Sam Gilman's dinner party, called her and asked her to go out with him. She said she couldn't as she had guests. He replied that all she had to say was that she had 'a sudden need of her ear trumpet and she would have to pick it up'. She giggled, made up a more convincing excuse, and left for the Sam Gilmans' place.

Marlon ran new movies in the living room and they ate hot dogs and went to bed. Next day, he invited her to his new apartment, which was over Carnegie Hall, directly opposite its predecessor.

When she arrived, the door was open. She walked into a big room, once used for dance rehearsals and furnished almost entirely with bongo drums. She had begun tapping away at them when Marlon, stripped to the waist, emerged from a side door, danced down the room, teasing her with his gorgeous semi-nudity, disappeared behind an opposite door, and then closed it behind him with a dancer's kick. He emerged dressed soon afterwards, smilingly demonstrating his talent on the drums. They walked off to pick up apples at a Seventh Avenue delicatessen, frozen chicken breasts and salad at a Sixth Avenue market. At Sam Gilman's, Marlon unfroze the chicken, roasted the apples in the fireplace, and joined the others present to see *Mr Peepers* on television. Soon afterwards, Anne visited him on the set of *On the Waterfront*. He liked to play games with her, calling her in a heavy German accent and saying that he was 'Count Von Huesen'. The couple often visited with Jocelyn and her husband Eliot Asinof, the Asinofs' child Martin, and their friends, the actor John Kerr and his wife. Anne watched fascinatedly while Marlon played with Martin, exchanging tongue twisters with him.

Marlon took Anne to a Forty-second Street theatre to see *The Wild One*. He had avoided previews; he wanted to see the picture in a theatre with an audience. They sat in the front seats, Marlon wearing the same cyclist's cap he wore in the picture. He covered his eyes with his hands during one scene, groaning, 'Oh, no! You can't look at this – it's too bad!' The sound of his own off-camera voice had him explaining, laughing, and moaning with embarrassment. He kept exclaiming, 'Look at my fat ass!' adding that from sheer boredom he had eaten constantly during the production.

They went to Anne's apartment afterwards. She had forgotten the key, and had to wake her roommate's mother, who was staying there. Marlon sank to his knees, his Navy regulation woollen jacket pulled up around his head, begging forgiveness of the old lady; as soon as she saw who he was, she burst into laughter. He continued into the apartment on his knees, swinging his arms like a wound-up toy soldier. He stayed on his knees, laughing, pretending to be unable to walk, in grotesque parody of his part in *The Men*, while he ate one cinnamon bun after another, washing them down with nearly a quart of milk while he kept the women helpless with mirth at his extravagant stories and jokes.

His relationship with Anne Ford was lighthearted. Never meant to be serious, it ended as quickly as it had begun.

During the making of *On the Waterfront*, Marlon had signed a two-picture deal with Darryl F. Zanuck, and he now had to face fulfilling that contract, which called for his services over a period of time to be agreed upon. He would be allowed to make appearances on the stage if called for between productions. The exact amount he would receive was not made public, but it is believed to be in the region of one hundred thousand dollars a picture. He had promised to make a movie of *The Egyptian*, based on the best-selling novel by Mika Waltari, a story of ancient Egypt to be made at Twentieth Century-Fox. Zanuck was holding him to the option. Marlon had seen only a brief outline of the story. He was intrigued by the theme of Sinuhe, a surgeon concerned with treating the poor in the world of Ramses, but he had disliked Philip Dunne's script, which he considered an example of Hollywood hokum. And Kazan was extremely offended by the order he got to finish shooting *On the Waterfront* so that his star could begin quickly Zanuck's absurd CinemaScope epic.

Brando hated *On the Waterfront* when he saw it. He had mixed feelings about having appeared in it at all, and exploded angrily when people mentioned it. No doubt part of this had to do with his struggle of conscience over appearing in a movie made by those who had informed before HUAC. Although he later forgave Kazan, for years he would scream with rage at the mention of his name. Upon the film's release, he refused Columbia's press office's pleas that he give press and radio conferences. Finally, pushed into a corner by the constant pleas of the studio publicity staff, he consented to talk to United Press and Associated Press representatives. He told them, 'I [am] fed up with the whole picture . . . The cold, Christ! And I was having problems at the time. Women trouble.' Asked about the big scene in the car with Rod Steiger, he said, 'There were seven takes because Steiger couldn't stop crying. He's one of those actors who loves to cry. We kept doing it over and over . . . The first time I saw *Waterfront* in a projection room with Gadge [Kazan], I thought it was so terrible I walked out without even speaking to him.'

He thought the picture's evasions and dishonesties were insupportable, and he regarded with total cynicism his nomination for an Oscar for his performance in the film. When he actually won, Marlon was stupefied. He was contemptuous of Bosley Crowther's description in *The New York Times* of his 'shatteringly poignant portrait,' his raving about '[Brando's] groping for words, use of the vernacular, care of his beloved pigeons, pugilist's walk and gestures, and . . . discoveries of love and the immensity of the crime surrounding him'. What was the matter with the world, that it hailed mediocrity in this manner, that it saw in him a superb star instead of a hardworking actor forced to compromise in the very unpleasant world of motion pictures?

10

Only hours after *On the Waterfront* was finished in December 1953, Marlon took a train back to Hollywood for the first meetings on *The Egyptian*. He told himself that at least he was cast as a decent physician opposed to the violent regime of the Pharaohs. But almost immediately he was thrown into a state of total dejection and irritation. He was no more impressed with Darryl F. Zanuck – or his studio – than he had been before.

Zanuck had the maddening habit of delivering small lectures filled with homilies. He kept reminding Marlon of the obligation an actor has to the studio, seemingly unaware that Marlon held the studio system in total contempt and thought its executives were dealers in shoddy merchandise. When Marlon told Zanuck he thought the script was bad, Zanuck refused to change it and said to him, 'Look at it this way, boy. You're in the trenches, see? And you've got to go over the top. You don't *want* to go over the top, but you've *got* to, see? Understand?' Marlon had no more respect for director Michael Curtiz, who had been assigned to the film. Curtiz was a flamboyant and foul-mouthed studio director. Marlon saw no artistry or even seriousness in Curtiz, no political or moral awareness, and no understanding of or feeling for the world of ancient Egypt. As though that wasn't enough his co-star was Bella Darvi, Zanuck's mistress and an untalented woman with a penchant for gambling and alcohol whose name had been formed from the first letters of

Zanuck's name and that of his wife, Virginia. After he met Miss Darvi, seeing at once that she wasn't an actress at all, he realized there was no way he could proceed with this film. It represented Zanuckdom at its worst: a phony, contrived story set in an era and a place that nobody at the studio really understood, filled with dialogue of stilted, pretentious silliness, and designed solely to fill the newly popular CinemaScope screen. Realizing the risk he was running legally, he did the unthinkable and walked out of the picture. He took the train to New York at the end of January.

This was a disaster for the studio. Spyros P. Skouras, the Greek multimillionaire who was chairman of Twentieth in New York, screamed at Zanuck, demanding Brando be brought back to Hollywood. The studio had spent a million in photographing exteriors in Egypt. Marlon's wardrobe was completed. The rest of the cast, led by Miss Darvi and Gene Tierney, had been rehearsed. Zanuck had no alternative but to file a lawsuit for several million dollars against Marlon for his refusal to appear in the film.

To add to Marlon's problems, he learned from his father that Dodie had collapsed while visiting with his Aunt Betty Lindemeyer in Pasadena. In a state of unrelieved anxiety, Marlon sought the counsel of his psychiatrist, Dr Mittelman. Mittelman informed the studio that his patient was quite unable to work, that he was very sick and confused, and that they would have to cast someone else.

That night at a party, Marlon ran into a very attractive girl who was working as a governess to the children of one of Bela Mittelman's psychiatrist colleagues. Her name was Jossane Mariani-Bérenger. Her father was a fisherman living in Bandol in the south of France. Dark-haired, ravishing, and barely twenty years old,

Jossane had a deeper effect on Marlon than any woman in his life since Movita. Now separated from both Movita and Anne Ford (who was now involved with someone else), Marlon became entangled in a serious relationship with Jossane.

By mid-February, Marlon was back in Los Angeles with her; through March, he spent every day at his mother's bedside, Jossane sometimes joining him. Dodie bore her suffering bravely, impressing him so much with her dignity that he told people for years afterwards she had taught him how to die. At the end of March, she was transferred to the Huntington Memorial Hospital, where tests showed that her liver and kidneys were almost completely gone. She passed away on March 31, 1954, at the age of fifty-five. Marlon, holding her hand, finally could keep back the tears no longer: he broke down and sobbed like a child. The funeral was attended only by Marlons Jr and Sr, Jocelyn and Frances, and Betty Lindemeyer.

In the meantime, Marlon's agents and lawyers met with Twentieth Century-Fox executives and made a deal. He would give them a partial financial settlement for his failure to show up for the start of *The Egyptian*, a sum that, along with the monies lost in Nebraska, virtually wiped out his cash reserves. He also would agree to make the movie *Desirée*, with a script by Daniel Taradash based on the novel by Anne-Marie Selinko, in which he would play Napoleon Bonaparte. The idea of acting the French military genius struck him as fundamentally ludicrous, but if he didn't want to be in debt for the rest of his life, he had no alternative. It was Zanuck's black joke that he should have chosen him, the epitome of blue-collar simplicity, as the ostentatious French emperor. Marlon hated the project, and his only consolation from the first meetings on was that Jossane Mariani-Bérenger would be present during the shooting. He took a house in Benedict Canyon and decided to make the best of a bad job. Only a few days into the film, he turned down the part of the itinerant stud in *Picnic* that was taken later by William Holden. The role reminded him too much of Stanley Kowalski in *Streetcar Named Desire*.

He hired Darren Dublin to act as his stand-in. Sam Gilman was absurdly cast at his insistence as Fouché, the French minister of finance. Phil Rhodes was again his make-up man, with Rhodes's wife Marie working as his secretary. Darren's wife, Florence, played one of Napoleon's sisters. He felt more comfortable when he was surrounded by these close friends. Only Carlo Fiore, who, after a period of abstinence, had again gone back to drugs, remained behind in New York.

Desirée's director was the charming, warm, intelligent, German-born Henry Koster, who says, 'Marlon had made only a superficial study of Napoleon. I had studied the subject deeply, because my father was a collector of Napoleon materials. Our house in Germany was full of Napoleon artifacts. Flags, uniforms, helmets, everything. Even buttons from Napoleon's own uniform.'

Koster says, 'Brando couldn't play Napoleon,' pointing out that Napoleon should have been acted as a power-hungry, dominant force who would always slam his fist on the table. Marlon, Koster added, made it clear he had been forced to do the part; he learned his lines the same morning he had to start shooting, and lost them by mid-afternoon. Koster had many angry exchanges with Marlon; off the set, they were friendly, and Marlon would come over to the home of the director and his wife Peggy on weekends, and invite them to his home. But on the set, every day was a protracted ordeal. Sometimes, he would even stop in the middle of a scene, and turn to Koster, mumbling indifferently, 'Is that the way you want me to do it?' Koster lamented, 'It was a terrible thing to do to me. We had to do it all over again, because he had interrupted the camera movement, and so it would go on. And on. There was endless tension and friction.'

Cameron Mitchell, who played Napoleon's brother Joseph Bonaparte, confirmed Koster's statement. He said that Marlon took advantage of Koster, who was 'very soft. He never hurt people . . . He was a nice man to work for, very pleasant.' Mitchell said that Marlon needed a hard taskmaster like Elia Kazan; he might hate Kazan's discipline, but without it he would rapidly lose respect. Mitchell described an incident in which Marlon nearly pushed Koster beyond the limits of exasperation. At the beginning of the scene, Marlon was seated on the marble fountain bowl in the pose of Rodin's sculpture *The Thinker*. When Koster said it was time to shoot, Marlon refused to move. Koster pleaded with him, asking him what was wrong. Marlon didn't reply. Everybody on the set was watching. According to Mitchell, Koster asked Marlon, 'What have I done? What is it?' Marlon didn't answer. Finally, the director sank to his knees. 'Please, Marlon, please,' he begged. By this time, Koster was almost in tears. Finally, Marlon mumbled something. Koster said, 'I didn't hear what you said.' Marlon murmured, 'I wish this fountain was full of chocolate ice cream soda!' Confused, Koster said, 'Chocolate ice cream soda?' Marlon said, 'Yeah, yeah, chocolate ice cream soda!' Koster pleaded, 'Why, Marlon, why?' 'Because I like chocolate ice cream sodas!' Marlon exclaimed. Company and crew burst out laughing.

'Marlon didn't give a damn. He was fucking Twentieth Century-Fox,' Cameron Mitchell says. He insisted that Marlon never did a single rehearsal: 'He would walk on to the set and go from chalk mark to chalk mark without the slightest show of interest. He flubbed and fumbled and fluffed his way through everything.' His accent was a simpering, high-toned British aristocrat's. At times, he imitated Merle Oberon, with her careful Anglo-Indian diction (she was cast as the Empress Josephine). To break the tension, he began to cut up even more than usual. He even brought a football to the set, and, just before a scene was about to shoot with all of the richly dressed extras in place on the set of a throne room, he initiated a touch football game with Mitchell, Gilman, Rhodes, and others of his gang. As they kicked the ball, it would smash the arc lights and cameras were knocked over as members of the crew joined in. Later, in the scene in which Napoleon crowns himself, there were almost a thousand dress extras. Marlon sneaked in water pistols for himself and Mitchell. The pair began squirting selected targets in the cast. As the game escalated they picked up fire hoses and aimed water all over the set, ruining costumes, wigs, and furniture. There was little Zanuck could do. He knew if he crossed Marlon, it would mean even further delays in shooting. The publicity department worked overtime, trying to conceal these shenanigans.

Shooting dragged on. Merle Oberon, who had been used to the more disciplined techniques of the old-time Hollywood, was frozen, upset, and tense during the work. Only Jean Simmons, cast as Desirée, put up with everything. Scene after scene had to be retaken as Marlon scratched his ass, his nose, or his crotch, complaining loudly that he had crabs or jock itch. Off the set, he continued to see Jossane Mariani-Bérenger,

195

but he was also, according to Mitchell, dating another girl. She was an actress under contract to the studio and was generally known as 'Little Miss Innocence'. One day, Marlon broke the shooting to drag all of his pals off to the Brown Derby Restaurant on Los Feliz Boulevard. They were chatting away when Mitchell suddenly heard a loud whacking sound. He said, 'The girl had hauled off and hit Marlon, hard, I mean, really hit him. I don't mean a gentle slap. Evidently, Marlon was doing a little extracurricular activity under the table. I thought, she's done the wrong thing. The moment a girl slaps Marlon, Marlon's interested. Doomsday for the girl!'

One day, Marlon told Cameron Mitchell, 'I'm trisexual.' Mitchell says, 'What the hell does that mean? I still don't know. I said to him, "Does that mean you do it on a tricycle?"' Mitchell remembers that Marlon replied with a belch.

During the picture, the Ethiopian Emperor Haile Selassie visited the set. He arrived with three heavily medalled generals and several captains, all speaking French. Koster, glad of this brief break in the ordeal of shooting the film, introduced the Emperor to 'Napoleon'. Selassie boasted a whole chestful of ribbons. Marlon, who was wearing only one medal, said to him, 'You won more battles than I did!' Selassie turned to stone.

Despite all of his misbehaviour, Marlon remained personally friendly with the Kosters and in their company revealed the other side of his character. The Kosters had a young girl staying with them, a former World War II refugee from Holland. She was acting as a babysitter and had a room in the house. One night, former singing star Deanna Durbin and her husband, a French film director, were visiting with the Kosters from France. Marlon, who wanted to meet Miss Durbin, joined them for dinner. The two stars went up to the girl, who was lying in bed recuperating from an accident in which she had broken her leg. After they left, the girl asked, 'Who was that man?' Koster told her, 'Just tell all the girls at school that Marlon was up visiting you, and see what happens.' From then on, Koster says she was the most popular child at school. Marlon was overjoyed to hear this. Later, when the Kosters came to his house, he donned an apron and cooked lamb chops for them in the kitchen, while Sam Gilman, who was living with him in Benedict Canyon, served the dinner. During that evening, Marlon was utterly charming, amusing, full of fun, completely different from the overgrown teenager who misbehaved daily on the set.

Not surprisingly, the resulting movie was a disaster, a hodge-podge from beginning to end. Some critics did find merit in Marlon's portrayal of Napoleon, though, and the fact is that despite everything he had done to wreck his own performance, there were moments when he was not entirely unconvincing. Regardless of its quality, *Desirée* turned out to be fairly successful at the box office, largely because of Marlon's star appeal.

When he was at last free of obligations on the shooting set of *Desirée*, Marlon flew off to attend the Venice Film Festival, where *On the Waterfront* was premiered. Jossane travelled with him; in Europe and back in New York, their relationship deepened. Cameron Mitchell and others implied that the affair was conducted publicly largely to promote *Desirée* because Jossane was French. But in fact, as Mitchell himself admitted, Marlon certainly had no desire to promote the film. By early October, Marlon arrived alone in Paris after yet another trans-Atlantic voyage. He stayed with his friend Herve Mille, member of the board of directors of *Paris Match*. Jossane had been staying with her parents in Bandol. The couple were seen together at various restaurants and even announced their engagement.

Jossane returned to Bandol, and Marlon travelled on to Nice, where he gave an interview to the press with shaving cream all over his face, announcing, in a surprising break from his usual refusal to discuss his personal life, that he would soon be leaving for Bandol, where he would be meeting with Jossane's parents. Once there, he was fascinated by her father, the weatherbeaten fisherman Paul Bérenger. On October 29, Bérenger inserted an advertisement in the local newspaper reading, '[We] are happy to announce the betrothal of [our] daughter, Jossane, with M. Marlon Brando.' The couple toured around the local roads on a motor scooter and spent evenings enjoying the bouillabaisse in the family kitchen. Reporters swarmed around the simple cottage, and for once Marlon cooperated with them, smiling cheerfully as he walked with Jossane down the streets under the trees, dressed in a French sailor's striped collarless shirt and white chino pants with a gaudy belt. But inevitably, the weight of such constant exposure began to wear on the family and the couple. The town of Bandol had been transformed into a grotesque circus with the press following their every move. Jossane's father was unmercifully teased by his fellow fishermen over the whole matter. Both he and his daughter were flatly accused of latching on to Marlon for money. Paparazzi even attempted to peep through their bedroom windows in the cottage to see if they were making love. They obscenely burst into church, taking shots of Jossane praying. When Marlon left for Rome, to discuss a possible appearance in *War and Peace*, Jossane was seen crying in the corner of a pew. Finally, to escape the pressures of her village, she flew to Paris and then New York, where she stayed at Marlon's Carnegie Hall apartment for three weeks until he returned. Meanwhile, Marlon drove off to Cannes, Nice, Florence, and the Italian capital with an old friend, actor Christian Marquand, whom Marlon had met on his first trip to Paris.

Then something happened that drastically upset the relationship. Marlon found out that Jossane had posed naked for eight paintings done by the Polish-born artist Moise Kisling. Marlon was appalled by the idea of spectators ogling his fiancée at Kisling's exhibition in Paris. His reaction revealed a surprising streak of midwestern puritanism. Nevertheless, their plans to marry were not changed. As though that weren't enough, a twenty-one-year-old American student, Henry Fennell, of Queens, New York, gave an interview to the *New York Daily News* stating that Jossane had broken off her relationship with him to take up with Brando, who 'had a lot of money and experience that I just didn't have'.

By the beginning of November, Marlon was cutting up again. He arrived at a press conference in Rome with a pretty blonde actress on his arm, denouncing all reports that he had 'skipped out' on Jossane as 'spittoon rubbish'. Asked who the blonde was, he said with a laugh, 'A little bobby-soxer type. I can't even remember her name.' The effect of these remarks on the girl was not recorded. Nor was Jossane's reaction. Meanwhile, Jossane was staying in Paris before leaving for New York on November 3. She told reporters, 'I'm very happy. My dream has come true.' Movita was asked for her comment by United Press correspondent Aline Mosby. She said, 'I do not think he will marry her soon. They probably are engaged, yes, but I do not think they will marry immediately. He's very charming, but he is a little immature for me . . . or rather I am a little mature for him. But I think he must be serious about her. He needs someone so desperately . . . He isn't the type to walk into something unless he's sure.'

On November 10, Marlon joined Marquand in Rome and the two set off in a British Aston Martin convertible for Florence, Lucerne, and Paris. They were fleeing mobs of hysterical fans, and the ever-persistent paparazzi. In New York, Jossane appeared on the Colgate Comedy Hour and was interviewed by the host Gordon MacRae for a fee of one thousand dollars. She said she hoped for a reunion with Marlon 'in ten days or so,' and that they would marry in June. When he arrived in Manhattan, they once again obligingly posed outside Carnegie Hall on the condition that the reporters didn't invade Marlon's apartment. However, their every move was followed. From the moment Marlon left the liner *United States* to the late afternoon when he sent four shirts to the laundry, they didn't leave him alone. Marlon said to *The New York Times*, 'In choosing a wife I don't think it's very important to question her nationality, providing she's not Joe Stalin's cousin.' When they took off together for the evening, they again smiled for the cameras. But Marlon was soon exhausted by all of the constant attention. He told *Newsweek*, 'The world will not wreck Jossane's and my love . . . I'm going to get a slouchy hat and a pair of dark glasses and creep up alleys. What a life!'

By the beginning of 1955, the gossip columns were full of reports of Marlon's extracurricular affairs – first with a black cabaret dancer, then with his old flame Rita Moreno. The passionate romance between Marlon and Jossane had grown lukewarm, either from the stress of conducting their private lives in public or from Marlon's resistance to long-term commitments. They parted amicably.

Meanwhile, Marlon began to consider appearing in the screen version of *Guys and Dolls* for Samuel Goldwyn. He had first been approached soon after the completion of *Desirée* and was attracted to the film because it offered a chance to work with Joe Mankiewicz again and because it was a role in a light comedy – a first in Marlon's film career. Asked by a reporter how he felt about playing Sky Masterson, the Broadway gambler who falls in love with a Salvation Army girl, he said, 'I know I can carry a tune, if the handles are big enough. But I've never sung anything that could be heard outside a shower. The idea scares me, but I think it's part of an actor's job to try new things.'

As a test of whether or not the studio needed to hire a voice double, he sang several numbers, including 'I'll Know,' for the composer Frank Loesser in Hollywood. He was appalled when he heard the recording and described it as 'the mating call of a Yak'. But Loesser told him, 'It's an untrained voice. But it has a pleasing, husky quality.' Marlon remained unconvinced, but decided to go ahead anyway, working hard with MGM vocal coach Leon Ceparro. He proved to be a quick study and surprised Ceparro with his singing after only two weeks of training. Sometimes, Marlon would break the vocal course by joining his trainer in an impromptu boxing match. He also learned to dance with Michael Kidd, the well-known choreographer, who described him as moving 'like a prizefighter: very light on his feet'.

Just before the shooting of *Guys and Dolls* began, Marlon received the Academy Award for Best Actor for

On the Waterfront. The movie had become a huge critical and commercial success. It received several Academy Award nominations, including Marlon for Best Actor, and Rod Steiger, Lee J. Cobb, and Karl Malden for Best Supporting Actor. This was the first time a movie had three performers competing in the same category. Eva Marie Saint was nominated for Best Supporting Actress.

Marlon told friends he would send a cab driver to accept the award for him. But to everyone's surprise, he arrived at the RKO Pantages Theater on Hollywood Boulevard, dressed formally in a tuxedo, along with Jay Kanter, Celia Webb, Aunt Betty Lindemeyer, and his father. Indeed, Marlon had agreed to present the award for Best Director. He was delighted, despite his avowed contempt for the Oscars, when he opened the envelope and discovered that Kazan had won. Kazan, hooked up to the coast by television, accepted the award in New York. During his speech, the director accidentally or deliberately placed the gold statuette face downward on the lectern. Marlon, who in later years never had a good word for Bob Hope, joined the master of ceremonies in a would-be humorous give-and-take. Hope said, 'Do you remember, Marlon, we talked about how I could get an Academy Award?' Of course, no such conversation had ever taken place. Marlon said, 'And you know I told you that you should hire a writer as good as Tennessee Williams.' Hope made a Sad Sack face and responded with, 'And *I* had to hire Tennessee Ernie!' After this somewhat laboured exchange, Marlon made his way backstage, only to find a policeman looming up in front of him, insisting on seeing his ID. When somebody explained it was Marlon Brando, the cop exclaimed, 'Gee! I didn't know the guy from Adam!'

Karl Malden presented the award for Best Original Screenplay to Budd Schulberg, and Frank Sinatra announced that Eva Marie Saint had won Best Supporting Actress. Like Kazan, Miss Saint accepted in New York. Several months pregnant, she announced, 'I may have my baby right here!' Then Bette Davis made a dramatic appearance on stage to present the Best Actor statuette. Her head completely shaven for her role in *The Virgin Queen*, she wore a jewelled skullcap. Marlon looked at her intently, parking his gum under the seat. She sounded delighted as she announced, 'And the winner is – Marlon Brando for *On the Waterfront*!' Marlon said, as he accepted the Oscar from Miss Davis, 'I can't remember what I was going to say for the life of me. I don't think ever in my life that so many people were so directly responsible for my being so very, very happy.' The evening was capped by Sam Spiegel accepting the Best Picture award for *On the Waterfront*, making a total of eight Oscars for the movie and placing it on a par with *Gone With the Wind* and *From Here to Eternity* in the annals of the award.

Marlon was looking forward to beginning work on *Guys and Dolls*, especially since he would act opposite Frank Sinatra, who had been cast as Nathan Detroit. Sinatra, however, did not share such eagerness to share the set with Marlon. The singer was painfully aware of having been passed over for the starring role in *Waterfront*, and he had also wanted to play Sky Masterson, the romantic leading role in *Guys and Dolls*. Accustomed as he was to star treatment of the highest order, Sinatra felt he had been upstaged and brought this attitude with him on that first day of production. According to Carlo Fiore, who was hired as Marlon's stand-in, when director Joe Mankiewicz introduced the two men, Marlon was effusively admiring while Sinatra could only return a cold smile more appropriate to a boxer shaking hands with an opponent.

Their working methods were polar opposites. Marlon liked to take a scene at a steady pace, probing into it, discussing the characterization with the director, weighing and measuring the balance and length of a sequence. Sinatra wanted to do everything quickly, on the first take, without fuss. Sinatra, the hard-core professional, had his whole performance worked out in his head, was letter-perfect down to the last line of every lyric he sang, and never even considered blowing an actor's gesture or word of dialogue. Marlon was unprepared.

During the first scene in Mindy's, a parody of Lindy's in New York, the tension on the set was unbearable. Sinatra had to eat cheesecake while listening to Marlon's dialogue. Marlon couldn't master the odd rhythms of the script, a sanitized version of Damon Runyon. One take followed another, until finally there were eight. 'One-Take' Sinatra lost his temper completely. He threw aside the cheesecake, prodded his fork into the tablecloth, and screamed at Mankiewicz, 'These fuckin' New York actors! How much cake do you think I can eat?' and he marched off the set. Mankiewicz went to see Frank in his dressing room, where Frank groaned about Marlon's Actors Studio Method approach. He came back and finished the scene, resenting every second of it. Again, Marlon would mumble, fumble a line, or have to discuss its meaning. By sundown Sinatra was livid. And that was only the first day of shooting.

In the weeks that followed, animosity between the two stars was given full and free expression. Marlon took to openly criticizing Sinatra's singing and told Mankiewicz, 'Frank's playing his part all wrong. He's supposed to sing with a Bronx accent. He's supposed to clown it up. But he's singing like a romantic lead. We can't have two romantic leads.'

In the end, Marlon didn't much like his performance in *Guys and Dolls* any more than he did any of his previous acting on film. He said later, 'In [that picture] I wanted to effect a frothy farce style, but I'm heavy-footed with high comedy.' Reviewers concurred with Marlon's own assessment of his debut in musical comedy. Nevertheless, the film was a box-office hit, which confirmed the value of star appeal in the studio system of making movies.

11

During the making of *Guys and Dolls*, plans were concluded for the formation of a new company, Pennebaker, Inc. (named for Marlon's late mother), intended as a means of support for his father, and as a tax shelter for Marlon. Fortunately for all concerned, Pennebaker was partly financed by Paramount Pictures, which hoped as a result of its participation to secure Marlon's services for future pictures. The partners, in addition to Marlon Sr, were George Glass, who had been an associate publicist with Stanley Kramer at the time of *The Men*, and Walter Seltzer, another well-regarded press agent. George Englund, an ambitious young would-be director and producer, was the fourth member of the partnership. According to Seltzer, the one surviving member of the Pennebaker board, Marlon took little or no interest in the company from the beginning. He gave the directors carte blanche to select properties, hire featured players, and make distribution deals through Paramount. And incredibly, despite his previous financial failures, Marlon still entrusted his father with his substantial earnings, allowing him to invest with a free hand.

Pennebaker's first undertaking was a film adaptation of Louis L'Amour's novel *To Tame a Land*. Alas, Marlon's interest was only passing, and the project was abandoned.

Penny Poke ranch in Nebraska was soon to be sold at a loss, a combination of inefficient management and natural disasters having forced its closure. In just a

In New York, late 1940s. He excited theater audiences in *Truckline Cafe* and *Candida*. *(Museum of the City of New York)*

Above: With Jessica Tandy in *A Streetcar Named Desire*, his insolent sexuality was unprecedented on the Broadway stage.
(Museum of the City of New York)

Left: The theatrical sensation of 1949.
(Wide World)

Above: With Vivien Leigh on the set of the film version of *Streetcar*. He was tender and thoughtful to the disease-stricken actress. *(Kobal Collection)*

Right: A young and gorgeous Shelley Winters had an intense love affair with Brando in New York. *(Wide World)*

The young movie star in Hollywood. *(Starchives/Starfile)*

Right: A bust by the Hollywood sculptor, Constantine, executed during the shooting of *Julius Caesar.* Brando hated it. *(Courtesy of Kenneth Kendall)*

Below: On the set of *Viva Zapata!* with director Elia Kazan and co-star Jean Peters, who later became Mrs Howard Hughes. The conditions were rugged and the shooting was exhausting. *(Phototeque)*

Above: With Eva Marie Saint and Karl Malden on the set of *On the Waterfront.* Brando won an Oscar for this controversial picture. *(Phototeque)*

Left: At the Academy Awards presentation in 1955 with Grace Kelly. Despite his loathing for the Oscars, he attended the ceremonies to receive his award. *(Wide World)*

Left: He accompanied Jossane Mariani-Berenger to the south of France in 1954, but their romance was ruined by an excess of publicity. *(Wide World)*

Right: On the set of *Guys and Dolls* with his dear friend, Tamar Cooper, who is the daughter of publicist Jack Cooper. *(Courtesy of Tamar Cooper)*

Right: Sultry, head-strong Rita Moreno. She tried to commit suicide when he rejected her. *(Wide World)*

Below: In the end, Brando despised the film *Sayonara*, directed by Joshua Logan (1.) and produced by William Goetz (r.). However, he fell in love with the country. *(Kobal Collection)*

He posed with his new bride, Anna Kashfi, in Hollywood in 1957. Their tormented relationship would include a fifteen-year custody battle over their son, Christian Devi. *(Wide World)*

Above: Brando directed *One-Eyed Jacks* after his arguments drove Stanley Kubrick from the project. One of their differences concerned casting Karl Malden. *(Kobal Collection)*

Left: The beautiful, tragic Pina Pellicer, discovered for *One-Eyed Jacks.* She committed suicide over the ill-fated love affair that followed her brief romance with Brando. *(Wide World)*

Right: The stunning Eurasian actress, France Nuyen, had a difficult relationship with him and was replaced in his affections by Barbara Luna.
(Wide World)

Below: On location in Tahiti with *Mutiny on the Bounty*. He fought with director Lewis Milestone but developed a lasting affection for the islands.
(Kobal Collection)

Above: Brando's political convictions were always apparent. Here, he marches in a demonstration for integration in California. *(Gene Daniels/Black Star)*

Right: His brief marriage to Movita was as unhappy as his first to Anna Kashfi. *(Wide World)*

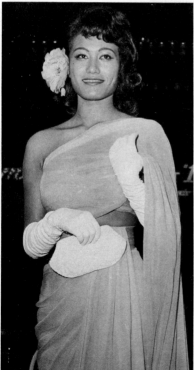

Above: Jocelyn Brando had a small part in the film of *The Ugly American* along with her famous brother. *(Phototeque)*

Left: He met the stunning Tarita while shooting *Mutiny on the Bounty*, and she remains devoted to him to this day. She is the mother of two of his children. *(Wide World)*

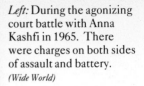

Left: During the agonizing court battle with Anna Kashfi in 1965. There were charges on both sides of assault and battery.

(Wide World)

Right: Actor/director Christian Marquand with starlet Ewa Aulin at the New York premiere of *Candy* in 1968. Marquand's close friendship with Brando infuriated Anna Kashfi.

(Wide World)

Right: Christian Devi Brando, age thirteen, was the object of protracted court battles between his parents. *(Wide World)*

Below: Marlon went to St. Paul in 1974 to lend his support to Indian activists who were on trial for their alleged involvement in the Wounded Knee incident. *(UPI/Bettmann Newsphotos)*

Above: With AIM leader Dennis Banks in Keshena, Wisconsin, in 1975, following the seizure of a monastery by the Menominee Warrior Society. *(Courtesy of the Shawano Evening Leader)*

Below: Brando's island paradise was battered by cyclones. It has recently been offered for sale. *(Tahiti Bureau of Tourism)*

handful of years, Marlon Sr lost all the money he had invested in it, which included most of Marlon's earnings to date. It can be estimated that Marlon's father lost him well over a million dollars (or $5–6 million in today's money) in Penny Poke and other schemes.

Marlon Sr rented a luxurious duplex apartment in an imitation Spanish building in West Hollywood, only a stone's throw from Marlon's recently acquired Spanish-style house on Laurel View Drive. (Marlon Sr had been in and out of Hollywood for some time, but only now had decided to settle permanently there.) To his associates, the old man seemed charming, gentlemanly, and subdued in his tweeds, with a pipe fixed semipermanently between his teeth, his manner schoolmasterly now in his more sober middle age. He was no longer the womanizer he had been in earlier years and would spend the day at the office and evenings at his modest home reading books on spiritualism, mysticism, and different forms of philosophy, or playing chess with Marlon or bridge with his partners and their wives or girlfriends. Yet Marlon continued to loathe the man as much as ever.

Seltzer recalls an incident in which some mail arrived addressed to Marlon Brando and his father accidentally opened it, thinking it was intended for him. Marlon Jr was furious, and told his father never to do that again. He also suggested that perhaps his parent should change his name. Marlon Sr said, 'I've had my name for over sixty years. Why don't you change yours?' Meanwhile, rumours were circulating that Marlon and Jossane Bérenger were still planning to marry – long after she had left his life. In June, Mike Sands, a twenty-six-year-old former prizefighter who was in love with Jossane, arrived at the Hollywood Plaza Hotel and called reporters to his room, announcing with a smack of his fist into his palm that he intended to settle the matter with Marlon man to man. He said, 'I love the girl, I feel she loves me, and I'm determined to find out Brando's intentions.' The two men never actually fought it out; Sands soon realized that Marlon had absolutely no interest in Jossane.

At that time Marlon formed an association that was to last most of his life – with Alice Marchak, a bright, blonde, attractive, and intelligent young woman who was his father's secretary and then his own. A movie buff, fascinated by Marlon, yet never involved with him romantically, Alice proved to be a mainstay of his life and a model of devoted efficiency under stress.

In 1955, Marlon embarked with George Englund on a documentary to be made for UNESCO, dealing with the problems of hunger and suppression in the troubled areas of Southeast Asia. More than ever, Marlon was concerned with the underprivileged and tormented peoples of what is known as the Third World. Still convinced that moviemaking contributed little to the world, he felt that only a commitment to the world's problems of poverty and their solution could justify him as a man and as a filmmaker. From the outset he decided to have Pennebaker finance this production, which had no name and for which no script had been properly developed.

In the meantime, to make money to support his plans, Marlon decided to embark upon a screen version of John Patrick's Broadway hit *Teahouse of the August Moon*. He had seen it four times in New York and had been lost in admiration for the witty, agile performance of David Wayne as Sakini, the Okinawan interpreter and humorous commentator on Japanese-American mores who formed the centre of the comedy. He saw a considerable and entertaining challenge in playing

Sakini himself, and a deal was struck with Metro-Goldwyn-Mayer. He had now achieved such extraordinary eminence that he was among the very first stars to obtain approval in the selection of a director. In this case, he settled on Daniel Mann, whose direction of such films as *Come Back, Little Sheba* and *I'll Cry Tomorrow* had impressed him. And he insisted from the outset that John Patrick write the screenplay, with no interference from the studio.

While the script was being prepared, Marlon befriended John Patrick. He would drive him around in his dilapidated-looking automobile, a bullet-riddled jalopy used in gangster pictures. Patrick wasn't comfortable as a passenger in this shaky contraption and, not surprisingly, Marlon got into a nasty accident while driving it. Marlon was taking Patrick back to the Beverly Hills Hotel one afternoon, and he nearly hit an elderly man; he screamed abuse at him. Soon after that, he actually did collide with another auto. As a result, he was given a ticket and had to appear in court to answer charges of reckless driving. When reporters invaded the courtroom at the hearing, he indulged in a Garbo-like flight from them, thus earning the headlines he was supposedly trying to avoid. As it turned out he was cleared of any liability in the matter.

In the fall of 1955, Marlon met a woman who was to change his life completely and plunge him into the first real emotional commitment he had ever known. Her name was Anna Kashfi, and she was destined to at once enhance and torment his existence. Fierce, challenging, very slender, and darkly beautiful, she was a woman whose origins were kept mysterious, although her Anglo-Indian accent was always evident. According to her story, she was born out of wedlock on September 30, 1934, in Calcutta, India, the illegitimate child of an architect named Devi Kashfi, a full-blooded Indian, and Selma Ghose, also of Indian blood, who later became his wife. Miss Kashfi claimed that when she was two years old her mother married William Patrick O'Callaghan, and she was taken by her stepfather to Darjeeling in northern India, where she attended school at a Roman Catholic convent. At eighteen, she said, she went to the London School of Economics. Her mother and stepfather were living in Wales at the time. She left the university because an Italian fell in love with her and took her to Rome.

Later, she scraped a living as a model in London. Although quite inexperienced, she was discovered by Paramount and introduced to the director Edward Dmytryk, who was preparing a picture entitled *The Mountain*, about a plane crash whose sole survivor was an Indian girl. Spencer Tracy, the male star of the picture, allegedly selected her after just one meeting in Paris. Her haunting looks and sensitivity made an impression in the film. Partly shot in Chamonix in the French Alps, the movie was finished in Hollywood.

One day in October 1955, she was lunching in the Paramount commissary when Marlon noticed her. He was, she improbably alleged, kissing and nibbling at Eva Marie Saint's neck. A. C. Lyles, assistant producer on *The Mountain*, introduced Kashfi to Marlon. Later that afternoon, Marlon called Paramount publicist Harry Mines and said he wanted to date Anna. Miss Kashfi was currently seeing an Italian pilot and wasn't interested. Several days passed. The phone rang at her apartment. A soft voice said, 'This is Marlon Brando. Do you remember me? We met in the commissary. A. C. Lyles introduced us.' He invited her to dinner. Her response was that she wasn't comfortable about going out with a complete stranger. In reply, Marlon offered to supply a chaperone. It was clever of him, because Indian women were customarily accompanied by chaperones when they went out on dates. She couldn't help but be charmed by the suggestion and laughingly agreed to see him – with the chaperone. However, when he turned up at her home for their first evening together, he didn't have a middle-aged woman with him, as she had expected. Instead, he had brought along George Englund. So, Anna Kashfi set out on her first date with Marlon Brando with two virile, handsome men as her escorts.

Incredibly, Miss Kashfi later claimed, she had never heard of Marlon Brando at the time of that first date. When she asked him what he did, he replied, 'I am the author of "Twinkle, Twinkle Little Star".' Nonplussed, she accepted the explanation. It was only the next day, when Spencer Tracy questioned her about her date, which had already made its way into the columns, that she learned who Marlon was. She was both embarrassed and upset, because by now she was aware of Brando's reputation as a womanizer, and she refused to go out with him again. Neither his pleas nor his gifts could change her mind.

In December 1955, after a brief trip to New York, Marlon attempted one more time to convince Miss Kashfi to go out with him again. She was everything he desired in a woman. Her dark, glossy hair, firm breasts, and long legs excited him. This time, she was unable to resist his charm. And, out of what she describes as sheer curiosity to see what he was like in bed, she went home with him at the end of the evening. She said he was pure Stanley Kowalski. They were watching television when he picked her up and carried her into the bedroom. She asked him as she lay in his arms if he was going to rape her, and he replied that rape was 'just an assault with a friendly weapon'. She later described his lovemaking as 'a well-rehearsed, polished performance, selfish, without warmth or naturalness'. She also added bitterly, 'Physically, Marlon is not well-appointed. He screens that deficiency by undue devotion to his sex organ. "My noble tool," he characterized it with some puffery.'

Anna consumed him utterly, as no previous woman ever had. His need for her was absolute. They made love at all hours of the day and night, insatiably devoured by lust for each other's bodies. They had little time at this stage to understand each other deeply. They began to be seen around Hollywood at certain obscure restaurants, but as always, Marlon hated the party circuit and refused to go to nightclubs or hotels. Anna learned to adjust to the constant pursuit of privacy that is the by-product of celebrity. Marlon scarcely even looked at another woman. His promiscuity ceased, at least for a time. Marlon would wake in the early hours of the morning feeling aroused, and, too impatient even to telephone her, he would drive to her apartment, ring the doorbell, and, when she opened it, rubbing sleep from her eyes, carry her headlong into the bedroom and make love to her on the spot. Then he would leave without even saying goodnight. It was the most unromantic relationship possible. Yet so complete was his fame and charisma, so enveloping his nature, that Anna Kashfi had no chance of escaping him. Both would have reason to regret the relationship before too long, but for now, theirs was a ferocious and overwhelming sexual obsession.

And of course no sooner had it begun than it was tested by separation. Marlon was committed to leave Los Angeles on an extensive trip through Southeast Asia to research his film for the United Nations Assistance Program. Following that, he would report to Japan in the spring to shoot *Teahouse of the August Moon*, a film he was looking forward to working in. He began to train for the part of Sakini by losing a great deal of weight; in fact, he had not been so slim since his appearance in *Truckline Café*. He also worked very hard to master Japanese and spent a great deal of time in Little Tokyo, near downtown Los Angeles, carefully studying the people there with his uncanny skill at capturing intonation and gesture.

Anna Kashfi could not accompany him on these trips. She was already involved in the film *Battle Hymn* with Rock Hudson, at Universal Pictures. While making the movie, she stayed with Hudson and his wife Phyllis at their Santa Monica beach house. Mrs Hudson was preparing for a divorce. Even though Marlon would often pick Anna up from the Hudson house, he was never close to Hudson.

In March 1956, after many delays, Marlon at last left for Hong Kong, Singapore, Manila, and Bangkok to scout possible locations for the UNESCO documentary. The writer Stewart Stern and George Englund accompanied him. His parting from Anna Kashfi was painful. He hated to be without a woman in his life and greatly resented the fact that she couldn't come with him. Determined not to be left alone in Japan, he invited his great-aunt June, Dodie's aunt and second daughter of Julia Gahan, to fly to Tokyo to join him. He also invited Jocelyn and her husband Eliot Asinof, who was having some success as a novelist in those years. Marlon also invited his old friend Phil Rhodes from the New York days, now a favourite of his regular entourage, and his wife Marie, who would act as stand-ins.

At a well-attended press conference in Singapore, Marlon launched an attack on Hollywood fan

213

magazines, calling them 'scavengers, against whom the libel laws give no protection'. He said, 'I have enemies in the film world, because I don't want to follow the dictates of certain companies or give interviews to columnists I don't know.' While railing against America, attacking its 'shoddy, vulgar and commercial' aspects, he also made great play with his gracious concern for Asian problems. He fussed over children with the enthusiasm of an electioneering politician. He met with Asian film studio chiefs, local dignitaries, and UNESCO representatives, charming everyone. He proclaimed that Asian reporters asked him 'intelligent questions instead of the foolish emphasis on my sex life which I have to tolerate in the United States'. It was only in Manila, where American movies were followed ecstatically by armies of fans, that he was mobbed as a star, and he grumbled to his travelling companions about such folly.

Little was done on the tour except to establish possible locations and important contacts in the areas. The story of the potential movie remained vague; it was destined to come to nothing. Marlon eventually would find a way of expressing his feelings about the American presence in Southeast Asia through a different project: the film version of the best-selling novel *The Ugly American*.

Marlon flew on to Tokyo on April 3, 1956, to begin filming *The Teahouse of the August Moon*. Three hundred teenage fans in school uniforms greeted him off the plane, and two Japan Airlines hostesses presented him with sheafs of flowers. Beaming, in excellent health, down to a mere 140 pounds for his role, he was full of enthusiasm for his trip. And now he was fascinated by Tokyo, which in those days was one of the most erotic and exciting cities on earth. By daytime a maze of smog-yellow, labyrinthine streets filled with the chattering of *pachinko* parlours, the stench of uncured fish, and the cries of vendors of every conceivable merchandise, at night it turned into a mad playground, with fanciful and crazy electric light signs that danced, rippled, flowed, and snaked up and down the buildings in so violent a profusion that beside them Broadway or Shaftesbury Avenue were caverns of darkness. Tokyo seemed to be a giant pop-art creation, a masterpiece of quasi-Western vulgarity.

Along with director Daniel Mann, Marlon's excellent co-star, Glenn Ford, cast as Captain Fisby, and the distinguished character actor Louis Calhern, cast as Colonel Purdy, Marlon stayed at Frank Lloyd Wright's Aztec pyramid of a hotel, the Imperial. Expeditions into the city involved hilarious pre-arrangements. Because none of the street signs was in English, Marlon had to have the instructions to reach his destination inscribed in Japanese characters by the doorman for the cab driver. Armed with this, he would proceed to the delightfully suspect and obscure quarters of the city.

During the day, he attended meetings at the Daiei Film Studios, the second largest (after Toho) in Japan. He and Daniel Mann turned out to have little rapport, and from the first Marlon developed an irrational dislike of Glenn Ford. He had somehow perceived Ford as little more than a conventional Hollywood actor, superficial and mechanical in his style. In turn, Ford had little admiration for Marlon's constant examinaton of the meaning of his role. It cannot have pleased Ford that Marlon's contract accommodated the star with great extravagance. He was to receive three hundred thousand dollars plus twenty-one thousand per week for every week the film ran over schedule. He could only be called upon for fittings, still photographs, tests, rehearsals, and script readings one week before and one week after shooting. He could not be asked to work more than eight hours a day, and he would never work on Sundays or public holidays. Ford had none of these privileges.

The two men never met in the evenings. Ironically, both were going through problems with the women in their lives at the time. Glenn Ford's marriage to Eleanor Powell was in ruins, and that had taken a visible toll. Marlon was equally frustrated. He missed Anna Kashfi, and even the most skilled attentions of Japanese geisha girls were no consolation. He countered that feeling of isolation by spending evenings with Phil and Marie Rhodes and Aunt June. And in a characteristic fit of nostalgia, he hired his former girlfriend Celia Webb, now a Mrs Meredith, to be his secretary, gofer, and general assistant during the production.

The company shifted from Tokyo to Nara, a typical Japanese tourist attraction, in which the delicate land-scape had been tortured into a fairy-tale setting of a deer park, a model village, and elegantly replanted trees. The old Nara Hotel had a grand, faded charm, and Marlon chose to occupy a room furnished in the Japanese mode. He relished the famous tubs, which were shared by men and women of all ages and types who bathed in the nude without embarrassment or shame. He was delighted by the attentiveness of the giggling Japanese girls whose very existence was a pretty and formalized self-parody. He wallowed in massages and nocturnal bathhouse encounters, ecstati-cally indulging himself. But he remained cool and distant towards his director and his co-star.

Almost from the first minute the company arrived in Nara, rain began to fall. As it thudded down with a

216

hard, grey monotony, Marlon was determined to make the best of a bad job. Holed up with his entourage, he studied Japanese with an instructor and from recordings, mastering the language to an amazing degree. He even managed to address a press conference in Japanese. He took pride in this new accomplishment, and somehow the days passed.

During the filming, Marlon renewed his friendship with Louis Calhern, whom he had first met during the making of *Julius Caesar*. Calhern admitted to Marlon that he had lately become depressed over a troubled affair he was having with a much younger woman. Because of his anxiety over the age difference and his own habitual drinking, Calhern had been unable to satisfy her sexually and was overwhelmed with feelings of impotence and ageing. Marlon did his best to calm his friend's troubled spirit.

Only five weeks after their arrival in Japan, on May 12, Louis Calhern was found dead in his hotel room. Marlon's telegram to John Patrick in America read, 'Lou died in his sleep last night, and I'm glad. He was so lonely and unhappy that he really didn't want to live.' Glenn Ford insisted on bringing in an American priest and on holding a wake, although Calhern himself was an atheist.

The rain broke long enough each day to allow for a twenty-mile car ride to the nearby Tobiki Village, where the villagers were paid by MGM for the cost of their crops because some filming took place in their fields. Mann filmed a diverting Jeep chase, followed by several more antic sequences marred only by the constant upstaging of one male star by the other. In the midst of that offstage struggle, the Nisei actress Machiko Kyo, cast as Lotus Blossom, the film's attractive heroine, proved to be a cool, perfectly controlled counterpoint to her fellow actors' misbehaviour.

Between the weather conditions and the lead actors who could not get along with the director or with each other, everyone at the studio felt that the only solution was to bring the unit home to California. Marlon would have preferred to wait until the rains broke, but the decision was made and the teahouse set was already constructed on the MGM backlot. Once the unit got back to Hollywood, matters only grew worse. Marlon kept Daniel Mann more at arm's length than ever. There was a scene in which Marlon had to stand on a platform talking to Ford about the Okinawans. According to Mann, both stars tried to hog the camera. First Ford would move up, and then Marlon. And Ford would say, as Marlon moved into the camera frame, 'Danny, are you sure you can see me?' Finally, Mann had had enough. He said to the two stars, 'This is ridiculous. This kind of competition is sheer self-indulgence. It's something I can't tolerate. It's shameful.' They more or less conceded his point, but soon afterwards they retired to the same competitive antics.

There was a scene in which Marlon had to talk directly to the audience in a speech that began, 'Lovely ladies, kind gentlemen.' Mann says that Marlon played the speech completely flat. By now, he and Marlon were barely speaking. However, there was no way Mann would allow such a meaningless and shallow delivery. He got down off the camera boom and politely but coolly asked Marlon to repeat the lines. Again, Marlon spoke without colour, without conveying anything. The way he delivered the words was like an artist without paint on his brush. Once more, the director descended to ask for more. Marlon coolly agreed to try again. It was useless. Mann had to resort to desperate measures. He went over to a Japanese woman extra and told her that when he gave her the signal she was to reach out and pinch Marlon's behind as hard as she could. She was startled, unable to believe what she had heard. Mann repeated the request. She nodded in agreement. Just as Marlon came by, she obeyed her instructions. Marlon jumped up. But he still didn't read the line correctly. Next time, she pinched harder – and with such vigour that Marlon's eyes were filled with tears. His final line in the speech was, 'Pain makes men wise!' And for the first time in many takes, he delivered the words with the required emphasis.

Marlon found it increasingly difficult to work with Mann and finally called John Patrick at his farm on the Hudson to ask him to take over. Patrick refused.

One personal matter that distracted him from concentrating on his performance was his concern for Anna Kashfi's health. During preliminary wardrobe tests for the film *Ten Thousand Bedrooms,* she became ill and was diagnosed as having tuberculosis. Although she had tried to keep the truth from Marlon, it became impossible when she had to be admitted to the City of Hope Hospital, where she was confined to her bed in a private room through much of the rest of the year. Marlon proved to be a devoted lover. He showered her with bouquets of flowers and other gifts so that her room soon filled with roses, boxes of chocolates, wind-up dolls, and souvenirs of his trip to Japan. And he treated her to private movie screenings in her room, including his favourite musical, the satirical *Singin' in the Rain.*

When he came to the hospital directly from the shooting set of *Teahouse,* he would enter her room wearing surgical mask and gown as called for by the medical staff, still dressed as Sakini in his complicated Japanese make-up, kidding her that he was a 'Tokyo physician,' Meshuggener Moto. It was painful and exhausting for Anna to laugh, but she was convulsed by his impersonation. He did everything he could to make her feel better. How could she fail to fall deeper and deeper in love with him?

They had long, intense conversations about philosophy and Buddhism. Anna was not a disciple of Buddha but was fascinated by the religion, and Marlon was attracted to the more pragmatic elements in Zen. They seldom discussed acting, and almost never his work.

Marlon narrated a documentary on the City of Hope Hospital as an expression of his gratitude to the staff for assisting in Anna's painfully slow recovery. When at last he had to go to New York to prepare another ill-fated Pennebaker project, accompanied by Aunt June, he called her constantly and sent her letters filled with his latest news.

When Marlon returned, he brought Anna Dodie's family bible, brooch, and earrings. He even gave Anna the pillow on which Dodie had expired. He poured out his heart to Anna and told her of his love for his mother and his pain over her drinking. Although he openly grieved over the loss of his mother, he told Anna, 'It's better she's dead. If she'd lived, I could never have loved you. She wouldn't have let me go.' And he began to cry. Finally, he slipped his mother's engagement ring on her finger.

12

On Thanksgiving Day, 1956, Anna was at last released
from the City of Hope Hospital. There was a double
celebration at the home of Eliot and Jocelyn Asinof at
Pacific Palisades. Jocelyn's sons by Don Hanmer and
Asinof were present. Marlon, thirty-two now, carved
the turkey, ate three helpings, then formally presented
Anna with a platinum-and-pearl engagement ring.
They agreed to keep news of their engagement out of
the papers.

Anna didn't move in with him to his house on Laurel
View Drive. Marlon found her a duplex apartment in
the same quasi-Spanish West Hollywood building
where Marlon Sr lived. As he moved Anna in, Marlon
bitterly criticized his father's womanizing and cruelty
to his mother. Anna soon had confirmation of Marlon
Sr's disposition. From across the courtyard she could
hear him screaming foul abuse at Alice Marchak. Anna
later wrote that on one occasion Miss Marchak even
shouted that she was going to slash her wrists because
she had grown so frustrated with her boss. During
those weeks, Marlon drove Anna around town in his
filthy, beaten-up car, which she described as 'strewn
with beer cans, stained hamburger wrappers, and discarded newspaper sheets'.

Their romantic bliss soon began to dissolve. These
two independent, challenging, strong, forthright and
opinionated personalities began to clash as they spent
more and more time together. Their constant proxim-
ity, so desirable at first, now began to grate. Marlon, as

always, needed his own space, and so, perhaps even more emphatically, did Anna. With a sense of sadness, they began to realize that, like so many involvements, theirs was not the easy pairing of complementary spirits. Indeed, they fought day and night. Yet Marlon and Anna were still deeply attracted to each other sexually; they remained creatures obsessed.

On a quick trip to New York to discuss the possibility of making the Louis L'Amour Western for Frank P. Rosenberg and Paramount/Pennebaker, Marlon began lusting for Anna and insisted she fly in to join him. Then he kept her waiting at the airport for two hours. Back at the hotel, they started arguing within minutes of arriving. He tried to appease her by taking her for a hansom cab ride through Central Park. It didn't work.

During the last months of 1956 Marlon had been engaged in discussions with Warner Brothers regarding a version of James A. Michener's best-selling novel of Japan, *Sayonara,* set during the Korean War. He was offered the part of Major Lloyd Gruver, a somewhat one-dimensional and colourless role in an improbable hearts-and-flowers romance. Gruver, serving with the US Army Air Corps, is on R&R leave in Kobe, and falls in love with Hana-ogi, member of a celebrated local dance group. Their secret and troubled affair is threatened by fear of discovery – both by her own monastic and disciplined society of dancers and by his military commanders. Marlon knew the film would not be high art, but he was tempted by the opportunity to beef up Pennebaker's finances and couldn't resist the idea of so early a return to his beloved Japan. It was typical of him that although he was engaged to Anna Kashfi, a part of him yearned to be several thousand miles away, to be free in another part of the world. Such obvious flights from romantic involvement were to anger women all through Marlon's life.

Marlon detested the work of *Sayonara*'s director, Joshua Logan, who had mounted the Broadway hits *South Pacific* and *Fanny* and the film versions of William Inge's popular plays *Picnic* and *Bus Stop.* However, Marlon hadn't forgotten that Logan had given Jocelyn a much-needed job in *Mister Roberts.* Logan had been planning *Sayonara* from as early as 1951. A man of extraordinary enthusiasms, highly strung and driven by demons, Logan suffered from sudden unexpected fits of depression. He was drawn to the exotic and had a passion for the Orient and the South Seas. Indeed, he had worked on Michener material years before *Sayonara* was written, adapting the author's *Tales of the South Pacific* (with Oscar Hammerstein) into the smash Rodgers and Hammerstein musical starring Mary Martin and Ezio Pinza. At the Tokyo Foreign Correspondents' Club in the summer of 1951, he and Michener had discussed the idea of a novel that involved the daring theme of an American-Japanese love affair. The resulting novel, *Sayonara,* became a best-seller after publication in 1954.

Logan planned to mount a show based on the novel on Broadway; he also wanted to import both the Kabuki theatre company and the Takarazuka dance troupe to New York, but the Japanese government nixed the idea (although in later years the Kabuki did tour in the US). The Japanese were also opposed to a film version of the novel; the matter even went to a very high government level, with the result that Logan was forbidden to use either one of these popular theatrical troupes in any movie. Between 1954 and 1956, Logan was engaged with Paul Osborn in writing the script and paid two visits to Japan, scouting locations and setting up particulars for film production. He was present in Tokyo at almost the same time that *Teahouse of the August Moon* was shooting. Given the successful release of *Teahouse* and Marlon's star status in Japan, Logan hoped his presence as the star could help overcome Japanese objections to the story and ensure that *Sayonara* would be an automatic international hit.

Originally planned for Columbia, the project moved over to Warner Brothers. William Goetz, a promotional hotshot married to Irene Selznick's sister Edith, was producer. Marlon met with Bill Goetz, Edie Selznick, Josh Logan, and Paul Osborn in the grand old Goetz mansion in Beverly Hills. Usually contemptuous of luxury, he was impressed by Goetz's collection of T'ang horses, Ming vases, and coromandel screens. He prolonged the conversation by urgently pressing the others to ensure that all of the Asians in the story had sufficient dignity. Then he arranged a second meeting, in New York at the Logans' apartment. During one of Marlon's quasi-political monologues, Logan began abstractedly pulling dead leaves off a wilting plant on his terrace overlooking the East River. Marlon was impressed by the delicacy of this gesture in so portly and seemingly heavy-handed a gentleman. And despite his misgivings about Logan's talents, he couldn't fail to respond to his considerable Old World southern charm and to his wife, Nedda, who he was fascinated to discover came from a family of vaudevilleans.

He told Logan that he hated the ending of the script, which echoed *Madam Butterfly.* The idea of an American Army officer walking out on a Japanese girl to a presumably conventional American marriage infuriated him. Logan promised to change the conclusion to a Japanese-American wedding scene, thus tying the story in more closely to Marlon's personal life as his marriage to Anna approached. The inducement of a three hundred thousand dollar salary plus percentages clinched the deal.

Red Buttons was cast as a blue-collar counterpoint to Brando. Ricardo Montalban was bizarrely cast as a Kabuki actor. And Miyoshi Umeki was chosen as Red Buttons's ill-fated girlfriend. Audrey Hepburn, who had a star reputation second to none in Japan, turned the part of Hana-ogi down because she did not want to play the role of an Oriental.

Early in 1957, after a prolonged search through Hawaii, Japan, and even France, a nonactress, Miiko Taka, was found for the female lead. The luscious Seattle-born Nisei, whose real name was Betty Ishimoto, was working the Mitchell Travel Agency in downtown Los Angeles when she went in for a reading at Warner's. Marlon was impressed with her from the first moment he saw her in Joshua Logan's office. Marlon took her off to a corner and talked to her, quickly discovering her sensitivity and intelligence. 'She's going to be okay,' he told Logan. She proceeded to read a sequence in which the character expresses her love for Major Gruver. Everyone, led by Marlon, was overjoyed. She had a natural, untrained talent, and they could hardly believe their luck. The only problem was that she had a discoloured tooth. Once her teeth were capped and she was taught the basics of singing and dancing, the problems were over. Marlon felt a little better about *Sayonara* now. Rather than identifying with his part to the point of having an affair with Miiko, he was fatherly and sweet to her from the beginning. His usual roughness with the women who fell in love with him disappeared entirely in this platonic relationship. Fortunately, Miiko had no romantic interest in him.

Accompanied by Carlo Fiore, Marlon flew to Honolulu without telling Anna. Then, characteristically, he relented and asked her to fly over to join him in the islands. Again, he was hours late picking her up at the airport. She was infuriated and demanded to know why they were even still engaged. As Marlon drove to the Coral Sands Hotel, she let go and slapped him across the face; the car weaved across the road, and he narrowly avoided winding up in a ditch. Still upset, she flew back to Los Angeles the next day. She was cast in another picture, *Don't Go Near the Water*, ironically opposite Glenn Ford, and she walked through her part in a state of miserable unhappiness.

In Hawaii, Marlon kept going over the script, rewriting lines, fretting about its synthetic elements. Carlo Fiore, who had cleaned up his drug-taking habits for the time being, was working with him on the Warner payroll as a dialogue coach, and he shared Marlon's view of the screenplay.

But Marlon was not only concerned with the dialogue; he was worried about his weight and the bulging belly he had developed. In response he started a crash diet to slim down by seventeen pounds. He and Carlo, who was already underweight, lived on raw vegetables and ran along Waikiki Beach every day. Marlon relived his days at Shattuck by throwing a football in the air to Carlo, who was decidedly nonathletic. One morning, Carlo awoke in his Coral Sands Hotel suite and found Marlon gone. Following an instinct, Carlo ran down to the local drugstore, where he found Marlon devouring a breakfast of cornflakes with bananas and cream, scrambled eggs with sausages and bacon, and a mountain of pancakes dripping with butter. When Carlo tried to drag him loose from this feast, Marlon began growling like an angry beast. In desperation, Carlo turned to the astonished breakfasters around them and shouted, 'I know this looks crazy. But Marlon's supposed to be on a diet for *Sayonara*. It's my job to see he stays on it!' Marlon told him not to make a jackass of himself, and at the same time poured maple syrup over the pancakes and ate every last bite. But after that, he did begin running and dieting again, with some success.

When Marlon arrived in Tokyo on January 12, 1957, he was greeted at the airport by Logan and several Japanese studio chiefs, who whisked him and Carlo off in a limousine from Yokohama to the capital. In the morning, Marlon, immaculately suited in dark grey, only slightly overweight at 170 pounds, appeared at an elaborate press conference. On this occasion he didn't address the reporters in Japanese but instead delivered a polished, carefully rehearsed, and well-thought-out talk on Japanese-American relations. The sincerity and intelligence of the speech, which he wrote himself – touching on such subjects as Buddhism, painting, music, dance and floral arrangements – overcame potential objections by the local press and won over all of those who felt that a miscegenation theme was insulting to the Japanese. He was not only the ideal choice for the part of Major Gruver, but also was clearly an excellent ambassador of goodwill and public relations representative for Warner Brothers. Still, in private he remained troubled by the essential thinness and contrivance of the Osborn screenplay.

Shooting began in Kyoto, a city of temples whose sombre beauty had a more authentic charm than the excessively formalized setting of Nara in *Teahouse*. Once again, the weather plagued the production. Marlon watched in despair as the rain poured down on the first day at the Miyako Hotel. Next day, the rain grew heavier, the light was hopelessly poor for shooting, and there were even snow flurries and haze. Just in the first week, five days of shooting were lost. Moreover, Miiko Taka was terrified of everything: the camera, Marlon (despite his supportive treatment of her), Logan, and the very thought of playing a part that would be seen by millions. Logan was forced to draw her aside and remind her of her professional responsibilities, telling her that he would no longer tolerate her behaviour. She promised to improve, and she did.

Meanwhile, Marlon became increasingly uneasy about Logan's direction of the picture. He tested him, asking him questions about gestures and movements, and was disconcerted when Logan told him to 'use your own judgement'. Logan's shifts of mood, from enthusiasm to bleak depression to irritation and back again, made Marlon restless and uncomfortable. Moreover, the rain reminded him all too vividly of the dreary experience of shooting *Teahouse.* Day after day was lost to the weather and dark skies.

At the beginning of February, the company and crew shifted to the grim industrial city of Osaka, where shooting was further delayed by weather and illnesses among the cast. Marlon succumbed to a nasty local virus and lay in bed with stomach pain and diarrhoea. Upon returning to the set he told Carlo he was going to test the director's skill. He was acting a scene with Red Buttons when, without warning, he made a grimace that was not called for by the script. Logan liked it and ordered it to be used. From that moment on, Marlon lost all faith in Logan's ability to control his acting and decided to walk through the part until the work was finished. His letters to Anna in Hollywood were full of expressions of his absolute contempt for the director. He even went so far as to turn up one day with his right arm in a sling, to provoke Logan. Logan, thinking the star had broken his arm, became visibly upset about the shooting schedule, and Marlon then began to wave the arm around, taunting, 'Too bad I can't move it like this!'

The weather continued to be dismal, and day after stormy day, he and Carlo, accompanied by Aunt Betty Lindemeyer, Marlon Sr, Celia Webb Meredith, and Phil and Marie Rhodes, all of whom had flown in to join him in Kyoto, sat around talking. Then something worse happened. Truman Capote arrived in Japan to fulfil a long-standing threat to profile Marlon for *The New Yorker.* He checked in at the Miyako Hotel carrying a bottle of hundred-proof Smirnoff vodka. Mincing into Marlon's suite, he put the vodka bottle on the table with as much ceremony as if it were an Academy Award. He told Marlon and Fiore a very curious story about how he and Leonard Bernstein enjoyed gossiping about their friends' questionable private lives and that Bernstein had secretly recorded Capote's outrageous revelations on tape. Soon afterwards, at a party, Bernstein played the recording and the guests sat stunned as the speaker system emitted Capote's squeaky voice revealing every scandalous detail about them. The party broke up in anger and embarrassment. For some reason, this all-too-revealing tale didn't alert Marlon to the dangerous bomb ticking before him.

Then Capote did something diabolical. Knowing Marlon's aversion to alcohol, Capote plied him with more and more shots of vodka until he completely forgot he was being interviewed, and began talking freely. When Capote brought up his own mother and his feelings for her, Marlon naturally felt compelled to mention Dodie and revealed far more than he should have about his mother's alcoholism. Marlon's inebriated commentary and recollections ranged from describing the broken nose he got during the fight with Nick Dennis in the boiler room backstage at *Streetcar,* to his contempt for the hearts-and-flowers nonsense of *Sayonara*. He angrily defended himself for not going back to Broadway, talked of working only for the money 'to put in the kick for my own company,' brutally imitated Joshua Logan's quivering and sad-eyed southern gentleman's behaviour but found a good word or two for Tennessee Williams. He added that he had seriously thought about giving up acting, that this kind of success didn't lead anywhere. 'You're just sitting on a pile of candy gathering thick layers of crust.' Marlon also described James Dean's constant attempts to 'get close' to him, and talked about doing the narration for a documentary about Dean to show he wasn't a hero – 'just a lost boy trying to find himself'. He talked of firing Alice Marchak when he returned to Hollywood, giving up the help and keeping house with the aid of a twice-a-week cleaning woman. The interview rambled on and on into the night and continued the next day. Marlon had lost all of his usual instinct for danger vis-à-vis his twittering, beady-eyed, undeniably brilliant companion. Capote cunningly played on Marlon's ego, his respect for great writers, and his need to talk about everything, which paradoxically worked against his obsession with privacy. The resulting scandalous profile ran in *The New Yorker* on October 27, 1957.

Almost two decades later, when the piece was included in a Capote collection called *The Dogs Bark*, the author had this to say about it and his famous subject: 'Of all my sitters, the one most distressed was the subject of "The Duke in His Domain," Marlon Brando. Though not claiming any inaccuracy, he apparently felt it was an unsympathetic, even treacherous intrusion upon the secret terrain of a suffering and intellectually awesome sensibility. My opinion? Just that it is a pretty good account, and a sympathetic one, of a wounded young man who is a genius, but not markedly intelligent.'

According to Carlo Fiore, 'Marlon and I must have fucked almost every Japanese girl involved with the picture.' One of the other girls left her mark: she bit both Carlo's and Marlon's tongues so deeply that they bled. One evening, Carlo took one of the Japanese girls in the cast to his bedroom. The girl suggested that Marlon join them. Marlon walked into Carlo's room and began to strip. 'Good night, Freddy,' he said, using his old nickname for Fiore. 'What do you mean, good night?' Fiore replied. 'This is my room and I found her first!' Marlon said, 'But *I'm* here now. Good *night!*' A moment later, he was naked, and Carlo was outside the door.

At last the company returned to Hollywood, and on April 3, 1957, Marlon celebrated his thirty-third birthday at a big party with a three-tiered cake and birthday salutations in Japanese and English.

Marlon had brought back Oriental costumes for Anna Kashfi, and he asked her to assume the role of a geisha dressed in her kimono, giggling behind a fan. She served him cups of sake while kneeling on a mat, and even cleaned his forehead with a hot cloth. At night, Marlon joined her in yoga; stark naked, his stomach flopping (he had gained more weight in Japan), he would prop himself up on his head against the wall, and his face would grow redder and redder. Then he would tumble exhausted into bed.

At that time, Rita Moreno, who had briefly visited with him in Japan, had taken to constantly calling him, in an attempt to resume their earlier relationship.

Apparently she succeeded in her resolve; Marlon was no longer willing to commit himself exclusively to Anna, and Rita was as exciting and gorgeous as ever. He couldn't resist her.

One night, as Anna was undressing at Marlon's house, she discovered a thick black wig on the bedpost. When she calmly asked who owned it, Marlon admitted it was Rita Moreno's. Anna became hysterical and demanded to be driven home. Next morning, Marlon's phone call to explain the situation was met with fury. Nevertheless, once more, she forgave him. Then, only a week later, she broke off the engagement because she was convinced that Rita was still sleeping with him.

As *Sayonara* was being completed, Marlon was drawn to another project: *The Young Lions*, adapted by Edward Anhalt from the World War II novel by Irwin Shaw. Marlon was offered the part of Christian Diestl, a decent German who has become a dangerous Nazi. At Marlon's first meeting with Anhalt and the director, Edward Dmytryk, he decided to accept the role, but wanted it changed. He felt that to make Christian Diestl too crude a Nazi would alienate the audience; he thought the character should be a complex personality, a man rather than a symbol. It was just over a decade since the war had ended, and to present a Nazi with even a slight amount of sympathy was exceedingly risky. Anhalt said, 'Marlon, like most actors, wanted to be loved, and I made the changes for that reason. And Marlon had script approval.'

Once again, Marlon decided to have Carlo Fiore, who had just married an attractive girl named Marcia Hunt, accompany him for the shooting of the picture in Europe. Like Marlon himself, Carlo never wanted his women to accompany him on foreign trips. With amazing callousness, he left his young bride behind in Hollywood, and they proceeded to New York en route to Paris. In France, Marlon became involved with the beautiful and hypersensitive Eurasian model and actress France Nuyen. Born in Marseilles in 1934, she had appeared as a young girl in *South Pacific* for Joshua Logan. She and Marlon had met a year earlier, and he had made her feel comfortable by speaking French to her. Miss Nuyen says that at the time she was utterly naïve, innocent, confused, and uncertain of herself. She entered into the relationship with Marlon without realizing for a moment that he was engaged to Anna Kashfi. She fell hopelessly in love with him, never questioning his total dedication to her. Carlo described her sitting at Marlon's feet, 'looking up at him adoringly'.

Montgomery Clift and Dean Martin were cast as American soldiers in *The Young Lions*. Like James Dean, Clift's name was constantly linked to Brando's as one of the three gods of the American screen, and Marlon's relationship with Clift had remained erratic and strange. Ever since the pranks in drag at Kevin McCarthy's home in Bedford Village in 1947, they had sparred around each other, edgily trying to decide whether they would be friends or enemies. Marlon admired Clift, but at the same time was made uneasy by his neurotic fragility. Clift had turned down *On the Waterfront* and *Desirée*, and Marlon had mixed feelings about his involvement in both of those films. Marlon had gone to see Clift in plays from time to time, although he seldom went to other actors' performances. Certainly, he knew that Clift possessed a more subtle and intellectual acting style than his own. Ironically, they shared the same agents – Jay Kanter in Hollywood and Edith Van Cleve in New York.

Their relationship warmed when Clift made a much-quoted remark: 'Marlon is continuously creative even with shitty material. He shows you what is going on inside himself.' At the opening night of *The Sea Gull* on Broadway, Marlon joined his old friend Harry Belafonte, Arthur Miller, and Marlene Dietrich in the enthusiastic crowd that mobbed Clift in his dressing room after his sensational performance. Marlon began to take a fraternal interest in Clift, trying to get him off booze and drugs, to stop his headlong passage into physical and mental disintegration. Marlon drove up to see Clift during the making of *Teahouse of the August Moon*. He begged him to clean up his act, assuring Clift that he was the best actor in America and praising him lavishly for his performance in *A Place in the Sun*. In response, Clift said he had deeply respected Marlon in *Streetcar*. According to the actor Jack Larson, Marlon said to Clift during that charged meeting, 'In a way I hate you. I've always hated you because I want to be better than you, but you're better than me – you're my touchstone, my challenge, and I want you and I to go on challenging each other.'

After Clift was involved in a horrifying car accident in which his face and body were smashed, Marlon again begged Clift to join Alcoholics Anonymous. 'You've got to stop this, you're killing yourself,' he said. In this basic way, these two stars were distinctly different. For all of Marlon's ambivalent feelings towards his work, his laziness, self-indulgence, and fits of excessive eating, he never had the streak of self-destructiveness that ruined Clift's admirable talents.

The idea of Clift appearing in *The Young Lions* impressed Marlon, yet he was in a way relieved that they would appear in only one scene together. He was shocked when he arrived in Paris and checked into the

Hotel Raphael to find an emaciated Clift, who had lost over twenty-five pounds for the role of Noah. He had never seen anyone look so gaunt, and moreover, Clift's face, despite plastic surgery, looked terrible, with his mouth marred by a vertical scar and the structure of his features permanently altered. Clift was tormented by the loss of his looks and the fact that the world would see him on the screen in this condition.

By contrast, Marlon's weight had blown up from 170 pounds to 190. His addiction to steaks and fried eggs didn't help, even though he avoided the rich Parisian cuisine. He began trying on blond wigs for his role of Christian, but found them exceptionally awkward and obvious, so he went to Carita-Alexandre's to have his own hair bleached. All of the hairdressers and mani-curists emerged to stare and giggle at him. At the end of the half-hour's treatment, he looked at himself in the mirror. His hair was an alarming shade of lemon yellow. Laughing, he clicked his heels, gave a Nazi salute to the mirror, and walked out of the salon.

Then an unfortunate accident took place. One after-noon, he went to the bar of the Hotel George V to join Dean Martin. Marlon was on the wagon after his experience with Truman Capote, and a large pot of boiling water was set up on the bar so he could make himself a cup of tea. The actress Liliane Montevecchi brushed by it, upsetting it. Marlon jumped up, yelling, 'Shit!' The hot water had scalded his genitals. Doubled up in agony, he pulled down his pants and ran with bare buttocks out of the bar while the phlegmatic French shrugged their shoulders at this alarming exit. Marlon raced back to his room at the Hotel Raphael, where Carlo Fiore found him in the company of a doctor who was smearing a yellow salve on his blis-tered penis. He said to Carlo, 'This would have to happen to me now in the middle of Paris in spring, with my prick in a sling.' He called Anna to tell her about it, and she suggested the newspaper headline, 'Brando Scalds Balls.' The joke soon turned sour. The company's insurance people insisted he be transferred to a hospital, and he lay there, depressed, watching the rain pour down outside the windows.

Released from the hospital and back at his hotel, he began fiddling with the script, even talking to Irwin Shaw about his ideas for revising the screenplay, much to the consternation of Anhalt and Dmytryk. The film began shooting at Chantilly, thirty miles north of Paris, and after a day or two of sunshine the rain came down. Somehow, during his days in bed, Marlon had lost the thread of the script and, according to Dmytryk, he was 'in the proper wardrobe, but had little idea of what the day's work was about'. The director told him what he was to do for the fourth time, but he didn't seem to comprehend. Eighteen rehearsals went by, followed by an equal number of takes. Finally, Marlon said, 'Oh, *that's* what the scene is!' After that, Marlon apparently decided that he would cooperate with Dmytryk. He began to act more seriously. 'He got the idea finally that *The Young Lions* was a good picture and buckled down,' Dmytryk said.

In August, the company transferred to Borego Springs in the California desert to shoot the sequences of North African warfare. Anna was busy completing her work in the film *Cowboy* when Marlon arrived; when she was finished, she checked into Marlon's suite. 'We had an ardent reunion and quick sexual gratification, the consequences of which were nine months in the development,' Anna wrote. When she confirmed that she was pregnant, Marlon was thrilled. Although he feared the responsibility of being a parent, he also felt the intense male joy of knowing that he would be a father. For a time, the couple grew closer, their bitter arguments temporarily forgotten. They walked together for hours, whenever there was a break in shooting, or on Sundays, discussing religion, life, and love. Anna became a sounding board for Marlon's endless investigations of inexplicable subjects. She watched him work for the first time, and was lost in admiration for his capacity to 'become' Christian Diestl. She marvelled at his complete commitment and integrity; now that Dmytryk had mastered him, he worked extremely hard, and there was the additional stimulus of Anna, carrying his child, just off the set, evaluating him as one actor judged another. In their nights together at the hotel, they at last found what she described as 'the most tranquil and perceptive period of our relationship'. Their troubled spirits discovered communion in the peace of the desert and the continuing excellence of the daily work.

However, there was always an unfortunate underside to the relationship. Anna, according to Carlo Fiore, was fiercely jealous of his friendship with Marlon. She suspected him of having a homoerotic interest in Marlon, since he was already at odds with his wife Marcia. At one point, she charged him directly with 'using him to further your own career,' and when Marlon turned to Carlo for his response, Carlo was too shocked to speak 'from the sheer impact of this viciousness'. Marlon said the charges must be true, as Carlo's hand was shaking violently. Carlo furiously replied that he was trembling because of the enormity of the disgusting lie, and Marlon just shrugged the whole thing off. But he warned Marlon not to marry Anna, that she would break up their long friendship if she could. When they left for Hollywood to finish the shooting, Marlon suggested that Carlo accompany them on the drive back. He refused, but Marlon insisted that he try to make a truce with Anna. Carlo reluctantly agreed, and so did the fiery Anna Kashfi.

It was a difficult drive back through the mountains, around hairpin bends above steep plunges. Sometimes, when another car approached on the narrow road, Marlon had to back to the edge to let it by. Marlon wasn't the greatest of drivers, and Carlo was terrified. Worse, when they stopped for coffee at a place high up in the Sierras, Anna talked Marlon into letting her take over at the wheel. When she announced as she did so that she was just learning to drive, Carlo was more petrified than ever.

What followed was something of a nightmare. Fiore said, 'She was one of the worst drivers I had ever had the misfortune to share a car with. Not only was she mechanically inept, but she had a great deal of difficulty keeping her eyes on the road.' Sometimes, as she approached an extremely dangerous curve, with a sheer drop below, she would turn around to talk to Carlo about something and Marlon would scream at her to keep her eye on the road. Marlon insisted he return to the wheel, but she refused. When they stopped for gas, Carlo said he would not get back in the car again. Marlon talked him into it and Anna continued to convey her two nervous passengers down the winding mountain curves.

They returned at last to Los Angeles, Anna to her apartment and Marlon to his house on Laurel View. As the filming continued at Twentieth Century-Fox studios, Marlon was faced with the fact that Pennebaker was floundering, with no viable script commissioned or project initiated. Marlon Sr was not managing the company productively because he was not terribly interested in movie production. And Marlon Jr maintained his attitude of indifference to what Pennebaker did. The company would option projects, commission scripts, and then abandon them because Marlon Sr and Jr simply couldn't make a final commitment. The able and dedicated Walter Seltzer and George Glass began laying out possible plans for a movie to be shot in Ireland, starring James Cagney, whose eventual title was *Shake Hands With the Devil*. (The film, directed by Michael Anderson, turned out to be only moderately good and not a box-office success.) But it would be some months before this film could be set in motion and the American and Irish shooting schedules satisfactorily meshed.

Marlon's behaviour was as eccentric as ever. Walter Seltzer recalls an episode in which he went to the Laurel View house to discuss some business with Marlon, who was failing to respond to requests for approval of certain Pennebaker moves. The house was filthy, strewn with newspapers, dirty glasses, and plates with half-eaten food. Then, according to Seltzer, to add to the general squalor, Marlon undid his fly and urinated into a dish-filled sink. On another occasion, when Marlon gave a party for some friends at his father's West Hollywood apartment, Marlon Sr retreated to his upstairs bedroom because of the loud music and people shouting and laughing. Then he came down and asked them all to leave. The painter Ron Mallory, who was present, recalled, 'The old man and Marlon went eyeball to eyeball. When Marlon refused to tell his friends to go home, Marlon Sr slapped him violently across the face and almost knocked him over. Marlon turned pale with anger, but didn't strike him back. We were all so embarrassed we literally picked up our things and fled.'

The Young Lions was released to great critical and commercial success in 1958. Marlon's sympathetic, intelligent, and perceptive playing of Christian received tremendous praise, and few found the picture's two hours and forty-seven minutes too lengthy. According to Edward Dmytryk, 'Marlon was as usual indifferent to the whole picture's success or failure. But when he finally got around to seeing it, I was amazed. He actually shook my hand and congratulated me on a job well done. I could hardly believe it.'

13

By late September, Marlon and Anna decided it was time to get married, if only to legitimize the child they were both certain would be a son. However, Anna's real father in New Delhi was opposed to the match and told her on the telephone, 'He's a bum. I don't care if he is famous, he's still a bum.' Anna angrily slammed the receiver down, cutting him off. Soon after, her half-brother called to tell her that her father had been murdered – shot dead in mysterious circumstances, his body rushed to the crematorium before anyone could investigate the crime. This was a devastating blow to her, despite her many differences with him. Marlon tried to cheer her up by forcing her to come with him to the Ambassador Hotel, where they danced for hours at the Coconut Grove before she insisted on going home and fell into bed for many hours of exhausted sleep.

In the wake of the announcement of their forthcoming wedding, Anna was besieged by demands from friends and family to break off the engagement. Her former fiancé, Rico Mandiaco, turned up and warned her she would be making the greatest mistake of her life. Then came an incident that gave her serious pause. One night, she and Marlon were wakened by a violent banging on the front door. It was Rita Moreno, screaming in a frenzied demand to be let in. When Marlon said he would go down and let her in, Anna shrieked, 'It's her or me. Make a choice – right now!' He told Anna he must deal with the matter personally, and Anna crept to the top of the stairs to eavesdrop on their conversation. She heard Rita shouting and Marlon calmly trying to persuade her to leave. Finally, Rita gave in and the front door slammed. As Marlon climbed the stairs, Anna told him she had had enough and was moving out. He told her to go if she wanted. She mockingly called him 'Rico' (after Rico Mandiaco) because she knew he hated that more than anything and he called her 'Rita,' since the mere mention of Rita Moreno drove her to anger. So, dishevelled and only partly dressed, Anna made her way down the stairs and out of the house, and drove to her apartment to lie awake all night. The next day, she packed up all of Marlon's gifts to her and returned them. He arrived with them at her doorstep and she finally weakened and let him in. They made up, setting the date for their wedding for October 9. But day after day, night after night, the quarrels went on. Miss Kashfi claims that Marlon was extremely worried about his child being 'of a dark colour'. He questioned her endlessly on her genetic background and even suggested she give birth in Hawaii to avoid the possibility of a black baby being seen in Hollywood.

The tortured couple drove off to Riverside for the marriage licence and blood tests, accompanied by George Glass and Walter Seltzer. Seltzer said, 'I wasn't impressed with Anna Kashfi.' There was even an argument over the nature of the ceremony itself. Anna wanted a Buddhist ritual; Marlon said that it would be impossible to find a Buddhist monk in Los Angeles. How about a Zen wedding? Anna flatly refused, regarding Zen as beneath her. Finally, Marlon decided he wanted an Episcopalian wedding, and Anna gave up the struggle and agreed.

Marlon had decided to hold the wedding at Aunt Betty Lindemeyer's house at Eagle Rock. He invited his

Aunt June along with her sister and brother-in-law; his grandma Nana had died two years earlier. Marlon's friends, scriptwriter Peter Berneis and his wife Ina, were best man and matron of honour, and the Louis L'Amours – friends of the bride and groom – were in attendance. Marlon refused to have his father present, telling Anna in anger, 'I'll bury him before I do!' Ironically, Marlon Sr remarried several months later – to Anna Parramore, who was several years younger than his own son – and didn't invite Marlon to his wedding.

Marlon bought the wedding band in Pasadena and drove to the ceremony in a dark suit, with a theatrical cloak flung over his shoulders and a homburg hat on his head. Halfway to Eagle Rock, Anna very nearly backed out of the whole thing. When she arrived, wearing a green and gold sari, Aunt June gave her a two-hundred-year-old lace handkerchief that Julia Gahan had treasured. Nervously, Anna placed the handkerchief in her bosom and Aunt June declared, 'How dare you take a family heirloom and put it in your undies!' Just as the wedding was about to begin, Anna decided that she had to have a bouquet of lilies. Marlon was furious, and everyone began calling different florists. No store had the Madonna lilies that she specified. Then Paramount Studios took the search to florists in other cities. Meanwhile, everyone had to wait, getting more and more irritable.

At last, Paramount found the lilies in San Francisco. They were flown down two days later. The forty-eight hours was an ordeal for everybody in the house. By the time the marriage took place, Anna was, by her own admission, drunk and would have, in her own words, 'said "I do" to a baboon'.

The ceremony was performed by the Reverend J.

Walter Fiscus, pastor of the Little Brown Church in the Valley in North Hollywood. Marlon was calm, Anna wobbly. As they drove off in Marlon's car, they suddenly realized they had made no arrangements for the honeymoon. After trying to decide what to do, they stopped and Marlon called Jay Kanter, who offered them his home in Beverly Hills. For some reason, they didn't want to spend the night at Marlon's house. Anna was disappointed that her suggestions for a cruise of the Pacific or a European tour had come to nothing. Her only comment on the wedding night was that it was not worth remembering.

The next day, she and Marlon drove to Palm Desert to stay with the L'Amours. Marlon and L'Amour spent the days firing at tin cans in the yard. Anna said, 'Marlon remained in a sulky mood throughout the week and refused to stir himself to any distance. At breakfast he entertained us by extinguishing cigarettes on the back of his hand. Of such events was made the soil of our honeymoon.' Paparazzi pursued them as they picked oranges or took rides into the desert, besieging L'Amour with questions about their day and nighttime habits.

Then came a surprise. Seeing the announcement of the marriage in England, a factory worker named William Patrick O'Callaghan announced in Cardiff, Wales, that Anna was not an Indian at all but his daughter. He said that she had been a former butcher's assistant and waitress and, paradoxically in view of his Irish name, 'as English as I am'. He said that her name was Joan, that she was born in Calcutta, and that she had lived there until she was thirteen, while he was a traffic superintendent with Indian railways. He said her wedding was 'a great shock' to him and that the wedding was illegal since Miss Kashfi had entered false statements to obtain the wedding licence. The matter blew up into a major furore. MGM revealed that Anna's payroll cheques were made out to 'Joanna O'Callaghan', and immigration authorities confirmed that she had entered the United States under the same name. An MGM spokesman said, 'Anna has always said she was Anglo-Indian . . . As far as we know, O'Callaghan is her stepfather.' Paramount, which had signed Anna for a part in *The Mountain,* said, 'The present Mrs O'Callaghan is probably not Anna's mother. It is our feeling that Mr O'Callaghan isn't telling the whole story.'

Olive Lindemeyer said that O'Callaghan's claim was 'completely false . . . I have known Anna for a couple of years and have talked to her about her family. She has told me about her father in India. He died a month ago. Her mother and father were divorced. Her mother is in Europe. Anna has never mentioned O'Callaghan to us.' George Glass told reporters that Anna had been grief-stricken over her father's death. Reporters besieged the O'Callaghan house in Cardiff. They demanded to know why Anna had such dark skin if she was purely English (or Irish). He told them, 'My mother was French. Many French people are dark. Joan takes after her grandmother.'

In tears, Melinda O'Callaghan stated that her daughter was in fact 'Joanna Mary'. It seemed that even her own parents didn't know Anna's 'real' name. Melinda said that she had 'never heard' of the alleged Devi Kashfi and Selma Ghose. Photographs of the O'Callaghans showed Melinda as a strikingly beautiful woman of middle years who had a strong resemblance to Merle Oberon, herself Anglo-Indian. The headlines went on and on: 'Why Has Our Daughter Disowned Us?' 'Come Back, Joanna, We Still Love You!' Anna told Marlon she had used the name of Joanna O'Callaghan on her passport to circumvent the limited Indian quota of the United States. She said she had had her true origins confirmed by Immigration and Naturalization, but had still been granted a green card allowing her to work. He said he was indifferent to the stories about her and that 'it's just some garbage rooted out by a flock of vultures'. However, he secretly sent out letters to detectives all over the world trying to find out the truth. He did not succeed.

During the weeks after the marriage, as the controversy swirled about their heads, Marlon gave a succession of parties to introduce his glamorous bride. Very nearly every major star in Hollywood came to their home on Laurel View; the Brandos were invited everywhere, because just about every woman in town wanted to see this mysterious 'Indian' Marlon had married. Between these frequent social events, several of them at the home of Anna's friends Humphrey and Lauren (Betty) Bogart, the couple continued to quarrel. Frequently, Anna claimed, Marlon disappeared for nights on end to stay with friends, including Peter Berneis, George Englund, and Sam Gilman. Marlon Sr assumed he had the right to supervise her accounts as her husband's business manager, and he went over every receipt she brought back from shopping, arguing over such absurdities as thirty-one cents paid for a toilet roll. He accused her of deliberately using Marlon to get rich, and she exploded and fired him on the spot. A major quarrel erupted between her and Marlon in December 1957 when they attended a preview of *Sayonara* in Beverly Hills. In one scene, Marlon was shown handing Miiko Taka a silk scarf wrapped around a present. Already jealous of Miiko, Anna went mad when she saw the scene because she remembered that Marlon had wrapped a scarf around one of her gifts when she lay in the hospital with tuberculosis. She stormed out of the theatre and disappeared for several days.

She didn't help matters by telling Hedda Hopper, 'Marlon leaves a lot to be desired as a romancer. He's just plain clumsy, and that's the truth. If he were not a film star, he wouldn't get to first base with women.' She told another reporter, 'I can't stand most of Marlon's friends – they're leeches – I resent them terribly. And, of course, they resent me too, because I am in the way.'

By New Year's Eve, Anna told Marlon he would either have to improve his behaviour or she would divorce him on the spot. She demanded that he move out of their home on Laurel View. Instead, they both left the house – to find a larger home to accommodate their child and give them more space from each other. After a considerable search, Anna located the perfect house: a big, handsome, Japanese-style residence at 12900 Mulholland Drive, high up in the mountains over Hollywood and Beverly Hills, with a tremendous view of the spectacular San Fernando Valley with its seemingly endless suburban sprawl set against violet-coloured peaks. From the moment he walked into the large, white-carpeted entrance hall, Marlon was delighted with the Oriental ambience of the house. He placed a large Chinese gong in the living room and delighted in banging it at every possible opportunity. He has remained in the house to this day.

They hadn't lived in the house for long when the couple discovered that during their absences the Italian cook arranged guided tours of the house, at fifty cents per head, during which she would announce such things as, 'Marlon and Anna sleep in this bed . . . This is where Marlon goes to the bathroom.' When Anna told Marlon of this, he laughed, saying, 'Surely the traffic would bear a dollar!' They decided to get rid of the woman. After they fired her, Henry Fonda called up and asked if the cook who had applied to him and given their name as a reference was any good. 'Grab her!' Marlon said. 'She's the greatest!'

Among the frequent guests at the Japanese house were Marlon's old friends from Paris, the actor-director Christian Marquand and the director Roger Vadim. Anna Kashfi wrote in her memoirs that on one visit, Vadim entertained the crowd with the grotesque account of a place in Paris called Le Canard Bleu, a nightclub that supplied live ducks for men to make love to. The duck was fixed in wooden stocks, with its rear exposed for intercourse. As the customers neared their climax, a waiter would decapitate the unfortunate bird. The twitching of the duck in its death agony caused the customers to experience heightened orgasms. Marlon, Anna reports, insisted on hearing this tale over and over again, and would exclaim at the end of it each time, 'Up your cloaca!'

In the early months of 1958, Marlon at last found a new film property that interested him. *Sayonara* had become a major success, confirming his worst suspicions about public taste as he still had no respect for the movie whatsoever. He had been virtually inactive since completion of production on *The Young Lions*. Now the genial producer Frank P. Rosenberg had come up with a novel entitled *The Authentic Death of Hendry Jones,* by Charles Neider, that he liked because it was, in his own words, 'the furthest west Western I had ever read'. A reworking of the story of Billy the Kid, it was set in part in Northern California along the Pacific Coast, which Rosenberg liked because it was a unique setting for a Western. He felt that the ideal person to write the screenplay was the up-and-coming, feisty Sam Peckinpah. The script was sent to Marlon through Pennebaker.

'In those days, Marlon was the greatest star in the world,' Rosenberg said. 'It took seven months even to get an answer from him. But he read the script in two days and we immediately had a deal.' Rosenberg added, 'Why was he attracted to it? Because the heavy in the story was called Dad, and of course he and his father never got along. Also, part of the story was laid in Mexico. He liked that.'

The first meeting was set up between Rosenberg and Marlon in Walter Seltzer's backyard. 'Marlon was wearing very thick shades,' Rosenberg said. 'He could see me, but I couldn't see into his eyes. He was very excited. But he said he felt it would take six months to get the script into shape.' The question arose of who should direct the film. Rosenberg suggested Stanley Kubrick, who had recently proven himself with such films as *The Killing* and *Paths of Glory.* Marlon insisted on seeing them and was impressed. He thought well of Kubrick, and when they met, they got on excellently. Kubrick brought in his friend Calder Willingham, author of a widely respected novel about a military prep school, *End as a Man,* to revise the script. Meetings to discuss the screenplay began in the summer of 1958 at Marlon's house on Mulholland. Everybody arrived at 9:00 A.M. and removed their shoes because of the teakwood floors. Among those present were Rosenberg, Kubrick, Marlon, Calder Willingham, and, from time to time, Carlo Fiore.

Fiore described Kubrick as 'always in motion, running his fingers through his hair, doodling on a pad, or diddling a loose bridge or shaky tooth at the back of his mouth'. There were many arguments as the collaborators dissected the script. Finally Willingham succeeded in producing a revised outline of the story. Both Kubrick and Marlon liked it, but Rosenberg argued that the outline was 'unfilmable' and could not be adapted into a screenplay. The producer much preferred the work Peckinpah had done on the script, and when he complained to Willingham, the author smugly said, 'You've got to have faith in my God-given gifts as a writer.' Rosenberg, alas, had no faith in those gifts, at least where writing films was concerned. Marlon then took Rosenberg behind a Chinese screen and whispered, 'Why don't you let Calder at least try to turn this into a screenplay?' Rosenberg reluctantly agreed.

Kubrick's assistant and Marlon's old friend Joe Sargent remembers that on one occasion, in the middle of an afternoon at the Pennebaker offices, they locked the doors, sat on the floor, laughed and giggled and hugely enjoyed a pornographic film. Sargent said, 'Suddenly I felt like a little boy with a bunch of other little boys playing hookey in the middle of the day.' Sargent feels that this kind of irresponsibility pervaded the preparation of the picture. 'There was a sort of cavalier attitude about doing less than very serious material . . . We weren't doing the work of art of the decade, but we were going to have fun.' Fifty pages into the script it was obvious that Willingham's efforts were hopeless. Joe Sargent said, 'Calder complained to Kubrick and me. He was terribly, terribly upset. He said, "I have suddenly discovered that I am the highest-priced secretary in Hollywood."' He would write a scene and Marlon would decimate it by deleting whatever he considered to be unnecessary. Ultimately, Marlon realized that Willingham just didn't share his own vision of the story and the characters. The writer had to go.

According to Carlo Fiore, Marlon undertook the task of Willingham's dismissal. He invited him to dinner in Los Angeles and fired him over the lamb chops. To ease the blow, he presented him with a farewell present: a costly rosewood chess table. Kubrick was unsettled by Willingham's departure (Willingham was later replaced by Guy Trosper). The star and the director then argued over casting. Marlon insisted that his old friend Karl Malden should play the part of Dad. Kubrick was opposed to this choice, because he felt that Malden was good at acting losers but didn't have the necessary strength to dramatize the contest of personalities in the story. Kubrick wanted Spencer Tracy. Marlon then revealed that he had promised Karl the part. Kubrick wanted Malden paid off, and claimed that Malden would accept such an arrangement if Tracy really wanted the part. But in the end, Marlon remained loyal to his friend from *Waterfront* and *Streetcar*.

The seemingly endless work dragged on. In the meantime, Marlon's marriage to Anna was already faltering, and he began seeing France Nuyen once more. Miss Nuyen said, 'Anna was completely out of the picture in Marlon's life when I met him again. For six months, I resisted him, but his humour, cleverness, and little-boy qualities finally succeeded in winning me over. He made me laugh. He was very sweet.'

Then on May 11, seven months after their wedding, Anna began to have contractions. Marlon and she were separated at the time, so she drove herself to the hospital and at 7:30 P.M. delivered a seven-pound, ten-ounce boy with blond hair, brown eyes, and dark skin. Reporters rushed to the hospital, and the news was relayed all over the world, but it was more than a day before Marlon turned up in the ward to see her. She greeted him, her baby nestled next to her, with bitter words: 'Well, Marlon, I hope he is the right colour for you!' Ignoring the remark, he began to weep and told her the child was 'wonderful'. Then he added, 'Thank God he looks more like you than me.' He promised to be more devoted from then on and decided on the spot to name the baby Christian, after Christian Marquand.* After considerable argument, they settled on Christian Devi. She has never called her child by the name Christian.

The new parents also disagreed over the question of circumcision, which she favoured for reasons of hygiene. Marlon told her, 'I've never been circumcised, and my noble tool has performed its duties through thick and thin without fail.' She charged him with being afraid of losing the foreskin, 'a psychological fear based on his own undistinguished pudendum'. But it was Marlon who won the battle. Despite his promises at Anna's bedside in the maternity ward, Marlon did not become more devoted – at least not to his wife. 'When the baby was several weeks old, Marlon walked into our home with Miss Nuyen on his arm,' Anna says. She claimed that France Nuyen walked into the kitchen, sniffed at the curry on the stove, and said Anna shouldn't be eating it while nursing the baby. Then she casually threw open the refrigerator door and took a mango from it. Anna fled to the bedroom in a fit of tears. She demanded that Marlon get France out of the house in thirty seconds. He did not. France denies the entire episode, but admits she may have forgotten the details of her only meeting with Anna.

* In later years, Anna has claimed that 'Marlon and Marquand ... displayed an affection towards each other that far overreached the usual expressions of friendship.'

It proved to be a difficult summer for the Brandos as Anna began to break under the pressure of such an untenable domestic situation. She admits to resorting to such drugs as Seconal and Nembutal, coupled with alcohol, for relief. Then, Marlon Sr's June wedding to the young Anna Parramore only exacerbated tensions in the household. Marlon exclaimed in anger, 'That goddamned son of a bitch . . . The way he treated my mother . . . And now this . . . To hell with him!'

In the fall, France Nuyen went to New York to star on Broadway in *The World of Suzie Wong*. She made an immediate sensation, and Marlon was overjoyed for her, and he flew out to be with her in an obvious display of extramarital activity.

That September, a terrible incident occurred at the house on Mulholland that sparked the final separation between Marlon and Anna. Anna's maid, a Japanese girl named Sako, was suffering from the extreme heat and asked if she could use the pool. Since Sako didn't swim, Anna said she shouldn't be in the pool unaccompanied and instead should take a shower and rest in her bedroom. When Anna later went to find Sako, there was no sign of her in the bedroom. Anna ran to the pool and was horrified to find Sako lying on the bottom. Anna's attempts to drag her from the pool were useless – she is a poor swimmer – so the firemen were called. They did their best to resuscitate the drowned girl, to no avail. In the confusion, the firemen and police thought that Anna herself had been drowned, and her death was announced over the radio. Marlon rushed home, and, according to Anna, he stared at her in utter disappointment.

When she saw the expression on Marlon's face, she realized she would have to leave him. She couldn't live with someone who wanted her to die. That day, she threw her clothes and make-up into suitcases and with her son she fled down Coldwater Canyon.

At that time, Anna was shooting the film *Night of the Quarter Moon*. Jay Kanter called her on the set. His voice trembling, he told her that he was up at Mulholland and Marlon had taken an overdose of pills and was about to drown himself in the pool. She left the set and sped up to the house, where she found Marlon standing fully dressed on the diving board. 'Jump, you son of a bitch, jump!' Anna screamed. Then she drove off.

With a divorce case obviously brewing, Anna retained an attorney, Seymour Bricker, and immediately charged that Marlon had been constantly unfaithful to her.

But since no formal demand for divorce had been filed, there was little Marlon could do. He was still in the midst of preproduction preparations of *The Authentic Life of Hendry Jones*, and his relationship with Stanley Kubrick was fast deteriorating. Their confrontations over selection of the scriptwriter and the other actors – with Marlon getting his way in both matters – had generated ill will between them. Then, when Marlon insisted on casting his recurrent lover France Nuyen as the Chinese girl in the story, Kubrick refused. Marlon chose to exercise his star's prerogative and told Frank Rosenberg that Kubrick had to go. Now, without a director – but with commitments from a cast of actors – the film was in trouble. In a bold move to salvage the project, Marlon announced that he would direct.

Because the title *The Authentic Death of Hendry Jones* was considered too cumbersome for theatre marquees, it was changed to *One-Eyed Jacks*. The film began shooting in the spectacular setting of Big Sur and Monterey. The female lead was the attractive but sensitive and neurotic Pina Pellicer, whom Frank Rosenberg had discovered in Mexico City. Marlon began a brief and casual affair with her. Painfully aware that he would be judged severely as a first-time director and would be suspected of vanity filmmaking, Marlon attempted to create a masterpiece in the genre of the Western. That approach, however, was tantamount to inflating a standard action picture into something that pretended to the status of art. Rosenberg recalls that shortly before Christmas, Marlon began filming a sequence in which his character was to sit on a rock gazing out at the surf. It was to be shot silent, without dialogue. Rosenberg took off to Carmel to buy some seasonal gifts for his children, and when he returned was astonished to see that Marlon was still seated on the rock and cameraman Charles Lang, Jr, had not been able to complete the shot. When Rosenberg asked Marlon what he was doing, he replied, 'I'm waiting for the right wave.' And he did wait, until there was almost no light, such was his mania for perfection. On another occasion, Marlon was to shoot a scene of a dog walking past a house. He spent hours fiddling with the composition until Rosenberg finally said, 'If you don't hurry up, the dog will be too old and the shots of it won't match!'

Marlon stayed at Monterey's Tickled Pink Inn as the shooting dragged on interminably. Paramount studio chief, Y. Frank Freeman, was annoyed by the costly slow pace of Marlon's filmmaking, but there was nothing he could do to speed things up. By now, Marlon's value at the box office was so high that Freeman could only endure these self-indulgent antics.

The company moved to Death Valley after Christmas.

The flight there in a DC-3 was extremely turbulent, and scriptwriter Guy Trosper was so overcome by fear that all he could do was hang on desperately to Walter Seltzer's arm. The company had just three months in which to shoot, because by April the heat there would become unbearable. Once again, Marlon was accompanied by his entourage, led by Sam Gilman, Carlo Fiore, and Phil and Marie Rhodes, and the evenings assumed a party atmosphere as the crew took over the Furnace Inn at Death Valley.

It was there that Marlon met an American Indian, Red Arrow, who taught him how to use a bow and arrow during the filming. The impoverished conditions of the Indian settlement disturbed Marlon, and he spent a great deal of time learning about their tribal history. Witnessing the Indians' circumstances formed a lasting impression for Marlon that later helped fuel his passionate involvement in the American Indian movement.

Marlon the director still worked as slowly as ever, and the film had fallen weeks behind schedule. Indeed, filming had taken so long that his weight had fluctuated enough to show the discrepancies from scene to scene. When the hot April weather finally arrived, the cast and crew were driven back to Hollywood where shooting continued on the Paramount backlot. By now, *One-Eyed Jacks* was drastically overbudget, and Rosenberg says that money was 'going out at a rate that rivalled only the current tapping of the United States gold reserves'.

Marlon did eventually complete the shooting of the film and then struggled through the protracted task of editing it. When, at last, he had what he considered a final cut, he invited Frank Rosenberg to view it. The producer sat through four and a half hours as the interminable story unfolded on the screen before him. When the lights came up, Rosenberg's only words were to ask where they should eat. Marlon suggested the Italian restaurant Chianti. After they had placed their orders, Marlon could restrain himself no longer and asked Rosenberg what he thought of the picture. 'What picture?' Rosenberg asked. 'That's not a picture, Marlon, it's just an assembly of footage.' Marlon did return to the cutting room, and the final version was at least brought down to a manageable length.

One-Eyed Jacks was ultimately released in 1961 to very mixed reviews and little box-office success. Despite some fine photography by Charles Lang, Jr, and expert performances by the entire cast, it was a slow, halting, and awkward movie that lacked rhythm and momentum. Marlon felt that the integrity of his picture had been compromised in the re-editing and was completely dissatisfied with the final version, even though he knew that Rosenberg could never have released a four-and-a-half-hour-long feature film. Marlon never directed another movie.

Towards the end of shooting *One-Eyed Jacks,* Anna had at last and inevitably filed a petition for divorce, charging that Marlon had caused her 'mental suffering, distress and injury'. On March 25, Marlon filed an appearance, stipulation, and waiver stating that the divorce was uncontested. The interlocutory decree was granted on April 22, 1959. At a meeting to show cause of action, Anna was present with counsel and her star witness, Kathy L'Amour, who confirmed the charges of deliberately inflicted mental suffering. She was granted custody of Christian Devi and visitation rights for Marlon were established. The property settlement called for $60,000 in cash to Anna, plus $500,000 over a period of ten years and $1,000 per month for child support, plus medical and dental expenses; in addition, she got a car, furniture, and jewellery. She was required to confer with Marlon regarding Christian's education and upbringing, and he would be allowed to see the child for just an hour and a half every other evening and at Thanksgiving, Christmas, and birthday celebrations. He would pay nursing or governess wages. The parents agreed to do nothing controversial in front of the child that could reduce his feelings for them.

The separation did not quell the explosively combative relationship between Marlon and Anna. That spring, while visiting Christian, Marlon became furious when Anna entered the room during his allotted ninety minutes with the child. According to her, he struck her and threw her to the floor, and she dragged herself to the door and ran to the kitchen. He raced after her and thrust a carving knife in her hand, ordering her to kill him. She screamed that he wasn't worth it, and then, 'he battered me again, slamming me against the kitchen wall. He stomped from the house.' But Marlon's version of the incident is that Anna entered the playroom, yelling that he 'didn't deserve to hold the baby'. She snatched Christian from his arms and he grabbed after her. When Anna went to call the police, he told her not to, but she insisted, and he responded by slapping her. Then he took her over his knee and spanked her and would only stop when Christian began screaming. When he finally left the house through the kitchen door, she came after him with a butcher knife and raised it to him. Marlon said, 'I told her to go ahead if it would make her happy. She threw the knife on the floor and came at me again, grabbing my hair. I freed myself and left.'

* * *

258

Before *One-Eyed Jacks* was released, the producers Martin Jurow and Richard Shepherd approached the great Italian star Anna Magnani, a close friend and former client of Jurow's during his years as a talent agent at William Morris, to star in the screen version of Tennessee Williams's *Orpheus Descending*. Based loosely on the classical legend of Orpheus, it was the story of a young man whose arrival in a small southern town disrupts that community because all of the women there are drawn to his sexual magnetism. Although Williams had actually written the play with both Brando and Magnani in mind, they both declined it, so Maureen Stapleton starred in the Broadway production with Cliff Robertson. Jurow had persuaded Williams that the play could be adapted for the screen with Magnani instead of Miss Stapleton in the leading role and another major actor playing opposite her. The producers made a deal with United Artists. Magnani was having an affair with Anthony Franciosa at the time and wanted him to be her co-star. The producers were attracted by the idea since Franciosa was a fine, virile actor with a powerful personality and would have been ideally cast. The only problem was that he wasn't a big name.

Meade Roberts wrote a very good adaptation with Williams, and the film version was retitled *The Fugitive Kind*. The producers had script meetings with Magnani and Franciosa on the script. Then, Jay Kanter let the producers know that Marlon was badly in need of money and was interested in discussing doing the film with them even though he had originally turned down the project. His divorce settlement with Anna Kashfi had drained his financial resources. Now the producers were faced with a major dilemma. It would be awkward to release Franciosa, but to secure a larger budget from United Artists and a major international market for the picture, they needed a star like Brando.

The producers went to see Marlon at Mulholland on a spring day in 1959. They took a deep breath and told him they could offer him a million dollars to do the picture – the largest amount ever paid to a star up to that time. He lit up like a firecracker. 'If you can get me a million, I'll make a movie,' he said.

The unfortunate Franciosa was dumped. Instead of fighting this decision, Anna Magnani ruthlessly decided she would much rather go to bed with Brando anyway, and Franciosa was disposed of by her without a shred of regret.

Sidney Lumet was hired as director. A very able craftsman with a fondness for controversial themes, Lumet had made a strong impression since the mid-fifties with several fine live television productions. A newcomer to motion pictures at the time, he had directed the admirable *Twelve Angry Men*.

Lumet lived in Manhattan and was married to Gloria Vanderbilt, and he would not work on the film if the production went on location away from New York. So, rather than head south, the unit moved into Milton, New York, near Poughkeepsie, a small town that was easily fixed up to look like a southern hamlet. From the beginning, the picture was in serious trouble. Magnani expected Marlon to satisfy her in bed now that she had disposed of her lover. However, there was some poetic justice left in the world: she didn't achieve her objective. Already middle-aged, voluptuous but not pretty, and possessed of a violent temper, she was far removed from the gorgeous women that Brando favoured. Although she never actually propositioned him, she gave every evidence of interest, and when she was snubbed she vented her anger on the shooting set.

Moreover, Marlon behaved very badly. He took endless takes to master scenes, and was exceptionally slow learning his lines. Neither the producers nor Lumet had the temerity to discipline their million-dollar star. He was respectful, polite, considerate and gentle – but totally uncontrollable. 'He was a god and he knew it,' Jurow said.

Magnani tried to match him in slowness. If he insisted on constant retakes, she would insist on more. If he would seem slow in a scene, she would reduce her usual Italian vitality to languor. In their love scenes, the actors notably failed to convey convincing passion, and their mutual antipathy was apparent to observant viewers. And yet, *The Fugitive Kind* is a fascinating film. Marlon played his part with a magical intensity and style far ahead of most of his peers. If working with him required infinite patience, it was worth it to the filmmakers because the results were powerful and unforgettable. And the supporting cast, led by Joanne Woodward and Maureen Stapleton, was consistently fascinating to watch.

But as always, Marlon was dissatisfied with both the picture he had just made and with his work in it. With feelings of defeat from the many compromises of moviemaking and the ways of Hollywood – yet drawn to the huge salaries – he again turned to compulsive eating to vent his frustrations. If Marlon had been reasonably fit and trim in *The Fugitive Kind*, now he ballooned to 195 pounds, which was more than he had ever weighed before. Much as he despaired over the loss of his youthful physique, he continued to consume food with abandon. Carlo Fiore remembered arriving at Mulholland Drive to find Marlon naked, sprawled over his huge bed, white, flabby, and sweating as he stared gloomily at his unused barbells and dumbbells.

14

As always in his life, Marlon would take up again with women whom he had seemingly dropped, and they apparently were willing to return to him on almost any condition he made. He had been flying to New York to see France Nuyen from time to time, and now decided she was 'the' woman in his life – at least for the time being. Miss Nuyen remembered how they used to travel in disguise. 'I lost count,' she said, 'of the false noses, wigs, make-up, false names, and accents we both had to use, most of which failed to work with the paparazzi. I even wore blonde wigs, which looked ridiculous on my Asian head.' The blonde wigs, of course, drew far more attention to France than her own raven-black hair. On one occasion, she recalled, Marlon posed as 'Dr Miles Graham of Omaha' (a version of his maternal grandfather Dr Myles Gahan), and his false nose was so ludicrous that she burst into helpless laughter. 'He wasn't so much afraid of the press,' Miss Nuyen said. 'He just wanted an excuse to be a big little boy and dress up and be someone else and see how long he could fool everybody.'

They decided to go to Haiti together. Marlon, who had never been there, hoped that mysterious island would be free from press intrusions, and he even arranged for them to live in a private house to avoid the tourists. This time they got away from New York in disguises that worked. Once on the plane, Marlon whispered to her, 'We've gotten away with it. Not a soul in Haiti will know who we are, anyway.' But when they landed and stepped down on to the tarmac, a uniformed brass band was lined up, led by a man playing a tuba, and there was a sign spread out with 'Welcome Marlon Brando' on it. Miss Nuyen said, 'He was very disappointed, his disguise meant nothing, he had been found out.'

In the Haitian capital of Port-au-Prince Miss Nuyen recalled that Marlon 'kept pressing the locals about the ethnography, customs, and habits, but nobody would answer him'. He was frustrated because he couldn't get responses to his endless probing questions. However, after considerable difficulty, he arranged to witness a voodoo ceremony. They had to hire a small plane to take them to a remote location in the mountains. 'We flew in this tiny, rickety thing,' Miss Nuyen said. 'I was petrified, thinking we would crash at any minute as we jolted through air pockets. I clung to him in fear. All I remember of the voodoo ceremony was fire, and drums, and dances.' She recalled Marlon dancing with the others, but 'somebody grabbed me and pulled me out of the circle'. Soon after that, they were on the plane back to Port-au-Prince.

They flew to Miami. As they walked into the airport, photographers swooped down on them. Already over-wrought from her experience with the voodoo ceremony, France was very upset by the flashing bulbs. Then Marlon suddenly took to his heels and ran, leaving her to face the cameras alone. When the *Miami Herald* photographer Douglas Kennedy began snapping pictures at close range, she hit him on the head with her pocket book and shouted, 'No interviews!' Marlon later explained his abrupt departure by claiming he had to confer with immigration authorities because his smallpox vaccination certificate had expired.

Back in Hollywood, there was more trouble with

Anna Kashfi. According to Marlon, she burst into his house one night while he was sleeping and hurled herself into his bed. When he told her to behave, she responded violently by slapping and biting him. Then, after he finally succeeded in ejecting Anna from the house, she tried to beat her way back in. When she broke through a window, Marlon seized her, threw her on to the bed, and tied her down with the sash from his robe. He summoned the police to have her taken off.

At yet another court hearing to air grievances regarding custody and visitation rights, Marlon complained that on one occasion when he had arrived with a new tricycle for Christian, Anna picked it up and threw it at him as he left. Anna did not deny the charges but said her actions were 'provoked,' and, at the November 18, 1959, hearing, Judge Aggeler ruled that Marlon could visit Christian three days each week from 5:00 P.M. to 7:00 P.M. and that Miss Kashfi must not be present during those visits. Following that ruling, Anna fled to London with their son. She checked into the Dorchester Hotel only to be besieged by the O'Callaghans, who insisted she should accept them as her parents. They even held a press conference in the lobby to criticize her behaviour. In the meantime, Marlon went to court, stating that Anna had abandoned her agreement to allow visitation, and that in fact she had 'allowed the child to run away from him'. When she returned, he arrived at her house to see Christian on Christmas Day, and Anna appeared, ordering him to get off her property. Later, Marlon charged that 'Anna became emotionally disturbed when she saw me and my companion and heaped vilification upon us. She deprived me of the opportunity of seeing my son, and slammed the door against me. I put my Christmas gifts on the front porch and left.'

The 'companion' referred to was yet another girl-friend, the exotic part-Hungarian, part-Filipino actress Barbara Luna, of whom Anna was savagely jealous. This exquisite beauty became the chief rival of France Nuyen, who by now was angrily on her way to London and Hong Kong via New York to make the screen version of *The World of Suzie Wong*. Marlon followed France to Manhattan and begged her to forgive him, but she proceeded in tears and a temper to London. Then, suddenly, she was dismissed from the cast of *Suzie Wong* and was completely shattered when it was announced that Barbara Luna would be taking her part. But instead, producer Ray Stark cast the virtually unknown Nancy Kwan. France returned to Hollywood, but her affair with Marlon was now at an end.

That summer, the problems with Anna dragged on, and in June 1960, she filed a brief against him, claiming that he had 'misjudged the best interests and welfare of our child'. She referred to his committing acts that 'tended to degrade himself and his family in society,' that earned 'public contempt, scorn and ridicule'. There was mention of her hiring Paul Gilbert, a Hollywood private detective, to spy on Marlon. In one hearing, Anna lost her head and fled from the witness stand. Concealed in the powder room, she refused to come out at the request of the bailiff, and only agreed to return to the stand after considerable persuasion. She repeated her charges that Marlon was 'an immoral man,' while Marlon responded that she had refused eight times to let him see his son. In the end, Marlon was granted further visitation rights under the separation agreement to be followed by the imminent finalization of their divorce, but he was cautioned to behave himself. Outside the court, Anna screamed at him,

'You criminal! You slob!' Her temper wasn't improved when, that summer, Marlon with typical unpredictability, went to Mexico and married Movita. However, the couple didn't live together after their first few days in that country. Some months later, Movita gave birth to a son, Miko.

The fights with Anna went on and on. Marlon was in an understandably bitter mood when, at the behest of Jay Kanter, he reported to MGM for exploratory discussions of a new film. Sol C. Siegel, the studio chief, had decided to remake the old classic *Mutiny on the Bounty*, which had originally starred Clark Gable and Charles Laughton; he wanted Marlon to play the mutineer Fletcher Christian. The earlier version had been shot mostly in and around Catalina Island off the California coast, with some second-unit work in Tahiti, French Polynesia. Siegel decided to shoot the new *Bounty* almost entirely in Tahiti, with just a few studio interiors where necessary. In this era of larger and more spectacular colour films, Hollywood producers were looking for appropriately spectacular properties. The story of the outbreak of violence in a ship's crew against the oppressive Captain Bligh had all the right ingredients: adventure on the high seas, passionate confrontations on the quarterdeck, exotic tropical settings, and the battle of good and evil.

Marlon responded to the theme of the rebellion against power, and he was fascinated by the story of what became of the *Bounty* mutineers. Exiled from society by their own choice, condemned in absentia by the London court, they turned what could have been a tropical paradise into a battlefield of conflicting egos, and by the end of a year all except one were dead. He was assured that the script would encompass both the mutiny itself and its aftermath – the life the mutineers had on Pitcairn Island – and on that basis agreed to sign a contract for five hundred thousand dollars plus percentages and overages. He was granted provisional script approval, easily obtained for him by Jay Kanter, since stars at the time already exercised extraordinary control over the material they performed.

The producer was a former USC football great, Aaron Rosenberg, and the director was Sir Carol Reed, who was chosen by MGM because of his British background and the fact that he had earned Marlon's respect through his direction of such classic movies as *Odd Man Out* and *The Third Man*. But Reed was an odd choice to direct a movie spectacle, since his proven strength lay in intimate, compressed stories, set in claustrophobic cities, and shot in stark black and white. Eric Ambler, author of international thrillers, was selected to write the screenplay, which he had begun as early as Christmas of 1959. His script failed to work, and after the expenditure of some $90,000, a new draft was commissioned in July of 1960 from John Gay. Gay's version in turn was scrapped and followed by new scripts written by William Driscoll, Borden Chase, and finally Howard Clewes and Charles Lederer. The total writers' bill on the picture came to $237,000, or well over a million in today's money. The task of finding fresh material from the story that had already been translated into a classic film proved problematic.

Trevor Howard was cast as the vicious Captain Bligh, and later, Richard Harris, Hugh Griffith, Duncan Lamont, and Chips Rafferty were added to the cast. Marlon was far from pleased with the way the final screenplay was shaping up, and he was especially disappointed that the idea of showing the Pitcairn survivors was dropped. He talked of getting involved in another film project – the story of Caryl Chessman, whose execution in the gas chamber at San Quentin that spring had been the object of protest demonstrations in which Marlon had participated. In the meantime, the *Bounty*, a boat that would serve as the shooting set, was being built in Nova Scotia for $750,000 and had to be shipped through the Panama Canal to Tahiti. Slightly larger than the original vessel, she was motor-powered; her top-heavy ballast was to prove a problem later on.

Marlon finally agreed to go ahead, despite his misgivings. So heavy was the studio's commitment to a late-fall starting date that they had to proceed without a complete script. Marlon and the production team briefly visited Tahiti in July, to get the lie of the land and to meet with the local contact men who could muster a very large cast of local citizens. Months passed, consumed in costume and make-up tests. At last, in mid-November 1960, the first batch of craftsmen went to French Polynesia to prepare the groundwork.

Marlon arrived on November 28, one of the first passengers ever to fly into the newly completed Papeete airstrip, and was immediately excited to be in the islands. The purple mountains, brilliant blue-green sea, and luscious vegetation intoxicated his senses. The gorgeous local girls who greeted him were gleefully available, without moral restraints, and intensely attracted to any man with white skin. They had no idea who Brando was.

Marlon moved into a modest, sprawling house in the local style and enjoyed walking about stripped to the waist, comfortably relaxed, thousands of miles away from courtroom battles and the Hollywood scene. Sir Carol Reed, with his dry sense of humour and sharp intelligence, was a congenial companion. The British supporting players were very much to Marlon's taste.

Youthful and vigorous, they wallowed with Marlon in the sensual delights of Polynesia.

The production began. Studio craftsmen had removed and replanted trees, diverted a river, built war canoes with local help, set up a laboratory for the daily rushes, shipped in equipment by a Swedish freighter, and organized buses for transportation. A massive catering truck was flown in and shipped from island to island on a raft. A local ferry, the *Ahi*, was effectively used to get everybody about. The first sequence Sir Carol shot at Bora Bora was a fishing scene, in which the young girls spread out in a human chain across an inlet, preventing the fish from slipping through the nets while the men bore down in boats and the *Bounty* crew ran out joyously to gambol with the beauties in the shallow water. There were over a thousand men and women in the shot. Two hundred painted war canoes made a brilliant splash of scarlet and gold against the smoky blue hills and mountains. The men threw stones attached to long ropes, beating the fish ahead. Twelve hundred pounds of fish were landed that afternoon.

Marlon discovered that many of the local girls were of mixed blood, born during the war as the result of the presence in Tahiti of the lusty Sea Bees. Assistant director Reggie Callow remarked later that you could meet one of the girls at Papeete's Grand Hotel, and half an hour later you were home in bed with her. Some of the girls even moved in with crew members and actors; a man could be taking a shower and suddenly see a young beauty standing naked in the bathroom doorway, announcing that she was the maid.

There were problems with the production from the beginning. The light was changeable, and a sequence that began at sea would have to be cancelled because of a sudden downpour. In the scene in which the *Bounty* arrives at the island, hundreds of war canoes butted out into the sound, only to be called back when a cloudburst drenched the extras and set the *Bounty* rocking violently at anchor. Efforts were made to shoot from a camera boat, but it proved too unstable in the swell, and the disappointed director had to stop once again. Sometimes, the morning would be bright and clear, but by midday the clouds had covered the sun, and by twilight rain blotted out all visibility. Moreover, the *Bounty* had become dangerously top-heavy now, with equipment, cameras, cables, and crew, and she rocked around like a cork in the waves.

Marlon became increasingly restive with all the production problems. Disagreements about the script continued to hold up shooting, as Marlon and Sir Carol worked out the actual construction of each scene. Essentially, though, they had a mutual respect, and Marlon – contrary to many published statements – was punctual nearly every day and never disrupted shooting for capricious reasons.

Another big scene shot in January was the native feast at which Captain Bligh, in an attempt to appease the native chief, is forced to execute an ungainly dance with the local girls. It was an episode featuring four hundred dancers and stretched the crew's considerable resources to the limit. Again and again, the scene was interrupted by rain.

Depressed and irritable, Marlon found solace in the company of a ravishing young girl named Tarita, who was cast, ironically, as his girlfriend in the story. Her origins were Chinese and Tahitian, and she was irresistible to him. With her exquisite sloping shoulders, her firm breasts, her flat stomach and wide hips, Tarita fulfilled Marlon's fantasies and became the embodiment of some South Seas goddess. A fine dancer who worked as waitress and part-time cook in a local café, she was involved at the time with a Danish chef. Much to the latter's annoyance, she fell in love with Marlon; but by the rule of the islands, a woman could drop one man and take up with another without compunction of any sort. There were no rules or sexual morals, in the Western sense, in Tahiti. She and Marlon immediately entered into an affair that grew into a relationship of intense personal communion and sympathetic warmth that continues until this day.

Marlon worked closely with Tarita, guiding her tenderly through her lines, and she responded with extraordinary sensitivity for a non-actress. Not only was her expression of love for Marlon genuine and moving to witness, she also had a certain amount of natural ability that came through when seen against his incandescent talent.

The project seemed plagued with delays, and in January 1961, Sir Carol Reed became ill with a combination of gallstones and heat prostration. And Richard Harris turned out to be a poor sailor – he got seasick aboard the rocking *Bounty*. Then in February, Marlon displayed his customary eccentricity and decided without warning to cancel all of the existing work and switch roles to the part of a lesser mutineer. Aaron Rosenberg flew to Hollywood to discuss this idea with his bosses. Not surprisingly, he was talked out of it. At last, the endless rewrites, delays and foul weather broke the project's back, and Sir Carol yielded to pressure from the studio to bring the company home.

Everything came to a halt. Ray Klune, vice president of MGM, demanded a shooting schedule and a projected completion date for the film. Assistant director Reggie Callow submitted an estimate of 139 days.

Klune, acting on President Sol C. Siegel's instructions, called for a 100-day completion. Then, at a meeting in Rosenberg's office with Marlon present, Klune asked Reed if he would guarantee to finish the movie in that time. Sir Carol said he could not, and MGM fired him. Marlon was furious over Reed's dismissal. Whatever differences might have existed between them, Marlon certainly respected the British director. They had established a working relationship that resulted in an improvement of the script on every page. And Reed had allowed Marlon to portray Fletcher Christian the way he saw the character – as a lisping dandy on the verge of effeminacy who is turned into a man by the conflict with Bligh. This switch of character halfway through the film was an inspired stroke on Marlon's part and undoubtedly gave the picture its chief strength.

Aaron Rosenberg had the responsibility of hiring a new director, and he selected Lewis Milestone, a Russian-born American director of great skill who was, unfortunately, at seventy, very far past his peak as a craftsman. Marlon was intrigued by the choice at first, since he was well aware of Milestone's great film, *All Quiet on the Western Front*. Milestone began directing the picture exactly a day after Reed left it, with an assistant filling in for a few hours while Milestone prepared the script pages. They began shooting sequences of the *Bounty*'s departure from Portsmouth Harbour at the commencement of the story and of the court-martial of the arrested mutineers towards the end. Whereas Reed had accepted Marlon's daily rewrites of the dialogue, Milestone was temperamentally incapable of working in that manner. He came from the old school, in which movies were made in a hurry and everybody toed the chalk line without asking questions. Milestone had no patience with the Actors Studio approach that defined Marlon's performances. This director could not tolerate his actors searching for meaning right there on the set. Within a week, they were at each other's throats.

Marlon's only consolation during those weeks was that Tarita had flown to Hollywood and was staying at the Bel Air Sands Hotel. He took great pleasure in showing her Los Angeles and seeing it through her innocent eyes; he even began to appreciate the city as he never had before. Just being with Tarita was an intense pleasure; she was so fresh, open, and sweet, and she had none of the awkwardness, shifts of mood, and challenging qualities he found in other women.

For some weeks, shooting continued at the MGM Studios. Then, on April 22, 1961, the unit returned to Tahiti to start all over again under Lewis Milestone. It was now that Marlon's behaviour became increasingly unprofessional. He was late arriving on the set again and again. The arguments over the writing were even more interminable and infuriating. Marlon moved to a new house, right on the beach, and this also slowed up the production. Throughout May, the rain and the heavy swells interrupted work, though not as seriously as before. Even Marlon got seasick during the protracted shipboard shooting of the mutiny itself in June. The tough, leathery old Milestone managed to stand up to everything, but one actor after another succumbed to dysentery or a variety of tropical illnesses. By July, a sense of hopelessness pervaded the cast and crew. Nor was Milestone's direction as strong and forceful as his predecessor's. The reshooting of much of Tahiti's welcome to the *Bounty* on July 23 and 24 was a nightmare of trying to match the existing shots. Marlon was ill again and again. And then there was an unmitigated disaster.

On July 25, the second unit shot a dramatic chase by canoe. Four craft were seen pursuing, under Bligh's orders, a group of runaway mutineers in canoes and being aided by natives. Assistant director James Havens handled the sequence with romantic dash, colour, and excitement. As the chase went on, the waves became violent and unpredictable, and the camera crew in motor-powered boats had trouble navigating the choppy surf. Finally, the lead canoe was struck broadside by a freak wave and hit the reef. Gashed open, the boat tipped sideways and flung every man aboard on to the jagged coral. One Tahitian was killed instantly, and other actors and extras lay everywhere, so injured that the reef was awash in blood. Doctors and nurses set up a field hospital in a nearby Chinese restaurant to tend the wounded. The tragedy blighted the production of *Mutiny on the Bounty* for good.

Yet the interminable work on the picture continued. Throughout the filming, Marlon had not been friendly with co-star Richard Harris, and by now frustrations with the project had tempers flaring all over. During the shooting of one sequence, Marlon was required to slap Harris on the face and exclaim, 'You bastard!' For some reason, Marlon couldn't bring himself to do this. Perhaps he was afraid that in view of his feelings for Harris, he might cause him real injury. Instead, he just barely tapped him. After three takes, Harris turned to Marlon and snapped angrily, 'Why the fuck don't you kiss me and be done with it?' Milestone gave up in October, and the picture closed down for several months while everyone tried to decide on the ultimate ending.

George Seaton, an able but undistinguished studio

director, was brought in to finish it in July. He directed Marlon in the protracted death scene. Marlon announced that he needed two hundred pounds of cracked ice. Assistant director Reggie Callow asked why, and Marlon told him not to think about it, just to get it. When it arrived, Marlon stripped down to shorts and lay on the ice until he was shivering violently. Taking the cue from his own mother's death and from the similar device used in *Truckline Café*, he had sought to 'get the death tremors'. However, despite all this care for authenticity, he failed to remember the lines in Tahitian he was supposed to utter with his dying breath. Callow took a grease pencil and wrote the words on Tarita's forehead. And then, when the scene was at last done, Marlon was so badly chilled he stayed in bed for three days and the production closed down again.

In one of the last scenes to be shot, Marlon had to appear drunk. Although he seldom drank alcohol, on the morning of the sequence concerned, he turned up with two bottles of Jack Daniels and announced, 'Everybody says I'm supposed to be a method actor. Well, by God, I'm supposed to be drunk in this scene and I'm going to be drunk, and so is everyone else.' He passed the bottles around and the whole cast got smashed. As a result, when the scene was finally edited, it didn't hold up and had to be cut.

In the end, the final budget had doubled from around $10 million to beyond $20 million. And the results were very far from what Sol C. Siegel wanted.

The troubled making of *Mutiny* could not be masked in the final release, and the movie was a colossal failure – despite its ravishing visual beauty and a very generous Oscar nomination for Best Motion Picture.

15

After the débâcle of *Mutiny on the Bounty*, Marlon found a film project that truly meant something to him because it would express themes sympathetic with his liberal views. With his old friend George Englund directing, he became involved in a screen adaptation of the popular and respected novel *The Ugly American* by William J. Lederer and Eugene Burdick, which dealt with American intrusions into Southeast Asian politics. The subject had been a concern of Marlon's since 1955 when he had initially explored making the UNESCO documentary with Englund. Now, seven years later, they had found a feature film property that covered the same ideas they had originally set out to probe.

The Ugly American fulfilled part of a multi-picture contract Marlon had signed with Universal, and the studio decided to make the film in Hollywood, with only backgrounds photographed in Thailand. Shooting on location in Asia had been considered, and now the film would lose a great deal of visual authenticity. Nevertheless, Marlon remained deeply committed to the project and immersed himself in the direction with George Englund. He was on his best behaviour throughout the production. Convinced that the movie presented an accurate picture of American bungling in the Orient, he didn't tamper with the script – although he still had difficulty remembering his lines.

The film turned out to be a well-intentioned but mediocre adventure into political commentary, relieved only by the appealing performance of the Japanese actor Eiji Okada, as a revolutionary leader, and by the skilful supporting performances of Pat Hingle and Arthur Hill. Marlon's sister Jocelyn played the part of Hingle's wife, and Marlon dutifully gave press interviews, stating that Jocelyn was 'the true talent in our family'. By this point, many of those in Hollywood who were exasperated by Marlon's anti-Americanism and unprofessional behaviour on the set were only too willing to agree.

During the shooting of *The Ugly American*, Marlon was briefly involved with a gorgeous Filipino girl, Marie Cui, whom he had first met in Manila on the way to do *Teahouse of the August Moon*. She had now settled in Los Angeles and occasionally appeared in Los Angeles nightclubs as a singer and dancer. In June 1962 she missed her period and told Marlon she was pregnant. But unlike the situation with Movita, this time he was convinced from the beginning that the baby was not his. He felt that he had an animal instinct about such things, and he was furious when Marie claimed that he was the father. However, he was determined that the child should have the best of care, and he sent Marie to his physician, Dr Melvin L. Sommer, in Beverly Hills.

Anna Kashfi heard about Marlon's affair, and once again her jealousy was inflamed. Now long divorced from Marlon, she could have no logical claim on him, yet she responded with the passionate anger of an offended lover. Propelled by her customary emotional fury, she arrived unannounced at Marlon's house. He had temporarily moved out of the Mulholland Drive residence and was occupying the old John Barrymore estate on Tower Road. Unable to raise anybody when she rang the doorbell, she discovered a door open at the side of the building and walked into the entrance hall. According to Anna, she then made her way upstairs to the master bedroom, where she found Marlon in bed with Marie Cui, who was naked. Marlon covered himself with sheets and blankets, while Marie, furious at Anna's sudden invasion, flung a lamp at her. Anna fled down the stairs. She alleged later that Marlon ran after her and threw her to the ground, beating her head against it as she burst into hysterical laughter.

When Marlon left her lying there and returned to the house, she broke into the kitchen, and Marlon grabbed her from behind, swung her around, and tied her hand and foot with ropes. A neighbour reported the fight to the police. When the cops burst into the house, Anna refused to make an assault charge. Challenged about this incident by a reporter, Marlon cryptically replied, 'I have ladies in my home for many purposes, including sexual. But I would not like to give the impression that people are invited to my home primarily for sexual reasons.'

By now, Marlon had allowed his press agents to release the news of his marriage to Movita and the subsequent birth of their child. The announcement came as a shock, as not even the most avid gossip columnist had suspected that Brando was again a married man. Anna Kashfi, of course, was furious when she heard the news.

Surprisingly, the news also infuriated Rita Moreno, who had apparently remained madly in love with Marlon. She now realized that she had lost all opportunity of taking Anna Kashfi's place in a marital relationship. In anger, she stormed up to Marlon's house and demanded to see him, and Marlon reluctantly admitted her. She began questioning him about the nature of his marriage to Movita – whether or not it was merely because of the child. He refused to reply. Then Rita reached into her handbag, took out a handful of pills, and swallowed them before he could stop her. An ambulance was called, and she was rushed to a hospital, where her stomach was pumped.

Three days later, Rita convinced Marlon into going out with her to discuss their tortured relationship. While they were driving it began to rain, Marlon lost control of the wheel, and they ran off the road. Rita's head smashed against the dashboard, and her face was severely cut. Blood gushed from the wound. Again, Marlon rushed her to the hospital. She said later, 'When I got to the emergency room, I was bloody and hysterical. The nurses almost had me calmed down when a bunch of photographers surged into the cubicle, shouting questions, popping flashbulbs. I was screaming, fighting them out of the room . . .' As if all that were not enough, Marlon and Rita had another violent quarrel, and Rita later slashed her wrists. Yet again, she was hospitalized and went around town wearing bandages, thus feeding gossip columns. At last, she began intensive psychotherapy and managed to accept that Marlon would never become involved with her again.

Marlon flew to Bangkok with George Englund for the world première of *The Ugly American.* He was received by His Majesty King Rama IX at the Chitlada Palace, and they discussed American-Asian relations; Marlon said he was 'touched and honoured by the invitation'. He said of the king, 'One tends to think that the system of monarchy belongs to an old, decadent, useless world. I was especially privileged and impressed that His Majesty not only is a king, but that he is alive to even the subtlest and ordinary kinds of information.

279

He certainly is concerned with the state of the world and the preservation of democratic ideals. He is not a man full of platitudes and drowned in formalities.'

At a press conference the next day at the Erawan Hotel, where he was staying, he gave a typically lively talk, enjoying his favourite role of the enlightened American abroad. Discussing M. R. Kukrit Pramoj, a well-known Thai newspaper publisher and former finance minister cast as prime minister in the picture, he mischievously brought a gasp when he described him as 'a dissembler, liar and thief'. He added hastily, 'Mr Kukrit told me he couldn't act, and then proceeded to prove he could act and in fact acted me off the screen. He stole the whole show.' He laughed, and the Thai reporters dissolved in responding mirth. He discussed the movie, saying, shrewdly, 'Some people will react as Barry Goldwater might. Some people will react as President Kennedy might. And the spectrum of reaction will depend upon the individual. There will be a wide variety of reactions within the State Department.' He pointed out that the film was critical of the United States, of the neutralists, and of the rightist régimes who 'make no reforms and are not willing to make reasonable and intelligent concessions for the establishment of democracy in their countries'. He noted that the picture was critical of Communism and then pointedly added, 'There will be an enormous and perhaps bombastic reaction in some areas against this picture in America. I think it is fitting. In the South today we have a situation that has brought great shame upon us as a nation, and many of us are entirely indifferent to that.' His impassioned speech cited numerous examples of racial discrimination in America and continued for more than half an hour.

Leaving Thailand, he went on with George Englund to Paris and then to Los Angeles for the American première. On April 15, 1963, he appeared at a press conference in Chicago before the local première and turned the tables on the gathered critics and reporters by demanding that they disclose whether they were told by their editors 'to slant reviews and articles'. They all responded in the negative, of course. Marlon assailed the misrepresentation of his personal and professional life in mass-circulation magazines – referring in part to a damning article that had appeared the previous year in *The Saturday Evening Post* about his prima donna-like behaviour on the set of *Mutiny on the Bounty* over which he had initiated and dropped a multimillion-dollar lawsuit. He virtually lectured the press: 'Where does a reporter or writer draw the line between legitimately dramatizing a subject and plainly distorting the facts to fit a preconception?' He added, 'A publication that prattles about morality on its editorial page is being two-faced by toying with the truth in news and features.' Not particularly chastened by this drubbing, the press gave an understandably cool account of the conference.

On April 18, he appeared at the Overseas Press Club in Los Angeles; three days later, he broke his normal rule against appearing on television interview shows and agreed to go on David Susskind's syndicated programme, *Open End*. Susskind made a deal with him in advance that Marlon would be allowed to attack the press, including Truman Capote, *The New Yorker*, *Time* magazine, and *The Saturday Evening Post*, as well as the world of journalism at large, on condition that he agree to discuss some aspects of his life and work in Hollywood. Asked why he objected so strongly to comments about him in the columns, he said, 'I have two children growing up in this community, and I think that they deserve protection as do their mothers.' He was accompanied on the show by Eugene Burdick, co-author of *The Ugly American*, and George Englund.

Deal or no deal, Marlon filled the entire programme sounding off against the press. He told Susskind, 'I have withstood raps, justified and unjustified – wrath, hatred, disregard, vulgarity, insults – for years and years.' He talked of 'clap-trap scatological journalism,' and he claimed, 'I have reached the point of no return, and it might be a fruitless, stupid and vain effort, but I cannot, will not, tolerate this kind of thing anymore.'

Susskind, in an attempt to change the subject, asked Marlon whether Tahitian women were 'beautiful and wavy' and given to 'exciting dances'. Marlon brushed aside the question and proceeded to a more elevated discussion of Tahitian society past and present. Unaware that he was criticizing several members of his own inner circle, he attacked 'phony well-wishers who display more teeth in their smiles as the star's income goes up'. With his typical sense of mischief, he attacked Susskind point-blank for having a cigarette-making sponsor whose product caused cancer. Susskind uncharacteristically accepted Marlon's behaviour with docile resignation – at least on camera.

On April 27, Marlon announced that he was about to begin work on a comedy, *King of the Mountain*, later retitled *Bedtime Story*, written by Stanley Shapiro and to be directed by Ralph Levy. David Niven and Shirley Jones would be the co-stars. He had wanted to appear in a comedy and was delighted when the picture, originally scheduled to star Rock Hudson and Cary Grant, became available. Shapiro's script appealed to Marlon's sense of humour, and he liked the role of

Freddy Benson – con man, mimic, and crafty seducer – an Army corporal at large in Europe who is involved in a number of escapades and fraudulent misadventures. A typical Benson trick as invented by Shapiro has him taking a picture of a German cottage and then telling the pretty young girl living in it that he is trying to find his grandmother's birthplace. When he shows her the picture he has just taken, she expresses surprise at the coïncidence. Inevitably, she takes him on a tour that terminates in bed. Much of the movie concerns Benson's rivalry with the elegant, unscrupulous cad Laurence Jamieson, played by Niven, as the pair pursue available females. The story's cheerful vulgarity was entirely compatible with one aspect of Marlon's nature.

Ralph Levy recalled that it was the first motion picture he had directed, having been involved mostly with television. He was surprised to find that even though Marlon liked the script, he wasn't fully prepared when work began. The entire unit had to wait while he took an extra hour to report to work from his dressing room. Such behaviour gave Levy qualms from the outset. He also felt that Marlon's pacing was 'slow for comedy. He tended to intellectualize things as we discussed scenes. I told him, "Marlon, you can't intellectualize, analyse or dissect comedy. If you deliberate too much it will ruin the picture's speed."' Marlon didn't seem to absorb this advice. Levy also noted that Marlon had a tendency to upstage Shirley Jones. 'At one stage, this was so irritating that I stopped work and called Marlon off the set. I told him what he was doing, and he said, "I'd like to kick you in the goddamned ass!"'

Levy described the first day of work, the scene in which Benson goes to the cottage to seduce the girl. 'As we began, with Marlon taking the photograph from behind a tree, I was amazed to see he had a cigar in his mouth. There was nothing in Stanley's script to say he should be smoking at all. It wouldn't have mattered so much, his springing this on me. But it was obvious from the way he handled the cigar that he didn't know how to smoke it. It looked completely unnatural and wrong. I stopped the shot and called him aside. We had a fifteen-minute discussion. I told him, I'm afraid rather bluntly, "If you feel you need the cigar as a crutch to help you with the scene, go ahead. But learn how to smoke it first." He was absolutely furious, but he did throw the cigar away.'

Levy pointed out that 'Marlon was eating compulsively through the work. There was a beach scene in which he was in swim trunks. He looked a little heavy when we shot it, but not enough to worry about. However, the camera is ruthless. It always adds ten pounds. When we saw him in the rushes we were horrified. We dropped the scene at once and had to reshoot it later, when the picture was finished, and he had had a chance to diet. It meant rebuilding the whole beach set.'

During the making of *Bedtime Story*, newspapers circulated reports that Marlon was suffering from a viral infection with a fever and that he was absent from shooting. However, Levy denies there was any sickness and claims it was just Marlon's way of not working. He kept calling for one thermometer after another because none would register an abnormal temperature. When he did show up on the set, sometimes he would tell cameraman Clifford Stine that he didn't like a particular angle and wanted it changed. Stine would alter the camera position as requested and then, when Marlon wasn't looking, move it back again.

On the other hand, Stanley Shapiro, who was also

on the set daily, had much fonder memories of Marlon's professional behaviour during the making of the film. He recalled, 'Marlon was almost never late. He was a dream to work with. We never had any trouble with him.' At the time, when the nationally syndicated newspaper gossip columnist Kate Cameron turned up on the set, Shapiro told her, 'I found Marlon punctual, courteous and considerate of his staff and his fellow players. He took direction like a lamb. There were no arguments, only discussions.' However, today Shapiro does admit that Marlon sometimes delayed shooting because he would not emerge from his dressing room until he had completed various meetings with representatives of civil rights organizations and visitors from Asia.

In 1963 the civil rights movement had heated up, and Marlon had become deeply involved in the cause. In July, as the last scenes of *Bedtime Story* were being shot, he had committed himself to participate in a demonstration in Cambridge, Maryland, where racial conflicts had resulted in the brutal treatment of blacks by the Maryland National Guard. He appeared at a mass meeting of the American Civil Liberties Union Arts Division at the Beverly Hills Hilton, along with director-writer-producer Phillip Dunne, actor James Whitmore, Nate Monaster of the Writers' Guild of America West, Samuel Goldwyn Studio attorney George Slaff, Mildred Walters of the Congress of Racial Equality (CORE), and Tom Neusom of the National Association for the Advancement of Colored People (NAACP). Marlon delivered a lengthy speech denouncing the widespread film industry belief that the public was not ready for a realistic portrayal of blacks in films. He asserted that actors could be instrumental in fighting discrimination since 'we can refuse to work in a picture if the Negro is not represented in it,' and he urged performers to stand together and pledge not to support production companies that upheld the principles of segregation. He added, 'Somebody said it was going to be a long, hot summer. We can do something now or let the situation get away from us and have it end tragically.'

Following that speech, he was publicly criticized by Caleb Anderson, president of the Hollywood Race Relations Bureau. Anderson blasted Marlon for allowing himself to be 'used' by the ACLU among other groups. He argued that Marlon was mistaken in his claims about Hollywood's treatment of blacks and cited the fact that eighty television and motion picture productions in the previous twelve months had accurately portrayed 'the Negro as he is today'.

In response, Marlon rejected all of Anderson's arguments. While these accusations were being hurled back and forth, Marlon was suffering from an unpleasant attack of pyelonephritis, an inflammation of the kidney. By July 18, as he was about to depart for Cambridge to join the demonstration, his condition had deteriorated to the extent that he was admitted to St John's Hospital in Santa Monica for tests and recuperation. In a state of frustration, he announced that he could not make the trip.

There, as he lay resting in the hospital, he was confronted with another crisis of a completely different nature. A stranger entered his room and introduced himself as William Lowe, a private detective. Then, without warning, Lowe handed him a packet of papers: Marlon was being sued for child support by Marie Cui, whose daughter, Maya Gabriella, had been born on February 27, 1963. In the document, Bernard B. Cohen, attorney for Ms Cui, claimed on her behalf that Marlon earned 'between half a million and one million a year, and that his net worth was in excess of one million,' that 'Plaintiff was conceived in Los Angeles, as a result of intimate relations between me and defendant, and said child was born in Manila, Philippines.' The mother added, 'I unequivocally state that during the period of conception of said child I did not have sexual relations with anyone other than said Marlon Brando, and that no one other than he could possibly be the father of said child.' Marlon's lawyers, Norman Garey and Allen E. Susman, responded quickly. They announced that Marlon was not the father and that undoubtedly a blood test would prove it. Depositions were taken on both sides. But after a protracted fight in the Superior Court the blood tests established Marlon's innocence in the matter, the case was dismissed immediately, and there was no appeal. Marie Cui later married and settled in Los Angeles, but continued to claim that the baby was Marlon's.

Perhaps because of the stress of this episode, Marlon began eating more ferociously than ever. By now, his once-powerful physique had turned even softer. At thirty-nine, he no longer had the metabolism of his youth, and his failure to keep up a régime of calisthenics or weight-lifting took its toll on him. He developed an unsightly paunch, and his weight blew up to a shocking 220 pounds.

On July 26, Marlon marched with 150 demonstrators to protest housing discrimination in an all-white residential tract in Torrance, California. Repeatedly interrupted by reporters bombarding him with questions, he was told by a police officer, 'You'll have to keep moving or you will be arrested. You are blocking the sidewalk.' Several demonstrators, including the

Reverend Morris V. Samuel, associate rector of the Episcopal Parish of East Los Angeles, and the Reverend Herbert Yates, of the Southwestern Presbyterian Church, were seized by law officers and lifted bodily into the paddy wagon. Marlon did not carry a placard, unlike most of the demonstrators; instead, he made notes as he walked. He was followed by three American Nazis carrying the sign, 'Brando is a stooge for Communist race mixture,' and by three young men in the uniform of the Ku Klux Klan. He told the press, 'I hope this demonstration will communicate to others the truth that discrimination does exist. Many people are not aware of what's going on, and anyone who believes in civil rights should take part in this.' As some reporters trampled on flowers, lawns, and shrubbery to get to him, he said, 'Some of the flowers are being stepped on today. But so are some people's civil rights.' A woman screamed at him that he was a 'Commie!' He didn't reply.

Then on August 24, Marlon was in New York to support a proposed boycott of public schools that was being organized by civil rights groups. When he was in New York, Marlon also appeared with Paul Newman at a special benefit performance attended by two thousand people at the Apollo Theater in Harlem to raise money for a planned march on Washington. Following the benefit, they proceeded to the Polo Grounds for a twelve-hour rally. The crowd was picketed by American Nazis and representatives of the National States Rights party, who carried Confederate flags and signs that read, 'Black and white is red' and 'Race mixing is a Communist conspiracy.'

From there Marlon flew to Gadsden, Alabama, and Birmingham at the invitation of CORE to continue his protests, accompanied by Paul Newman, Anthony

Franciosa, and actor Virgil Frye. In Gadsden, the heart of staunch southern conservatism, they were attacked violently by Mayor Lesley Gilliland, who accused them of rabble-rousing tactics. Marlon, Franciosa, and Frye sought a meeting with Gilliland, but he refused to talk to them and warned that if they violated the law by damaging public property or inciting a riot they would go to prison.

Unable to confer with Gilliland, the three men proceeded to the Republic Steel Corporation plant in town, where they confronted the officials with charges of racism in their hiring practices. They then proceeded on foot to the Goodyear Rubber Company, whose guards at the gate refused to admit them. Frustrated, they called a press conference out in the street where a grim-faced Marlon told reporters, 'We are here as devoted and peaceful representatives of goodwill, not as agitators, interlopers or interferers.' He added, 'Southerners can point to the North and accuse us of hypocrisy, insulated and restricted thinking just as easily as the finger can be pointed the other way.' A crowd had gathered around the reporters, TV cameramen, and radio correspondents. Some people cheered Marlon's speech, others jeered him, and a few threw pebbles and pieces of dirt. Marlon, Franciosa, and Frye felt satisfaction at having provoked such strong reactions.

This somewhat uncomfortable if well-intentioned journey to the South had an unfortunate result for Universal. According to Stanley Shapiro, 'Bedtime Story was not shown in many southern theatres. This affected its commercial success considerably. Moreover, some theatres showed the picture with David Niven's name alone on the marquee. This was a great setback, as Marlon's was the name that brought the public in.' For years, many southern newspapers harshly attacked all of Marlon's movies.

After Marlon had established a high profile in the civil rights movement, columnist Jack Anderson disclosed the fact that the FBI was tapping Marlon's telephone. Marlon turned up on *The Tonight Show* and *The Today Show* to air his views. At the same time, Marlon's private life was as confused and muddled as ever. Tarita continued to live in Tahiti. He remained married to Movita; she was seeking a divorce, but so far there had not been a hearing on it, and the question of a property settlement was unresolved. Anna was constantly fighting him over the time he could spend with Christian, and now he also had to deal with Movita on visitation rights to see Miko. It was understandable that he should want to make a permanent home for himself in Tahiti. Late in 1963, he flew to Polynesia three separate times to negotiate for the purchase of an atoll at a price variously given as $50,000 or $250,000. He had another motive for wanting to settle in the South Seas: his concern over the possibility that a nuclear war could wipe out much of the life of the Northern Hemisphere. He felt the need to seek out a healthy and self-sufficient environment for Tarita and any children they would produce. Marlon had considered buying land in Bali, but there was unrest in Timor and that magical island no longer offered utopian possibilities. Instead, he settled on Teti'aroa, a coral atoll situated north of Tahiti, twenty-five miles off Point Venus, where Captain Cook had landed in 1769.

Resembling a blue-green necklace strung across the sea, the cluster of small islands had a history marked by corruption, bloodshed, and sexual abandon. Legend had it that the mythical warrior Tafa'i had created

Teti'aroa by pulling a great sea beast on his straining fish line up from the ocean floor, cutting the creature into segments, and watching it rise in its bloody fragments through the foam to float there fixed forever, to be assaulted by the powerful beating of the Tahitian surf.

The thirteen islets surrounded a closed lagoon of opalescent water that changed colour from a pale ethereal blue, to a garish turquoise, to a menacing green. The warrior kings used the atoll as places of punishment or debauchery, and Tahitian King Pomere I in the eighteenth century travelled there to indulge in the pagan orgies that the Christian missionaries would not tolerate. The royal concubines were stuffed with food to render them fatter and thus more appetizing to their royal lovers. And there, too, the voluptuous and self-indulgent girls and youths of the Arioi Society travelled in groups of five hundred by brilliantly painted canoe to fornicate pleasurably on the sand.

For scores of years, the atoll was virtually uninhabited. In 1904, it was bought by a dentist, Dr Will Williams, whose granddaughter in turn sold it to Marlon. He bought it sight unseen, then took off to examine his new purchase. The voyage of discovery was shocking, marvellous, and unforgettable: the dream of a twelve-year-old-kid, straight from the pages of *The Coral Island*, *The Blue Lagoon*, or the glossy *National Geographic* magazines he had pored over during school detentions at Libertyville.

He went across from the main island with four Tahitian crewmen, aboard a rowboat unequipped with an outboard motor, following the same route as nineteenth-century travellers before him. The passage to landfall on the lagoon edge was a tormentingly narrow, dangerously shallow and windswept entrance through surf, over coral that was so sharp it could make a severe dent even in the steel plates of a large ship. So tremendous was the swell that the crew gave up the attempt to make the passage from the south and circled the atoll to enter from the north side. By the time they were in sight of their destination, they realized the only way they could land was to shoot a wave into the very mouth of the northern channel. But when they tried, the captain miscalculated and the boat missed the crest of the breaker and was sucked dangerously back into the ebbtide, drifting out into a mountainous sea.

At that exact moment, another giant comber caught the vessel amidships and slammed her sideways. The occupants were flung in a daze of blue water and foam into the jagged, awaiting mouth of the coral reef. Terrified and exhilarated all at once, Marlon was sure he was going to die. If he stayed aboard, he would risk being swamped as the boat capsized, pinned under the scuppers and crushed by the supply boxes. If he jumped, the waves could smash him head-first on to the razor-sharp coral. He chose to stay aboard. He and the other men in their frail craft were sent hurtling on to the crest of the reef and scattered bloodily about.

Bruised from head to foot, bleeding from dozens of wounds, Marlon and his companions crawled on their hands and knees to the peaceful, pale waters of the uninhabited island's central lagoon. Their boat was totally foundered and they had no way out and no radio with which to communicate. For two days and nights, they managed to tend their wounds and subsist on coconut flesh and milk and native-grown beans. When a rescue vessel arrived, she too was smashed against the reef. It took a third craft to bring the castaways to safety.

It was one of the best times Marlon ever had in his life. A kid at heart for all his sophistication, he thoroughly enjoyed this dreamlike adventure. After such a baptism of fire, it was inevitable he would fall in love with Teti'aroa. The constant changes of light, from pale grey-gold to scarlet, the sudden drenching rains, the overwhelming nights of haunted, velvety darkness and great lemon moons intoxicated him. The brilliant stars were like great lamps hanging above his head, not the dim, twinkling paste jewels of the Northern Hemisphere. He loved nearby Bird Island, with its thousands of winged creatures sweeping from their palm tree nests to scoop up fish with their beaks. Here was a mortal paradise where neither telephones, television, newspapers, nor commerce would intrude.

He could have stayed there, gloriously alone, or with Tarita, for the rest of his life. He almost certainly had enough money by then to earn sufficient interest to allow him to live simply the rest of his days. Yet, unpredictable and strangely perverse as ever, he decided to turn this paradise into, of all things, a tourist resort. How can one explain so astonishing an aberration? He, who despised slavish fans, who dreaded the presence of the Ugly American, who loathed the idea of an invasion of his privacy, actually chose to disrupt the very hiding place he had found for himself.

With a combination of thrift, respect for the ecology, and midwestern horse sense, he constructed his hotel almost entirely of indigenous materials, ferrying in many of them from neighbouring islands or from Tahiti itself with considerable difficulty by outboard motor launch across the tricky reefs. He used palm wood and leaves, and he began to plan windmills that could utilize the tradewinds for making grain. But of course, if he was to make the place work, he needed plumbing and other modern conveniences; he decided against air conditioning, though, as the constant breezes supplied at least some relief from the humidity.

A small community formed around him. The centre of his tiny world was his own thatch-roofed hut on a beach's edge surrounded by palm trees. It was basically just one large room with a double bed covered in mosquito netting, a cheap refrigerator, a gas cooking stove, and window shutters made of palm fronds. There was a flush toilet and a shower, but otherwise he held to his fondness for simplicity. His colony was tiny and self-contained. It was led by Harry Rittmeiser, a German who had spent World War II in prison in Papeete as Tahiti's sole POW. Tall, husky, and blond, Rittmeister was overseer, major-domo, chief lieutenant of the kingdom. Len Kell, a former California schoolteacher, and his French wife, Monique, were others who lived there, and gradually other island lovers moved in, surrounding Marlon with strength and affection. But he soon had to pay the price of his fame as others arrived who wanted to entrap him in discussions of his performances in *Streetcar*, *The Men*, or even *Desirée*.

Anna was ill that year, suffering from symptoms of what appeared to be epilepsy and alcoholism, as well as periods of extreme depression. Marlon suddenly became sympathetic to her. Apparently, he was concerned about her appalling physical condition. In one letter to her from Tahiti, he wrote that he would 'cut off my arm if it would help you'. He added that she must realize that when he didn't call it was not from forgetfulness so much as remembering when Christian called on the phone crying to say he didn't want to hear his son cry with the operators listening. But he concluded, 'I know that I am still an upsetting factor in your life, and I don't want to make it any worse or be in any way an irritation.' In spite of that, he continued to be a tease, and on one occasion he called Anna saying, 'I want to tell you something before you read it in the newspapers. I have terminal cancer. I'm going into the hospital for a biopsy.' Anna called Jay Kanter and the L'Amours for an explanation. Could it possibly be true? It wasn't, of course: he had just gone in for a checkup to see if he had an ulcer.

In January 1964, to finance the hotel project, Marlon agreed to make a new film, *Morituri*, for Darryl F. Zanuck. The script had been written by Daniel Taradash, author of the screenplay of *Desirée*. Based on a book by Werner Luedecke, former German naval attaché in Tokyo during World War II, it was the story of the voyage of a German freighter in 1942 from Tokyo to occupied France. Brando was to play the part of Robert Crain, a German living in India, who acts as a secret agent for the British on board, posing as an SS officer in order to ensure the British capture of the vessel, which carries a large cargo of valuable rubber. Much of the drama springs from the relationship between the taciturn Captain Mueller, who was to be played by Yul Brynner, and the double agent Crain.

Aaron Rosenberg, who had by now forgiven Marlon for the events of *Mutiny on the Bounty*, was producer. The director chosen was Bernhard Wicki, an imposing master craftsman whose film *The Bridge* had greatly impressed Marlon. Zanuck had little to do with the picture, since, according to Taradash, he had already lost his grip over the studio and his son Richard was more or less in charge. At first Darryl had interfered constantly with the script, reducing it to nonsense, but Richard had overridden him, and Taradash's revised draft appealed strongly to Marlon. He very much wanted to play the part of an anti-Nazi. He had trimmed down over the months on Teti'aroa and was ready for the camera.

One night, Daniel Taradash received a telephone call. A heavy Russian voice on the phone announced that the caller was the well-known character actor Akim Tamiroff. Taradash had never met Tamiroff but admired his work on the screen. He was delighted when Tamiroff said that he had just read the script and it was a masterpiece, a brilliant achievement in the art of writing. Suddenly, Taradash began to smell a rat. And no sooner had suspicions entered his mind than the voice at the other end of the line broke into uncontrolled laughter. It was Marlon.

Richard Zanuck decided to charter a vessel named *The Blue Dolphin*; it had been built in Scotland just before World War II and for years sailed under Chinese registry. The ship was currently laid up in very poor condition in Yokohama Harbor, Japan. Taradash, Wicki, and Rosenberg flew to Tokyo to make the arrangements for the transfer of the old tub to Catalina Island, where the film would be shot.

Taradash recalled the ordeal of the early script conferences on the movie at Marlon's house on Mulholland. They were no less unpleasant than the meetings with Zanuck at an earlier stage in New York. Taradash, Wicki, and Rosenberg would turn up at the house at nine A.M. as arranged: 'We would sit until eleven or later, when Marlon would stagger in wearing a robe and start playing with his huge St Bernard dog, using a basketball because of its size,' Taradash said. 'He hacked away at the script in a most infuriating manner, even cutting out one complete character, that of a young girl on board the ship.' This was torture for Taradash, who had won the Academy Award for *From*

Here to Eternity and was one of the most respected writers in Hollywood.

Script conferences continued at Twentieth Century-Fox. Marlon would 'turn up three hours and more late, announce that he had been drinking all night and had a hangover'. (Marlon must have been pulling Taradash's leg, because he still scarcely touched alcohol.) Taradash continued, 'Marlon would curl up in a large chair and we would at last start to go over the script, and either he wasn't paying attention at all, or if he did so he would suddenly say, "I think my character would do so and so and so and so." His idea of rewriting was how would Marlon Brando act in the situation.' Taradash reminded Marlon that just because he hadn't heard anybody talk like Robert Crain, that didn't mean that Taradash's interpretation of Crain's speech patterns would be incorrect. 'It was like having a script conference with a foetus,' Taradash said.

The days and nights of conferences dragged on unbearably. At last, shooting began in the choppy waters off Catalina, using the ship as a set. The cast had to scramble over greasy catwalks in the ship's engine room in temperatures over 100°F. In one scene, actress Janet Margolin had to get out of a rubber raft in a heavy swell. In another, actor Hans Blech was hung over the side of the ship at the end of a rope and fell into the water. Taradash took off to Egypt with his wife for an anniversary trip, and when he returned was informed of the quarrels that had taken place on the set at Twentieth Century-Fox. 'Bernhard told me that Marlon went totally to pieces at the studio,' Taradash said. 'At one stage, Marlon actually ordered Bernhard off the set. I had never heard of such a thing. It was monstrous.' Aaron Rosenberg charged that Marlon and his own circle of friends, including Wally Cox, who played the ship's morphine-addicted, crumbling doctor, would disappear into Marlon's trailer and spend the whole day rewriting the screenplay, emerging at sundown with pages that had to be shot into the night. As an example, Rosenberg showed Taradash one of the most important scenes in the picture, in which Marlon was in a cabin with Janet Margolin. Marlon crossed the cabin, opened the porthole, and returned to his place on the bunk for no apparent reason. 'Why did Marlon go over there, Aaron?' asked the scriptwriter. And Rosenberg replied, 'Because his goddamned lines were on the idiot board outside the porthole!'

Taradash says that Marlon had ruined a good scene for Miss Margolin, in which she told how the Nazis had forced her to make love to her own brother at gunpoint while they watched. 'I dreamed that scene up, and it could have shattered an audience, but Marlon slashed it to ribbons,' Taradash said. 'Brando was like a dog who gets a bone and runs with it, and you can't catch the dog.' But although the film ended up being a commercial failure and far from what Taradash or Aaron Rosenberg intended, it is fascinating to watch today. Wicki's direction and the glittering black-and-white photography of Conrad Hall have a virtuoso authority. Yul Brynner makes a real character of the ship's captain. Marlon is excellent too: playing in a flawless German accent, looking in first-class physical condition, he subtly suggests the tension and stress of acting out the role of a double agent. Marlon's old friend from *Arms and the Man*, William Redfield, and Wally Cox, vivid and convincing in his playing, make strong impressions in the supporting cast. But the subject was not of pressing public interest when the film was released in 1965, and the American public failed to identify with an almost entirely foreign set of characters. *Morituri* went down the drain.

Soon after the long-drawn-out ordeal of *Morituri* ended, Marlon had shocking news. His father, from whom he was still estranged, had developed a large, irregular black mole on the back of one hand. Somebody had pointed out that it might be dangerous, and the old man checked with a physician, who informed him that it was a melanoma, a deadly malignancy. It was too late to operate, and he was told that the cancer would spread and kill him in a matter of months. Walter Seltzer, probably his closest friend, recalls that he took the news bravely. His wife Anna proved to be a great support to him in his state of extreme psychological shock. Marlon Jr was devoted. He completely buried all of his hatred and acted, according to Walter Seltzer, 'exactly as a son should'. There was nothing now except to wait for the painful and protracted end. He felt no storm of grief as he had felt when he knew his mother would die; this time he felt empty and dispossessed.

He also faced the closure of Pennebaker. By now, it had become totally absorbed into the structure of Universal Studios and no longer existed as a separate entity. Its pathetically meagre assets were dispersed and its board of directors disbanded. Seltzer recalls a conversation he had with Marlon in the last stages of the company. Marlon was complaining to him about the desperate plight of millions of starving Indians, Ethiopians, and other Third World people. Walter finally had had enough of Marlon's bleeding heart. He turned to him and said, referring to himself and his partners, 'How about three starving Jewish executives?'

Meantime, Marlon succeeded in obtaining temporary custody of Christian for the unusual period of two months. In one of her rare calm moods, Anna didn't fight him over the arrangement. He wanted to take the boy to Tahiti, and she had to admit the trip would benefit the youth, who was not robust and vigorous. The fresh air, saltwater, and marvellous local produce, plus plenty of swimming and running along the beach, might put some flesh and sinew on him.

He took off to Teti'aroa in the fall of 1964. Aunt Betty Lindemeyer accompanied Marlon and his son. By now, the hotel on the atoll was in advanced stages of construction. Bernard Judge, a California architect of great ability, had worked doggedly month after month to create a structure that would effectively reflect its tropical environment. The central building had a pandanus roof structure without walls, supported only by upright posts. It was similar to buildings constructed in ancient times for Tahiti's successive monarchs. The central building of what was in effect a compound comprised of a large entertainment area, an airy dining room, and a well-equipped kitchen. The floor was made of cement. Storage buildings were scattered through the sprawling property, which covered several acres. The guest bungalows were octagonal and of pure Tahitian inspiration. Each bungalow had a bedroom raised four or five feet above ground level to escape flooding during storm activity and had walls and roofs made of coconut palm leaves. The main framework for each small structure was built with local kahaiha wood, with a floor of the same material, and finely crushed coral used for motifs in the bathroom and shower. These bungalows were in fact quite spartan, with only a water basin of seashells and a fairly primitive shower.

Marlon was in the process of building a new house a few hundred yards away on the edge of the atoll to escape the activity caused by tourists. His earlier rented homes in Tahiti had been quite elaborate. The first one, which he lived in during the shooting of *Mutiny on the Bounty*, was a sprawling colonial residence overlooking the sea in the Mahina district. His second home, in the Paea district, closer to the beach front, was a one-storey, three-bedroom house with bamboo walls. His latest home was not much more than a cabin, a native hut with the crudest and most unsophisticated of furnishings. It only contained a bed, chairs, shower, toilet, and bathroom. It was ideal for him. With his distaste for ostentation and the glittering life of movie stars, he could live there in true beachcomber's style.

Christian responded exactly as Marlon and Anna hoped he would. He grew bronzed, fit, and strong in this marvellous, still unspoiled environment. Marlon frequently took his son with him to the other islands he owned, partly to avoid staring tourists, and also to allay his underlying fear of kidnapping.

In that time, Marlon ordered further development on Teti'aroa. He began to lay plans for an airstrip, which was built between 1967 and 1968. This, along with the hotel, would ensure a source of revenue for Tarita and his children by her, when they should come along. She was already pregnant with the first child, Simon Teihotu. The atoll also provided a tax write-off since, for the first few years at least, Teti'aroa would represent a negative cash flow. He started arranging to rent tourists motorboats to reach Teti'aroa. New equipment to construct the hotel was brought over through the difficult reefs by an old US LST boat and dumped on the reef, at which point it was ferried to shore by small craft. Marlon would not allow construction of a temporary dock to receive this equipment or opening of a pass in the reef by blasting the coral with dynamite. Such solutions would have drastically affected the local ecology.

So Marlon became thoroughly immersed in the development of his island paradise and divided his time between Teti'aroa and Los Angeles. The final months of 1964 passed without incident – until another violent and traumatic episode occurred in December.

16

At two A.M. on December 7, 1964, the ring of a telephone awakened Marlon in his bedroom on Mulholland Drive. The Los Angeles Police Department was on the line, and the detective told Marlon, 'We are at Mrs Brando's house. Your son Christian called us because he couldn't waken his mother . . . Could you come here immediately, please?'

Marlon hung up, threw on a pair of jeans, and drove to Anna's house in Brentwood. Police there told him that Anna had been taken to the UCLA Medical Center because she had attempted suicide with an overdose of drugs. He was horrified to find empty liquor bottles strewn all over the house, and six-year-old Christian crying, hungry and terrified. Instead of going to the hospital, he took his son home to Mulholland. Christian screamed and twisted around on the bed, and Marlon was distressed to see him in this condition. Although he hated to leave his son, he had to shoot some additional scenes for *Morituri*, which had been withdrawn from its original preview showings for more work when initial audience reaction had been very unfavourable.

Marlon was at the studio at approximately one P.M., when Anna Kashfi, who had left the hospital unnoticed, arrived at Mulholland. She somehow succeeded in breaking through a wooden fence, then smashed a window and burst into the kitchen. She was armed with a loaded gun. She flung herself on Alice Marchak, who was taking care of Christian, hit her violently, and flung her headlong to the floor. Then she tossed a kitchen table through a plate-glass window and leapt through it, carrying Christian in her arms. The child was hysterical; this was kidnap. When a distraught Alice called Marlon at the studio, he drove back in anguish to find her story confirmed by the staff. Meanwhile, Anna fled to the Bel Air Sands Hotel, where, oddly enough, Tarita had been staying, and hid there with Christian. Detectives had located her whereabouts, and Marlon, who was armed with a special emergency court order to assume custody, charged the lobby accompanied by Sergeant Ed Hall of the LAPD, attorney Allen Susman, and two private detectives. A ferocious fight ensued with Anna. With her long black hair streaming over a pink nightgown and white bathrobe, Anna attacked hotel manager Sterling Peck, desk clerk Beverly Ross, and hotel detective James Briscoe. She was arrested on the spot.

Marlon and the police carried Christian down the corridor to escape her clutches as she fought with the police and broke loose for a moment, screaming after them. She managed to elude their grasp as she ran headlong through the lobby and hit a police sergeant across the face. At last, they caught up with her and threw her – handcuffed – into a paddy wagon that took her to the precinct. When she got to the West Los Angeles Police Station, she fought so violently with a policewoman and a male officer that she was covered in bruises before she could be transferred to the Van Nuys Women's Prison. But once in the car, she jumped out on to the kerb and refused to get back in until an officer thrust her into the seat. Then she refused to move over to allow room for the policewoman to sit down. 'You're going to have to make me move!' she screamed. Finally, she was forced to the centre of the seat, where she sat and glowered as the car took off for Van Nuys.

Marlon drove immediately to the superior court in Santa Monica, where he obtained temporary legal custody of his son on the ground that his wife was dangerous, carried a gun, and presented a threat to the child's safety. In turn, Anna petitioned to regain Christian. The trial date was set for February. Anna was permitted to leave the prison on bail. She charged that Marlon was living with Tarita out of wedlock and that it was an unsuitable household for her son.

In February 1965, the case was heard in Santa Monica Superior Court. It was the couple's fourteenth court appearance on the matter of custody. Under oath, Marlon testified that he had only married Anna because she was pregnant and he wanted to legitimize the baby. He described his former wife's consistent pattern of irrational behaviour. 'On one occasion she attempted to stab me; this occurred in front of the boy. On several other occasions, she threatened to kill me, the child, and herself.' Anna's doctor described her fits of depression and elation, her hysteria, and the fact that even a glass of beer could make her seem drunk. He told of her grand mal seizures and the drugs he gave her to help control them. A maid talked of Anna entertaining naked men in her bedroom. A psychologist testified that Christian had become 'a tense, fearful, terrorized youngster who is very hypersensitive and is unable to maintain attention or relate well to most adults . . .' Officials of Christian's Montessori school said that he was 'emotionally disturbed, totally incapable of facing reality, experiencing behaviour problems, and working far below his intellectual potential'. They testified that since Brando had taken custody of the child, he had greatly improved. It was ruled that young Christian

305

must temporarily go and stay with Frances and Dick Loving in Mundelein, Illinois, so he would not be exposed to such ordeals again. Anna was ordered on probation for psychiatric examination for six months.

Anna was furious with the ruling and responded by hurling herself from the courtroom, banging the swinging wooden doors, and announcing to the crowd of newspaper men, 'This baby is my whole life. I bore him. Where in hell was Marlon Brando when the child was being brought up? I am not through fighting. I will subpoena the judge and the whole goddamned court.' By contrast, Marlon acted with exemplary restraint, speaking in a soft voice and picking up a woman reporter's glove when she dropped it as he left the courthouse. Just as he was entering his car, an old woman ran up to him and hit him hard over the head with her umbrella. 'How could you take a child from its mother?' she screamed. Holding his head, he made his way into the autombile.

While Marlon took Christian to Illinois, Anna was enjoined from annoying, molesting, harassing, threatening, interfering with, or in any way causing embarrassment to Marlon. Meanwhile, a team of neurologists and psychologists were appointed to take Anna through a rehabilitation programme.

When Marlon visited Mundelein, Dick Loving recalled, 'He never talked about his career. Even if we asked him something, he would make a brief, dismissive comment. Instead, he talked about people and behaviour. He liked to discuss the natural phenomena of weather and season, the behaviour of animals, and tell stories about family animals, particularly Duchess.

'Christian stayed with us and Marlon visited often,' Loving went on. 'Christian was midway between Kitty and Zoe, our kids, in age. He went to the rural school with my kids. He didn't adjust too well.' Loving remembered that the boys at the school fought like 'little maniacs'. He said that Christian was 'a charming little devil of a kid. His main impulse in life was to win over the adults to his side. When you caught on to that, it encouraged him to try harder.' Loving observed that Marlon 'related to Christian as a patriarch. As the rest of the family did. He enjoyed the role.'

Exhausted by this new struggle with Anna, Marlon somehow summoned the energy to make a new movie, *The Chase*, based on the play and novel by Horton Foote. Neither had enjoyed great success, and now Lillian Hellman had adapted the story for the screen, combining elements in both the dramatization and the work of fiction. Despite Marlon's misgivings about the lacklustre commercial history of *The Chase*, he was talked into making the film by Sam Spiegel, to whom he had remained grateful since *On the Waterfront*. The director was the admirable Arthur Penn, and Jane Fonda, Robert Redford, and Angie Dickinson were among the cast.

The Chase was a somewhat rambling affair set in Texas; Marlon played a decent, liberal small-town sheriff who fights injustice and seeks to protect Robert Redford's Bubber Reeves, a prison escapee. And Marlon felt a personal involvement in the story of tension between white and black, rich and poor, the privileged and the underprivileged.

Shooting began in May at the Columbia sound stages and then moved over to the specially borrowed Warner Brothers backlot and the Columbia Ranch, where the Texas town had been carefully reconstructed. Once again, Marlon was surrounded by his favourites, Phil and Marie Rhodes, Sam Gilman, and Carlo Fiore. Jocelyn Brando, to his great delight, was added to the cast. He got along well with the slight, scholarly Arthur Penn, who tolerated his constant 'improving' of lines, despite their having been written by one of America's leading playwrights. 'We had a good interchange of ideas,' Penn said. 'Marlon told me at the outset that he would present his ideas, and that if I didn't like them I should tell him so. That's the way it was. Most of his notions were excellent.'

Arthur Penn, with his fiercely independent style and New York training, definitely was not cast from the Hollywood mould, and he appreciated Marlon's approach to acting and his constant rethinking of lines to add freshness to the performance. But Lillian Hellman was disgusted by the changes and disowned the film. Jane Fonda, still very young and far from the powerful figure she is today, found it difficult to adjust to Marlon's consuming personality: 'I felt sucked into it,' she said. For years afterwards, she kept party guests entertained as she imitated his careful and moody delivery, face sullen and blank, eyebrows moving, body stiff, as she dredged a new line from her toes up through her body until at last it erupted through her mouth in a well-nigh incomprehensible mumble. Marlon himself admitted that nobody imitated him better.

As always, Marlon had difficulty even with the lines he himself had written. In one speech, he had to refer to a man in jail named Lester Johnson, but he upset Penn by calling the character Bubber Johnson. Penn reminded him of the correct name. On the second take, Marlon got the Lester right and the surname wrong. He talked about 'Bubber Richards'. When the script clerk reminded Marlon that Bubber's name had been changed from Richards to Reeves in the script, and was a different character anyway, Marlon merely made a face. He was not in a mood to be apologetic.

But despite his seeming inability to remember the actual words of Lillian Hellman's script, Marlon was reaching out for the truth of the character, and at times his acting had a startling realism and power. For a sequence in which Sheriff Calder was beaten on his way to rescue Bubber Reeves from the lynch mob, Phil Rhodes and he worked out his make-up: face and shirt drenched in blood, bruises on cheeks and forehead. Cigar stuffed into Marlon's swollen and distorted face, he staggered out of the courthouse and fell down the steps, bringing a gasp from some of the extras. Angie Dickinson, who played his girlfriend, helped him strap his gun belt on. And again and again, the shot had to be redone, either because doors opened too far, revealing studio arc lamps, or the position of the camera was wrong. And Marlon repeatedly, knees buckling, fell down the steps on his behind. At the end, as the shot was finally completed, Marlon groaned, 'My butt's sore, you know that?' Director, fellow actors, crew and spectators all laughed as the tension was broken at last.

In scenes that took place later in the story, Marlon and Phil Rhodes worked out that the Sheriff's bloodstains would be dry now and brownish. They used chocolate syrup on the shirt to create the appropriate effect. The patience required to attain this attention to detail had not been Marlon's signature in recent years. Clearly, the combination of Hellman, Penn, Redford (who was just beginning to emerge as a major star), and Fonda brought out the best in him. Indeed, Redford has commented, 'It was fascinating working with Marlon. And he understood how much my part meant to me. I had been in prison when I was a kid. Marlon knew that.' Alas, *The Chase* was destined to be neither a critical nor commercial success.

In the meantime, as Marlon remained involved in work on that film, Anna went on trial for assault and battery; this was a follow-up to the previous case at Santa Monica Superior Court, at which Marlon had obtained temporary legal custody of Christian on the ground that his wife was dangerous. She was now being charged with assault against the policeman at the Bel Air Sands Hotel. Marlon tried to avoid being served papers as a material witness. He hated the thought of another harrowing legal hearing, and when police arrived at Mulholland early in the morning with the necessary papers, he sent his two St Bernards to chase them off the property. The officers sat at the gate, waiting for his return, as Alice Marchak brought them coffee and cakes.

Finally, they did manage to serve him at Columbia Studios. Under oath, he stated that Anna suffered from 'psychoneuroses, which at times caused hysterical blindness . . . barbiturate poisoning . . . occasional malnutrition . . . a psychological and physical addiction to barbiturates, alcohol, and,' he added oddly, 'tuberculosis'. Anna was convicted and fined two hundred dollars or thirty days in prison. She paid the fine.

The trial was over on July 13, 1965. Meanwhile, Christian was still staying with Frances and Dick Loving in Mundelein. Initially, they had found him nervous and uneasy, but half a year of the healthy life on the farm had been beneficial, and the simple family life was what he needed. Soon, Christian became a totally mischievous, outgoing, normal boy who easily played with the neighbourhood kids. According to Loving, Christian seemed altogether more self-confident, and the escape from the custody battle proved enlivening and revivifying for him. In a curious episode, later mentioned by Dick Loving, Christian, and others, the family took an effigy of Anna and significantly buried her in the soft soil of the farm – as though to expunge her memory.

In a startling reversal, Judge A. C. Scott returned full custody of Christian to Anna, with Marlon retaining secondary rights. However, the couple was forbidden to annoy, molest, or harass each other. Scott felt strongly that a child should not be without his mother. When the decision was made, Anna picked up Christian and ran from the courtroom, terrified Judge Scott might change his mind.

This was a grievous blow to Marlon, and he anguished over it. Very depressed, he embarked without much enthusiasm on preparations for a new film project – a Western called *The Appaloosa*, to be directed by the Canadian Sidney J. Furie. Marlon was cast as an old saddle tramp, a buffalo hunter by trade, named Matt Fletcher, whose Indian wife is murdered. The action centres on his pursuit of a Mexican bandit. The screenplay was more or less conventional material, which the director worked hard to overcome with fancy camera angles and lighting. Locations were in Utah, where Furie experimented with extremely realistic effects, aided by the inventive and crusty old cameraman Russell Metty, who had worked with Orson Welles. Furie and Marlon had a very uncomfortable working relationship that was not helped by Marlon's lack of enthusiasm for the material. Furie, known as an enfant terrible at the age of thirty-two, was extremely feisty, and the pair of them fought over scenes in arguments that went on into the night. At one point, Marlon refused to shoot a scene at all. Later, Furie threatened to leave for England and not come back.

'Making a picture is like waging war,' Furie said. 'This was no exception. I expect trouble. I'm ready for it. It's part of the creative process.' He added, 'I knew Brando would be tough to direct. Our first meetings were disastrous. In the first session, Marlon asked me, "What makes you think you know what actors are all about?" I told him he didn't want to work for anyone except Elia Kazan, and since he couldn't get Kazan he'd have to have me.'

Marlon had wanted to do the picture in Mexican make-up. 'He looked like Genghis Khan when he did that, and I refused to allow it,' Furie said. 'I won the battle finally.' At the end of shooting, Furie did have a grudging respect for Marlon. The director had, in the end, grown somewhat accustomed to arguing with his leading actor over dialogue – even when the sun was about to go down, and the whole scene would be lost one minute later. Furie said, 'It got you down sometimes, but he was gutsy. A tremendously creative guy.'

Just before *The Appaloosa* began shooting, Marlon had flown to London briefly to discuss making a film, *A Countess from Hong Kong*, with his childhood idol Charlie Chaplin as director. The script was not very satisfactory, but Marlon could not resist making a movie with one of the few artistic geniuses of the screen. Apart from the uncomfortable Norman Mailer party at which he had met Chaplin briefly before fleeing with Shelley Winters into the night, he had not encountered Chaplin before. But he retained a deep admiration for Chaplin's liberalism, as expressed in such devastating attacks on modern industry and fascist regimes as *Modern Times* and *The Great Dictator*.

A Countess from Hong Kong had originally been written by Chaplin in the 1930s as a comic vehicle for his then-wife, Paulette Goddard, but had never been filmed. Marlon would play Odgen Mears, a millionaire diplomat sailing from Hong Kong to San Francisco on board a luxury liner. Mears meets a penniless Russian emigrée, the Countess Natasha, who has been working since her teens as a dance hostess. She stows away in Mears's cabin; he threatens to expose her, but she announces she will accuse him of kidnap if he does so. Most of the action concerns his continuing and farcical efforts to hide her from the crew of the vessel.

Shooting began at the Pinewood Studios outside London on January 25, 1966. It was preceded by script meetings. Exhausted from jet lag, Marlon fell asleep in the middle of the first discussion. Chaplin laughed and forgave him; the relationship between the two men was warm. However, Chaplin made clear that he was aware of Marlon's constantly changed and improvised lines, and the seventy-six-year-old director stated that he wouldn't tolerate such interference with his writing. Marlon wasn't pleased with this announcement but, in view of his respect for Chaplin, reluctantly accepted the conditions.

Work progressed slowly, first because Chaplin's methods belonged to an earlier era, and second because he was not in good health and came down with influenza following some exceptionally long shooting schedules that dragged far into the night and wore down his strength. Chaplin proved susceptible to the virus that was sweeping London at the time. When he came back on the set, he was irritable, pale, and tired. Marlon was quickly disillusioned about Chaplin's directorial abilities, realizing that the great man was far past his peak. He was especially annoyed by Chaplin's habit of acting every scene out for him as though Marlon had never been in a picture before. Nor did he admire his co-star, Sophia Loren. He felt she belonged to the school of actresses that were mere movie queens, coasting along on their physical beauty and charm, and he didn't believe she had the correct timing or understanding of English to effectively handle a comedy of this kind. Sulking, Marlon turned down an invitation to attend the royal command film performance in mid-January, where he was to meet Queen Elizabeth II. When Sophia Loren also turned down the invitation, the press began to rumble. This was considered a direct insult to the palace.

Marlon never adjusted to Chaplin's old-fashioned style of direction, with such instructions as, 'Don't denote anything in your face. Keep your voice up.' It had nothing to do with Marlon's preferred method of inventing his own performance as he went along. So, Marlon listened and absorbed Chaplin's direction carefully but then interpreted the lines in his own manner. Marlon acknowledged that Chaplin could teach him something about playing comedy and sometimes allowed the director to control his delivery. But more often than not, his own instincts would take over and he would pace the scene as he thought best. Within weeks, Marlon was simply walking through his part, responding to Chaplin's instructions with indifference.

The atmosphere on the set was far different from Hollywood. The crew addressed Chaplin as 'sir,' and Marlon's usual gags and fooling around were strictly forbidden.

As shooting continued, Marlon increasingly resented the way Chaplin treated him as though he were an inexperienced beginner. The director would choreograph a cabin scene down to minute details, moving extras on and off the set. Then he would seek to improvise 'business' – the technical executions of farcical gestures – for Brando, show him how to belch when he drank a glass of Alka-Seltzer or how to move Sophia Loren into a closet with a smooth, balletic movement.

Sophia Loren tried to overcompensate for the feebleness of her lines by mugging, a technique that Chaplin encouraged. In contrast, Marlon tried to compensate by underplaying, smoothly and coolly coasting through scenes. This wasn't what Chaplin wanted at all. And after two months, just about everyone connected with the film, except the director himself, realized it was going to be a disaster.

On April 19, Marlon became ill. The stress of trying to please Chaplin and himself and the constant irritation of the day-and-night shooting caused him to have a contracting colon. The pain became so severe he had to check into University College Hospital in London for tests. He struggled out of his sickbed to complete some pick-up scenes for *The Appaloosa*, shot by Sidney Furie at Elstree Studios in Middlesex, and then, feeling terrible, went on to Pinewood to finish work on *A Countess from Hong Kong*.

This was probably Marlon's nadir. Added to his ordeal was the insufferable way Chaplin treated his son Sydney, who played a small part in the picture. Marlon hated Chaplin's cruelty towards Sydney; he was reminded of his own father. Handsome, powerfully built, Sydney had all of the qualities of a motion picture star. But he couldn't possibly compete with his famous father. The conflict between them was painful. Brando said, 'He was a mean man, Chaplin. Sadistic. I saw him torture his son, humiliating him, insulting him.' The ghastly ordeal went on and on.

Marlon missed Christian painfully. He told friends he wanted to return to Los Angeles to see him as soon as possible. Once the picture was ended, he flew to California to spend time with his son and then

315

proceeded alone to Tahiti to see Tarita and his newborn son – their first child – Simon Teihotu. After a long stay there, he travelled in June with Sammy Davis, Jr and Burt Lancaster to Mississippi to help the civil rights marchers there. The three men appeared at public meetings and joined with the demonstrators in their long walks from one town to another. It was a peaceful protest that passed without dramatic incident.

At the time, Marlon was also in discussions by telephone, and later in person, with producer Ray Stark to make a film called *Reflections in a Golden Eye*, based on the novel by Carson McCullers, which had been in the works as a potential movie for many years. Elizabeth Taylor, cast for the leading female role, had wanted to make the movie since the early 1960s when she first discussed it with Stark in Mexico on the set of *Night of the Iguana*. She was drawn to the plot of an army wife in the Deep South, whose husband, suffering from sexual impotence, is a closet homosexual obsessed with a soldier who indulges the eccentric habit of riding nude on horseback through the surrounding countryside. When Taylor first talked about the part with Stark in Puerto Vallarta, Mexico, she felt very strongly that her close friend Montgomery Clift should play the part of Major Weldon Penderton opposite her. Richard Burton was mentioned as possible director, and also for the part of Mrs Penderton's lover. However, Clift was opposed to Burton and didn't want to work with him. Burton ultimately backed out, and Miss Taylor decided to approach John Huston to take over the job of directing. Clift, who had mixed feelings about Huston based on the experience of making *The Misfits* and *Freud* with him, accepted this arrangement.

The production was delayed again and again. Mont-

gomery Clift's mental and physical health had deteriorated, and in mid-1965 he was in even worse shape.
After making a wretched film entitled *The Defector*, he
sank into suicidal depressions that led him into heavy
doses of Demerol. Then on July 22, 1966, a friend
found him dead on his bed. A grief-stricken Elizabeth
Taylor was determined to proceed with the film.

Six previous scripts, including those written by Francis Ford Coppola and Christopher Isherwood, were
abandoned. John Huston settled on the British novelist
Chapman Mortimer to undertake the adaptation.
Huston himself worked on the screenplay with his
long-term assistant Gladys Hill, while Carson
McCullers, who suffered from very poor health, gave
her blessing to the project.

Now came the crucial question of casting Major
Penderton. At first, Marlon turned down the script
because he was uneasy about playing a latent homosexual. Rumours of his own leanings in that direction had
already circulated without his playing such a controversial part. When Huston and Stark approached Jack
Warner to advance them the million dollars necessary
to secure Brando – assuming they could overcome
Marlon's reluctance – Warner turned them down. Producer and director talked to one star after another, but
all, including William Holden and Robert Mitchum,
rejected the role, either because of the homosexual
stigma or conflicting schedules.

Finally, Jay Kanter called Stark to express Marlon's
change of heart about the picture. He had seen *Who's
Afraid of Virginia Woolf?* and very much admired
Elizabeth Taylor's performance in the film. And now
that he had read Chapman Mortimer's first-draft screenplay of *Reflections*, he was intrigued by the project.
Marlon remained tied to Universal under a multi-
picture contract, but Stark managed to convince

317

Universal Studio chief Lew Wasserman to 'loan' Marlon out for this film. Then, without major studio backing, the producer secured Marlon for $750,000, plus $150,000 in bonuses and 7½ per cent of the gross profits. Such an arrangement was virtually unprecedented in Hollywood, since even the biggest stars seldom retained more than a percentage of the net profits, which seldom amounted to anything once all the studio's costs were covered. Elizabeth Taylor would receive $1 million plus additional sums; she was adamant that the film be made in Italy because her husband Richard Burton was scheduled to be there at the same time, shooting another movie, and she would not be separated from him. Also, by making the film in that country, she would avoid paying some US taxes because special arrangements were available for American citizens who lived abroad for a minimum number of months. The picture, of course, was totally unsuitable for an Italian location, since it was a quintessentially American subject. So Ray Stark was faced with the nightmare logistics of beginning a film in Long Island at the end of September, to make sure the leaves were still green, and of finishing in Rome not later than the middle of October, somehow matching these totally disparate sceneries. 'I wonder if Gucci makes straitjackets?' Ray Stark wrote to Elizabeth Taylor on October 11, 1966.

In the midst of all these negotiations, Marlon began to waver a little. Huston worried that his star might back out and invited Marlon to visit with him at his home, St Clerans, a romantic mansion in Ireland. Once there, Marlon read the revised draft of the screenplay and took off into a gothic thunderstorm for a long walk, brooding over the part and whether he dared play it. He returned with his mind made up. Marlon decided to take the gamble of playing the kind of figure the American public would find repellent. It was perhaps his bravest decision as a performer.

Before *Reflections* began shooting, Marlon flew to India. The Bihar famine, then making headlines all over the world, had wiped out millions of Indians in that state, and Marlon was haunted by the horror of the crisis. He wanted to see the conditions at first hand, and he took with him an 8mm movie camera in hope of shooting footage that could be used by UNICEF for fund-raising purposes. The sheer weight of the poverty and suffering was unbearable; while walking through a field in one drought-ridden province, he picked up a starving child who looked at him with huge, tortured eyes and then died. He told UNICEF's Jacques Danois in a filmed interview, 'I have seen ugliness beyond describing. Despair and horror ... [I saw] children covered with sores from head to foot [who] can't open their eyes and their hair is falling out ... It was [for me] a baptism of fire.'

He told Danois, 'It is time to realize that if we don't care for all peoples irrespective of their colour and political disposition, [to make sure that they] are a community of people, then there is a very good expectation that we simply won't survive as a species.' Marlon plunged into fund-raising functions, and made personal donations to the UNICEF famine-relief programme.

Back in New York, before *Reflections* began, he worked with UNICEF officials in the film division to edit his 8mm documentary, but the quality was understandably very poor, and it proved impossible to blow it up to 16mm or 35mm for public showing. Pieces of it were later used in UNESCO-inspired TV programmes.

It was difficult for Marlon to return to commercial film-making after this shattering experience. But he was determined to keep his promise to Ray Stark and director John Huston and make *Reflections in a Golden Eye*. The shooting began on Long Island at the Nassau Community College, known during World War II as Mitchell Field. In the barracks, hangars, commissary, and administration buildings, the harrowing action was played out. Other scenes took place at the Long Island Freight Yards in Garden City, the Pine Lawn Virginia Railway Station, and the Garden City Hotel. Two white Lippizaner stallions were borrowed from the famous Vienna riding school for scenes that involved extensive riding. Marlon was given a tame young mare, and according to Huston, 'Marlon was terrified of the horse.' This is inexplicable, because he had ridden extensively in *One-Eyed Jacks*, and as a country boy had been raised among horses and was in the saddle at the age of eight. Such fear of horses was, however, consistent with the character of Major Penderton, who was fragile and feminine inside his powerful bulk. He did have a problem with a Lippizaner when the location was shifted to Italy. In a scene in which he had to ride the horse headlong through woods, catching a glimpse of a nude soldier in the clearing, he suddenly felt his mount get out of control. It galloped so fiercely in response to his whip that it very nearly threw him.

While Marlon was making *Reflections in a Golden Eye*, Tarita turned up in Rome with one-year-old Simon Teihotu. She was pregnant with their second child. Two paparazzi hid outside Marlon's home on the island of Tiberia (Rome's island across from the ghetto on the River Tiber) for hours, hoping to trap him with his girlfriend and his child. At last, the front door opened and Marlon showed a guest out. He was carrying his baby in his arms.

The paparazzi photographed him. Marlon set the child down and charged across the street at the two men. He hit one of them with a right uppercut and jumped on the other one, pummelling him violently until the man broke free. He then took a champagne bottle and chased the photographers down the street. Furious, he called the American ambassador and other officials in the middle of the night, demanding that he be given protection from further incidents of this kind.

The forty-two-year-old Marlon gave his best performance in years in *Reflections*. Happy to have Tarita at his side, he reported promptly to the set every day and concentrated on holding his own with the admirable surrounding cast. The cameraman Aldo Tonti said, 'He impressed us all with his quiet professionalism and discipline. He was first on the set; punctual and sober. No fuss. When Liz Taylor appeared she was late and followed by a trail of assistants, fans, the more the better. Brando was serious and couldn't stand fawners and camp followers and fans.' Although Marlon claimed that he did the film strictly for money, nothing could have been further from the truth. The imposing and strenuous Huston fascinated Marlon. The great director seemed to be inexhaustible, working endless hours with Tonti to ensure a look that reflected the title: a rich, burnished glow.

But however vivid and striking the movie was, Carson McCullers's tortured vision and the themes of impotence, homosexuality, nudism, and psychological torment were far from what the American public wanted to see. And Marlon's fans were put off by his assumed effeminacy. The picture never took off, and the critics were blind to its merits.

Marlon was embittered by this result. He had worked hard, for a change, and to little avail. Moreover, Marlon had still further domestic troubles. Years after their divorce, Movita stated she had another child by him. Now she was seeking support from him, not only for their boy Miko, but for this new baby, whose name was Rebecca. Movita wanted five thousand dollars per month for herself, and three thousand dollars per month for the two children. She took action so that Marlon couldn't sell their mutual property. Judge Edward Brand presided over the case. Marlon and his lawyers Allen Susman and Norman Garey (the latter was also the legal representative for Marlon's agent MCA and would soon become in effect his full-time agent and business manager), researched Movita's background carefully. They alleged that she had been married to her previous husband at the time she wed Marlon. They managed to reduce the alimony and child support considerably. Four years later, Marlon charged she was living with another man and tried to terminate the alimony payments. He did not succeed.

In the wake of *Reflections in a Golden Eye*, Marlon felt a strong desire to continue filming in Europe. Not only did the on-location productions give him a tax write-off, but as usual he preferred to work outside the United States. On a brief visit to Paris, Marlon's old friend Christian Marquand asked him if he would appear in *Candy*, a film based on the novel by Terry Southern and Mason Hoffenberg that was a parody of Voltaire's *Candide*. This would be Marquand's second film as director. Marlon only played a small part in the film, as Grindl, an Indian guru, involved in teaching the innocent Candy the seven stages of sexual mysticism. With long, streaming hair, a caste mark on his forehead, and dressed in a skimpy cotton garment,

Marlon still looked surprisingly muscular, his flabby waistline disguised by the camera angles. Giuseppe Rotunno, who photographed *Candy*, was fascinated to be working with Marlon. 'I knew from seeing him in *The Men* how completely he understood the camera and what it could do. There was a scene when you saw him from the back as he wheeled himself down a long corridor. He hung his head slightly to one side. The gesture and the way he sat were extraordinary.'

In shooting *Candy*, Rotunno noticed that 'he had an extraordinary mask or face, which he managed to direct and command with masterly concentration. When the time came for shooting, he would take his time in order to isolate himself into concentration and sink into the character. He would resurface *as* the character. He had one peculiar trait that singled him out. His pauses and silences were as powerful as his speech. He didn't use the requirements of the script but 'lived' the pauses to create suspense. If he had to walk up to a house and ring the bell, he wouldn't do so automatically but would have a series of expressions, hesitations, gestures, which would express every thought going through his mind in a given situation.' *Candy*, Rotunno continued, was 'a cheerful film'. He added, 'Everyone was in a good mood. Brando got on with everyone and fit into the general cheerful atmosphere. We would all eat together as we shot in Rome – we took over the whole of the Dear Studios.' As it turned out, *Candy* was a critical and commercial flop.

On a visit to Hollywood soon afterwards, Marlon was approached by the producer Elliot Kastner to appear in *The Night of the Following Day*, based on *The Snatchers* by Lionel White, a kidnap novel with resemblances to the Lindbergh case of the 1930s. Stanley Kubrick had originally owned the film rights, but the Breen Office imposed a ban on kidnap stories in the belief that such plots provided inspiration for criminals. Kubrick eventually released the rights, and it was optioned by the director Hubert Cornfield, who had made *Pressure Point* and *The Third Voice*.

Cornfield wrote a script with Robert Phippeny, but again it proved impossible to get the project cleared by the censors. Finally Cornfield decided the only way it could be made was to present it as the sustained nightmare of a young girl who imagines she is kidnapped by crooks. This approach would give the story a strong sexual undertone, suggesting that perhaps she wanted to be a victim.

Originally, Yves Montand was slated for the lead role, but other commitments prevented him from going ahead, and Richard Boone was to take over. However, when Kastner talked to Jay Kanter, who had turned producer, the two men agreed that a deal could be made for Marlon, with Kanter as part of the package, and the picture to be released through Universal under Marlon's long-term contract. Boone, surprisingly, accepted a subsidiary role in the film.

Inexplicably, after some very generous film deals in recent years, Marlon was now in need of money. According to Cornfield, Marlon was forced to accept half salary, and took a somewhat malicious pleasure in telling people he was only doing the film for cash. Cornfield first met him in London, at the Hilton Hotel. 'He was very nice, very polite,' Cornfield says. 'As I left, after the meeting of all parties concerned, and he helped me on with my coat, he said, "Let's make a little money together." Not, let's make a good film. This surprised me.' Cornfield, an embattled and underrated artist of the screen, had expected Marlon to be equally dedicated to making fine motion pictures.

Marlon used the occasion to get a job for Rita Moreno. Despite the tormenting years of their affair and her attempted suicide on his living-room floor, he retained a loyal affection for her. She was married now with a small child, and she needed the work since her career after *West Side Story*, in which she had made a sensation and won an Oscar, had not flourished. He persuaded Elliot Kastner to let her replace a French actress, Nicole Courcel.

The cameraman Willy Kurant was withdrawn from Orson Welles's film *The Deep* to shoot the picture which went on location to Le Touquet, a French seaside resort on the English Channel swept by icy winds and driving rain. The Bristol Hotel there was, according to Alice Marchak, who turned up for most of the shooting, draughty, damp and depressing. The dismal days on the dunes, in a house with a sinister atmosphere in the dripping forests of Normandy, weighed on Marlon's spirits.

As in his other works, Cornfield gave no names to the characters. 'People have no names in dreams,' he said. 'But Marlon insisted he have a name.' So, as in *The Man*, he was oddly called his own nickname, Bud, in the picture.

There was no rapport between Marlon and Cornfield. 'It wasn't fun directing him,' Cornfield said. 'Working with Marlon *sucked.* Direction is a collaborative effort. Marlon gave me no collaboration. He would ignore me. We would argue again and again.'

At times, Marlon tried to give realism to the scenes, actually turning up drunk for one sequence. As usual almost a teetotaller, and on a diet now that gave him a lean, trim appearance, he had consumed a whole bottle of whisky for an episode in which Rita Moreno was lying in a bathtub drugged. In another episode, he struck her so violently that he shocked her into tears; Kurant has suggested that Marlon overdid the blow to her face 'out of revenge. He had never forgotten his affair with Rita.' Cornfield denied this, contending that Marlon merely followed the script.

At times, Marlon was so obviously bored he would just turn to Cornfield and say, 'Hey, what do you want me to do?' According to Kurant, Marlon even forgot Cornfield's name at times, so uninterested was he in the director. Finally, relations between them broke down completely. When they got to Paris, there was a scene in which a police car follows the kidnappers. 'Marlon had the idea that his character would hail the cops' car, as though it were a taxi. I hated this idea. I said, "Marlon Brando might do that, but Bud wouldn't."' So tremendous was the quarrel that followed that Marlon went to Elliot Kastner and announced he would no longer have Cornfield direct him. Instead, Richard Boone was chosen to take over. The result was an embarrassing and ill-directed sequence completely out of accord with the rest of an intriguing, cleverly directed picture. By now, Cornfield was dejected, and his visions of making an artistic movie had evaporated in the weeks of difficult work with his recalcitrant and dissatisfied star.

This was a low point in Marlon's career; he had made one failed movie after another and Night of the Following Day was no exception. Although he continued to act with all of his old power and magnetism, although he could command in the range of $1 million per picture, he seemed to have lost his magic for appealing to the mass public. His days of renewed glory were just around the corner; meanwhile, he was totally indifferent to the critical and commercial failure of his films. Now, he was primarily concerned with his children, Tarita, his Tahitian developments, and his obsessive concern with Third World problems. Making movies was still just a means to an end, a way of securing the future for his family and helping the underprivileged.

17

Marlon had become deeply concerned with the affairs of the Black Panthers, whose militant activities constantly made headlines in the 1960s. At this time of the most extreme polarization in American society, Marlon's sympathies, as always, lay not with the establishment, but with those who represented the forces of revolt in the country. He was horrified to learn of the death of Bobby Hutton, a seventeen-year-old Black Panther, shot by police in Oakland during a gun battle in which another Panther and two police officers were also wounded. Bobby Seale, chairman of the local Panthers, told the press that Hutton had been mown down in cold blood. Once the police had unsealed the scene of the incident, Marlon joined a group of citizens to inspect the house where Hutton died. Then he appeared at a rally of nearly two thousand mourners held within earshot of the County Courthouse Jail where Huey Newton was being held on charges of murdering a policeman. Marlon addressed the throng through a public address system set up on a flatbed truck, saying, 'That could have been my son lying there. The preacher said that the white man can't cool it because he has never dug it. I am trying to dig it. That is why I am here.' He added, 'You've been listening four hundred years to white people and they haven't done a thing . . . I'm going to begin right now informing white people what they don't know.'

A few days later, he announced that he would join forces with Mrs Martin Luther King to 'carry the banner for the cause' of her recently assassinated husband. He went on to refer to the series of political assassinations that were occurring at the time, openly blaming the government, which he also charged with eliminating free speech by repressive action. Simultaneously, he declared that he would not, as previously announced, be appearing in the leading role of *The Arrangement*, Elia Kazan's screen version of his own novel. He explained that he was too distracted with the country's racial crisis to devote himself to the part, which would be taken by Kirk Douglas instead. In late April, he appeared on *The Tonight Show* with Johnny Carson to announce that Martin Luther King's murder had jolted him into 'trying to rectify the situation we are in. Nothing is really going to change unless I do it, unless the trombone player, the guy watching TV with a can of beer all do it.' He revealed that he, Barbra Streisand, Paul Newman, and columnist Drew Pearson were pledging 1 per cent of their earnings from now on to the late Dr King's Southern Christian Leadership Conference. Carson told Marlon he would do the same.

On May 10, 1968, Marlon publicly pledged his support for the Poor People's Campaign March of seventeen hundred persons on Washington. At the same time, he was in Albuquerque, New Mexico, along with Joan Baez, appearing at a public rally for marchers' funds, and he stated that he would dedicate the rest of his life to the civil rights movement. He increased his financial commitment from one to twelve per cent of his income.

At the time he told the United Press that his new policy was only to make movies that were of 'appropriate significance'. So when the Italian director Gillo Pontecorvo began planning to make *Queimada*, later

329

retitled *Burn!*, a film about a seventeenth-century revolution in the Caribbean, the project seemed natural for Marlon. It was the story of Sir William Walker, a British government agent who arrives on the fictitious island of Queimada to bring about a revolution that will replace the Portuguese colonial despotism with a no less reprehensible British equivalent. Pontecorvo said, 'I wanted Brando for the part of Sir William. I was convinced he was the greatest actor the cinema ever had. And this conviction was strengthened now. His capacity of expression added to his facial mobility and somatic features were unique . . . He was the only actor in the world who was capable of laughing with one eye and weeping with the other.'

However, Pontecorvo had a severe struggle to secure Marlon for the role of Walker. He went to United Artists for backing, but they were extremely reluctant. Following the series of box-office flops that included *Reflections in a Golden Eye* and *The Night of the Following Day*, Marlon was no longer considered bankable. While the director's struggle with UA continued, he met with Marlon at Mulholland. Marlon had seen and admired Pontecorvo's brilliant left-wing, anti-French *The Battle of Algiers*. Pontecorvo's script wasn't ready, but he told Marlon the story, and before he was even finished, Marlon agreed to take the part of Sir William. 'Our political ideas were in the same sphere,' Pontecorvo said. 'While I am an independent Italian left-wing thinker, he is an American independent left-winger. We both liked the idea of an ideological adventure film. He completely agreed with the ideas behind it. He was concerned with the idea of film as a medium serving a political purpose.' United Artists was eventually convinced to gamble on Marlon, and Alberto Grimaldi became the producer of the picture. Marlon was offered and accepted $750,000 as his fee.

Sir William Walker, with his constant scheming, his steady disintegration into corruption, alcoholism, and breakdown, was a part Marlon could certainly get his teeth into. He approved the decision to shoot the picture on location in the mountains and jungles of Colombia, South America, using local facilities in Cartagena. He was aware that making *Queimada* that summer would be difficult given the heat and rugged terrain, but those conditions did not lessen his commitment to his impassioned director.

On his way to Cartagena from Miami, he boarded National Airlines Flight 64. He had grown a long beard, shoulder-length hair, and a pigtail. As he got on to the plane, he said, jokingly, to a stewardess, 'Is this the flight to Havana?' Suspecting that he might be a hijacker, the stewardess immediately reported to the captain. Neither recognized Marlon, and as a result, the captain insisted he leave the plane at once. He was furious, but the plane took off at 12:15 A.M. without him.

Twenty-four hours earlier, another National Airlines flight had been hijacked and flown to Cuba with thirty-five people aboard.

Extremely angry, Marlon managed to find a flight to Jamaica, where he boarded another plane for Colombia. At first, as the shooting began in torrid conditions near Cartagena, on mountain roads that crumbled into chasms, the relationship between director and star was good. But the language barrier soon became a problem. Marlon spoke very little Italian, despite his sojourn there during *Reflections in a Golden Eye*, and Pontecorvo was not fluent in English, and was baffled by American terminology. The two men unsuccessfully tried to converse in French before they finally gave up and resorted to an interpreter. Pontecorvo said, 'We ended up missing out on essential nuances and created misunderstandings which in the long run contributed to the creation of great tensions and the deterioration of our relationship.' In those early weeks, Marlon, according to the director, 'showed real professionalism and cooperation, despite all the difficulties of working under the torrid conditions of subtropical Colombia amid the noise and confusion of an Italian production and with non-professionals as actors and extras'. The second lead was played by an illiterate Colombian black named Evaristo Marquez. A magnificent physical specimen, Marquez had been discovered by the director when he saw Marquez, stripped to the waist, riding a galloping horse through a rain forest. Pontecorvo decided then and there to hire this man for the part of the powerful dock worker José Delores, who becomes a revolutionary under Sir William Walker's influence.

At first, Marlon not only accepted this untrained actor but also helped him a lot in his performance. 'Marquez,' Pontecorvo said, 'had to speak in sounds which could produce lip movements similar to English, but since he didn't even have an idea of what dialogue was, Marlon would put his hand on Evaristo's shoulder or knee in order to give him the cues for his lines. He went even further: he stood behind the camera and mimicked the facial expressions for Evaristo to imitate.'

The misunderstandings between Marlon and Pontecorvo inevitably increased, and the situation affected Marlon's attitude towards Marquez. Pontecorvo said, 'He became impatient and demanded I substitute someone for Evaristo. I told him he would have a week's trial. In which I would shoot with him alone, without Marquez.' Meanwhile, Pontecorvo's wife and an assistant coached the untried actor off-set, and the director decided that after a week, they would decide whether to keep him or take on another actor. Finally, they decided to keep Marquez. And, Pontecorvo said, 'Marlon went into a rage and kept insisting that both of us would have to pay for the consequences. He didn't forgive me, and started seeing me as a monster.'

Pontecorvo admits that he and Marlon were badly matched. As a maniacal perfectionist, the director says he was difficult to put up with. This put off the hypersensitive Brando. Their hatred for each other reached what Pontecorvo calls a 'terrible crescendo'. Due to Marlon's sensitivity and moody nature, what started off as mere discomfort gradually developed into loathing. 'Marlon saw me as his antagonist in whom he accumulated the attribution of all the negative aspects and criticisms he felt about the situation,' Pontecorvo said. 'Anything that disagreed with him in the film was all my fault.'

Their conflict reached a tremendous climax when Pontecorvo required Marlon to do forty-one takes of a scene near burning fields. Driven beyond exasperation, Marlon 'exploded in raging cries. It looked as if the film would be stopped for good.' At this stage, it was clear that the two men had a totally opposite view of a film's purpose. For Pontecorvo, it was the mirror of a single person. The actors must simply serve an artistic vision. Marlon, of course, simply could not tolerate such an approach, which negated his own creative contribution.

And as if this ideological conflict were not enough, there was the sheer physical torture of making the film. Marlon was fat again and out of condition, and despite his familiarity with heat and humidity he found the suffocating conditions of Colombia unendurable. The cameraman Marcello Gatti said, 'Although Brando had an air-conditioned villa to live in in Cartagena and an air-conditioned trailer on location, he suffered badly. The humidity was at least ninety to ninety-five per cent. We had to travel a hundred kilometres a day, to and from the shooting location in the mountains, on terrible dirt roads. We were given a pack of grains of salt to put into water, which we drank in quantities of ten litres per day.' Gatti added that a truckful of water was driven out to the set; there was disinfectant in everything, in the ice for the whisky as well as in the bathtubs.

'Marlon's fair, delicate complexion broke out into a terrible rash,' Gatti said. 'The make-up man had to intervene all the time to cover it up. You could tell the poor guy was sick, and as time went by more and more he needed to get away.' Marlon took long breaks and flew to Los Angeles. The film was delayed month after month. Finally, Gatti said, the situation became so desperate that when Marlon went to the airport, 'The entire crew, all of us, assistant directors, make-up people, costume designer, electricians, fifty in all rushed to the airport to stop him. He agreed to come back, and we all went to the Hilton, where he offered us champagne and we danced together.'

Then Marlon charged the director with paying the black extras less money than he paid the whites and supplying them with inferior food. He discovered that a wardrobe woman's son was feverish and had vomited a hookworm after lunch. She told Marlon that Pontecorvo wanted to finish the shot before the child was treated. Marlon screamed at a chauffeur, 'Take the kid to the fucking hospital right now!' As the car drove off, Marlon told a reporter later, 'If Pontecorvo had been taller, I would have fucking fought with him. I really would have punched the guy out.' From that day on,

Pontecorvo carried a gun. 'He laughed, but actually he did have a gun on his belt,' Marlon said. Pontecorvo revealed a superstitious streak that further irritated Marlon: the director carried lucky charms in his pocket, refused to discuss the picture on Thursdays, ordered everybody wearing purple off his set, and wouldn't allow red wine to be served at lunch.

Pontecorvo denies that he mishandled the extras. He said that, according to Italian rules, there were three categories of such players, and they were always paid three different salaries. Naturally, he added, the lowest-paid category was for the blacks in the crowd scenes. Pontecorvo insists that he was not influenced in the least by racist feelings. Pontecorvo adds that Marlon 'would be furious with me if I raised my voice in anger when a black extra was incompetent. But I felt that I should treat incompetence in black man and white with equal firmness.'

With only a few days left to shoot, and more than sixty days missed due to his absences, Marlon walked out of *Queimada* after a particularly violent quarrel. Producer and director were left in an impossible position, with a huge financial commitment and an unfinished movie. Weeks went by. Producer Alberto Grimaldi pleaded with Marlon to return. But he flatly refused to return to Colombia under any circumstances. After discussing several possibilities, Grimaldi settled on Morocco, of all places, as the new location. At least it was dry. Marlon finally yielded and agreed to return to work there. It was a nightmare trying to create an environment exactly identical to that found in the wilds of South America.

In Marrakesh, a partial reconciliation took place between director and star, and the best scene in the picture was shot there. That was the sequence in which

Sir William Walker tried to convince José Delores to choose his freedom. A morning went by with nothing accomplished. The dialogue was too lengthy, and the exposition boring. Finally, Pontecorvo hit on the idea of cutting the dialogue to a minimum and using Bach's partita 'Come, Sweet Death' as the emotional accompaniment to the lines. When the shooting recommenced after lunch, Pontecorvo, without warning Marlon, had someone put on the record. Pontecorvo said, 'Since Brando is like an ultrasensitive animal, he was so moved by the music that he performed one of the most extraordinary scenes he ever played. The entire crew was moved to tears, and exploded into applause. Brando was stunned, and according to Marcello Gatti, he and Pontecorvo embraced each other at the end of this extraordinary scene. Pontecorvo, however, denies this, adding, 'When Marlon and I parted in Marrakesh, we didn't even say good-bye.' Later, when Marlon saw the film, in a gesture of forgiveness he invited Pontecorvo to Hollywood to discuss a possible film about American Indians, *Wounded Knee*. That project never came to fruition.

In England, through the offices of Jay Kanter, he became involved in an intriguing movie, *The Nightcomers*. The point of departure for Michael Hastings's script was Henry James's celebrated short story, *The Turn of the Screw*, about the tortured life of a governess who guiltily becomes attracted to the head of a household in Victorian England when she is put in charge of two children. She struggles for possession of their souls with two diabolical and tormented spirits – those of the dead nursemaid Miss Jessel and her lover, the brutish valet Peter Quint. Michael Hastings, working in collaboration with the director Michael Winner, was inspired to tell the story of Jessel and Quint before the events that Henry James described. In collaboration with Elliot Kastner and Alan Ladd, Jr, Jay Kanter offered Marlon the part of Quint. It was a difficult role, that of an Irishman of persuasive charm and sexual magnetism who gradually perverts his infant charges and subdues and tortures Miss Jessel until at last both die. She perishes by drowning in an icy lake, because the children have made a hole in the rowboat bottom, while the young boy, Miles, shoots two arrows into Quint's head. Now, the murdered couple will return to haunt the living.

The film was shot in the depths of winter near London. Stephanie Beacham, who would later star in *The Colbys* on television, was cast as Miss Jessel. She recalled, 'I will never forget meeting Marlon for the first time. He had an immediate instinct for my sense of unease and fear; he was like an animal. He had a farm boy's simplicity and directness. He understood me completely before we had even had a chance to speak. I have never seen such an instinct in anyone.'

She remembered that before they began work, he showed her a list of his films and remarked how this one had been done because of a divorce payment or that one because of business setbacks. 'He had no other interest in them retrospectively.'

The film probed the connections between passion and sexual domination, and the scene in which Brando tied Miss Beacham to a bed was acted with startling intensity under the direction of Michael Winner. She remembered that in playing the sequence, both she and Marlon 'went far beyond the bounds of anything that had been seen on the screen before'. Some of the sequence had to be cut because of its extreme sexual frankness. She recalls, 'Marlon had such a mischievous sense of humour! The call came for everybody to go to lunch – before we had finished the sequence. He got up off the bed and made his way to his dressing room. Naturally, I assumed I would be able to wriggle out of the knots he had tied quite easily. But imagine my feelings when I discovered I simply couldn't free my wrists! After several members of the crew tried to untie me, without success, Marlon finally returned and took care of the problem . . . I'm not sure that I thought it was very funny at the time.'

In another sequence, in which Miss Jessel was seen drowning in an icy lake, the actress suffered from exposure and extreme cold, and momentarily fainted. Michael Winner insisted on continuing with the sequence for the sake of realism, and Miss Beacham was instructed to pretend to be dead as Marlon lifted her out of the water. She said, 'Of course, since I was supposed to be a corpse, I couldn't even shiver or move a fraction of an inch. The shot went on and on until finally I gave up and insisted on knowing what was going on. Marlon told me that the reason the sequence was taking forever was that he wanted to make sure the lake weed frond over my eyes was in exactly the correct position.

'Later in the day, after we finally got through this impossible scene, Marlon had to pick me up,' Miss Beacham continued. 'But either accidentally or on purpose he let me slip through his arms, and I fell with a crash! I always suspected that he deliberately dropped me!'

The end of shooting of *The Nightcomers* came with Marlon's shrugging realization that his career was at a low ebb. Movie after movie failed at the box office. *Morituri*, *The Chase*, *The Appaloosa*, *A Countess from Hong Kong*, *Reflections in a Golden Eye*, *Candy*, and *The Night of the Following Day*, were followed by the financial disaster of *Queimada*. Even Brando's star stature could not endure a decade of such unsuccessful films, and Hollywood now viewed him as positively unbankable. Coincidentally, the heavy burden of debt incurred by supporting his two ex-wives and his several children (Christian with Anna, Miko and Rebecca with Movita, and Simon Teihotu and Tarita Cheyenne with Tarita), combined with some questionable investments, had left him in a very poor financial state despite the vast sums he had earned. Marlon could be had for a very modest price indeed.

It was from this deepest of professional troughs that Brando would emerge to regain his title as the world's greatest star. Mario Puzo was a little-known author whose career had been limping along with modest sales and indifferent reviews. Then came his novel about an organized-crime family, *The Godfather*; the book rose with amazing rapidity to become the number-one best-seller in the country, with sixty-seven weeks on *The New York Times* best-seller list. It also became the fastest-selling novel in paperback up to that time. Even the reviews were good.

Puzo had sold the film rights early on to Paramount for a mere $12,500 option payment against $50,000 with escalators. He was appalled when he read an article stating that Danny Thomas was being considered for the role of the imposing patriarch, Godfather Don Corleone. Nothing could have been further from Puzo's vision of the character; he was determined from the outset to have Marlon Brando play the role. So the novelist called Marlon out of the blue to urge him to consider the part. Marlon, however, did not respond with even the slightest interest. Not having read the novel, his impression was that *The Godfather* was just another gangster thriller.

Francis Ford Coppola was assigned to direct. He had come off a series of failures, including *The Rain People* and *Finian's Rainbow*, but studio head Bob Evans was convinced that as an Italian himself Coppola would be ideal for the project. The hunt continued for an actor to play Corleone. Several, headed by Ernest Borgnine, were mentioned, and the attorney Melvin Bellie was said to be anxious to act the part. However, Coppola, after many meetings and interviews with unknowns, felt finally that only two actors were great enough: Laurence Olivier and Marlon Brando. Tentative inquiries showed that Olivier was suffering from a severe illness and would be neither insurable nor available to play the role.

When Coppola and producer Al Ruddy brought Marlon's name before Paramount's board, they were unequivocally told that he was out of the question. Not only was it widely known that Brando had suffered a decade of failures and that the audience had evidently lost interest in him, but he was also notoriously difficult on the set. And, despite the huge success of the novel, the film was given a tight production budget and a short schedule for shooting. Paramount had recently made some expensive mistakes – notably *Darling Lili* and *Paint Your Wagon* – and their last big gangster movie, *The Brotherhood* with Kirk Douglas, had not attracted moviegoers. Another multimillion-dollar flop would threaten the studio's solvency. Hence, they were not feeling expansive towards Marlon and his tendency to complicate productions with script rewrites and prima donna behaviour.

Preproduction discussions began and continued in an atmosphere of tension and anxiety. Coppola decided to rewrite Puzo's first-draft screenplay, and during this arduous work Puzo reiterated his desire to have Marlon play Corleone. Soon, everybody wanted to be in the picture. Rod Steiger, already middle-aged and fat, wanted to play Michael, who was slim and twenty-five years old. Finally, Al Pacino was cast in that role, and James Caan secured the part of Sonny Corleone. As for Marlon, Ruddy and Coppola finally wore away the objections of the Paramount brass. It was agreed they would ask Brando to do the unthinkable: a screen test. It was the first he had made since 1946, when he had gone into Twentieth Century-Fox, New York at the behest of Meyer Mishkin. By now, Marlon had read the book and loved it. Not only was he impressed by the power and forcefulness of Puzo's writing, but he understood instantly the point the novelist was making: that since America was run by the corporate mentality, it was inevitable that crime would be institutionalized in the United States. In effect, criminals were simply business tycoons whose cover was less effective than that of the people running the major corporations. Nor were Marlon's motives entirely those of a standard liberal looking for a way to expose the evils of society. With his usual sharp instincts, he smelled a big commercial success, which he badly needed.

Coppola and a cameraman went up to the house on Mulholland. They were received by Marlon in a Japanese kimono, his hair drawn back in a ponytail in the Indian style. He had applied some shoe polish to his hair and stuffed some Kleenex in his mouth to widen his face. Phil Rhodes had helped him create the look of a coarse, harsh, obstinate figure, his jaw jutting out with bulldog determination and his mouth a hard line of determination. Without the artificial latex skin that a studio make-up department would have supplied, he still managed at forty-seven to seem a man well into his sixties. The camera started turning. Marlon came to life in the lens. Director and cameraman returned to Paramount. The executives saw the film along with several other actors' tests. 'Fuck!' 'Who's that?' 'Shit, the guy's terrific. Who is he?' were among the responses in the darkened room. When Coppola and Al Ruddy told them who he was, they were astounded. It was agreed at once that Marlon would take the part.

He was paid five hundred thousand dollars with a percentage of deferments. This turned out to be a tremendous deal for him. He began preparing for the part with a concentration that belied once more his public contempt for his art and recalled his earlier days of dedication and youthful ambition. Al Ruddy recalled that Marlon went to New York and met with mobsters in clubs in Greenwich Village, observing them at close quarters. He picked up their mannerisms with his customary skill; he learned much from them of a gangster's way of life.

Simultaneously in 1971, Al Ruddy held meetings with mob leader Joe Colombo, making a deal with him whereby the gangs would not interfere with the shooting on condition that the word 'Mafia' was never mentioned on the screen. The newspapers got on to this deal and dragged Ruddy through a gruelling press conference in New York. Reporters peppered him with questions, charging him with castrating his own property in order to enter into a partnership with organized crime. Paramount's Stanley Jaffe fired him for one day because of the adverse publicity, then rehired him the next on the instructions of Charles Bluhdorn, head of Gulf and Western Industries, which owned the studio.

Shooting took place in Manhattan and on Staten Island, with some studio interiors. Marlon loved working with Coppola. Ruddy said, 'From the beginning, Marlon was committed to his part completely. He refused to go to the locations in a limousine, and instead was picked up from his hotel in a station wagon. Though he needed to be visually cued in on the beginnings of his speeches, he remembered them with an accuracy and conscientiousness he hadn't shown in fifteen years.' The actors, led by Al Pacino and James Caan, were deeply in awe of him. 'In a sense, Marlon had "created" these guys,' Ruddy explained. 'Without him, they would never have existed. They just stood there frozen when they first met him. Marlon strolled on to the set as they stood lined up to meet him. In an instant, he cracked a joke or two, relaxed, fooled around, made fun of them, let them make fun of him, and before ten minutes was up they were all one big gang together. During the shooting, they never stopped kidding each other, and in fact Jimmy Caan and Al Pacino were constantly sneaking up behind the cameraman and making weird faces at Marlon when he was playing particularly difficult scenes. He hated tension on a set, conflict, competition of any kind between him and the rest of the cast.' The tension, Ruddy added, was rapidly broken and everybody was at Marlon's feet. 'His naturalness and lack of bullshit deeply appealed to those tough men. They loved him, and he loved them.'

In his big sequences – in which Don Corleone refuses to participate in drug deals, barely escapes a murder attempt, tries to arrange a truce between the rival gangs, and dies on camera in his garden – Marlon made an unforgettable impression. The stuffing in his mouth and the dental device that further distorted it gave him a look of extreme cruelty, while his haunted dark eyes, circled with black make-up, stared out as though from a private inferno. The greatest scene was in the garden. There were problems in shooting it. The location

343

manager had found the perfect spot: a compound in Staten Island, for which the art director designed a highly photogenic wall. Tomato plants were planted to create a vivid and colourful background. But rain washed them away, and Ruddy took his courage into his hands and asked Marlon if he would work a few extra days without charging heavy overages so that the plants could be replaced. He only hesitated a second before he agreed, and when his lawyer Norman Garey objected, he overruled him. Ruddy was lost in gratitude and admiration.

Another problem with the scene was that it couldn't be rehearsed or done in many takes because of the presence of the five-year-old boy playing the Don's grandson, who shares with him his final moments. Therefore, Marlon had to do it perfectly in one long sustained series of dying gestures. Right in the middle of the sequence, without warning Coppola or Ruddy, he pulled an irregular piece of orange peel out of his pocket and pushed it into his mouth, startling the child as much as he startled his producer and director. It was a trick he had often used to surprise Christian and Miko when they were very young. Coppola kept the camera rolling. He let the scene play in full, knowing that Marlon had made the right decision.

During the shooting, Marlon looked for ways to relax. He and James Caan joined in the adolescent practice of mooning, baring their asses whenever the opportunity arose. At one point, they were driving down Second Avenue. James Caan said, 'I was in a car and Marlon was in another. As my car drove up beside his, I pulled my pants down and stuck my ass out of the window. Marlon fell down in the car with laughter.' In one scene, right on camera, Caan entered a room to find Marlon thrusting his buttocks into the air. During the big wedding scene, Marlon, Caan, Pacino, and Robert Duvall all dropped their shorts and stuck their behinds in a row into the extras' faces.

In one scene, following the attempted assassination, Marlon as Don Corleone had to be carried up a staircase of his house on a gurney. The extras hired to lift him found his two-hundred-pound weight too heavy and gave up. Instead, members of the film construction crew took over. But while they were being dressed as paramedics in white coats, Marlon asked the assistant director Fred Gallo to get him some sandbags and place them inside the gurney. Then he lay down on the sandbags. 'You should have seen those guys trying to carry the gurney up the stairs,' Gallo said. 'Their veins almost popped out of their necks! The fucking thing must have weighed about four hundred pounds. Marlon got the biggest laugh out of that.'

In the wake of the picture's completion, Shana Alexander interviewed him for *Life* magazine. He had just completed redubbing his part to correct passages that were unintelligible because of his mumbling. He told her, 'I felt the picture made a useful commentary on corporate thinking in this country.' He added that if the Cosa Nostra had been black or socialist, Corleone would have been dead or in jail. But because the Mafia patterned itself so closely on the corporate structure, it prospered. Marlon added, 'The Mafia is so American! To me, a key phrase in the story is that whenever they wanted to kill somebody it was always a matter of policy. Before pulling the trigger, they told him: "Just business. Nothing personal." When I read that, McNamara, Johnson and Rusk flashed before my eyes.'

Initially, as the film was being made, it had been attacked by Italian pressure groups as defamatory of the whole community. Letters poured in threatening demonstrations, boycotts, or strikes. Yet, once the movie was finished, it instantly found acceptance at nearly every level of press and society. The critics were virtually unanimous in declaring it a major work. Although it ran three hours, and the studio talked of trimming it, Ruddy and Coppola fought for its full length and won. Vincent Canby in *The New York Times*, Pauline Kael in *The New Yorker*, and just about every major reviewer, except John Simon, gave the movie its due. *Newweek*'s Paul D. Zimmerman summed it all up when he wrote, 'There is no longer any need to talk tragically of Marlon Brando's career. His stormy two-decade odyssey through films good and bad, but rarely big enough to house his prodigious talents, has ended in triumph.' Calling *The Godfather* the *Gone With the Wind* of gangster movies, Zimmerman went on, '[Once] he was hailed as the greatest actor of his generation. Now, at forty-seven, the king has returned to claim his throne.'

Like Marlon, Coppola saw the picture as a metaphor for America. The director explained, 'Our society, like the Mafia, is transplanted from Europe; it is a capitalistic, profit-seeking body; it believes that anything it does to protect and sustain itself and its family is morally good.' Coppola added that he saw a parellel between the cruelty and harshness of the Mafia and American interference in South America; he felt that the Mafia invasion of North America was equivalent to the United States infiltrating Latin American countries under CIA cover, an equally criminal procedure. Wasn't the picture unreal? 'Okay, yes, it's unreal. But it's a fairy story, an allegory. It's the story of a royal family. Could I show these people as monsters in their own homes? No one would go to see it.'

The Godfather went on to become the top-grossing

film of its day. But until it was released, Marlon was among the least bankable of the major stars. He began casting about for a change of pace.

At this time, the Italian director Bernardo Bertolucci had decided to embark upon *Last Tango in Paris*, a film in which a couple would act out their deepest sexual fantasies. At first, he thought of using two men; but there was still a good deal of public disfavour where gay themes were concerned, and he reworked the story for Jean-Louis Trintignant and Dominique Sanda. However, those actors were just not big enough stars to overcome the controversial nature of the film, and Bertolucci could not secure a distribution deal for the picture. It was the film's producer, Alberto Grimaldi, who had been involved in *Queimada*, who ultimately suggested it would be an original idea to cast Brando. Grimaldi said, 'Brando had the personality and charisma which could allow for an easier public absorption and reception of the considerable shock which such a film would provoke. Marlon was contacted and agreed to meet the director and producer. He had very much admired Bertolucci's movie *The Conformist*.'

Just three days after producer and director had concurred on Brando, Marlon happened to be staying at the Hotel Raphael in Paris. As Marlon encountered the handsome young Italian filmmaker, he spent a long time staring at him, listening to him talk, and observing his face, particularly his eyes, his body, and his movements, until at last he was convinced that he was in the presence of a sincere, honest, and gifted artist. At that meeting, the director only briefly sketched the story for the actor. Bertolucci recalled that Marlon had very little to say and was clearly just using conversation as an opportunity to observe him. The two men parted. Now it became a matter for Grimaldi as producer to find backing for the project – and immediately there was a problem. Grimaldi found that Marlon was virtually unfinanceable. 'He was very poorly rated at the time, and I had to try companies from all over the world,' Grimaldi said. 'No one was interested, no one was willing to take the risk, especially with such a film . . . But finally, despite their fear that it might stain or throw a shadow over their image, United Artists, after much reluctance, agreed to a co-production with me. The final film only cost $1,430,000, of which UA put in $800,000. Marlon took very little up front.'

Meanwhile, as the negotiations went on, Bertolucci flew to Los Angeles to continue his discussions with Marlon at Mulholland Drive. The director had the shrewd intelligence not to discuss the film itself. Instead, the two men talked about everything else under the sun, most notably the Indian issue. Bertolucci said, 'I believe what convinced Marlon to accept the part was the fascination of experimenting with a new working method. That is, the idea I've always had about cinema: it is not the actors who have to conform and fit the script, but it is the characters who must conform to the actors.'

Brando later commented on Bertolucci for *L'Europeo*, saying, 'He appeared to me as a man who is capable of extracting from an actor the best of himself and also of teaching him something. A man capable of doing something new, of tearing away all conventions, of overturning psychologies and renewing them, like a psychoanalyst.'

Before work began, Marlon met with Maria Schneider, the unknown girl who was cast opposite him as the woman who shared with him a totally self-contained erotic experience. Brando called her 'an extraordinary person, of great strength and intensity.

We lived out our characters entirely. The complicity between us was the complicity of two ghosts to whom we had lent our bodies.'

The central figure of *Last Tango* is a broken-down, middle-aged American living in Paris who has reached the nadir of his existence. He becomes involved in a violent, kinky sexual marathon with a young woman he randomly selects. At their first meeting, he has sex with her while wearing an overcoat. Ripping off her pants, he mounts her against a wall and then on the floor with a despairing display of ageing virility. He regards her with sadistic contempt as they play out a scenario of sexual dominance and submission. 'What will you do if I die?' she asks. 'Learn to fuck a dead rat,' he answers. On the face of it, the intent of the script was to expose the futility in modern society of seeking a mindless hedonism. At an early stage in the action, while the overcivilized figure played by Marlon's character is discovered in the depressing, once-elegant apartment he occupies, the script indicates that the music must turn to a South Seas conventional melodic line, ironically commenting on the fact that Tahiti is a million miles removed from this rancid setting.

As Bertolucci began to film the story in the early months of 1972, the intended intellectual detachment of director and star began to fall apart. They became accomplices in the theme itself, along with Maria Schneider, cast as the self-appointed victim of the protagonist's sexual misadventure. Marlon began rewriting the dialogue more excessively than he had ever done before. The action ground to a halt one day when, encouraged by his director, who shot him in a protracted close-up, Marlon actually dropped into personal remininscence as though he, not the character, were being filmed. He spoke with sentimentality and not a little exaggeration of his father as a drunk, telling the story of how he was commanded to milk a cow when he wanted to take a girl out for the evening; when the cow shat on his shoes, he was bitterly disgusted and disappointed. He spoke tenderly of watching his dog Dutchie gambolling around, presumably in Evanston, among the flowers in front of the frame house where the family lived.

Marlon was deeply impressed with the way the film developed. He told Adriano Botta of *L'Europeo* in March 1973, 'This was a true film. I'll add that it is humane and poetic. In our daily life almost everything is squalid, scandalous or odious. Things which are too true always give us a sense of annoyance, of nausea, and this film is true. It is difficult to create a work of art at any time and expect to be understood by everyone.' Asked by Botta whether there was anything autobiographical in his character in the film, Marlon replied, 'Only a certain desperate melancholy. A gloomy regret. A hatred for oneself. All men, when they reach my age, unless they are absolute idiots, must feel a sort of emptiness inside, a sense of anguish, of uselessness. And consider my generation. It is horribly hybrid, torn by painful contradictions.'

Last Tango in Paris created an immediate and overwhelming international sensation. The sound of Marlon tearing Maria Schneider's underpants as he mounted her caused instant shock waves. This was the first time that a major star had appeared in a movie that explicitly displayed sexual intercourse. A chance to see one of the great popular figures of the age actually engaged in sex was irresistible, and moviegoers flocked to theatres in the United States and Great Britain. *Last Tango* was banned in Italy. Despite the most desperate efforts by Bertolucci, the courts would not yield, declaring the picture to be disgustingly obscene. The judges, in reaching their ultimate decision, referred to sequences in which Maria Schneider seemingly inserted her fingers in Marlon's anus, and episodes in which he sodomized her while compelling her to renounce the Church, family, love and all other human values.

Thirteen years later, while filming in Peking, Bertolucci commented, 'The banning of the movie in my home country was a very strong blow. I suffered emotionally and physically from this drastic act that was both violent and utterly devoid of understanding. For thirteen long years that ban has continued. I long to see it released in my homeland. To see what emotional impact it would have on Italians today. I insist that the film is not really a work of violence or crudity; that its action lies in the unconscious, in the mind of the film, in its emotions. It was essentially a romantic film, an innocent work.'

Bertolucci continued, 'In making *Last Tango*, my obsessive question was, "Is it possible for a man and a woman to have a relationship outside of traditional social patterns?" That is why I decided to place the relationship between the couple in a room, an anonymous room deprived of all identity, as were the characters, who had even renounced their own names. When they had no identity they were innocent and protected. But the moment they came in touch with the outside world, their innocence turned to anguish and guilt. That was the point of the film.'

The reviews were generally favourable. Pauline Kael in *The New Yorker* hailed the work as a masterpiece, a revolutionary creation equivalent to Stravinsky's *The Rite of Spring* and a revelation of Marlon's extraordinary gifts. By contrast, some critics found the film repellent; John Simon, in a skilfully argued critique, analysed the film's disconcertingly misogynistic elements and its emphasis on squalor. However, whatever view one took of the movie, nobody could deny that it changed the face of movies as completely as *Streetcar* had changed the face of the theatre. Once again, Brando, by exposing his own sexual compulsions with unique daring before the world, was instrumental in expanding an artistic medium. The movie was a huge hit, and following the sensation of *The Godfather*, which became one of the biggest box-office successes of all time, Marlon had permanently secured his position at the very top of the superstar category.

18

In the middle of shooting *Last Tango*, Marlon was faced with another lurid and unsavoury situation in California. On February 28, Anna exercised her right of access to Christian and picked him up from his school in Ojai. She drove him to her home in Los Angeles. She was only supposed to keep him for the weekend, but he developed bronchitis and her doctor advised her to keep him with her for several more days. The doctor, she claimed later, recommended that Christian be taken to Mexico for a vacation.

With her friend James Wooster, she drove Christian to Mulholland Drive to collect some travelling clothes and a suitcase for the journey. When they arrived, Marlon's Japanese housekeeper Reiko Sato refused to admit Anna. She had orders from Marlon that Miss Kashfi must never enter the house.

Christian told Miss Sato that he wanted to stay and that he didn't want to go to Mexico with his mother. The boy looked ill and was coughing badly, and the housekeeper was reluctant to let him go. She quarrelled with Anna, who insisted Christian pick up his things and come out of the house. Uncertain what to do, Miss Sato called Norman Garey, who despatched private detective Jim Briscoe to assess the situation.

Garey followed Briscoe to Mulholland. There, he insisted Anna leave at once, but she would not. Anna later alleged that he beat her brutally. Garey in turn claimed that she broke a window and snatched Christian from the house, bundling him into a blue pickup truck and driving off with him down the hill, with James Wooster at the wheel. According to the press accounts, Anna struggled with police, who arrived on Garey's instructions, and Christian volunteered to go with her to prevent any further trouble.

Garey called Marlon in Paris to tell him that Anna had made off with Christian, and asked what he should do. Marlon, who had just come off a harrowing day with Bertolucci, was beside himself. He instructed Garey to get a restraining order against Anna. Garey complied, but by that time Anna and Christian were already in Baja California and couldn't be traced.

Meanwhile, having entrusted Christian to Wooster's care, she returned to California. When she later arrived back at the motel in Baja, Wooster and her son were gone. Anna then ran to a local Mexican police station and spoke incoherently of kidnap. In a state of hysteria, she made her way back to Los Angeles, where she created a scene on a city bus, allegedly abusing the driver and other passengers. The driver ejected her from the bus and summoned the police. Charged with being drunk and disorderly, she spent the night in jail.

The story was in papers all over the world the next day. Marlon called Norman Garey and insisted that Christian be found. Garey recommended detective Jay J. Armes of El Paso, ironically named because he lost his hands in an accident and was equipped with prosthetic devices. Marlon remembered meeting Armes, who had played a bit part in one of his movies. He called Armes directly with the dramatic words, 'I want you to find Christian.'

Meanwhile, Mexican federal police traced the blue pickup truck travelling south. Armes picked up the trail in his helicopter at the village of Puertecitos. Once on the ground, he drove with several officers to a tent camp. They found Wooster, five other men with beards and shoulder-length hair, a fifty-one-year-old woman, and a nude girl in a sleeping bag. The officers lined up the suspects at gunpoint against a sea wall and demanded to know Christian's whereabouts. According to Armes, James Wooster replied, 'What Christian?' But another man, Allen H. Davos, said, 'He's in that tent.' Armes was horrified to find Christian shirtless and shoeless, coughing with bronchitis, frightened and confused, trying to hide under some clothing. Wooster said, 'Okay, we weren't going to hurt the boy. Anna promised us ten thousand dollars to keep him here. To hide him for a while . . . to prison the boy.' Another man confirmed the offer. Armes searched the camp and found it was supplied with several months of food and drink. The entire group of eight was conducted across the border and told never to return. Armes escorted Christian back home. At seven A.M., Marlon met with Christian at the Los Angeles Airport, following an all-night flight from Paris. He was beside himself with worry over the boy. Anna, who was still awaiting trial for her drunk and disorderly behaviour on the bus, filed an assault charge against Norman Garey, stating that he and 'ten others' had beaten and injured her at Mulholland on March 5. She wanted punitive damages of over $1 million, and general damages of the same amount. Nothing came of this case.

On March 13, at a custody hearing at the Santa Monica Superior Court (Marlon did not press kidnapping charges), the group of alleged kidnappers was identified by Armes. He told of the boy's state of terror and described how Christian had tried to flee the car and vanish in the desolate countryside on their way back from Mexico. Christian was not present in court, as Judge Laurence J. Rittenband felt it would be better for him to wait in a back room.

Marlon testified that if he were allowed to take Christian to France he would make sure he had proper schooling there. Clinical psychologist Dr Evelyn Troup, who had been appointed by the court to advise in the matter, recommended that Christian be allowed to undertake the trip. Miss Kashfi did not appear. The outcome was that Marlon was granted the right to take his son to Paris, and was given sole custody for the next twelve months. As Marlon left the courthouse with the nervous and frightened thirteen-year-old boy, who looked painfully thin and frail, a paparazzo rushed up to him to take a picture. Marlon grabbed hold of the photographer and pushed him off the sidewalk. Norman Garey pulled Marlon loose from the man and bundled Marlon and Christian into a waiting car.

Marlon was overjoyed to have Christian with him during the remaining weeks of *Last Tango in Paris*. When the shooting was over, he took him for an Easter trip to Tahiti and then to Sun Valley, Idaho, for spring skiing. For a year, Anna was forbidden any contact with the boy.

Anna made further charges against Marlon as she returned to court in her continuing battle for Christian's custody. She claimed that Marlon encouraged Christian to steal a 'Yield' sign from a crossroads on Mulholland Drive and allowed the boy to conceal the sign in the house while denying any knowledge of the matter to the police. She told a curious story of the Sun Valley ski trip, describing how Marlon pushed Christian, dressed only in a bath towel, out of a hotel room on to a balcony and locked the door. Since the day was bitterly cold and Christian wasn't strong, the boy grew hysterical and beat on the glass, insisting he be admitted. Anna said, 'Marlon dropped his pants, pressed his buttocks to the glass, and yelled, "Here, climb into this!" The story, combining sinister allegations of both pederasty and incest, was told under oath, yet it made little sense and was never explained further in court. The outcome of the hearing was inconsequential. The couple would share custody, even though Anna fought bitterly to prevent Marlon from having access to his child.

Then, in July 1972, Marlon became embroiled in yet another fight. This time he was fighting his former wife Movita, whose lawyer, Peter Notras, charged that Marlon had stopped paying alimony to Movita in September 1971, that he had ignored a court order to continue $1,400-a-month payments, and had failed to supply support for his children Miko and Rebecca. Movita also claimed that Marlon had promised to finance her purchase of an abalone fishing company, from which she had hoped to make a profit, and which she had said would earn her an income that would make his alimony payments unnecessary. She insisted that he had broken his promise. Marlon lost the case. Peter Notras told *Los Angeles Times* columnist Joyce Haber on July 3, 'If Mr Brando doesn't resume payments, I suppose we'll try to take him for everything he's got.' He did resume them.

Months later, Marlon suffered a terrible blow when his beloved Wally Cox, only forty-eight, was found dead at his home on Roscomare Road in Bel Air. Pat Cox had called the Bel Air Patrol at 7:30 A.M. Although there was a near-empty bottle of Palcidyl, a sleeping tablet, on the night table, some evidence of drinking, and a badly typed note in the typewriter, Los Angeles Court Coroner Thomas Noguchi stated that Cox's death was due to 'severe coronary disease due to arteriosclerosis'. He had lost much of his confidence in the wake of the disappearance of *Mr Peepers* and its successor, *Hiram Holiday*, from television, and the small role he had as a radio operator in *Morituri* was indication of how far his career had sunk. His memoirs, *My Life as a Small Boy*, had received little attention.

Marlon was devastated when he heard the news, and he gave what comfort he could to Pat Cox. When a wake was held for Cox's friends, headed by the Everett Greenbaums, he hid in the bedroom, apparently to escape inquisitive people.

Wally had despised funerals and to deflect the press the story was put out that arrangements had been made with the Neptune Society and that Marlon scattered Wally's cremated ashes at sea. Instead, he was said to have taken the urn to an unknown place in northern California, where the ashes were thrown into the wind. Marlon later told a *Playboy* reporter he kept the ashes with him in his house in Tahiti.

It was certainly no consolation to him in that tormented time to learn that he would probably win the Academy Award for *The Godfather*. Since his last appearance at the Oscars almost twenty years earlier for *On the Waterfront*, he had never ceased to express his contempt for the ceremony and everything it represented. He arranged to send a friend of his, a half-Apache young woman named Sacheen Little Feather, to act as his representative at the 1973 Awards. He worked out a lengthy speech in which he attacked the misrepresentation of Indians on the American motion picture screen. The Wounded Knee trial was taking place at the time, and the lavish awards ceremony struck Marlon as an absurdly trivial event, in contrast.

Marlon had already refused to accept a New York

Film Critics Award and the Foreign Press Association Golden Globe. He sent telegrams forty-eight hours before the Oscars to these groups, stating, 'I respectfully ask you to understand that to accept an honour, however well intended, is to subtract from the meagre amount left. Therefore, to simplify things, I hereby decline any nomination and deny anyone representing me.' The telegram continued, spewing forth a barrage of complaints about the government's treatment of blacks and Indians, an imperialistic foreign policy, and the curtailment of a free press. When attempts were made to reach him for comment, Alice Marchak said he was 'somewhere in the Pacific'. She did not advise the Academy whether Marlon would attend. At the last minute, she got hold of tickets from Howard W. Koch, president of Paramount Studios and producer of the Awards show. She helped Sacheen Little Feather dress for the occasion in Native American clothing and jewellery. Meanwhile, Daniel Taradash, who was quite familiar with Marlon's capacity for difficult behaviour from *Morituri*, was now president of the Academy and faced the evening with apprehension.

Right up to the last minute, Marlon was rewriting the speech. At 6, with the doors of the Dorothy Chandler Pavilion closing at 6:30, he still wasn't ready. At 7, he was busy scribbling yet another draft. Sacheen and Alice began watching the show on television and could see their two empty seats.

At 7:30, with the telecast well underway, Marlon at last handed Sacheen the finished pages. By 8:30, she and Alice were at the Music Center, where a guard led them to a side door, and they made their way to the seats. Alas, the stage manager had filled them during the first commercial break, so the two women waited beside an exit door. Meanwhile, backstage, Howard

Koch learned of their arrival when someone announced, 'My God, Marlon Brando sent the Indians to get us!' Koch conferred anxiously with Daniel Taradash. Afraid of an activist incident, Koch took Alice and Sacheen out into the lobby and told them that he wouldn't allow a disturbance. When he saw the four-page speech Marlon had written, he told Sacheen that reading it was out of the question. In anger, she insisted she would go ahead, and he threatened to cut her off the air. After a conference with Taradash, Koch then told Sacheen she could have exactly two minutes, and if she were one second over he would have her bodily removed from the stage.

Seats were found for Sacheen and Alice next to James Caan. Nominees for Best Actor were announced. Liv Ullmann and Roger Moore opened the envelope. The winner was Marlon. Sacheen ran up to the stage, and Roger Moore charmingly handed her the award. Sacheen refused to accept it and turned to the crowd to announce that the time limit prevented her from reading Marlon's prepared speech. She stated that Marlon could not accept the award because of the treatment of American Indians in movies and on television, and also because of 'the recent happenings at Wounded Knee'. She added, 'I beg at this time that I have not intruded upon this evening, and that we will, in the future, in our hearts and our understanding, meet with love and generosity. Thank you on behalf of Marlon Brando.' There was no applause. The remaining presenters were predictably cynical. Rock Hudson announced Gene Hackman and Raquel Welch as presenters of the Best Actress Award with the meaningful words, 'Often to be eloquent is to be silent.' Miss Welch said of the actress nominees, 'I hope none of them has a cause.'

Clint Eastwood added a comment: 'I don't know if I should present the Best Picture Award on behalf of all the cowboys shot in John Ford Westerns over the years.' Watching the telecast at Mulholland, Marlon was disgusted by these gratuitous insults. Daniel Tardash said, 'We let Sacheen go just four seconds over two minutes. One more second, and I would have escorted her out. If Marlon had any class, he would have come down here and said it all himself.' At a press conference that night, Michael Caine said, 'I agree entirely with what Marlon did, but I think he should have stood up and done it himself instead of letting some poor little Indian girl take the boos ... If you're going to make a humanitarian gesture, I think a man who makes $2 million playing the leader of the Mafia should at least give half of it to the Indians.' Charlton Heston told the reporters, 'The American Indian needs better friends than that.' Jane Fonda was one of the few who thought Marlon had made the right decision. Then Rona Barrett revealed that Sacheen Little Feather was really Maria Cruz, Miss American Vampire of 1970, who had made some freakish publicity appearances for MGM's horror spoof *House of Dark Shadows*.

Chief Dan George, a Squamish Indian from Canada, who had won Best Supporting Actor nomination two years earlier for *Little Big Man*, told the press that Sacheen Little Feather's speech came ten years too late. He said that treatment of his people on the screen was 'accurate and decent' now, and that it was a very long time since the American Indian had been portrayed as a savage. The rest of the Indian community was divided on the issue. Grace Thorpe, daughter of the Indian Olympic athlete and football star Jim Thorpe, termed Marlon's refusal as 'absolutely delightful,' and she attacked the treatment of Indians in certain films as 'a gross distortion of the truth'. She noted that Greeks, Italians, and Mexicans were hired to play Indians in films and cited the case of the female Indian lead in *A Man Called Horse*, who was played by a Greek beauty-contest winner. She ignored the fact that she had approved the casting of Burt Lancaster in the title role of *Jim Thorpe – All American*. The episode brought out the worst in several movie executives. One studio referred to Sacheen as 'Marlon Brando's Jewish Indian,' and another said, 'I'm sick of these bleeding-heart liberals like Brando who grow fat on the capitalism they despise.'

On April 12, 1973, Anna Kashfi yet again petitioned the Los Angeles Superior Court to secure her right to custody of Christian. She asserted that Marlon had not used 'sufficient parental control and discipline' over their son since the preceding May 10, when he had taken him to Europe. Then she argued that Marlon's role in *Last Tango* and the way he had chosen to treat his recent Academy Award were poor examples of behaviour for Christian that had caused the boy to suffer ridicule and embarrassment among his peers. Anna lost the case.

On June 12, Marlon taped *The Dick Cavett Show*. It was an uncomfortable occasion. Marlon behaved with obvious impatience and mischievousness, clearly revealing his disdain for television talk shows. He refused to discuss his movies or his private life, and Cavett became visibly embarrassed and uncomfortable. Marlon made cruel fun of his host by repeatedly asking Cavett why he was fiddling with notes, and called attention to the bell-like sounds that announced commercial breaks. Every time he tried to swing Marlon towards a discussion of *The Godfather*, *Last Tango*, the Academy Award, and any other subject of public interest, Marlon refused to say anything and forced Cavett into a give-and-take of exceptional tedium on the subject of the Indians.

Marlon's dislike was not for Cavett, but for television and for the public's consuming interest in celebrities. In fact, after the taping, Marlon even went to dinner in Chinatown with a remarkably sporting and forgiving Cavett. Paparazzo Ron Galella chased the two men down the street, and when he asked Marlon to remove his sunglasses for a shot, Marlon yelled at him and delivered a hard right hook to the jaw. Galella fell down bleeding on the sidewalk, then struggled to his car and drove in agony to Bellevue Hospital, where doctors applied nine stitches to seal the cut and fixed a metal brace in his fractured jaw. The next day, Marlon went to the Hospital for Special Surgery with a swollen right hand that, according to press reports, had become infected. It was an unpleasant ending to an already disagreeable experience.

Upset and worn out after this experience, Marlon sought a change of scene. He took off for Omaha, perhaps hoping to find there some indication that there was still an unspoiled and innocent world buried in the American heartland of his past. But to his disappointment, the city was just like any other American commercial centre in 1973. He took a quick drive in a cab past his birthplace and kindergarten school and ate a sandwich in a coffee shop. Then, without ceremony, he left town.

19

In this period of the early 1970s, Marlon embarked upon an extraordinary adventure in politics. Always obsessed with the causes of minorities, by now deeply read in the horrifying history of Indian genocide, Marlon helped to found, finance, develop, and support the militant organization known popularly as AIM, the American Indian Movement. Comprised of members of various tribes who found a common purpose in defying the US establishment and drawing attention to the sufferings of the original Americans, AIM's methods ranged from political lobbying to demonstrations and civil disobedience.

With his commitments to his family and his career, Marlon obviously could not actually run AIM. Instead, two powerful figures of the Indian societies came to dominate its activities under Marlon's careful strategic guidance. Russell Means was an Oglala, born on Pine Ridge Reservation in South Dakota; a man of forceful and single-minded determination, Means had a demanding, consuming energy that was evident in his absolute commitment to the movement. Marlon was proud to count him a friend, and they met repeatedly in Los Angeles and elsewhere as AIM took shape.

The other leader of AIM was the more subdued Dennis Banks, a native Minnesotan who had gone through the usual American Indian experiences of unemployment, hunger, and homelessness. Marlon admired Banks deeply and saw in him a moderating influence within AIM that would counter the extremists in the organization.

In addition to underwriting AIM, Marlon also supported Hank Adams, who founded the Survival of American Indian Associates. While Marlon's financial connections to the Indian movement were not publicized, his aggressive stance in support of the cause became public knowledge.

Starting in April 1973, Marlon became distantly involved in a chain of incidents that secured AIM's outlaw status in the eyes of local and federal authorities. Earlier that year, Sarah Bad Heart Bull's son Wesley had been stabbed to death by a white businessman in a barroom brawl in Buffalo Gap, South Dakota. The grief-stricken mother demanded that the accused killer be charged with murder – not involuntary manslaughter – and arrived with Banks and two hundred AIM members at the Custer County Courthouse in South Dakota. The heated confrontation escalated to a violent riot in which Sarah Bad Heart Bull was beaten, and the guards resorted to shooting tear gas into the crowd inside the courthouse. Nearly overcome by the fumes, Banks led a group who smashed open the windows in an effort to get fresh air. Banks and his companions were able to escape, but they were later charged with damaging state property and inciting riot. Marlon sent substantial funds to Sarah Bad Heart Bull along with food and wrote to her in support.

Throughout the following year, Banks lived a desperate existence, moving from one trouble spot to another, keeping Marlon apprised of his activities. When Banks called Marlon in October 1974, it was to inform him that two AIM members had been charged with the murder of a white cab driver who had been found stabbed and hidden in a drainpipe at an AIM camp in southern California. Marlon posted their bail. The two defendants were later acquitted for lack of evidence against them.

Meanwhile, Marlon was engaged in soliciting support for AIM around the country. He was helped by Lucy Saroyan, daughter of the writer William Saroyan, and Ethel Kennedy, Robert Kennedy's widow. His old schoolmate Harry Belafonte, as well as Arlo Guthrie and Buffy Sainte-Marie, also joined him. Although he found it contradictory to don formal wear for such a political cause, he did so to preside over a $150-per-plate fund-raising dinner at the Waldorf-Astoria that featured a traditional Indian menu. Marlon arrived at the affair flanked by three Indians in tribal uniform.

The evening was a mixture of enlightenment and embarrassment. Dick Cavett's emceeing of the occasion was widely criticized. After clumsily announcing that several Yakima tribe members had been placed inappropriately at the back of the room, he awkwardly cut off the Yakima chief in mid-speech to announce the late arrival of New York State Governor-elect Hugh Carey. Marlon delivered an immensely long speech in which he unleashed his impassioned feelings. In the course of the address, he described a moving occasion on which Banks had taken him to meet a medicine man of the Ojibway tribe, who played the tribal drum for the first time in over thirty years in his presence. The meeting took place at night in a tiny hut in the middle of winter, with everyone present stripped to the skin. Marlon said, 'We were all naked there, at four-thirty in the morning, freezing cold in this little . . . hovel, sitting next to our brothers. I had a sense of brotherhood there more than I suppose anywhere I've ever been – and it was dark, and they brought the stones in, and they poured water on, and they put tobacco on, and we passed the pipe around, and every man took the drum, and he beat it four times . . . Each man present spoke of his personal anguish, and several began to cry.'

At the end of 1974, Marlon attended a hearing at the federal courthouse in Lincoln, Nebraska, to determine the federal court's jurisdiction over the defendants in the Wounded Knee incident. He arrived in the company of Dennis Banks and Russell Means. Marlon was given an opportunity to discuss the case with Judge Warren Urbem in his chambers, and there expressed his desire for proper justice. Then, Marlon took a front-row seat and, arms folded, listened intently to the proceedings for an hour, staring directly at Judge Urbem's eyes.

As he left the building at day's end, he announced to the one hundred gathered reporters and photographers on the courthouse steps that he was going to give away his land, including forty acres in Agoura, California, an apartment house in Anaheim, his house on Mulholland Drive, and Frannie's farm at Mundelein to the Indians. That night, he appeared before an audience of six hundred at the University of Nebraska campus, where Indian leaders gave him a pipe of peace. He said, 'I don't believe in honours of any kind. It puts people in some kind of condescension. This is not so much an honour as it is an inspiration. It humbles me. This means more to me than the Academy Award because it reaffirms me as a person.' Talking of Indian misery and despair, he said, 'We have invited these people into oblivion, but they won't go!'

When newspapers circulated the story that Marlon was giving away all of his property, his sister Frannie in Mundelein was in a state of shock. She told newspapers that her farm and the land surrounding it would be disposed of 'over my dead body'. She called the farm in Mundelein 'the family homestead' and insisted there must be some mistake. Marlon assured her it would not be part of his gift to the Indians. Two weeks later, on the last day of 1974, he stood on a muddy, rain-swept hilltop near Liberty Canyon in Agoura, California, with Senator John B. Tunney and several members of the Survival of American Indians Association. He handed over the deeds to forty acres of the Santa Monica Mountains to Semu Huaurte, medicine man of the Red Wind Association of twenty-three tribes, with apologies for being 'two hundred years too late'.

The property consisted of forty acres of rolling, dusty hills forty miles northwest of Los Angeles off the Ventura Freeway and was worth about two hundred thousand dollars. To a triumphant roll of tribal drums, Marlon proceeded to hand the medicine man a quit-claim form and stated that he hoped with the approaching United States Bicentennial, the gift would serve as an example for righting the wrongs committed against the Indian nations. Huaurte said that the land would probably be given to the Chuwala Indians, original owners of the tract. Then the Indians performed consecration rites, intoning incantations.

The land transfer, however, was not without complications. On January 4, 1975, John F. Hamilton, of Pacific Palisades, Los Angeles, who held the mortgage on the land with his brother James and sister Janet, told the press that the Indians would be inheriting a heavily encumbered property with repayments that would amount to as much as twenty thousand dollars a year. Everyone had assumed that Marlon owned the land outright. But in fact, he hadn't paid so much as a dime on the principal. As a result, the property lay in limbo for eleven months, until at last Norman Garey announced that full payment had been made. Marlon's critics used the unfortunate situation to support their claims that his involvement with the Indian movement was not much more than a publicity stunt.

In the meantime, yet another incident involving members of AIM and other militant Indians was unfolding that would draw Marlon inextricably into the fray. During the early hours of New Year's Day of 1975, forty Indians, identified as the Menominee Warrior Society, had invaded the caretaker's cottage next to the abandoned Alexian Brothers' Noviciary two miles from Gresham, Wisconsin. They held the caretaker and his family at gunpoint and seized the compound, which was surrounded by 225 acres of fields. The Menominee Indian group issued the demand that the property be given back to the tribe because it had once been Menominee land and its lease to the Alexians had run out. AIM enthusiastically sanctioned this repossession, and Marlon, in his unequivocal support of Banks and Means, expressed his approval. However, the Menominee Reservation Committee, the official tribal organization, was utterly opposed to the action.

The police threw a cordon around the building in which the Indians had barricaded themselves, and Judge Gordon Myse attempted to negotiate with one of the group's leaders, Neil Hawpetoss. Shawano County sheriff Robert Montour forbade food to be passed through the blockade, in the hope that the Indians would be forced by hunger to abandon their stand. Then, in an effort to compromise, Alexian Brother Florian Eberle offered to set up an Indian medical facility in the building if the group would quit peacefully. They refused.

Five days later, Wisconsin Governor Patrick J. Lucey

ordered the National Guard to the scene. He permitted some food to be sent to the Indians, who had endured freezing conditions without electricity or plumbing. Banks and Means arrived, and Marlon promised to follow shortly. Outside the police cordon, supporters of the Menominee group gathered, as did some armed locals who threatened to storm the building to remove the Indians.

When three Indians walked out of the monastery on January 11, they were immediately arrested. The following day, Dennis Banks issued a national appeal for donations to buy the compound from the Alexians. Apparently Marlon was not directly approached. As the situation remained at a stalemate through the month, local residents became increasingly frustrated and angry, and they demanded that the National Guard besiege the compound.

Marlon finally arrived at the scene to lend assistance to the negotiations. He conferred with Banks and with Father James Groppi, a Milwaukee activist priest who was also seeking a resolution to the crisis. Marlon was allowed to cross the police line and enter the noviciary. Once inside, he met with Neil Hawpetoss and his cohorts, who were milling about in great confusion, many of them suffering from the cold of the unheated building and from the inadequate supplies of food and drink. The stench from the broken plumbing, the gloomy and shabby rooms, and the tormented determination of the occupants created a scene more striking and dramatic than any Marlon had experienced in motion pictures.

On the night of February 1, as Marlon sheltered with his companions, gunfire broke out in the snow. Several vigilantes from the local citizenry had finally taken the law into their own hands and were peppering the building with bullets. Other locals were apparently exchanging gunfire with National Guards, who were under orders to maintain a moderate and balanced situation. Marlon climbed up to the building's roof to witness the exchange of gunfire, where bullets flew past his head.

Some Menominee Indians objected to Marlon's presence, feeling that he was there simply for the publicity. They played a brutal joke on him, by decapitating a horse that they had eaten because they were starving and putting the head in his sleeping bag in a parody of the famous scene in *The Godfather*. He burst into tears when he found it, realizing yet again, and more painfully than ever, how little actors meant in the scheme of things.

Marlon spent three nights in the building until, on February 3, the Alexian Brothers agreed to sell the compound to the Menominee Indian Society for one dollar. However, after a protracted negotiation between the Alexians and the Menominee Indians, it became clear that the cost of maintaining the compound far exceeded the resources of the tribe, and the offer to sell the land was withdrawn. Instead, the Alexians presented the property to another local charitable group called Crossroads. Marlon was embittered by the final outcome.

The first half of 1975 was marked by a string of disturbing incidents involving AIM members as the movement grew more militant. Marlon was called upon to post $54,000 bail for Russell Means and two others when they were charged with first-degree murder in the shooting of another Indian. Only Means was ultimately acquitted. Then in June, Means suffered a gunshot wound when a Bureau of Indian Affairs officer shot him during a scuffle on the Standing Rock Indian

Reservation in North Dakota. Means was charged with obstructing an officer in the course of performing his duty. That same month, two FBI agents were shot and killed while attempting to serve warrants on the Oglala Sioux Reservation in South Dakota. AIM leader Leonard Peltier was sought for the crime.

In the midst of these events, Marlon apparently found himself in need of money for his Tahitian ventures, his divorce alimonies and child support, and to provide bail and other help for his friends in AIM. As a result, he accepted a new film role. It was in Arthur Penn's Western *The Missouri Breaks*, which was to be shot in Billings, Montana, in the mid- and late summer. The story involved a highly eccentric hired gun, played by Marlon, fond of riding about in a woman's dress and bonnet, who is brought in by a wealthy rancher to rub out a gang of cattle rustlers led by a gleeful Jack Nicholson. Nicholson had agreed to make the picture for a fee of $1.25 million if Marlon were to co-star. The producer was Elliott Kastner, of the ill-fated *Night of the Following Day*, and Jack Nicholson had recently taken a house next to Marlon's on Mulholland Drive. Marlon had asked for half a million dollars a week, but United Artists had countered with an offer of 1 million plus 2½ per cent of the gross, and Marlon agreed.

Weighing a shocking 250 pounds, Marlon arrived in Billings, a sprawling, ugly industrial town surrounded by trailer camps and oil wells set in a featureless, dusty landscape flanked by ice-capped mountains. Thomas McGuane, author of the screenplay, was infuriated, like many writers before him, by Marlon's interference with the script before and during the shooting. Marlon remained unhappy with the material and was determined to ham it up without restraint. Marlon drifted through the shooting, and couldn't remember his lines. He had them posted all over the set and even on other actors' bodies, or simply improvised dialogue. Accompanied by the shrilling of grasshoppers in the sagebrush, skittering puffballs, and grass seeds, shooting took place on and around a ranch outside of Billings in hundred-degree weather. Dramatic thunderstorms disrupted shooting with lightning and massive threatening clouds; when the storm ended, the heat resumed with severity.

Marlon spent most of his spare moments talking to his Indian activist friends by telephone from his mobile home, a massive and handsomely equipped trailer that he lived in during the making of *Missouri Breaks*. He wandered about, often in his Mother Hubbard costume, tenderly picking up bright green grasshoppers and studying their physical structure. On one occasion he dropped a loudly ringing creature straight into the mouth of sleeping actor Randy Quaid, who woke to find his tongue and gums swollen from painful bites. He collected stones from the Yellowstone River, licked them and polished them, and delighted in showing them to visitors. Sometimes, he would wade into the river in front of the cast and crew, and on one occasion caused widespread gasps and laughter as he bit a live fish in half and swallowed it.

During the filming, two FBI agents arrived on the set to question Marlon. Leonard Peltier was still being sought, and Russell Banks – out on bail pending a trial over the events at the Custer Courthouse – had disappeared. Marlon refused to disclose anything, even though he almost certainly knew the approximate location of these men. In fact, he later admitted he played a role in Banks's escape from justice, albeit an indirect one, since he was tied up in Montana at the time.

He spent his nights alone, meditating, studying the potential for wind, methane, and windmill power for Teti'aroa, and examining records that could assist him in providing support for his activist associates.

After the tedious work on the picture was ended, he returned to his real purpose in life. He made his mobile home available to refugees Peltier and Banks. This was, of course, in contravention of federal law. He told *Playboy* in 1980, 'For me to be put under indictment for aiding and abetting an American Indian who was forced to go underground due to political pressure – the entire thing was fraught with a very special kind of concern that it did not get too large.' In fact, Banks and Peltier had gone underground to avoid criminal charges against them – Banks for evasion of justice and Peltier for first-degree murder.

On November 13, Banks and Peltier were seen in Oregon, travelling east in a convoy led by the mobile home. Next day, Oregon State Troopers were ordered to keep the caravan under close surveillance. Misunderstanding those instructions, they ordered the vehicles to stop at gunpoint. The troopers ordered everyone to get out and lie down on the road shoulder. Peltier emerged from the trailer, and as he sank to his knees on the asphalt, he screamed a warning to Banks, who was still inside, apparently at the driver's wheel. Banks made a rapid getaway under gunfire, distracting the police so that Peltier also was able to take to his heels and jump over a fence. Several others in the group were arrested.

Hours later, the deserted mobile home was found on Highway 80. Examining the registration, a patrolman discovered that it was under Marlon's name. It was found to contain a cargo of dynamite, firearms, hand grenades, and detonators. A paper bag pulled from under the front passenger seat contained a service revolver that belonged to one of the murdered FBI agents. The bag also allegedly had Peltier's thumbprint on it. Peltier was now among the most wanted fugitives in the country.

According to his interview in *Playboy*, Marlon gave Banks a refuge in his house in Teti'aroa, where the fugitive remained for several weeks. In January 1976, Banks decided to cease this pleasant if meaningless exile in the South Seas and return to California. Arrested and charged in Oakland, he was held on one hundred thousand dollars' bail on the old charges of the 1973 Custer incident. He insisted that he had committed no crime, had been unlawfully convicted, and would be killed instantly by vigilantes if he returned to his home state. Then-Governor Jerry Brown successfully fought his extradition. But in April of the following year, Leonard Peltier was found guilty on the two counts of murder in the first degree and at last report was serving two successive life sentences at Leavenworth Prison.

Banks remained in California for nine years, where he taught at an Indian school in the town of Davis, still under Jerry Brown's protection. When Governor George Deukmejian took office, Banks no longer had sanctuary in California, and he fled to the Onondaga Indian reservation in New York State, hiding under local protection for a year and a half. Finally, worn out by a life in hiding, Banks surrendered to the original South Dakota police officials who had charged him during the riot years earlier and accepted a fourteen-month sentence in jail. He was at last released on parole and went to live on Pine Ridge Reservation, South Dekota, where Russell Means had also found at least a provisional home.

Marlon never lost his intense fascination with these men's activities. But the decision in 1985 of certain members of AIM to support the contras in Nicaragua caused him great anguish. Their motive was apparently to assist the Meskito Indians of that country who, Means felt strongly, were threatened with total genocide by the Sandinistas. By a supreme irony, Marlon now found part of his funds in AIM being used for what is widely felt to be a CIA-run rebel operation. Marlon was shocked into complete silence by this action, and Means's own brother, William, head of the AIM International Treaty Council, told Bella Stumbo of the *Los Angeles Times Magazine*, 'This is just another of [Russ's] sensationalist, publicity-seeking stunts.'

In 1975, at the age of fifty-one, Marlon was approached by Francis Ford Coppola to appear in the director's most ambitious film to date: *Apocalypse Now*, a version of Joseph Conrad's novel *Heart of Darkness*. Yet again, the money was a temptation. And at least the picture seemed to be about something: a serious and poetic exploration of the horror of the Vietnam War, as seen through the eyes of an Army man, Willard, sent to liquidate the demented Colonel Kurtz, who had gone mad in a jungle compound. In discussions with Coppola, Marlon agreed that the movie would help to illustrate the Vietnam War as an act of insanity, and that Kurtz was simply a scapegoat, a victim. Moreover, Kurtz would be shown in the film as a man who had lost his taste for war, who had been appalled by the cruelty and viciousness of the US military force in the region. Marlon welcomed the thought of returning to the Philippines.

In February 1976, before he went on location for *Apocalypse*, Marlon surprisingly declined the

NAACP's Humanitarian Award, saying, 'It makes me happy to think I have been of some help to those who are less fortunate than myself... [but] I don't think there is a white man who can know what that black experience is, and it's in that spirit that I will respectfully decline this honour.'

Confrontations between white authorities and Indian activists continued throughout 1976. Meantime, the Coppola unit and stars settled into the Philippines to begin a protracted and unpleasant shooting schedule that would drag on for months. Harvey Keitel, cast as Captain Willard after several stars turned down the part, fought with Coppola, who charged him with acting 'too feverishly' and dismissed him. Coppola flew to Los Angeles, bumped into Martin Sheen at the airport, and hired him on the spot. Then Sheen collapsed with a heart attack. The production was also beset by natural disasters: an earthquake, a typhoon, tropical rain storms. Shooting was delayed for months. The art department was ordered to build a temple in the mode of Angkor Wat up the Pagsanjan River, and industry rumours hold that actual corpses were used in some scenes. The excesses of the film have become legendary.

Marlon arrived in Manila from Hawaii in August. He was well over 250 pounds, despite a drastic attempt to diet at the last minute to make more convincing his performance as a former Army man. He had shaved himself completely bald, and as it turned out, Coppola was delighted with the look. His formidable presence would certainly lend an unrivalled power to the final sequences of the picture, and probably no other actor could have delivered the requisite personality and presence. With the picture's theme of the search for and the discovery of a mysterious, remote, and mythical figure, only a man who himself was a myth and a mystery could have done justice to the part.

During the filming Marlon was comfortably lodged at Caliraia, a sprawling, comparatively luxurious settlement for the Filipino well-to-do, with comfortable cottages and villas surrounded by palms up the Pagsanjan River valley. The house that Coppola had thoughtfully provided, with its bamboo furniture and rattan blinds, rather resembled a Hollywood movie idea of a tropical residence, and was certainly far more spacious and comfortable than Marlon's thatched hut in Teti'aroa.

Alice Marchak arrived during the shooting and immediately fell ill. The tropical heat proved too much for her. As she lay in her room, she openly complained to crew members that her whole life had been absorbed in tending to Marlon. In a reversal of roles, Alice became the focus of Marlon's concerned attention each day, as he tended to her every need. Witnesses on location were fascinated to see this enormous man, humble as a small boy, nervously knocking at Alice's door, asking to be let in, then fussing over her with extreme patience as she recuperated. .

Embarrassed by his weight, Marlon insisted on a body double for longshots in the film. He reworked the script in conference with Coppola and introduced passages from T. S. Eliot and other authors, fragments of metaphysical thought, expressions of pity for the conditions of the Vietnamese, and poetic meditations. The scenes in Kurtz's compound achieved a terrifying force, in which Marlon's still, Buddha-like presence exerted an appalling power. The homoerotic slaughter scene in which, instead of fighting his execution by the half-naked Sheen, Marlon accepted it passively, wallowing orgiastically in his own blood like the water buffalo being ritually carved apart by the local tribe, was the most extraordinary in the film. The flare of torches, the ebony darkness, the dying Kurtz murmuring, 'Horror, horror!' created Marlon's most astonishing moment on the screen.

20

In the wake of making *Apocalypse Now*, Marlon did not cease to be troubled by the prolonged struggle with Anna Kashfi. She sued him for $2 million, charging him with failing to allow her to visit Christian. Nothing came of this case, and as Christian grew into his teens, still a willowy boy with his mother's long, slender limbs and a distinctly Indian look, he declined to see his mother at all. Marlon, by general agreement, was a devoted father, anxious for the best for his son; he was closer to him than to Miko or Rebecca, Movita's children with him, although Simon Teihotu and Tarita Cheyenne in Tahiti were his adoring and constant companions.

In the meantime, Marlon always needed more money to pour into Teti'aroa. He relied more and more on his lawyer, Norman Garey, who had assumed the roles of legal adviser, agent, and business manager. Jay Kanter had since moved into the film industry full-time as a producer and later as a studio executive. Marlon and Garey were also locked into an intensely close personal friendship, and the actor regarded him as a brother and a counsellor. Garey's upward mobility was startling, and by 1979 he represented Francis Coppola, Gene Hackman, Kenny Rogers, Donna Summer, Elton John, and Quincy Jones among many others. One of his most spectacular achievements was getting Marlon an unprecedented deal: $3.7 million for twelve days' work as Superman's father in the film of that name, produced by Alexander Salkind. Tennessee Williams was heard to crack, 'Marlon must have been paid by the pound.'

Before he began work on this elaborate spectacle film, Marlon had much to take care of. In Teti'aroa, his hotel was flourishing in its fifth year. He was developing a coconut plantation, improving the bird sanctuary island, setting up windmills, and had local craftsmen working on canoe building and weaving, while fishermen also developed the local saltwater grounds. He was like a benign version of Colonel Kurtz, moving majestically in his flowing mumus with big straw hats through his personal kingdom. His vast bulk, considered so disgraceful in the Northern Hemisphere, meant nothing in the islands.

He worked hard to encourage field missions to investigate the history and ecology of the islands, investing a great deal of money so that scholars under his patronage could unearth the rich and fascinating history of the atoll. Under his sponsorship during the 1970s, Professor Koshiko H. Simoto of the Department of Archaeology of the Bishop Museum of Honolulu conducted field work in Teti'aroa and discovered interesting details of the Arioi society's use of the Isle of Rimatu'u by their high chiefs and ruling families for reckless debaucheries. Simoto confirmed, through dating relics found in ancient dwelling sites, that the atoll had first been settled in the fifteenth century.

Marlon shuttled between this idyllic island existence and the harsher world of Hollywood. His romantic life was as complex as ever. He had dated Lucy Saroyan for a brief time; they remain friends. He also had an affair with an ill-fated woman named Jill Banner. A tiny, appealing former actress who talked in a low-pitched, sexy, drawling comic voice like Mae West, she eternally fascinated Marlon. According to Marlon and

Wally Cox's old friend Everett Greenbaum, Marlon was fiercely possessive of this intriguing girl. 'I used to take Jill for rides in my aeroplane,' Greenbaum recalled. 'Every time Jill went flying with me, Marlon got furious. They had a fight and then made up. Marlon bought her a golden apple made of solid gold studded with emeralds, rubies, and diamonds. She wore it around her neck. Then they went to some island in Hawaii, and Marlon had an argument with her on the beach and he yanked the apple off and threw it away in the ocean.'

Greenbaum added, 'Jill was killed in a terrible car crash. I was at the funeral. I didn't see Marlon. But I heard afterwards he was hiding in the trees next to the burial ground.' Fearful of the attentions of the press, Marlon, as at Wally Cox's funeral, didn't want to be seen, even by the other mourners. Yet, paradoxical as always, he did turn up for the funeral of someone he didn't know: the grand old comedian Jimmy Durante. He wasn't present, by contrast, at the funeral of Anne Ford, his girlfriend during the making of *On the Waterfront*, who was brutally murdered that year when intruders burst into her Hollywood home. Like so many men of his age, now well into his fifties, he experienced the inevitable passing of old friends. Carlo Fiore had finally succumbed to the effects of years of drugs and passed away in the Veterans' Memorial Hospital in Westwood, Los Angeles, at the age of fifty-eight. Another very close friend of many years, the actor Sam Gilman, suffered two heart attacks and would later die of cancer. These were grievous blows that made the past seem painfully far away. When Marlon called Darren Dublin, whom he had not seen for many years, to discuss the 'good old days' with him, Dublin could only cynically reply, 'What good old days?'

As always, whenever he was especially tormented, Marlon over-ate. By 1979, his weight had swelled up to over three hundred pounds. He went on a crash diet, only to slip back with nightly raids on the refrigerator. On one occasion, Phil Rhodes found him haemorrhaging on to his pillow. Rhodes attributed this to Marlon's eating an entire gallon of ice cream at one sitting.

Somehow, he managed to squeeze down his more-than-fifty-inch waistline to appear as the trim, dynamic George Lincoln Rockwell, führer of the American Nazi party in the 1960s, in Alex Haley's *Roots: The Next Generations* on television. His long association with the Jewish ideal that had inspired him in *A Flag is Born* drove him to impersonate this fascist figure. He appeared in just one sequence, based on an actual incident, in which Haley, played by James Earl Jones, who had once met Marlon in Africa, interviewed Rockwell. Seated before a large portrait of Hitler, with a display of American and Nazi flags – a juxtaposition that delighted Marlon – he acted with all the force he could muster, greatly pleasing the director John Erman.

Later that year, after a long sojourn in Teti'aroa, Marlon flew to England for his grotesquely overpaid twelve days' work on *Superman*. He acted the hero's father on the planet Krypton with an otherworldly quality. When he spoke of his dying planet, and of his desire to have his son experience the healthy, vibrant, plant-yielding life of fertile Earth, Marlon might easily have been talking of his desire for Christian and his other children to seek the still pure and unsullied land and water of Teti'aroa.

When he was in Los Angeles he came to appreciate the company of his neighbour Jack Nicholson and the actress and restaurateur Helena Kallioniotes. One Saturday night, with Jack, Helena, LeVar Burton, Art

Garfunkle, and Jack's girlfriend Anjelica Huston, he went to the Reseda Roller Skating Rink. Each of them wore bomber jackets with nicknames stamped on them. It was a glorious night, during which he played as a kid again. Spectators were astonished to see his vast form, some three hundred pounds or more, spinning around the rink on skates.

In 1979, the land he had given to the Indians was again the cause of controversy. Intended for use as a tribal colony, a kind of free reservation, it remained a windswept, dusty, and useless region. Motorcyclists in leather jackets reminiscent of the characters in *The Wild One* held dirt races there; construction crews dumped refuse on it; and coyotes claimed the land as their own. The county board of supervisors was blocking development there, chiefly due to the lobbyings of Sierra Club president David Brown, who claimed that extensive building would threaten what was left of the parklike nature of the environment, and that fire, landslide, and earthquake hazards threatened anyone who settled there. Furthermore, Brown asserted that, despite promises by Indian groups, the Chumash Indians, who had allegedly owned the original site, had never been consulted during development planning.

Hank Adams of the Survival of American Indians Association charged Brown with being a racist in the guise of an environmentalist. Ironically, Marlon found himself in the position of attacking the Regional Planning Commission for not allowing development to go through, since the taxes and insurance on the land were a hardship to the Indians.

Further trouble engulfed the question of the Anaheim apartment house that he had donated. It had been the focus of protracted discussion and threatened litigation because many of the elderly tenants who had

384

been there since the building's construction strongly objected to eviction orders from the new owners. Residents in nearby buildings complained about the late-night parties held by their new Indian neighbours. Finally, the properties were sold and used to provide support not only for individual Indians but for AIM and the Survival of American Indians Association, along with other activist groups. It was a good deal of this money that was allegedly directed to support the contras in Nicaragua.

In April 1979, Marlon appeared with his friend, Governor Jerry Brown, at a Push for Excellence rally at Dodger Stadium. He addressed the Indian cause in a lengthy and impassioned address in the company of George Peppard, Lou Gossett, and football players Tony Davis and Larry McCutcheon. Simultaneously, Norman Garey failed to put together a satisfactory deal with the Salkinds for Marlon to appear in *Superman II*. Although many of Marlon's scenes for the sequel had been shot, Garey lost what could have been a tremendously lucrative arrangement involving little or no extra work because he made excessive demands on the producers.

Instead, later in 1979, Marlon committed for a considerably lesser sum to play the oil tycoon Adam Steiffel in *The Formula*, a script by Steve Shagan about the search of an irascible detective played by George C. Scott for the killer of a close friend. In the search, the cop determines that the murdered man was disposed of because of his knowledge of an international oil cartel conspiracy involving a secret Nazi hydrogenation formula smuggled out of Germany at the end of World War II. It was a conventional thriller plot, but the idea of international oil cartels that threatened to ruin the environment intrigued Marlon. He felt that the movie, under its conventional surface, would say a great deal about the current state of the world, and he was drawn to the idea of playing a monster business-man not so far removed from Don Corleone in *The Godfather*.

After going over the script with a fine pencil, marking up suggested changes, Marlon invited Shagan and the director John Avildsen up to Mulholland. Garey told the two men at ten A.M. one morning to wait for the summons to the house. After five hours they still hadn't had a word, and they called Garey to beg him to let them go out for just thirty minutes to attend to some business. He told them to stand by and in just a few seconds he would pick them up.

They stayed at Mulholland until well after midnight. Marlon peppered them with questions about politics, Indians, and other matters. As the light faded, they found themselves seated in complete darkness. When Shagan asked Marlon why he didn't put on the lights, he replied with a laugh, 'Stop being such energy junkies!' A Japanese girl glided in and delicately lit the candles. Shagan spent much of the evening staring glumly at a NO SMOKING sign. At last, seemingly impressed by their comments on the issues that most concerned him, he stood up and said he would do the picture. But he added gloomily, 'Of course, it won't be a hit. But nothing serious ever is.'

Shooting began at the oil fields at Newhall, continu-ing in Bel Air, at the old Conrad Hilton estate, and in the Security Pacific Bank building in Westwood, where a suite of offices was converted into the headquarters of the oil tycoon Adam Steiffel. For some years now, Marlon had been using earplugs when acting certain scenes, memorizing what other actors would say, and watching their lip movements, while at the same time cutting out all extraneous sounds. For this picture, he took the device a step further and arranged for the character of Steiffel to be equipped with a hearing aid. Unable to memorize lines, as always, he had someone read them to him through wires leading into the aid. His co-star George C. Scott was perplexed that Brando would need such a device. Scott was from a different school, in which actors learned their lines, followed the script, and got on with the job. When Marlon constantly juggled with the words, 'You have the soul of a Swiss,' Scott couldn't take it any longer. 'It wore me out,' he said.

At one point, Scott asked him, 'What are you going to say this time?' and Marlon replied, 'What the fuck does it matter? You know a cue when you hear one!' Marlon hated his co-star's habit of smoking four packs of Lucky Strikes a day and forbade Scott to smoke in actual scenes. Of course they did have one thing in common: they had both turned down Academy Awards and had a well-publicized contempt for the industry that had made them rich.

Marlon played his part with rather less than his customary skill, never quite conveying the correct flavour of power and authority of an international oil cartel honcho. An effort to create a character that was charming, soft, and indulgent on the surface, but utterly ruthless underneath, never came together. The glint of danger never appeared in his eyes. Then Marlon insisted on adding a sequence free of charge after the entire movie was shot. Unwisely, Shagan and Avildsen went along with this request. The scene showed Adam Steiffel with a large fishing net, dipping it in his swimming pool and pulling out an unfortunate frog which is wriggling about in the torments of chlorine poisoning. This act of tenderness, accompanied by a would-be ironical speech about the dangers of pollution, achieved little. It fatally softened the character of Steiffel, rendering all of his other actions incomprehensible, instead of showing that there were paradoxical decencies in every man.

Marlon had curious obsessions in those years. He invited Everett Greenbaum to Tahiti to explain his plans for scooping algae out of the Teti'aroa lagoon to feed the hungry of the Third World. It was a decent, ambitious plan, virtually impractical in view of weather conditions, but he began plunging money into it. He decided he should fly his own plane in and out of Papeete. Greenbaum tried to train him in flying for his pilot licence in Burbank, California, but he, in Greenbaum's words, 'got scared and never wanted to fly again'. And in an effort towards self-sufficiency in Teti'aroa, he tried to learn welding, and set about fashioning a table with a drill press. But, according to Greenbaum, he became frightened of the flying metal sparks and abandoned the pursuit. He put all of his welder's accessories into the yard at Mulholland and they rusted until they were useless. He thought of teaching Christian to fly, set up a meeting with Greenbaum to launch the boy, then father and son failed to turn up.

His interrupted or uncompleted plans went on and on. There was talk of his undertaking a film version of the life of Picasso, an artist he deeply admired, but the project never came to fruition. It is variously reported that either Garey blew the deal or Marlon couldn't come to terms on the script or even that he wouldn't lose enough weight for the part. He toured a Caribbean turtle farm to see forty thousand endangered creatures; he talked extensively with the ambitious Adrian Malone, British producer of *Cosmos* with Carl Sagan, about a television series entitled *Quest*, about the Sand Creek massacre of Cheyennes in 1864, that supplanted his earlier notion of bringing the Wounded Knee story to film. This also fell apart. CBS embarked on the project, but script and casting problems proved insurmountable. He plunged into discussions with George Englund, planning a movie entitled *Fan Tan*. That project also disintegrated. By the eighties, the conservative political shift in the country was startling to such a committed liberal as was Marlon. His alienation from society had always been there, of course, but now he experienced the estrangement that comes with age. He faced the end of his acting career as well as the dominance of another generation's values. Then, in August of 1982, he experienced one of the most shattering blows of his life. Marlon was informed that Norman Garey had locked himself in his den and shot himself in the head with a .38 Smith & Wesson revolver. Why would the most successful deal-making lawyer in Beverly Hills want to end his life when he was only in his mid-forties? The answer was a classic lesson in the dangers of high-level film industry existence that Marlon had spent so much of his life excoriating. Garey had been taking an antidepressant which had severe after-effects on its users, causing feelings of inadequacy after a transcendental high. Marlon was shattered with grief by the loss and by the need to face his own mortality.

After the painful ordeal of Garey's funeral, Marlon understandably spent more time than ever in Teti'aroa among the palms and beating surf and soothing blues and greens of the lagoon. Not only did he continue to work on the windmill technology and the plankton farm, but he also worked out elaborate plans for the University of French Polynesia, an educational institution that would enable students in the region to open up their minds to the wider world. Among those to whom he gave his patronage was the distinguished anthropologist Professor Jean Dorst of the Muśee d'Homme in Paris. Dorst intended to coordinate with Jacques Cousteau and the Berkeley Research Center. Thirty or forty scientists would work under his aegis. Polynesian students would study not only the history, ecology and botany of the islands, but also the ecology of the lagoon. This magnificent venture would soon acquire a new and irresistibly romantic name: The University of the Sea.

But the ill fortune that dogged so much of the actor's life struck yet again. No sooner had he completed detailed blueprints and conducted conversations with his academic colleagues than devastating cyclones swept down on Tahiti, smashing Teti'aroa to pieces, splintering the palms, ripping off the leaves, and flooding the thatched huts that composed his hotel. In despair, he was forced to postpone his university project, while he attempted to rebuild the severely damaged resort. Finally, with resignation, he put up the entire atoll for lease.

But even before the cyclones virtually wiped him out, he had other major problems. His next-door neighbour on Mulholland Drive was brutally murdered by intruders and the Hillside Strangler struck in his neighbourhood. He was constantly being backed into corners by tourists who wanted to talk about his films. Yacht charter guests and local unauthorized fishermen preyed on his private empire or flooded ashore on dinghies to haunt his beaches and sully his waters. Reporters turned up to harass Tarita and his children. He chased them off, but more turned up.

He also suffered from conflicts with his son Christian, who in many ways had the appearance and manner of an early 1960s hippie. Taking after his mother, the young man was still quite unlike the young Marlon in build. His dark skin and drawn-out look, his edgy, sometimes fierce personality alternating with periods of reflectiveness and romantic daydreaming, had more to do with Anna Kashfi than with his father. He loved to bodysurf and considered a career as a model – he had the physical beauty for the job – but then backed out at the last minute before signing with an agency. Sometimes, he would turn up in the islands and spend time with his exceptionally handsome half-brother and -sister, both of whom inherited Tarita's ravishing good looks. Christian had a long and stormy affair with the beautiful Italian-American Laura Funio and later married a young woman, Mary, who worked in a boutique on La Cienega in Los Angeles.

After trying various jobs, Christian pursued a career as a tree surgeon in the mid-1980s. Now in his early twenties, he went for long periods without talking to his father at all, although he did renew contact with his mother after many years. Marlon realized the boy needed a home of his own, and he generously bought him a house in rustic Laurel Canyon. Miko Brando, Movita's son, became a bodyguard to rock star Michael Jackson; Rebecca led a more subdued and modest life at college in Arizona.

In 1980, Marlon underwrote a campaign against the making of a mini-series based on the best-selling novel *Hanta Yo* by Ruth Beebe Hill. Alex Haley's *Roots* had been a huge success, and producer David Wolper wanted to make *Hanta Yo* an Indian equivalent for ABC Television. Marlon objected to the fact that Ruth Beebe Hill was not Indian and had written a book about an ancestry that was not her own. Moreover, historians of the Lakota and Dakota tribes told him that the portrayal of those tribes in Miss Hill's pages was not accurate, and that she had distorted the tribal languages. In a coordinated effort with the Black Hills Treaty Council, a powerful Indian group, Marlon presented a protest to David Wolper and ABC. After months of negotiation between the producer and the Indians Wolper yielded and agreed that the name *Hanta Yo* would not be used in the mini-series, and that there would be no reference in it to Lakota and Dakota Indians. The result was a very poor effort entitled *The Mystic Warrior*. Few Indians agreed to work in the film at all. According to the Indian journalist Geri Keams, 'Although the mini-series was ridiculous, the Lakota and Dakota people won a victory by forcing Wolper to change its name and by discrediting it publicly. The message was loud and clear: Indian people will not allow themselves to be distorted in television and film.' Marlon funded the anti-*Hanta Yo* campaign from beginning to end.

And so, at present, this greatest of American actors, this powerful and humanistic man, finds himself at a standstill in his sixties. While he remains a passionate supporter of the cause of the American Indian Movement, he has been silent on the subject of certain members' support of the Nicaraguan contras. He now appears to be disillusioned with Teti'aroa. His visits there to see Tarita and their children, Tarita Cheyenne and Teihotu, have become increasingly infrequent in the mid-1980s. The hotel and its atoll are up for sale, but given the threat of cyclones, no buyers have come forward. He spends most of his time in his isolated Japanese house high above the flat, smoggy, featureless sprawl of Los Angeles. He is surrounded by guard dogs, sound-bugging devices, the watchful eyes of video cameras. Tourists, fans, and sightseers are discouraged or driven off the property. Only Phil Rhodes, whom he met before filming *Julius Caesar*, remains from the old days.

He is still haunted, tortured by the past. When a visitor to his house admired a painting of his mother over the fireplace, he said, 'Yes, she was beautiful. What a pity she spent most of her life on the floor.'

He reads more than ever now, hungrily consuming books on philosophy, the history of Jewish and Indian genocide, psychology, mysticism, and explorations of life after death. He searches restlessly, sleeplessly, for an answer to the overpowering questions that still disturb him: whether life has any meaning, whether man is redeemable, and whether the power of love can save a corrupt and cruel world. No adherent of any specific religion, he is in many ways deeply spiritual: in his worshipping of the great and good heroes of history, and in his need to be surrounded only by positive thoughts and feelings. Physically, he has become a disaster: Despite sporadic efforts to diet, he is still a looming 350 pounds. Even now he could command over $3 million a picture, and the mere presence of his name in a movie will ensure a film's colossal international market. Yet such matters interest him little. He is alone and able to think his thoughts out in full. And then there is the ever-present thought of decline and death, and again, the abiding and impenetrable mystery of existence. One wishes him peace. Let him have the final word.

When one stops seeking to find out who one is, one has reached the end of the rope. I have spent my whole life trying to know myself. If one is interested as I am in the history and conduct of mankind, one should begin with the material nearest to hand: oneself. That's what Socrates and the other philosophers did. But of course, it's a challenge. Man is, isn't he, afraid when face to face with himself? I am . . .

ACKNOWLEDGEMENTS

Writing this book would not have been possible without much excellent help from people all over the world. Gary Luke was my patient, able, and excellent editor. Peter Kelly bore the brunt of the research. Geri Keams checked and researched the American Indian aspects of the work. Anthony Slide handled the formidable task of copying six thousand pages of documented information. Tamar Cooper interviewed many close friends and family members. Donatella Ortona talked with the Italian colleagues. Earl Schenck did the difficult on-the-spot work in Tahiti. Darcel Dillard talked to Brando's New York City associates. France Nuyen broke twenty-five years of silence to talk about Brando. Jean Peters (Mrs Howard Hughes) gave her first interview on any subject in thirty-five years. Walter Seltzer provided a steadying hand throughout; as partner of Marlon Brando, Sr he was privy to much that has not been published hitherto. Frank P. Rosenberg, producer and friend of Brando, read the manuscript and gave unselfishly of his own time. My agent, Mitch Douglas, was a tower of strength. Bob Flood in Omaha, Paul Smith in Shattuck, Minnesota, Bob Seidenberg in Libertyville and Jim Newton in Evanston were all very helpful, tracking down people from Brando's childhood. Paula Larabure and Herbert Nusbaum of the now sadly vanished MGM were kind in giving me unprecedented access to studio files and so were Dr Robert Knudson and Ned Comstock at the Dohney Library of USC. David Shepard and David Bradley were, as always, of tremendous assistance and unstinting support. I drew also from conversations with Marlon Brando on the set of *The Chase* and on a brief visit he made to Australia where he evinced great interest in Aborigines.

Among over a hundred interviewed were:

Richard Stockton; Ruth Woolf; Mildred Milar; Glenn Miller; Frank Underbrink; Don Hanmer; Julia Cameron; Dick Denman; Barbara Wright; Maria Ley Piscator; Elaine Stritch; Meyer Mishkin; Edward Silver; Ruth Alley; Harry Belafonte; Blossom Plumb; DeWitt Bodeen; Mildred Natwich; Everett Greenbaum; Richard Loving; Darren Dublin; Joseph Sargent; Eddie Jaffe; Stanley Kramer; Marie Cooper; Richard Erdman; Roberta Haynes; Ken Kendall; Ken Du Main; Laslo Benedek; Mary Murphy; Daniel Taradash; Henry Koster; Al Ruddy; Mrs Henry Koster; Cameron Mitchell; Hope Holliday; Daniel Mann; Victoria Shellin; Charles Lang; Martin Jorow; Trevor Howard; Stanley Shapiro; Ralph Levy; Conrad Hall; Aldo Tonti; Jacques Danois; Bernardo Bertolucci; Gillo Pontecorvo; Alberto Grimaldi; Hubert Cornfield; Willy Kurant; Marcello Gatti; Stephanie Beacham; Anita Terrian; Jim Bailey; Francis Ford Coppola; Laura Funio; Jean Dorst; Giuseppo Rotunno; and Pasqualino de Santis. I found Alice Marshak's memoirs interesting, especially in the matter of Brando's shipwreck in Tahiti, which he described to her; local interviews filled in more detail. Anna Kashfi's *Brando for Breakfast* and Carlo Fiore's *Bud: The Brando I Knew* were much the best books available to date and provided valuable source material augmented by interviews and news accounts. Robert Lewis's excellent memoirs and Brian Garfield's book on the Actors Studio were the source of much information and so was the detailed file at the University of Southern Illinois on the New School. In all, 35,000 documents,

300 books, and countless newspaper clippings were read for this work, and the films were seen and reseen by me thanks to Robert Gitt, David Bradley, and Video Journeys, Inc.

Index

ABC, 391
Academy Awards, 158, 165,
    179, 367
    The Godfather, 358–63
    On the Waterfront, 9, 188,
        201–3
Actors Studio, 103, 104, 117–18,
    149–50, 204, 273
Adams, Hank, 365, 384
Adler, Ellen, 91, 104, 139
Adler, Luther, 71, 83, 134
Adler, Stella, 48–50, 62, 64–5,
    71–3, 83, 91, 134, 137
Alexander, Shana, 345
All My Sons, 96
Ambler, Eric, 267
American Civil Liberties Union
    (ACLU), 285–6
American Indian Movement
    (AIM),13, 256, 358–62,
    364–76
    Academy Awards and,
        358–62
    Alexian Brothers' Novitiate
        and, 13, 368–72
    contras and, 376, 385, 392
    fugitives and, 373–5
    Hanta Yo and, 391–2
    leaders of, 364
    MB's donation of property to,
        367–8, 384–5
    murders involving, 371–2,
        374–5
    Wounded Knee trial and, 358,
        367, 389
Anderson, Jack, 290
Anderson, Maxwell, 71, 74,
    76–7

Anhalt, Edward, 232, 236
Apocalypse Now, 11, 376–9
Appaloosa, The, 311–12, 315
Arletty, 123
Armes, Jay J., 354–5
Arms and the Man, 178
Arrangement, The, 329
Asinof, Eliot, 169, 186, 213, 221
Atkinson, Brooks, 85, 110
*Authentic Death of Hendry
    Jones, The*, 248, 254
Avgerinos, Milton, 27–9
Avildsen, John, 386, 387

Balsam, Martin, 149
Bankhead, Tallulah, 72, 91–6,
    98
Banks, Dennis, 13, 364–5, 367,
    370, 374–5
Banner, Jill, 381–2
Barnes, Howard, 76
Barrett, Rona, 361
Barrymore, John, 117, 165
Baxley, Barbara, 149
Beacham, Stephanie, 337–8
Beauvoir, Simone de, 123
Bedtime Story, 282–5, 289
Belafonte, Harry, 47, 57–8, 234,
    366
Belli, Melvin, 340
Benedek, Laslo, 170–76
Berneis, Peter, 243, 246
Bernstein, Leonard, 229
Bertolucci, Bernardo, 347–52
Bihar famine, 13, 319
Birmingham Veterans Hospital,
    131–4, 135
Black Hills Treaty Council, 392
Blacklist, 179

Black Panthers, 13, 328
Bluhdorn, Charles, 342
Bobino, 53
Bogart Humphrey, 158, 246
Boomerang, 159
Bond, Rudy, 145
Boone, Richard, 324, 326
Borgnine, Ernest, 340
Bors, Dr Ernest, 135
Botta, Adriano, 9–10, 350
Brand, Judge Edward, 322
Brando, Christian Devi, 241.
    251–2, 257–8, 294, 315,
    339, 380
  adulthood of, 390–91
  custody battles over, 257–8,
    264–5, 290, 303–7,
    310–11, 353–7, 362, 380
  with the Lovings, 306–7, 310
  mother's breakdown and,
    303–7
  in Tahiti, 300, 301
Brando, Dorothy (Dodie), 11, 15,
    18–36, 42, 65, 80, 105,
    110
  alcoholism of, 24–5, 32, 51–2,
    60, 63, 66–7, 70–71, 78,
    128, 130, 185, 229
  childhood of MB and, 28–34
  death of, 191–2, 220
  Dramatic Workshop and, 60,
    62
  Omaha Community Playhouse
    and, 22–5
Brando, Frances (Frannie), 20,
    21, 24, 30, 31, 32, 33, 63,
    65, 78, 110, 120, 192,
    367–8
  on Evanston, 26–7
  marriage of, 89, 90, 127, 150,
    177
  in New York, 42, 43, 45–6,
    87–8
Brando, Jocelyn, 20, 21, 24, 28,
    31, 32, 63, 65, 78, 110,
    170, 179, 192, 221

Asinof and, 169, 186, 213
Hanmer and, 33–5, 127, 150
in New York, 42
success as an actress, 119–20,
    277, 307
Brando, Marlon,
  acting and, 5–7, 8–9, 10, 11
  Academy Awards and, 9,
    158, 165, 179, 188, 201–3,
    358–61
  Adler and, 49–50, 71, 72–3
  Chaplin and, 312–15
  Clurman and, 72–5
  'death tremors,' 275
  Denman on 38–9
  disdain for, 9, 54, 64, 67, 73
  Dramatic Workshop and,
    47–63
  hearing aid and, 387
  Kazan and, 100–103,
    104–6, 194
  Method approach, 204, 216,
    275
  mumbling and, 74, 75, 83,
    137, 151, 165, 189, 204,
    308
  in musical comedy, 201,
    203–5
  Pontecorvo on, 329–30, 336
  rearranging dialog, 67, 174,
    175, 185, 226, 232, 251,
    272, 295–8, 308, 312,
    313, 349, 372–3, 377–8
    386
  rehearsing and, 175, 193–6,
    204
  Rotunno on, 323
  voice and, 162–5
  The Wild One and, 176–7
Americans in Southeast Asia
    and, 212–15
anti-Americanism of, 277, 280
athletics and, 39
auto accident of, 209
Avgerinos on, 27–9
Bankhead and, 91–6

Beacham on, 337–8
birth of, 20
body-building and, 36–7, 88, 105, 121, 146, 261
boxing and, 113
broken nose of, 113–14, 163, 230
causes of, 9, 10, 82, 151, 163, 179, 208, 267–8, 276, 279–82, 299–300, 326–7, 328–9
  American Indians, *see* American Indian Movement (AIM)
  civil rights, 13–14, 285–90, 316, 328–9, 334–5, 377, 388–9
childhood of, 20–42
children of, 277, 281–2, 290
  Christian Devi, *see* Brando, Christian Devi
  Miko, 266, 277, 278–9, 290, 322, 339, 357, 391
  paternity suits, 277, 286–7, 322, 339
  Rebecca, 322, 339, 357, 391
  Simon Teihotu, 301, 316, 320–21, 339, 380, 392
  Tarita Cheyenne, 339, 380, 392
Clift and, 77, 103, 233–5
clothes and, 10, 11, 68, 129
Coopers and, 129–31
Cox and, 15, 30, 87–90, 118–19, 148, 357–8
Cui and, 277–8, 286–7
Denman on, 39–40
death of friends of, 357–8, 382, 389–90
described, 5–6, 7–8, 20–21, 38–9, 50, 64, 88, 99, 106, 130, 131, 299, 322–3, 325–6
  weight of, 39, 187, 213, 214, 226–7, 231, 235, 256, 261, 284, 287, 333, 345, 372, 378, 383, 393

as director, 254–5
eccentricities of, 52, 81–2, 87–8, 103, 130, 134, 145–6, 239, 271–2, 372–3
Erdman on, 134–5
in Europe, 122–7, 179, 197–201, 320, 322–3, 324–6
fame and, 126, 141, 209, 214, 294–5, 392–3
family of, 18–21
father and, *see* Brando, Marlon, Sr., MB and
finances of, 9, 101, 111, 189, 192, 208, 215, 225, 259, 267, 318, 324, 326, 330, 337, 339, 342, 371–2, 374, 380–81, 383, 385
  Marlon, Sr. and, 122, 127–8, 143, 177, 206–7, 238–9, 299
forged photograph of, 166
in Greenwich Village, 45–7, 342
in Haiti, 262–3
Hanmer on, 33–6, 52
Haynes and, 139–41
health of, 39–40, 42, 113–14, 146, 235–6, 273–4, 295, 315, 333–4
Hollywood and, 8–9, 56–7, 100, 111, 121, 127, 129, 147, 157–8, 165–6, 175, 188, 190, 213–14, 261, 387, 393
home of, 246, 277–8, 392–3
homosexuals and, 177, 213, 230, 316–17
interviews and, 111, 121–2, 129–30, 142, 143, 148, 176, 188, 198, 199–200, 214
  Alexander, 345
  Capote, 229–31
  Cavett, 13, 362–3
  L'Europeo, 9–10, 14

Susskind, 281–2
Jaffe on, 116–17
in Japan, 214–18, 222, 227–9
Koster on, 193–4
Kramer and, 128, 130
languages and, 149, 213. 217, 332
lawsuits against, 191, 192, 281, 310, 322, 368, 380
Leigh and, 145–7
makeup and, 152, 154, 165, 341–2
Marchak and, 208
Milar on, 29–30
military service and, 37–40, 41–42
Miller on, 33
Mitchell on, 194–6
Moreno and, 14, 167–8, 200, 241–2, 278–9
nickname of, 20, 132, 326
Nuyen and, 12, 233, 251, 252, 254
paparazzi and, 198, 200, 244, 262, 320–21, 356, 363
Peters on, 155–6
Pontecorvo and, 329–36
practical jokes of, 58, 67–8, 103, 114, 116, 133–4, 144–5, 175, 195, 344–5
on the press, 281–2
psychiatry and, 106, 128, 191
Quinn on, 154–5
religion and, 220, 242, 393
Ruddy on, 343
sex and, 7, 9–10, 211–12, 236, 247, 252, 277–8, 351
Stritch and, 54–6, 61
in Tahiti, 14, 15, 268–75, 290–94
   see also Teti'aroa
in Thailand, 279–81
Tarita and, see Tarita
Underbrink on, 33
Williams and, 98–100
Winters and, 104–5, 137–8, 141

women and, 7, 9–10, 14–15, 37, 49, 67, 71, 91, 104–5, 137–41, 155–5, 167–8, 191–2, 246–7, 262, 268, 269, 278
engagements, 112, 197–201, 207, 220, 221–2, 224–5, 226
wives of, see Castenada, Movita; Kashfi, Anna
Brando Marlon, Sr., 10–11, 15, 18, 20, 23, 25–26, 32–4, 37, 79, 110, 192, 229, 246
death of, 299
MB and, 32, 35, 36, 37, 42, 80–81, 238–9
investments of, 122, 127, 143, 177, 206–7, 238–9, 299
second marriage and, 243, 253
secretary of, 208, 221
Brando, Miko, 266, 277, 278, 290, 322, 339, 357, 380, 392
Brando, Rebecca, 322, 339, 357, 380, 391
Brando, Simon Teihotu, 301, 316, 320–21, 339, 380, 392
Brando, Tarita Cheyenne, 339, 380, 392
Brandow, Eugene, 18, 20
Breen, Joseph (Breen Office), 139, 142, 157, 172, 173, 323
Bridges, Lloyd, 179
Briscoe, James, 304, 353
Brown, Governor Jerry, 375, 385
Browne, Arthur, 180, 182
Brynner, Yul, 295, 298
Burdick, Eugene, 276, 282
Burn!, 329–36
Burton, LeVar, 383
Burton Richard, 316, 318
Buttons, Red, 225, 228

Caan, James, 341, 343, 344–5, 360
Cagney, James, 239
Caine, Michael, 361
Calhern, Louis, 161, 166, 171, 215, 217
Callow, Reggie, 269, 271, 275
Cameron, Julia, 36
Cameron, Kate, 285
Canby, Vincent, 346
Candida, 78–81, 91, 99
Candy, 11, 322–3
Capote, Truman, 36, 229–31, 235, 281
Carnovsky, Morris, 159
Carson, Johnny, 329
Castenada, Movita, 14, 155–6, 168, 171, 174, 178, 177
  alimony battles, 322, 357
  breakup with MB, 182, 185, 192
  divorce of, 290
  on engagement of MB, 199–200
  marriage of, 266, 277
Cavett, Dick, 13, 362–3, 366
Champion, 126
Chandler, Joan, 117
Chaplin, Charlie, 138, 312–15
Chaplin, Sidney, 315
Chapman, John, 80, 110
Charley's Aunt, 59
Chase, The, 307–10
Chase, Borden, 267
Chekov, Anton, 150
Chessman, Caryl, 267–8
Christians, Mady, 65, 67
CIA, 376
City of Hope Hospital, 219–20, 221
Civil rights movement, 285–90, 316, 328–9, 334–5, 377
Clewes, Howard, 267
Clift, Montgomery, 77, 103–4, 138, 176–7, 233–5, 316–17

Clurman, Harold, 48, 71, 72–5, 76–7, 137
Cobb, Lee J., 179, 202
Cocteau, Jean, 91
Cohen, Bernard B., 286–7
Cohn, Harry, 181
Colombo, Joe, 342
Columbia Pictures, 180, 181, 188, 307–8, 310
Communism, 159, 170
Contras, 376, 385, 392
Cook, Donald, 92
Cooper, Jack, 129–31, 137, 141, 165
Cooper, Marie, 130–31, 137, 141, 165
Cooper, Tamar, 141
Copper, The, 148
Coppola, Francis Ford, 317, 380
  Apocalypse Now and, 376–7, 378–9
  The Godfather and, 339–47
Cornell, Katherine, 77–8, 79, 80
Cornfield, Hubert, 324–6
Corridan, Father John, 180
Countess from Hong Kong, A, 312–15
Cousteau, Jacques, 390
Cox, Eleanor, 87, 89
Cox, Pat, 357
Cox, Wally, 110, 141, 148, 166, 297–8
  apartment of, 90, 104
  death of, 357–8, 382
  friendship with MB, 15, 30, 87–90, 118–19
  Mr. Peepers and, 161
Crawford, Cheryl, 103
Crossroads, 371
Crowther, Bosley, 143, 158, 188
Cruz, Maria, 361
Cry Havoc!, 60, 163
Cui, Marie, 278, 286–7
Cukor, George, 110
Curtis, Tony, 47
Curtiz, Michael, 190

Dane Faith, 81, 91, 104, 139
Danois, Jacques, 319
Dantine, Helmut, 95
Dapper Dan, 131, 137
Darvi, Bella, 190–91
Davis, Bette, 203
Davis, Sammy, Jr., 316
Davis, Tony, 385
Dean, James, 176–7, 230
Deep Are the Roots, 159
Defector, The, 317
de Havilland, Olivia, 139
De Niro, Robert, 8
Denman, Dick, 38
Dennis, Nick, 113, 145, 230
De Sica, Vittorio, 125
Desiree, 192–7
Deukmejian, Governor George, 375
Dickinson, Angie, 307, 309
Dietrich, Marlene, 234
Dmytryk, Edward, 210, 232, 236, 237, 240
Don't Go Near the Water, 226
Douglas, Kirk, 329, 340
Dramatic Workshop, 47–63, 99, 169
Driscoll, William, 267
Dublin, Darren, 51, 58, 62, 66, 68, 91, 110, 139, 193, 382
Dublin, Florence, 193
Duncan, Ronald, 91
Dunne, Philip, 188, 285
Durante, Jimmy, 382
Durbin, Deanna, 196–7
Duvall, Robert, 345
Dyer, Chouteau, 53, 58, 59–60, 62

Eagle Has Two Heads, The, 91, 94–5, 103
Eastwood Clint, 361
Eberle, Brother Florian, 369
Egyptian, The, 187, 190–92
Eisler, Hanns, 48
Elizabeth II, Queen, 314

Englund, George, 206, 208, 213, 246, 276, 279, 389
Erdman, Richard, 132, 134–5
Evans, Bob, 340
Evanston, Illinois, 25–31, 32–3

Fan Tan, 389
FBI, 14, 290, 372, 373, 375
Fiore, Carlo (Freddie), 58–62, 66, 68–9, 80–81, 84, 105, 110, 112–13, 168
  death of, 382
  drug addiction of, 106, 112, 178–9, 182, 193
  Kashfi and, 238
  MB's film career and, 178, 183–4, 203–4, 226, 228, 231, 232–3, 235–6, 249, 251, 256, 261, 307
Fiscus, Reverend J. Walter, 243–4
Flag is Born, A, 82–5, 116, 137, 162
Fletcher, Nuba, M., 39, 41
Foley, Gregory, 22
Fonda, Henry, 24, 25, 119, 248
Fonda, Jane, 307, 308, 309, 361
Fontaine, Joan, 139
Ford, Anne, 14, 185–7, 382
Ford, Glenn, 215–18, 226
Ford, John, 180, 361
Foreman, Carl, 132
Formula, The, 11, 385–8
Forsythe, John, 103
Four on A Heath, 40
Franciosa, Anthony, 259, 288–9
Freeman, Y. Frank, 255
Fugitive Kind, The, 259–61
Funio, Laura, 391
Furie, Sidney J., 311–12, 315

Gahan, Julia, 19, 213, 243
Gahan, June, 213, 216, 220, 243
Gahan, Dr. Myles, 19
Galella, Ron, 363
Gallo, Fred, 345

404

Garey, Norman, 287, 322, 344, 353–4, 355–6, 369, 380, 385, 386, 388–9
Garfield, John, 97, 101, 149
Garfunkle, Art, 383–4
Garland, Judy, 134
Garland, Robert, 67, 85
Garson, Greer, 161
Gas, 52
Gassner, John, 48, 52
Gatti, Marcello, 333–4, 336
Gazzara, Ben, 47
Gentlemen's Agreement, 160
Ghose, Selma, 210, 245
Gielgud, John, 161, 163–4
Gilbert, Lou, 160–61
Gilbert, Paul, 265
Gilliland, Lesley, 289
Gilman, Sam, 178, 185–6, 193, 195, 197, 246, 256, 307, 382
Gilmore, Virginia, 72
Glass, George, 206, 239, 242, 245
Godfather, The, 9, 11, 339–46, 358–62
Goetz, William, 224
Golden Globe Award, 359
Goldwyn, Samuel, 201
Gossett, Lou, 385
Grant, Cary, 382
Greenbaum, Everett, 81, 88, 358, 382, 388
Greenwich Village, 45, 46, 342
Griffith, Hugh, 267
Grimaldi, Alberto, 335, 347–8
Groppi, Father James, 370
Group Theater, 103
Guernsey, Otis L., Jr., 143
Guthrie, Arlo, 366
Guys and Dolls, 203–5

Haber, Joyce, 357
Hackman, Gene, 360, 380
Hagen, Uta, 122
Haile Selassie, Emperor, 196

Haley, Alex, 383, 391
Hamilton, John F., 368
Hammerstein, Oscar, II, 65
Hanmer, David, 119
Hanmer, Don, 33–6, 42, 45, 52, 63, 90, 119, 127, 150, 221
Hannele's Way to Heaven, 53
Hanta Yo, 391–2
Hardwicke, Sir Cedric, 79, 80
Harris, Julie, 151–2
Harris, Richard, 267, 271, 274
Hastings, Michael, 336
Havens, James, 274
Hawkins, William, 85, 110
Hawpetoss, Neil, 369, 370
Hayden, Jeffrey, 183
Haynes, Roberta, 139–41
Heart of Darkness, 376
Hecht, Ben, 82–6
Hedda Gabler, 149
Hefner, Bessie (Nana), 19, 20, 36, 128, 130–31, 138
Hefner, June, 20
Hefner, Ollie, 19, 128, 138
Helburn, Theresa, 48
Hellman, Lillian, 307, 309
Hepburn, Audrey, 225
Heston, Charlton, 361
Hill, Arthur, 277
Hill, Ruth Beebe, 391–2
Hillside Strangler, 390
Hingle, Pat, 277
Hoffman, Dustin, 8
Holden, William, 193, 317
Home of the Brave, 127
Homolka, Oscar, 65, 67
Hope, Bob, 202
Hopper, Hedda, 129, 130, 143, 247
Houseman, John, 161–4
House Un-American Activities Committee (HUAC), 159, 170, 179, 180, 188
Howard, Trevor, 267
Huaurte, Semu, 368
Hudson, Rock, 213, 282, 360

Hunt, Marcia, 232, 237
Hunter, Kim, 6–7, 101, 110,
    144–5, 158, 179
Huston, Anjelica, 384
Huston, John, 161, 171, 317, 320
Hutton, Bobby, 328

Ibsen, Henrik, 149
Inge, William, 223
I Remember Mama, 64–70, 78,
    122
Isherwood, Christopher, 317
Ishimoto, Betty, 225
Is Zat So?, 40

Jaffe, Eddie, 115–16
Jaffe, Sam, 160
James, Henry, 337
Jennings, John T. Wilson, 29
Jews, 49, 71, 82–6, 137, 383
Jim Thorpe – All American, 362
John, Elton, 380
Johnson, Malcolm, 180
Jones, James Earl, 383
Jones, Margo, 99
Jones, Quincy, 380
Jones, Shirley, 282
Judge, Bernard, 300
Julius Caesar, 11, 161–7
Jurado, Arthur, 132, 136
Jurow, Martin, 259, 261

Kael, Pauline, 346, 351
Kallioniotes, Helena, 383
Kanter, Jay, 139, 144, 163, 202,
    244, 254, 295, 380
    as MB's agent, 126, 127, 128,
        152, 173, 233, 259, 266,
        267, 317, 324, 336, 337
Kashfi, Anna, 14, 209–13, 391
    background of, 209–10, 241,
        244–6
    breakup with MB, 251–4
    conflicts with MB, 221–3, 226,
        241–3, 246–7, 257–8,
        263–6, 277–9

divorce of, 257–8, 264–6
engagement of, 220–22,
    224–5, 226, 233
Fiore and, 237–8
home of, 246–7
illnesses of, 219–21, 294
marriage of, 242–4
Moreno and, 231–2, 241–2
pregnancy of, 236–7
real name of, 244–6
son of, *see* Brando, Christian
    Devi
suicide attempts, 14, 303
Kashfi, Devi, 210, 241, 245
Kastner, Elliot, 323–5, 337, 372
Kaufman, George S., 48
Kaufmann, Boris, 184
Kazan, Elia, 149, 155, 158–60,
    312, 329
    On the Waterfront and,
        179–89, 201–3
    A Streetcar Named Desire
        and:
        screen version, 142, 144–7,
            157–8
        stage version, 96–7,
            98–111, 113–14, 122
    Truckline Cafe and, 72, 74–7
    Viva Zapata! and,
        150–57, 160–61
Kazan, Molly, 96, 103
Keams, Geri, 392
Keitel, Harvey, 377
Kendall, Kenneth, 165
Kennedy, Douglas, 263
Kennedy, Ethel, 366
Kerr, Deborah, 161
Kerr, John, 186
Kidd, Michael, 201
King, Martin Luther, 13, 328–9
Klune, Ray, 271–2
Koch, Howard W., 359
Koster, Henry, 193–4, 196–7
Kramer, Stanley:
    The Men and, 126–7, 128–9,
        131–2, 136, 138

The Wild One and, 169–76
Kronenberger, Louis, 76
Krupa, Gene, 34, 111
Kubrick, Stanley, 249–51, 254,
    323–4
Kukrit Pramoj, M.R., 280
Kwan, Nancy, 265
Kyo, Machiko, 217

Ladd, Alan, Jr., 337
Ladies in Retirement, 59
Lamont, Duncan, 267
L'Amour, Kathy, 257
L'Amour, Louis, 206, 222, 243,
    244, 295
Lancaster, Burt, 97, 146, 316,
    362
Lang, Charles, Jr., 255, 257
Larson, Jack, 234
Last Tango in Paris, 11, 347–52,
    353, 356, 362
Laurel and Hardy, 51, 89
Laurent, Arthur, 126–7
Lederer, William J., 276
Lee, Shavey, 149
Lee, Sondra (Peanuts), 114–15
Legion of Decency, 157
Leigh, Vivien, 10, 142, 144–7,
    158
L'Europeo, 9–10, 14, 348, 350
Leverett, Lewis, 159
Levy, Ralph, 282, 283–4
Lewis, Robert (Bobby), 67, 92–4,
    103, 117
Lewis, Sinclair, 48
Ley, Maria, 47, 54, 58
Libertyville, Illinois, 33–7
Liebling, William, 97–8
Life magazine, 119, 128, 345
Lindemeyer, Elizabeth (Betty),
    20, 23, 32–3, 128, 130,
    138, 191, 192, 202, 229,
    242, 300
Lindemeyer, Olive, 245
Little Feather, Sacheen, 358–62
Loesser, Frank, 201

Logan, Joshua, 223–4, 227–8,
    230, 233
Logan, Nedda, 224
Loren, Sophia, 313–14
Los Angeles Times, 357, 376
Loving, Richard, 89, 110,118,
    120, 127, 150, 177,
    306–7, 310–11
Lowe, William, 286
Lucey, Governor Patrick J.,
    369–70
Lumet, Sidney, 260
Luna, Barbara, 265
Lyles, A.C., 210

MacArthur, Charles, 83
McCarthy, Kevin, 77, 103–4,
    118, 233
McChesney, Nan Prendergast,
    31
McClintic, Guthrie, 77–8, 79, 81
McCullers, Carson, 316, 317,
    321
McGuane, Thomas, 372
McGuire, Dorothy, 23, 24, 46
McLaglen, Victor, 138
McNally, Andrew, 25
MacRae, Gordon, 200
Madame Butterfly, 224
Madwoman of Chaillot, The,
    139, 141
Mafia, 345–6
Magnani, Anna, 259–61
Mailer, Norman, 138, 312
Malden, Karl, 72, 77, 160,183,
    202, 203
    One-Eyed Jacks and, 251
    A Streetcar Named Desire
    and, 7, 101, 110, 144, 158
Mallory, Ron, 239
Man Called Horse, A, 362
Mankiewicz, Joseph L., 161,
    162–3, 164–5, 201, 204–5
Mann, Daniel, 209, 215, 218–19
Marchak, Alice, 208, 221, 230,
    303–4, 310, 325, 378

March of Drama, The, 52
Margolin, Janet, 297–8
Mariani-Bérenger, Jossane, 191–3, 195, 197–9, 207–8
Marquand, Christian, 199, 200, 248, 252, 322
Marguez, Evaristo, 332
Mars, Janice, 178
Martin, Dean, 233, 235
Marx, Harpo, 83
Mason, James, 161
Matthau, Walter, 47
Mayer, Louis B., 96, 100, 107, 109
Mealey, Hudson (Hockey), 39
Means, Russell, 13, 364, 367, 369, 370, 371–2, 375
Means, William, 376
Men, The, 11, 126–39
    filming of, 134–5
    preparation for, 131–4
Menominee Warrior Society, 369, 371
Meredith, Burgess, 73, 78
Meskito Indians, 376
Message from Khufu, A, 40
Metro-Goldwyn-Mayer (MGM), 161, 165, 167, 181, 209, 217, 218, 245, 266, 267, 271, 272, 273
Michener, James A., 222, 223
Milar, Mildred, 29–30
Milestone, Lewis, 272–3
Mille, Herve, 198
Miller, Arthur, 96, 180, 234
Miller, Glenn, 33
Miller, Paula, 159
Mines, Harry, 210
Mishkin, Mayer, 56, 341
Missouri Breaks, The, 11, 372–3
Mister Roberts, 119, 127, 179, 223
Mitchell, Cameron, 194–5
Mitchum, Robert, 317
Mittleman, Dr Bela, 106, 128, 191

Monaster, Nate, 285
Montalban, Ricardo, 225
Montand, Yves, 324
Montevecchi, Liliane, 235
Montur, Robert, 369
Moore, Roger, 360
Morehouse, Ward, 85
Moreno, Rita, 14, 167–8, 200, 231–2, 241–2, 278–9, 325
Morituri, 295–9, 303, 358
Morris, Maynard, 56–7, 64, 65, 73, 123–4
Morros, Borris, 82
Mortimer, Chapman, 317
Mosby, Aline, 199
Motion Picture Code (Breen Office), 107, 139, 142, 157–8, 172–4, 323
Mountain, The, 210, 245
Mr. Peepers, 161, 186, 358
Muni, Paul, 48, 82–5, 162
Murphy, Mary, 171, 174–5
Music Corporation of America (MCA), 56, 64, 97, 111, 126
Mutiny on the Bounty, 266–76, 281
Myse, Judge Gordon, 369
Mystic Warrior, The, 392

NAACP, 377
Naked and the Dead, The, 138
Nathan, George Jean, 77
Nathan, Vivian, 150
Natwick, Mildred, 77–9, 81
Neal, Patricia, 103
Nelson, Barry, 77
Neusom, Tom, 285
Newman, Paul, 8, 288, 329
New School for Social Research, 149
    Dramatic Workshop of, 47–63, 99, 169
Newsweek, 176, 200, 346
Newton, Huey, 328
New York City in 1943, 43–4

New York Daily News, 80, 110, 199

New Yorker, The, 67, 229, 230, 281, 346, 351

New York Morning Telegraph, 53

New York Film Critics Award, 358–9

New York Herald Tribune, The, 76, 86, 143

New York Journal-American, The, 67, 85

New York Post, 76, 110

New York Sun, 85

New York Times, The, 67, 76, 80, 85, 110, 143, 158, 188, 200, 346

New York World Telegram, The, 85, 110

Nicaragua, 376, 385, 392

Nichols, Frederick W., 29

Nichols, Lewis, 67, 76, 80

Nicholson, Jack, 372, 383–4

Nieder, Charles, 248

Nightcomer, The, 336

Night of the Following Day, The, 323–7

Night of the Quarter Moon, 254

Niven, David, 282–3, 289

Noguchi, Thomas, 357

Northwestern University, 29

Notras, Peter, 357

Nuyen, France, 12, 233, 251, 252, 253, 254, 262–3, 265

Oberon, Merle, 195

O'Callaghan, Melinda, 245, 264

O'Callaghan, William Patrick, 210, 244–5, 264

Odets, Clifford, 159

Oklahoma, 104

Olivier, Laurence, 8, 144, 146, 163, 340

Omaha, Nebraska, 17–25, 363

Omaha Community Playhouse, 22–5, 48

Omaha World Herald, 23, 25

One-Eyed Jacks, 15, 248–51, 254–7, 320
  direction by MB, 254–7

On the Waterfront, 179–89
  Academy Awards for, 9, 188, 201–3

Orozco, José Clemente, 47

Osborn, Paul, 223, 224, 227

Oscar awards, *see* Academy Awards

Pablo, 99

Pacino, Al, 8, 11, 341, 343, 345

Palance, Jack, 113

Palestine, 84–6

Pal Joey, 177

Panic in the Street, 142

Paramount Pictures, 181, 206, 210, 213, 243, 245, 339, 340, 342

Parramore, Anna, 243, 299

Parsons, Louella, 129, 143

Patrick, John, 166–7, 208, 209, 217, 219

Paxton, John, 171, 172, 173, 174

Pearson, Drew, 329

Peck, Sterling, 304

Peckinpah, Sam, 249

Pellicer, Pina, 15, 255

Peltier, Leonard, 373, 374, 375

Penn, Arthur, 308, 309, 372

Pennebaker, Inc., 206, 208, 220, 222, 239, 249, 299

Penny Poke Ranch, 122, 127, 143, 177, 192, 206–7

Peppard, George, 385

Peters, Jean, 152, 153, 155–7

Petrified Forest, The, 117

Picasso, 388

Picnic, 193

Pinewood Studios, 313

Pinky, 160, 180

Piscator, Erwin, 47–9, 52–3, 62, 99, 169

Playboy magazine, 125, 183, 358, 374
Play Me a Song, 141
Plumb, Blossom, 59–60, 62–3, 68, 92–3, 104, 139
PM, 76
Pomere I, King, 291
Pontecorvo, Gillo, 329–36
Powell, Eleanor, 216
Power of Darkness, The, 53
Power, Tyrone, 151
Prince of Players, 177
Pump Room, 133
Puzo, Mario, 339, 340

Quaid, Randy, 373
Queimada, 329–36, 347
Quinn, Anthony,122, 151, 154–5

Rafferty, Chips, 267
Rama IX, King, 279
Ratner, Herbert, 178
Redfield, William, 178, 179, 298
Redford, Robert, 307, 309
Red Wing Association, 368
Reed, Sir Carol, 267, 268–9, 270, 271–2
Reflections in a Golden Eye, 11, 316–22
Reunion in Vienna, 117
Rhodes, Marie, 193, 213, 216, 229, 256, 307
Rhodes, Phil, 178, 195, 213, 216, 229, 256, 307, 383, 393
    makeup and, 154, 165, 193, 309, 341
Rice, Vernon, 76
Riders to the Sea, 52
Rittenband, Judge Laurence J., 356
Rittmeister, Harry, 294
Robbins, Jerome, 103
Roberts, Meade, 259
Robertson, Cliff, 259
Robinson, Edward G., 86

Rockwell, George Lincoln, 383
Rodgers and Hammerstein, 65, 223
Rogers, Kenny, 380
Rooney, Frank, 169
Roots: The Next Generation, 383
Rosenberg, Aaron, 267, 271–2, 295, 297–8
Rosenberg, Frank P., 222, 248–50, 254–7
Ross, Beverly, 304
Rossellini, Roberto, 125
Rotunno, Giuseppe, 323
Ruddy, Al, 340, 341, 342–4, 346
Russell, 148, 156, 161
Rutkoff, Peter M., 48

Sagan, Carl, 388
Saint, Eva Marie, 181, 183, 184–5, 202, 203, 210
Sainte-Marie, Buffy, 366
Saint Joan, 52
Sako, 253
Salkind, Alexander, 381
Samuel, Reverend Morris V., 287–8
Sandinistas, 376
Sands, Mike, 207–8
Sarah Bad Heart Bull, 365
Sargent, Joseph, 114–15, 250
Saroyan, Lucy, 366, 381
Sartre, Jean-Paul, 123
Sata, Reiko, 353
Saturday Evening Post, The, 281
Saturday Review, 176
Saul, Oscar, 142
Sayonara, 222, 223, 224, 225, 227, 230, 231, 232, 248
Schack, Roberta, 139–41
Schary, Dore, 163
Schnee, Thelma, 149
Schneider, Alan, 117
Schneider, Maria, 10, 348–9, 350–51

410

Schulberg, Budd, 179, 180, 184, 203
Scientific and Cultural Conference for World Peace, 170
Scientific American, 88
Scofield, Paul, 161–2
Scott, Judge A.C., 311
Scott, George C., 385, 387
Scott, William B., 48
Sea Gull, The, 234
Seale, Bobby, 328
Seaton, George, 274–5
Seltzer, Walter, 206, 207, 239, 242, 249, 256, 299
Selznick, David O., 96, 100
Selznick, Edith, 224
Selznick, Irene, 96–7, 98, 100–101, 102, 110, 111, 114, 121, 122, 224
Sganarelle, 53
Shagan, Steve, 385, 386
Shakespeare, William, 161, 164
Shapiro, Stanley, 282–3, 284–5, 289
Shattuck Military Academy, 37–41
Shaw, George Bernard, 78–9, 178
Shaw, Irwin, 232, 236
Sheen, Martin, 377
Shepherd, Ann, 72, 76
Shepherd, Richard, 259
Sherwood, Robert, 83, 117
Siegel, Sol C., 272, 275
Sierra Club, 384
Simmons, Jean, 195
Simon, John, 346, 352
Simoto, Koshiko H., 381
Sinatra, Frank, 181, 203–5
Skouras, Spyros P., 191
Sloane, Everett, 135
Sommer, Dr Melvin L., 277
Southern Terry, 322
South Pacific, 223, 233
Spellman, Cardinal, 157

Spiegel, Sam, 181, 203
Stanislavsky, Konstantin, 49
Stanley Kramer Company, 129
Stapleton, Maureen, 103, 259, 261
Stark, Ray, 265, 316, 317, 320
Steiger, Rod, 47, 181, 183, 184, 188, 202, 341
Steinbeck, John, 150
Stern, Stewart, 213
Stine, Clifford, 284
Strasberg, Lee, 48, 49, 103, 149
Streetcar Named Desire, A, 11, 96–120
    Kazan and, 101–6
    New Haven opening, 107–9
    New York opening, 109–10
    screen version of, 138, 141–7, 157–8
Streisand, Barbra, 329
Stritch, Elaine, 47, 54–6, 58, 59, 60, 61–2
Stuart, Bishop George, 25
Superman, 9, 380, 383
Superman II, 385
Survival of American Indians Association, 365, 368, 384
Susman, Allen E., 287, 304, 322
Susskind, David, 281–2

Tahiti, 14, 15, 268–75, 290–95, 300–301, 316, 326
Taka, Miiko, 225, 228, 246
Tamiroff, Akim, 12, 296
Tandy, Jessica, 6, 101, 102, 108, 109, 110, 113, 116–17, 122, 123, 142
Taradash, Daniel, 12, 295–8, 359, 360, 361
Tarita, 270-71, 273, 290, 293, 305, 316, 320, 326, 390, 391, 392
Taylor, Elizabeth, 316-17, 318, 321

Teahouse of the August Moon, 208, 213, 214–20, 224, 234

Teti'aroa, 290–91, 375, 380, 381, 383, 388, 389–90, 392
cyclones at, 15, 390, 392
hotel at, 293–4, 300–302, 380, 381, 390, 392

Tetzel, Joan, 67

Theater Arts, 22

Thomas, Danny, 339

Thompson, Dorothy, 86

Thorpe, Grace, 361

Tierney, Gene, 191

Time magazine, 158, 281

Today Show, The, 290

Tonight Show, The, 290, 329

To Tame a Land, 206

Tracy, Spencer, 210, 211, 251

Tree Grows in Brooklyn, A, 72, 159

Trosper, Guy, 251, 256

Troup, Dr Evelyn, 356

Truckline Café, 71–9, 95, 275

Tunney, Senator John B., 368

Twelfth Night, 53, 56, 58, 60, 62

Twentieth Century-Fox, 150, 153, 155, 177, 187, 191, 192, 194–5, 297

Ugly American, The, 214, 276–7, 279-82

Ullmann, Liv, 360

Umeki, Miyoshi, 225

Uncle Vanya, 150

Underbrink, Frank, 33

UNESCO, 208, 213, 214, 276, 319

UNICEF, 13, 319

United Artists, 129, 181, 260, 330, 348

Universal Studios, 276, 289, 299, 317, 324

University of Nebraska, 367

University of the Sea, 390

Urban, Joseph, 47, 52

Vadim, Roger, 248

Van Cleve, Edith, 64–5, 73, 91, 95, 97, 98, 101, 177, 233

Vanderbilt, Gloria, 260

Van Druten, John, 65–6, 70

Village Vanguard, 118–19

Viszard, Jack, 172

Viva Zapata!, 150–57, 160

Wagner, Earl M. (Duke), 40

Wallach, Eli, 118, 149

Wallis, Hal, 97

Walter, Francis E., 160

Walters, Mildred, 285

War and Peace, 52, 199

Warner, Jack, 157, 181, 317

Warner Brothers, 139, 141, 157, 222, 224, 225, 227, 307

Wasserman, Lew, 318

Webb, Cecilia (Celia) d'Artuniaga, 46–7, 51, 58, 62, 66, 68, 71, 81, 91, 98, 104, 111–12, 139, 202, 216, 229

Webb, Jack, 132, 136

Weill, Kurt, 82, 84

Weisbart, David, 147, 157

Welch, Raquel, 360

Welles, Orson, 78, 135, 325

West, Mae, 177

Whitmore, James, 285

Wicki, Bernhard, 295, 296, 298

Wild One, The, 176–8, 186

Williams, Tennessee, 47, 96, 97, 98–100, 105, 109, 112, 142, l49, 230, 259, 381

Williams, Dr Will, 291

Willingham, Calder, 249–50

Winchell, Walter, 115

Winged Victory, 46, 52

Winner, Michael, 336–8

Winters, Shelley, 47, 104–5, 134, 137, 138, 141

Wolper, David, 391–2

Wood, Audrey, 96, 102

Woodward, Joanne, 261
Woolf, Ruth, 27
Wooster, James, 353–5
World of Suzie Wong, The, 253. 265
Wounded Knee, 336
Wright Barbara, 38, 41
Wright, Reverend Douglas, 36
Wright, Teresa, 137
Wyler, William, 144
Wyndham, Donald, 112

Yates, Reverend Herbert, 288
Yiddish Theater, 49, 71
Young Lions, The, 232–6, 240

Zanuck, Darryl F., 150, 151–2, 180–81, 187-8, 190–91, 192, 195, 295
Zanuck, Richard, 296
Zimmerman, Paul D., 346
Zinnemann, Fred, 131, 136
Zionism, 82–6, 115, 137